The Founders on
God and Government

The Founders on God and Government

Edited by
Daniel L. Dreisbach,
Mark D. Hall,
Jeffry H. Morrison

ROWMAN & LITTLEFIELD PUBLISHERS, INC.
Lanham • *Boulder* • *New York* • *Toronto* • *Oxford*

ROWMAN & LITTLEFIELD PUBLISHERS, INC.

Published in the United States of America
by Rowman & Littlefield Publishers, Inc.
A wholly owned subsidiary of The Rowman & Littlefield Publishing Group, Inc.
4501 Forbes Boulevard, Suite 200, Lanham, Maryland 20706
www.rowmanlittlefield.com

PO Box 317
Oxford
OX2 9RU, UK

British Library Cataloguing in Publication Information Available

Library of Congress Cataloging-in-Publication Data

The Founders on God and government / edited by Daniel L. Dreisbach, Mark D. Hall,
Jeffry H. Morrison.
  p. cm.
Includes bibliographical references and index.
ISBN 0-7425-2278-4 (hardcover : alk. paper) — ISBN 0-7425-2279-2 (pbk. : alk.
paper)
1. Christianity and politics—United States—History—18th century. 2. United
States. Declaration of Independence—Signers—Religious life. 3. United States.
Constitution—Signers—Religious life. 4. Statesmen—United States—Religious
life. 5. United States—Religion—18th century. I. Dreisbach, Daniel L. II.
Hall, Mark David, 1966– III. Morrison, Jeffry H., 1961–
BR520.F68 2004 ℓ.ℓ
322'.1'097309033—dc22

2004007920

Printed in the United States of America

♾ ™ The paper used in this publication meets the minimum requirements of
American National Standard for Information Sciences—Permanence of Paper
for Printed Library Materials, ANSI/NISO Z39.48-1992.

To my sisters and brothers—Anne, John, Elizabeth, Priscilla, and
Peter—and their families.
—D. L. D.

To Miriam, Joshua, Lydia and Anna, with love.
—M. D. H.

For my father and mother, Donald and Jeannine Morrison.
—J. H. M.

Contents

Foreword: Religious Liberty

Michael Novak

It is an honor to introduce this new volume by a great new generation of students of the American founding. The preceding generations achieved a great deal, but they inevitably slighted some important themes in American legal and political history, as does every generation. Those of us who read history avidly, but with a strong interest in religion and philosophy, have again and again been disappointed in how little one can learn on these subjects from recent scholars. Economic and social factors seem to have preoccupied them, not religious practice. Again and again, I have picked up books on Washington, say, or Madison, or many another figure, only to find few if any lines on their serious considerations of religion. It may have been true that nineteenth-century historians were too enmeshed in (Protestant) Christian images to grasp the distinctive contours of religion in America from a larger perspective and, therefore, some turn to the secular was possibly healthy. Yet, as is often the case in all things, even good turns eventually go badly.

In particular, scholars since about 1950 have thoroughly misconstrued the high achievements of the founding generation with respect to religious liberty. They seem insensitive to, perhaps bewildered by, the extensive practical accommodations between religion and state that the founders worked out. Recent scholars have also failed to grasp the comparative advantage of Judaism and Christianity among world religions, that is, their rare and sophisticated understanding of liberty of conscience. Neither the Hindu nor the Muslim conception of God gives so much attention to the freedom of the individual before God, a God who asks to be worshiped "in spirit and in truth" (Josh. 24:14; John 4:23). Even American deism seems to owe more to Jewish and Christian concepts of God than to ancient pagan religious philosophies. The most common form of deism in the founding generation appears to have been the worship not of the god of Plato, Aristotle, Cicero, or even Descartes, but the Jewish-Christian God (Creator and Providence), abstracted from the historical particulars of Judaism and Christianity.

As a consequence, historians since 1950 do not place the American founding in a true international perspective. They seem uncommonly cut off from its historical roots in centuries of philosophical reflection on God, creation, and the proper relation of rational creatures to their creator. Such materials were consciously in the minds of graduates of elite colleges during the founding period, from the Unitarians or "broadminded" Puritans of Harvard and Yale to the Anglicans or evangelical-minded scholars of the College of New Jersey (Princeton) and King's College (Columbia). Final examinations and public declamations were designed to get these matters straight in the minds of all. For from such conceptions flowed conceptions of liberty of outward action and internal free choice, as these flow from careful deliberation, on the one hand, and from willing acceptance of full personal responsibility before God and man, on the other.

Judaism and Christianity taught their adherents to practice an interior life in the presence of an all-seeing God, an inner life known to them and God alone. This inner life (described at length in John Bunyan's *Pilgrim's Progress* and other books of piety and fiction) was held to be beyond the reach of the state or, for that matter, even of brothers and sisters, parents, or friends. Duties to one's Creator were held to be inseparable from the self and not transferable to any one else; they were "unalienable." This particular vision of a man's interior life is not part of the universal inheritance of humankind; its specific narratives, horizons, and concepts were worked out in Jewish and Christian history over many centuries. While there are many divergences between Protestant and Catholic versions of this vision of the interior life of Christians, the Americans of the founding period drew to a remarkable extent from traditions of reason they held in common with Catholics (through the Anglican Richard Hooker and the "Puritan Scholastics," among others) and to a commonsense reading of the political history of the Bible. One rarely finds among them the disdain for "reason" common among some of the reformers in Europe, on the one hand, or the total disdain for the Bible found among many of the "enlightened" in Europe, on the other.

The tone one finds in the public documents of the founding period, from *The Federalist* to the many state and regional declarations, constitutions, proclamations, political pamphlets, and newspaper disputations on public questions, is that of practical reason, drawing heavily on experiences that everyone can verify in daily observation, the reading of history, or argument drawn from the common Bible. This tone of voice is distinctively American. Its religious roots lie in the adoption of Aristotle as the model for Christian intellect by St. Thomas Aquinas in the thirteenth century, as well as in the pervasive use of Aristotle by the common law, on the one hand, and by international lawyers following Vitoria and Suarez, on the other. Prof. Richard E. Rubenstein's stunning discoveries in *Aristotle's Children* (2003) explain how civilization-changing the adoption of Aristotle was in preparing the way for the later scientific revolution.

As I write these words in early 2004, 244 Muslims have recently been trampled to death by unrestrained, surging crowds in Saudi Arabia making the annual hajj. Asked about these deaths and how they might have been avoided, the official in charge of pilgrimages shrugged and affirmed, "It is the Will of God. The Will of God cannot be prevented." So great is the liberty given God's will in this official's understanding of reality that there is apparently no room for human forethought, resolution, action, and responsibility. To God everything, to man nothing.

The concept of God in Muslim thought and in Christian (and also Jewish) thought is in such matters profoundly different, as is the concept of human responsibility and the understanding of the way in which God's freedom and human freedom interrelate. One can see in the American founding, as the essays here gathered into one another's happy company demonstrate, the workings of a God who wishes to be worshiped in spirit and truth, in the honesty of conscience within, and in uncoerced exercise in the public square of daily life, among men and women who are free, independent, self-reliant, cooperative with one another in civil society, and responsible for their own destiny. This is, as the world goes, a unique God, and these men and women are, in their way of relating to him, a unique people.

Three features of this collection deserve to be singled out for the reader's attention. First, the book focuses on the theme perhaps most neglected by other students of the founding, the intelligent and self-conscious religious views of the founders. The impress of the God of Abraham, Isaac, and Jacob on these views is unmistakably deep, even when the idiom in which his character and actions in history are discussed is practical, related to actual events in then contemporary history, and rather more commonsensical than strictly speaking theological or academic. The founders were lawyers, planters, builders of estates, pioneers, and, if ministers of the gospel (as a handful were), they were just the same practical men and builders of buildings and institutions in their own right. The presence of God was part of the air they breathed, and their thoughts about him were, if not often original, notably intelligent, searching, and self-critical. Most of the founders did not stand still in their religious lives; they pondered, changed, reconsidered, learned from experience, tried out new conceptions, and moved forward. They often examined their own pilgrimages along the way to take their bearings, recognize their changes of direction, or mark their progress. Their religious thinking was almost never merely rote or dictated by convention. Few ended precisely where they had begun.

The least orthodox of the lot were Thomas Jefferson (who described himself as something close to a Unitarian), Benjamin Franklin (who wrote to an inquiring president of Yale that, as close as he was to the age at which men typically die, he would know "soon enough" by direct evidence what to think of the divinity of Christ), and maybe James Madison (although Garrett Sheldon's essay in this volume challenges the conventional wisdom in this regard). Nearly all the other signers of the Declaration of Independence and the Constitution were publicly rather more devout and more orthodox than these three.

Ever since the Supreme Court decisions in *Everson v. Board of Education* (1947) and *McCollum v. Board of Education* (1948), the views of religion imputed by the Court to Madison and Jefferson have been surrounded by so much glare that it has been hard for other jurists, lawyers, or even historians to see in fair detail the actual religious landscape of the founding period and the 171 years that preceded 1947. That brings up the second notable merit of this book. This timely collection introduces other founding fathers, beyond Jefferson and Madison, several, it might be said, "forgotten founders," about whose religious views so much less is known, men like John Witherspoon, George Mason, Charles and Daniel Carroll, and James Wilson. But the old standbys are present. Jefferson and Madison are each represented by an essay, as are George Washington and Benjamin Franklin, not to mention the formidable John Adams, "the father of the nation's independence."

All in all, this volume permits an all too rare and suitably serious look into the power and depth of the religious views of these great personages, to whom the whole world today is manifestly indebted. Indeed, it may be doubted whether the world ever knew so little about so many to whom it owed so much, and, particularly, whether it knew so little about their views on religion and liberty, the two themes that seem now most likely to determine the course of our own twenty-first century.

The third feature that I cherish in this volume is that its authors pay extensive attention to the public documents to which these founders contributed—not so much, that is, to their privately held religious views, but to those views whose public expression seemed to them most important. They wanted these public expressions of religion to express the consent of the people as a whole and to protect the institutions of liberty they were in the process of establishing, legitimating, and commending in perpetuity.

As Alexis de Tocqueville pointed out in *Democracy in America*, America was most distinguished from continental Europe by the fact that here religion and liberty were seen to be interdependent. Each had been present at the founding. Each had heightened the prestige of the other. Each continued to nourish the other. The public expression that the founding generation gave to their long-deliberated, carefully chosen religious formulations, therefore, is of the highest religious interest. It is of much higher interest, even, than the record of their personal convictions, cherished in the privacy of their souls or communicated solely to their spouses, their children, and their extended families. Their public religion belongs to the inheritance of the nation as a whole.

This public inheritance is, furthermore, of rare international value. For the comparative advantage of the public religious convictions of the people of the United States is, first, that they allow for the religious liberty even of those who do not share the religious views of Jews or Christians and even of those who declare themselves to be agnostic or atheist. Their comparative advantage is, second, that they protect religious liberty on premises that are not relativist, nihilist, or cynical. In other words, a commitment to religious liberty, or liberty of conscience, does not entail a commitment to the moral equivalence of any and all points of view. On that premise of moral equivalence, there would be no intellectual defense against the will to power. For if it were true that reason has no capacity for deciding that one point of view is better than another, then the power of decision would have to be vested outside of reason, in raw power or something like it. On that foundation, neither liberty nor civilization could ever be secure. The possibility of liberty requires the possibility of truth. As it is written, "The truth shall make you free" (John 8:32).

The commitment of a civilization to the idea of truth does not require the belief that any one person actually possesses the truth. All that it requires is respect for rules of evidence on the part of all. If all of us are subject to the rules of evidence, we are each servants of such truth as humans may come to. The truth is not our servant; we are its servants. If others show us superior evidence, we must allow that they are correct. Even in those who are our opponents, we may see some truth, just as even in our own views, we may be led to see some error. It is in this way that civilized people learn to argue with one another and to settle disputes by argument in the light of evidence, if not in one meeting, then over time and after sufficient reflection on all sides.

It is on this ground, indeed, that Thomas Jefferson (as I suggested earlier, perhaps the least orthodox of the founders) drew a portrait of the Christian idea of God as a necessary premise for his argument in favor of religious liberty. "Well aware that . . . Almighty God hath created the mind free, and manifested his Supreme will that free it shall remain," he wrote in his Bill for Establishing Religious Freedom in 1779,

> That all attempts to influence it by temporal punishments or burthens, or by civil incapacitations . . . are a departure from the plan of the holy author of our religion, who being Lord of both body and mind, yet chose not to propagate it by coercions on either, as it was in his Almighty power to do, but to extend it by its influence on reason alone.

It was this view of God's relation to truth, and this view alone, that allowed Jefferson to assert a natural right of human beings to religious liberty. To that extent, I would argue, Jefferson's argument for a natural right is in this case not merely a philosophical argument, but, rather, a philosophical argument that in one of its premises borrows a Christian conception of God. I suppose it is legitimate in a philosophical argument to borrow a concept from wherever one will, so long as one is honest and forthright about that, as Jefferson surely is.

It might not be so easy, I imagine, for a Muslim scholar to make such a step from the classical view of Allah to the religious liberty of every individual. About Hinduism, Buddhism, and Shinto, on these matters I also have my doubts. So far as mere secular philosophy goes, it does seem to be true, as Alasdair MacIntyre sadly asserts in *After Virtue* (1981), that the long-cherished project of the Enlightenment to discover a universal ethic based upon reason alone has ended in failure, or, more precisely, in relativism, subjectivism, "nihilism with a happy face," and other such forms of take-your-pick. Post-Enlightenment ethics has been reduced, in effect, to an individual *boo!* or *hurrah!* As we have seen, a commitment to some principle less than finding the truth provides no reasonable basis for either civilization or liberty.

In any case, this book represents an exciting collection of no small importance to world civilization just as the twenty-first century opens. For, once again, questions of religious liberty in the building of new nations have moved front-and-center onto the world stage. Neither Europe nor the rest of the world has in the past paid much attention to the world-altering originality of the American experiment in liberty. Yet, on nothing, and on nothing so important for the future of the world, were our forebears more brilliant in their originality than in their way of reasoning about religious liberty. If the achievement of religious liberty is the luster of our country, as it most assuredly is, our failure to study both its origins and the winding, slowly ascending sources of its brilliant realization has been our singular shame. But now no longer. For that we are all in the debt of the editors of this splendid volume, the first in an important series that they are hereby launching.

Michael Novak
Washington, D.C.

Preface

In recent years, political scientists and historians have gained an appreciation for the important relationship between religion and politics. With respect to the founding era, a few scholars have argued persuasively that religion was far more influential than many twentieth-century scholars recognized or acknowledged. Books such as Ellis Sandoz's *A Government of Laws: Political Theory, Religion, and the American Founding* (1990), Barry Alan Shain's *The Myth of American Individualism: Protestant Origins of American Political Thought* (1994), and Michael Novak's *On Two Wings: Humble Faith and Common Sense at the American Founding* (2002) have painted a vivid picture of how religion impacted the political theory and practices of the founding generation. Perhaps by necessity, most scholars who have addressed these matters have painted with broad strokes.

One avenue for understanding more fully religion's contributions to the American founding is examining the role of religion in the political thoughts and deeds of individual founders. The task of identifying and describing the influence of a particular faith or belief system on an individual's life and thought is, to be sure, difficult. Nevertheless, it is an undertaking that we believe can provide useful insights not only into the examined lives, but also into the society and times in which they were lived. To be successful, such an examination requires both a critical analysis and a willingness to take religion seriously. This combination has been rare among students of the founding era, but it is one we aspire to in this book. We hope our commitment to providing a fair, balanced treatment of the founders examined in this volume is evident in the pages that follow.

In *The Founders on God and Government,* we bring together some of the best students of specific founders who are willing to take religion seriously. We asked each author to write a chapter that, in addition to providing a brief biographical sketch, identified the profiled founder's religious beliefs and denominational affiliations, as well as examined the relationship, if any, between his religious beliefs and political thought. Of particular interest to us was how the selected statesmen, each of whom played a vital role in the founding of the American republic and its institutions, viewed the relation of religious truth to civil authority, especially as such views were expressed in public acts and words uttered in an official capacity. We were also interested in whether standard scholarly treatments of these figures had given adequate attention to religion and its public role in their lives. Several chapters are followed by one or more documents from the pen of the profiled founder that provide insight into the draftsman's thought and the themes of this volume. In addition, we asked Barry Alan Shain to write an essay reflecting on the current state of scholarship in religion and politics in the founding era.

Although we encouraged the contributors to follow the above pattern, we did not insist on absolute uniformity. Our authors come from a variety of backgrounds, and they bring to this project diverse disciplinary perspectives, methodological approaches, and styles of scholarship and documentation. Accordingly, the essays do not address their subjects in lockstep fashion, but each provides a concise and focused treatment of its founder's view of religion and civil government. In some cases, essays offer new interpretations or arguments. Others pull together arguments that their authors have made elsewhere, often in book form. In either case, we believe that this collection makes a useful contribution to the literature by compiling concise and informative essays on eleven influential founders. We hope that both scholars and the general public will read them for enlightenment and pleasure.

We are grateful to the many institutions and individuals—named and unnamed—who helped make this book possible. We start by thanking each contributing author for completing his essay in a timely and professional manner. Many of these essays originated as papers delivered at the American Political Science Association annual meetings or as John Courtney Murray lectures at the American Enterprise Institute for Public Policy Research in Washington, D.C. We are grateful to the many discussants in both forums, whose valuable comments refined these essays. We are particularly indebted to Michael Novak and Graham Walker for organizing the Murray lectures and helping us to conceptualize this volume. We are grateful to the Witherspoon Institute of Princeton, New Jersey, for a subvention at a critical juncure. Our editors at Rowman & Littlefield Publishers made the process of putting together a volume of this scope and size far more enjoyable than it might have been. We particularly appreciate the labors of editors Laura Roberts Gottlieb, Terry Fischer, and Mary Carpenter and their predecessor, Stephen Wrinn. Finally, we thank the publishers and journals that granted permission to reprint material in this volume.

On a personal note, Daniel Dreisbach is grateful for the generous research support of American University, the Virginia Historical Society (for an Andrew W. Mellon Fellowship), and Gunston Hall Plantation, which made possible his contribution to this volume. He also acknowledges the assistance of librarians and archivists at American University, the Virginia Historical Society, and the Fairfax County Public Library. For their endless patience and good humor during the course of this and other projects, he thanks his wife, Joyce, and two daughters, Mollie Abigail and Moriah Esther. Mark Hall would like to express his gratitude for the support of George Fox University and the research assistance of Rachel Sparks, Susanne Cordner, and Karlyn Fleming. He is especially thankful for the patience and love offered freely by his wife, Miriam, and children, Joshua, Lydia, and Anna. Jeffry Morrison thanks the faculty and staff of the James Madison Program in American Ideals and Institutions of the Department of Politics at Princeton University for a visiting fellowship during 2003–2004, and Regent University for ongoing institutional support. He is also deeply appreciative of familial support and grants of toleration from his wife, Melissa, and children, Alex and Ella.

Even before they were laid in their graves, the founders, both individually and collectively, excited the imagination of the American people. They continue to fascinate and inform the public mind today. Biographies of both famous and forgotten founders sit atop national bestseller lists, and politicians and jurists continue to make frequent appeals to their words and precedents. We hope this book makes a useful addition to the literature on the founding in general, and to religion's contributions to American civic culture, in particular. Given the continuing influence of the founders on political and legal thought, we believe this collection of essays will cast light not only on the past but also on the future of the American experiment in liberty under law.

1

Religion and the Common Good

George Washington on Church and State*

Vincent Phillip Muñoz

> Individuals entering into society, must give up a share of liberty to pre-
> serve the rest. The magnitude of the sacrifice must depend as well on sit-
> uation and circumstance, as on the object to be obtained. It is at all times
> difficult to draw with precision the line between those rights which must
> be surrendered, and those which may be reserved.
>
> —George Washington, letter submitting the proposed constitution
> to the president of Congress, September 17, 1787[1]

George Washington's political thought regarding church and state
never has been thoroughly articulated. Most scholars assume that on
matters of religious liberty Thomas Jefferson and James Madison
speak for the founding generation. The near-exclusive concern with
Jefferson and Madison can be traced to the landmark 1947 Establishment Clause case *Everson* v. *Board of Education*. In *Everson*, the
Supreme Court presumed, first, that the founding fathers shared a uniform understanding of religious freedom and, second, that Jefferson
and Madison most authentically represented the founders' views.[2]
Ever since, most constitutional scholars have uncritically accepted
Everson's presumptions.[3]

George Washington, however, was no less dedicated to securing religious freedom than his second and third presidential successors. In
a 1783 letter he testified that "the establishment of Civil and Religious

---

*A different version of this chapter was originally published as "George Washington and Re-
ligious Liberty," *The Review of Politics* 65, no. 1 (Winter 2003): 11–33.

Liberty was the Motive which induced me to the field [of battle]."[4] Washington, moreover, offers a different understanding of the right to religious freedom than Jefferson and Madison, at least as they are usually interpreted. Like many, if not most, leaders of the founding generation, Washington believed a pious citizenry was indispensable to republican government and, therefore, that civil government could and should endorse religion. On questions of free exercise, he believed the right to religious liberty to be limited by the legitimate duties of republican citizenship. If we make the attempt to understand Washington's thinking, we shall see that he offers a theory of the right of religious freedom that reveals the diversity of thought within the founding generation and that speaks to the First Amendment religion controversies continually before the nation's courts.

Unlike Washington's political philosophy on church–state matters, his personal religious opinions have been the source of much scholarly speculation. Paul Boller's classic study, *George Washington and Religion*, offers the most comprehensive account of Washington's beliefs.[5] The numerous quotations Boller assembles reveal that Washington espoused belief in the existence of a good and providential God. As discussed below, Washington's speeches and letters frequently invoke the "Supreme Being" and the "All Wise Creator," who "wisely orders the Affairs of Men."[6] Boller concludes that Washington was a deist.[7] John West Jr. points out, however, that Washington's belief in divine providence means, by definition, that he could not be labeled a deist.[8]

Washington clearly did not possess the anticlerical spirit that animates some Enlightenment figures, but less clear is the strength and depth of his interior conviction is less clear. Washington rarely spoke about Christ, and he usually referred to the divine in only the most general terms. Toward the end of his life he wrote, "in politics, as in religion, my tenets are few and simple."[9] The simplicity of his faith is captured in a short passage he wrote three months before his death:

> I was the *first*, and am now the *last* of my father's Children by the second marriage who remain. When I shall be called upon to follow them, is known only to the giver of life. When the summons comes I shall endeavour to obey it with a good grace.[10]

Washington's religious practices reflect the same ambivalence captured in his written words. He was a lifelong member of the Anglican Church in Virginia, in which he was baptized, married, and served as a godfather for the children of various relatives and friends. Yet, Washington attended church services only infrequently.[11] We may say with confidence that Washington believed in a good and providential God, but other than these basic tenets, we can say little with certainty about the content of his faith.

WASHINGTON'S POLITICAL DIFFERENCES WITH MADISON

Deducing Washington's political philosophy of church–state matters is not an easy task. Because he does not offer a singular document on religious liberty, we must extrapolate his political theory from his political practice, including the letters and writings that belong to it. When one turns to Washington's practical politics regarding religion, one cannot help but be struck by how different they are from Madison's. Whereas Madison sometimes attempted to separate religion from politics,[12] Washington consistently sought to use governmental authority to encourage religion and to foster the religious character of the American people.

Washington, for example, initially was not opposed to Patrick Henry's general assessment bill, the proposed statute that sparked Madison to write his "Memorial and Remonstrance against Religious Assessments." Writing to George Mason, a leading assessment foe, Washington explained,

> Altho [*sic*], no man's sentiments are more opposed to *any kind* of restraint upon religious principles than mine are; yet I must confess, that I am not amongst the number of those who are so much alarmed at the thoughts of making people pay towards the support of that which they profess, if of the denominations of Christians; or declare themselves Jews, Mahomitans or otherwise, and thereby obtain proper relief.[13]

In the same letter, Washington further explained, "As the matter now stands, I wish an assessment had never been agitated and as it has gone so far, that the Bill could die an easy death; because I think it will be productive of more quiet to the State, than by enacting it into a Law."[14] Washington opposed Henry's measure not because it violated the principle of religious liberty, Madison's principal argument, but because the bill caused unnecessary political turmoil.

Washington's opinion of the propriety of military chaplains reflects a second difference from Madison's. Madison thought taxpayer-funded chaplains violated constitutional principles.[15] If such a thought crossed

Washington's mind, he never said so. As commander in chief of the Continental army, Washington sought not only to procure chaplains for his soldiers, but also to insure that the Continental Congress offered a salary generous enough to attract "men of abilities."[16] Chaplains, he believed, helped to improve discipline, raise morale, check vice, and fortify courage and bravery while securing respectful obedience and subordination to those in command.[17] Washington, moreover, did not make chaplains available only to those who wanted them. He repeatedly commanded his soldiers to attend Sunday services if the war effort permitted it. "The General," he declared in one such typical order, "requires and expects, of all Officers and Soldiers, not engaged in actual duty, a punctual attendance on divine Service to implore the blessings of heaven upon the means used of our safety and defence."[18] The "regularity and decorum" with which the Sabbath was observed, Washington explained following another such order, "will reflect great credit on the army in general, tend to improve the morals, and at the same time, to increase the happiness of the soldiery, and must afford the most pure and rational entertainment for every serious and well disposed mind."[19] It would also reduce "profane cursing, swearing and drunkenness," he said on another occasion.[20]

General Washington also commanded his soldiers to observe special days of "Fasting, Humiliation and Prayer." Sometimes he issued orders to comply with resolutions passed by the Continental Congress, but on other occasions, in particular after key victories or successful strategic operations, Washington relied upon his own authority. After receiving news of the conclusion of an alliance with France in 1778, he issued the following:

> It having pleased the Almighty ruler of the Universe propitiously to defend the Cause of the United American-States and finally by raising us up a powerful Friend among the Princes of the Earth to establish our liberty and Independence up[on] lasting foundations, it becomes us to set apart a day for gratefully acknowledging the divine Goodness and celebrating the important Event which we owe to his benign Interposition.[21]

Washington brought to the presidency the practice of declaring special days of prayer and thanksgiving, which brings forth another sharp difference from Madison. Madison issued four official religious proclamations during the War of 1812, but he later maintained that such measures violated the spirit of the Constitution.[22] Washington took no such view. He issued two official presidential proclamations for days of prayer and thanksgiving, the first on October 3, 1789, in response to a request by Congress and the second on January 1, 1795, apparently on his own initiative.[23] Nothing indicates that Washington hesitated in any way when issuing them.

The proclamations themselves, moreover, speak in defense of their own propriety. Both start with a statement of duty. Washington begins the first decree, "Whereas it is the duty of all nations to acknowledge the providence of Almighty God, to obey His will, to be grateful for His benefits, and humbly to implore His protection and favor."[24] The first paragraph of his 1795 statement similarly maintains,

> In such a state of things [exemption from foreign war and the existence of domestic tranquility] it is in an especial manner our duty as a people, with devout reverences and affectionate gratitude, to acknowledge our many and great obligations to Almighty God and to implore him to continue and confirm the blessings we experience.[25]

Madison's proclamations, by comparison, all begin with the bland assertion that the Congress has called for a national proclamation. He does not emphasize the propriety or duty of giving thanks to the Almighty. If Washington thought that the American people had a duty to recognize and acknowledge God, surely he did not think it improper for the president to facilitate its performance.

Washington's official religious presidential proclamations reflect his deliberate intention to solemnify public statements and occasions. All of Washington's most important public addresses include religious language. His 1783 "Circular to the States," the closest thing to a national or presidential speech in American history prior to 1789, ends with an earnest prayer for God's "holy protection." His first inaugural address, similarly, begins and ends in prayer. Toward the beginning of the speech, Washington states,

> It would be peculiarly improper to omit, in this first official act, my fervent supplications to that Almighty Being who rules over the universe; who presides in the councils of nations; and whose providential aid can supply every human defect; that his benediction may consecrate to the liberties and happiness of the People of the United States, a Government instituted by themselves for these essential purposes. . . . In tending this homage to the Great Author of every public and private good, I assure myself that it expresses your sentiments not less than my own; nor those of my fellow citizens at large less than either. No people can be bound to acknowledge and adore the invisible hand which conducts the affairs of men, more than the people of the United States.[26]

At the first inaugural Washington also added the phrase "So help me God" to the end of the presidential oath of office, and he began the tradition of swearing the oath on the Bible.[27]

The use of taxes to support religion, the appointment of military chaplains, the propriety of issuing religious presidential proclamations, and the deliberate inclusion of sacred language in public ceremonies reflect the distance between Washington and Madison on the proper disposition of government toward religion. Washington did not think that the state must be "strictly separated" from religion. He agreed that religious worship was a natural right and that the purpose of government was to secure the rights of man, but he did not translate those general principles into Madison's specific limitations on the powers of government.

WASHINGTON'S DEFENSE OF GOVERNMENT SUPPORT FOR RELIGION: THE FAREWELL ADDRESS

Washington's most definitive political statement regarding religion, in fact, pertains not to the limits of government power, but rather to the propriety of governmental support. In his Farewell Address, Washington's valedictory statement to the American people,[28] he explains why republican government must endorse religion:

> Of all the dispositions and habits which lead to political prosperity, Religion and morality are indispensable supports. In vain would that man claim the tribute of Patriotism, who should labor to subvert these great pillars of human happiness, these firmest props of the duties of Man and citizens. The mere Politician, equally with the pious man ought to respect and to cherish them. A volume could not trace all their connections with private and public felicity.[29]

Religion and morality are indispensable because, Washington explains a few lines later, "'Tis substantially true, that virtue or morality is a necessary spring of popular government."[30]

Washington's reference to virtue as the "spring" of popular government is Montesquieuian. In *The Spirit of the Laws*, Montesquieu teaches that each form of government relies upon a "principle" or "spring," by which he means the ruling passion that sets the regime in motion and perpetuates its existence.[31] The principle or spring of republican government, Montesquieu claims, is virtue. By virtue he does not mean the classical moral virtues or even human excellence more generally, but rather what he called political virtue, self-sacrifice for the common good.[32] In the Farewell Address, Washington uses virtue and morality in both their classical and their modern Montesquieuian senses. Washington follows the classical teaching insofar as he explicitly connects individual virtue to human happiness. Yet, his analysis is also distinctly modern and Montesquieuian insofar as he makes virtue and morality instrumental to political life, not the aim of politics. Virtue and morality are needed for public felicity because without them, "Let it simply be asked where is the security for property, for reputation, for life, if the sense of religious obligation *desert* the oaths, which are the instruments of investigation in Courts of Justice?"[33] Washington venerates virtue and morality because they prompt citizens to act in a decent, truthful, and law-abiding manner. Virtuous citizens govern themselves voluntarily and respect the rights of others, thereby reducing the need for government to secure rights through the coercive force of law. Virtue and morality are indispensable because they make self-government possible.

Washington recognizes that for most men most of the time, virtue and morality are not choice-worthy in and of themselves. Republican government needs religion because virtue and morality depend on religious faith:

> And let us with caution indulge the supposition, that morality can be maintained without religion. Whatever may be conceded to the influence of refined education on minds of peculiar structure, reason and experience both forbid us to expect that National morality can prevail in exclusion of religious principle.[34]

Washington concedes that a few may be good on account of their education, but the less refined many require the fear of eternal damnation and the prospect of eternal salvation to fortify their characters. Washington's view of human nature is soberly low; he reaffirms Madison's portrait of human nature in *The Federalist* No. 51 that men are not angels. Yet, Washington's accommodation to human nature's lack of virtue goes beyond Madison's prescription. Whereas *The Federalist* accepts human nature as it is—and therefore emphasizes the separation of powers and checks and balances—Washington focuses explicitly on shaping the moral character of the American people. He endorses the use of religion for political purposes, something that Madison labeled "an unhallowed perversion of the means of salvation."[35] Washington thought the Madisonian position failed to respect reason and the lessons of experience, both of which taught that patriotic republicans ought to recognize and endorse religion because only a religious citizenry could sustain republican self-government.

GOVERNMENT SUPPORT OF RELIGION AND
THE COMMON GOOD

Washington's critique of Madison's position brings forth an obvious question, especially to modern sensibilities colored by the last fifty-five years of Supreme Court jurisprudence: Did Washington think that government support of religion was compatible with religious freedom? Does support not favor religion over irreligion, thus violating the neutrality that religious freedom guarantees? Washington's answer is relatively simple: religious liberty does not require governmental neutrality toward religion. He believed that republican government ought to favor religion and discourage irreligion, because religion favors republican government.

The more difficult question, one that Washington was obviously aware of, but never addressed theoretically, is, How can government support religion without inviting discord among competing religious sects? Government support of religion invites irreconcilable theological differences to enter into the political arena. While one can speak of supporting religion in the abstract, it is difficult to do in practice. All religions are particular; general support of religion inevitably results in the support of some particular sects and not others. Positive government action can easily trigger partisan politics along religious lines, pitting sects against one another for scarce political resources and inviting political strife among groups unable to reconcile their differences. Madison sought to avoid this dilemma by denying religion as such direct government support, thereby limiting sectarian politics.

From Washington's perspective, Madison's approach ignores the reality that republican government requires religion. Separating religious morality from state support unnecessarily destabilizes the very foundation upon which republican government rests. Yet, the manner in which Washington chose to support religion reflects his awareness of the problem that such support entails. In his public speeches and writings, Washington used only nonsectarian language. His first inaugural address includes fervent supplications to "that Almighty Being who rules over the universe," homage to "the Great Author of every public and private good," and humble supplications to "the benign Parent of the human race."[36] His presidential proclamations of days of prayer and thanksgiving recognize "that great and glorious Being who is the beneficent author of all the good that was, that is, or that will be"[37] and render hearty thanks to "the Great Ruler of Nations."[38]

Washington's support of military chaplains also reflects the delicate balance that he sought to maintain. He not only wanted chaplains, but chaplains of every denomination so that each soldier could attend his own religious services. When the Continental Congress sought to appoint chaplains by brigade, rather than at the regiment level, Washington protested. Because brigades were larger than regiments, the likelihood of unanimity of religious sentiment was reduced. Washington feared that the reduced number of chaplains could have "a tendency to introduce religious disputes into the Army," that is, disputes over the denomination of the chaplain to be secured. Brigade chaplains, moreover, "in many instances would compel men to a mode of Worship which they do not profess." If employed incorrectly, military chaplains, whom Washington thought were absolutely necessary to the war effort, could have a deleterious effect by introducing "uneasiness and jealously among the Troops."[39] Washington recommended to Congress that chaplains remain assigned at the level where most soldiers would have a chaplain of their own religious persuasion, thereby minimizing religious discord.

Washington's efforts to maintain military chaplains at the regiment level exemplify how he thought government could and should support religion, yet maintain respect for the individual's rights of conscience. He included within the right of conscience the right not to be compelled to practice a mode of worship that one does not profess. He did not extend this to a more general right to abstain from worship, however, because he did command his soldiers to attend religious services. But if military superiors expected their soldiers to attend religious services, they ought to provide chaplains of the soldiers' denominations.

Washington also excluded from the rights of conscience a right not to be taxed for the support of religion. Military chaplains were legitimate because they supported the war effort, which itself was directed at the common good. Insofar as religion contributes to the common good, it is a legitimate object of taxpayer dollars. Washington thus explicitly disagreed with Madison's claim in the "Memorial" that compelling even three pence for the direct support of religion violated the principle of religious liberty.[40] Washington was always very careful, however, to link public support of religion to a public good. In the case at hand, Washington explicitly connected military chaplains to the discipline and morale of the armed forces. Washington's definition of the public good was expansive—it included the formation of individual's characters—but, nonetheless, he did not promote support of religion as an end in itself.

Washington's position is thus most similar to that of those who have suggested the "secular purpose" rule for establishment clause jurisprudence—government may support religion so long as its puts forth a legitimate secular reason for doing so. He probably would have disliked the term *secular purpose,* as that term itself is unnecessarily hostile toward religion, and instead would have favored "civic policy" or just "the common good"—government may support religion insofar as it does so in a manner that supports the common good. Washington would have disagreed with today's "strict separationists," who claim that government may not favor religion over irreligion. He also would have disagreed, although less emphatically, with "nonpreferentialists," who claim government may support religion if it supports all religions equally. Washington's position is more discriminating. Government should support religion because religion supports republican government. By implication, government ought not support those religions that maintain principles hostile toward republicanism or advocate behavior contrary to good citizenship.[41]

THE LIMITS OF THE RIGHT TO
THE FREE EXERCISE OF RELIGION

Just as concern for the common good sanctions governmental support of religion, it also defines the legitimate limits of the right to religious free exercise. When Madison recognized the right of religious liberty in "Memorial and Remonstrance," he specified limits on the realm of legitimate governmental action. Washington agreed with this formulation, as did all social contract theorists and practitioners at the time. He disagreed with Madison, however, on where the lines demarcating the right of free exercise should be drawn. Whereas Madison sought to establish the precise rule that government may not be cognizant of religion[42] and, therefore, may not act in a manner that penalizes religion as such, Washington found the natural boundaries of the right to free exercise established by the reasonable demands of maintaining the social contract. To put the matter in more Washingtonian language, Washington held that the right to religious liberty must recognize the legitimate demands of good citizenship.

Washington addressed this theme most directly in a series of letters written soon after his assumption of the presidency. Upon his election, Washington received numerous congratulatory letters, including letters from churches of several religious denominations. Washington's response to these groups captures the truly revolutionary character of the American regime. As Harry Jaffa has written and as Washington sought to make clear, for the first time in human history political citizenship would no longer be based upon religious affiliation.[43] In an act of the highest statesmanship, Washington staked his considerable personal prestige on the new nation's commitment to religious freedom. In doing so, he not only demonstrated his personal commitment to this right, but pledged the nation to it as well.

These letters make clear that religious freedom does not supplant the duties of republican citizenship. Washington's epistle to the Baptists of Virginia captures the theme of his postelection letters. In their letter to Washington, the Baptists expressed concern that the Constitution did not sufficiently secure the liberty of conscience. In his response, Washington assured them, "I would have never placed my signature to it [the Constitution]" if he thought the general government might render the liberty of conscience insecure. He continued, then, to explain and define what the liberty of conscience secures:

> For you, doubtless, remember that I have often expressed my sentiment, that every man, conducting himself as a good citizen, and being accountable to God alone for his religious opinions, ought to be protected in worshipping the Deity according to the dictates of his own conscience.[44]

The right to liberty of conscience secures the freedom to worship the Deity according to the dictates of one's conscience. This means that government ought not impose a mode of worship upon an individual that he or she finds objectionable.

But what about individual modes of worship that the government finds objectionable? To take an extreme, but historical, example, what about the Aztec religion, which ordained the sacrifice of human beings in supposed obedience to a divine command? If government prevents this, does it fail to protect the individual's rights of conscience? And what if government commands the performance of acts that an individual believes violates his religion? May government legitimately prescribe such actions?

Washington's answer to these questions is clear: a condition of civil society and, thus, of a government capable of protecting the rights of conscience is that individuals must conduct themselves as good citizens. In his letter to the Baptists, the modifying clause "conducting himself as a good citizen" defines the limits of the right to liberty of conscience. The right to religious freedom does not include the right to perform actions contrary to the duties of citizenship. The state possesses no affirmative obligation to tolerate actions opposed to good citizenship, including religiously motivated actions. And the state may legitimately expect all citizens to perform the reasonable duties of citizenship, even those that religious citizens find objectionable. Washington does not define here what the obligations of good citizenship include, but whatever they are, they stand as a precondition to having one's rights secured.

Washington faced this difficult issue concretely in his dealings with the Quaker religion. Most Quakers at the time interpreted their religious precepts to forbid any kind of participation in the armed forces. Washington encountered Quaker pacifism as early as 1756 during the French and Indian War, when six Quakers were drafted into the Virginia militia and sent to serve under his command. In Washington's own words, they would "neither bear arms, work, receive pay, or do anything that tends, in any respect, to self-defence."[45] He faced similar resistance throughout the Revolutionary War, which I shall discuss below. In 1789, the Quakers wrote to Washington to explain their principle of pacifism and "to assure thee [Washington], that we feel our Hearts affectionately drawn towards thee, and those in Authority over us."[46] Washington's response to the Quakers is a model of magnanimity and charity, especially considering that it comes from a life-long military commander. Nonetheless, it is less than an absolute endorsement of the Quakers, and it delivers a stinging criticism. Washington writes,

> The liberty enjoyed by the People of these States, of worshipping Almighty God agreeably to their Consciences, is not only among the choicest of their *Blessings*, but also of their *Rights*—While men perform their social duties faithfully, they do all that society or the state can with propriety demand or expect; and remain responsible only to their Maker for the Religion, or modes of faith, which they may prefer or profess.
>
> Your principles & conduct are well known to me—and it is doing the People called Quakers no more than Justice to say, that (except their declining to share with others the burthen of the common defense) there is no Denomination among us who are more exemplary and useful Citizens.[47]

Washington recognizes the rights of conscience as a liberty enjoyed by all Americans and, thus, by the Quakers. At the same time, however, he refuses to recognize the political legitimacy of their refusal to take up arms. Society and the state can properly expect all citizens, even religious pacifists, to share in the burden of the common defense. To the extent that the Quakers refuse to fight in defense of their country and of their rights, even if for religious reasons, they are not exemplary or useful citizens.

Perhaps in anticipation of the Quakers' disappointment with his polite but stern rebuke, Washington concludes his letter charitably:

> I assure you very explicitly that in my opinion the Conscientious scruples of all men should be treated with great delicacy & tenderness; and it is my wish and desire, that the Laws may always be as extensively accommodated to them, as due regard to the Protection and essential Interests of the Nation may Justify and permit.[48]

When perceived religious obligations conflict with fulfilling the duties of citizenship, Washington's "wish and desire" is that the laws may be accommodating. To wish and desire that such may be the case is to express a hopeful opinion of a particular outcome, but it by no means promises that outcome or in any way indicates that the state has an affirmative obligation to reach it. Washington, moreover, explicitly calls attention to limitations on making legal accommodations to religion. The protection and the essential interests of the nation—that is, the common good—must first be recognized and secured. Washington establishes a clear hierarchy when religious practices clash with legitimate obligations of citizenship: the political is higher than the religious. Religious individuals must accommodate their conscientious scruples to the essential interests of the nation in matters of reasonable social duties.[49]

We see this same formula in Washington's letters to the Roman Catholics in America[50] and to the Hebrew congregation in Newport. In the latter, perhaps his most famous address to any religious society, Washington writes,

> It is now no more that toleration is spoken of, as if it was by the indulgence of one class of people, that another enjoyed the exercise of their natural rights. For happily the Government of the United States, which gives to bigotry no sanction, to persecution no assistance requires only that they who live under its protection should demean themselves as good citizens, in giving it on all occasions their effectual support.[51]

In two beautiful sentences, Washington recognizes the revolutionary character of the American regime. The rights and privileges of U.S.

citizenship do not depend on religious affiliation. These rights, however, are conditioned by corresponding duties, the first of which is that every individual must "demean" himself as a good citizen.

Washington's letters contain a twofold approach to the protection of religious liberty. On those matters that do not involve the essential interests of the state or the duties of good citizenship, the state should remain quiet. The state, for example, cannot properly dictate the tenets of any religion or prescribe any particular mode of worship. The state, moreover, cannot condition the rights and privileges of citizenship on the basis of religious affiliation. The most sacred rights of republican citizens, the rights to property and to participate in rule through voting and holding office, for example, cannot depend on one's theological beliefs or lack thereof. On matters involving the essential interests of the state or the duties of citizenship, however, the state has no obligation to recognize religious dissent. If it so chooses, the state may accommodate conscientious religious scruples—Washington expressed his wish and desire that it would—but it has no obligation to do so. On matters pertaining to the essential interests of the nation and the duties of good citizenship, religious individuals can only expect to be tolerated.

The manner in which Washington dealt with Quaker pacifism during the Revolutionary War offers a revealing case study of the degree to which he understood religious liberty to include an element of toleration only, with toleration defined as a conditional willingness to bear with that which one disagrees. At times, General Washington sought to accommodate the Quakers' refusal to bear arms. When the war shifted to Pennsylvania in early 1777, for example, he wrote to the Pennsylvania Council of Safety that "it is absolutely necessary, that every Person able to bear arms (except such as are Conscientiously scrupulous against it in every Case), should give their personal Service, and whenever a part of the Militia is required only, either to join the Army or find a Man in their place."[52] Washington did not mention the Quakers by name, but it is fair to assume that he anticipated their religious objection to military service. Later in that same year, he sent home several Virginia Quakers who had been drafted into the militia.[53]

At other times, however, Washington was much more harsh toward the Quakers, especially those in Pennsylvania whose neutrality was interpreted by many to be, in effect, pro-British Toryism. In May 1777, he wrote to Pennsylvania governor William Livingston, "I have been informed by Colo. Forman, that the Quakers and disaffected are doing all in their power to counteract your late Militia Law; but I hope, if your Officers are active and Spirited, that they will defeat their evil intentions and bring their Men into the Field."[54] During the British occupation of Philadelphia, Washington's ire peaked. When giving orders to impress supplies from the countryside, Washington twice commanded his officers to "take care, that, the unfriendly Quakers and others notoriously disaffected to the cause of American liberty do not escape your Vigilance."[55] In March 1778, Washington went so far as to order his officers to prevent Quakers from entering Philadelphia so they could not attend their religious services, "an intercourse," Washington explained, "that we should by all means endeavour to interrupt, as the plans settled at these meeting are of the most pernicious tendency."[56]

The Quaker situation Washington faced anticipates the contemporary Free Exercise jurisprudential question of whether religious citizens possess a right to exemptions from generally applicable state actions that burden religious exercise. The Quakers of Washington's time made the same claim that Seventh Day Adventists,[57] the Amish,[58] and members of the Native American Church[59] have made before the Supreme Court: equal respect for religious freedom requires exemptions from neutral but burdensome laws. Although one should hesitate to apply actions from one historical context to another, a Washingtonian interpretation of the free-exercise clause would not admit a constitutional right to religious exemptions. Washington did not treat the Quakers' religious pacifism as a right. He was inclined to accommodate the Quakers' sincere religious exercises, and, at times, he was willing to permit the Quakers not to fight. But he never acted under the presumption that the right to religious freedom entitled the Quakers to different treatment because of their religious beliefs. His order to his officers to be vigilant in impressing Quaker property, moreover, reflects his belief that they had failed to contribute their fair share to the war effort and that their refusal to fight, whatever the reason, was in some sense unjust to other more dutiful citizens. His command to prevent Quakers from attending religious services, furthermore, clearly evinces his belief that religiously motivated actions could be prevented if they were antithetical to the interests of the nation. Washington permitted or constrained Quaker religious exercises as the common good dictated. His actions during the war perfectly match the theory expressed in his presidential letters to the various religious denominations. And although Washington writes against mere "toleration" in his letter to the Hebrew congregation, his understanding of religious liberty, both as espoused in his letters and reflected in his actions, contains an important element of this principle.

For the most part, Washington did not force Quakers into combat. He attempted to minimize the tension between the Quakers and the war effort, just as he sought to minimize religious disagreements within the army by maintaining chaplains at the regimental level. Washington's consistent attempts to reduce conflict between government and religious sentiment indicate that he would support discretionary legislative or executive religious accommodations. But although religious exercises are of the rights of mankind, they are legitimately and necessarily limited within civil society. Just as religion should be encouraged and accommodated as much as possible because it is profoundly connected to the moral foundations necessary for good government, religious exercises legitimately can be limited when required for the common good.

This brings forth a final set of questions: If Washington respected individuals' sincerely held religious beliefs, why then, when these beliefs came into conflict with the interests of the nation, did he favor the government over the individual? Why not favor the individual's perception of his religious duties over the government's interests?

Again, Washington does not offer a theoretical discussion or a carefully articulated explanation of his position. In a letter to the general assembly of the Presbyterian Church, however, he gives a brief indication of how he thought the tension between an individual's religion and governmental interests could be resolved. The Presbyterians were the first religious group to write to Washington after his election to the presidency. Their letter was full of high praise. In particular, the Presbyterians testified,

> [We] esteem it a peculiar happiness to behold in our chief Magistrate, a steady, uniform, avowed friend of the Christian religion, who has commenced his administration in rational and exalted sentiments of Piety, and who in his private conduct adorns the doctrines of the Gospel of Christ, and on the most public and solemn occasions devoutly acknowledges the government of divine Providence.[60]

Washington's response to the Presbyterians, like all of his responses to various congregations that wrote to him at this time, mirrors their letter to him. The Presbyterians' letter began by announcing their adoration of God for giving to the United States a man of such talents and public virtue. Washington's response, in turn, begins by thanking the Presbyterians and reiterating his dependence on the "assistance of Heaven" for his arduous undertakings.[61] The Presbyterian letter then praises Washington for his Christian character. Washington's response at this point takes an interesting turn. Rather than reiterating his Christian beliefs, he offers a statement on the new nation's dedication to the principle of religious liberty, even though the Presbyterians' letter did not broach the subject. At the very point that the Presbyterians become sectarian, Washington becomes ecumenical. He indirectly instructs the Presbyterians on the nonsectarian character of the new American regime. While he will affirm his reliance on providence and heaven, he will not explicitly invoke the name of Jesus Christ.

Here we see a subtle, yet instructive, example of Washington's strategy for minimizing the conflict between the duties of citizenship and the sentiments of religion. The United States can avoid unnecessarily highlighting tensions between civic duties and religious sentiments if it avoids sectarian rhetoric and policy. Washington's letter then goes one step further. He writes,

> While all men within our territories are protected in worshipping the Deity according to the dictates of their consciences; it is rationally to be expected from them in return, that they will be emulous of evincing the sanctity of their professions by the innocence of their lives and the beneficence of their actions; for no man, who is profligate in his morals, or a bad member of the civil community, can possibly be a true Christian, or a credit to his own religious society.[62]

Government can rationally expect that all religious citizens will be good citizens because no true religion would encourage its followers to be bad members of the American civil community. I highlight Washington's use of the word "rationally," because in it lies the ultimate justification for the government's encroachment upon an individual's religious sentiments. The American polity, founded upon the self-evident truth that "all men are created equal," is in its founding principles and constitutional government a rational regime. It accords with the transcendent principles of "nature and nature's God" as apprehended by man using his natural reason. And thus, that which is essential to the common good of the nation is itself reasonable, defensible, and just.

The religious sentiments of "bad members of the civil community," including those who fail to fulfill their civic duties for religious reasons, can legitimately be limited because these sentiments cannot possibly be true to Christianity or, Washington suggests, to true religion simply.

The precepts of true religion and good citizenship are not in tension in a regime grounded upon the principles of "nature and nature's God." In demanding good citizenship and only sometimes tolerating religious actions that contravene good citizenship, the state offends neither true religion nor a rational understanding of justice.

CONCLUSION

Washington's twofold approach to the right of the free exercise of religion—government noninterference grounded on right regarding matters not affecting the common good, and discretionary toleration for matters involving the duties of citizenship and the essential interests of the nation—is perfectly compatible with his Establishment Clause position of government support of religion. Both approaches, in fact, emerge from the principle that the state may permissibly take action to foster the common good of the community. Washington thought religion not only a moral duty for the individual, but also a public good for the polity. He thought it proper, accordingly, to support and endorse religious sentiments that support the common good. The state, similarly, may legitimately limit religious exercises so long as those limitations are connected to the common good. On matters that do not concern the common good—and most religious exercises would fall into this category—the state ought not impose unnecessary limits.

George Washington did not participate in the drafting of the First Amendment (of course, neither did Thomas Jefferson). One cannot and ought not claim that a Washingtonian understanding clearly represents the original intentions of the drafters or the ratifiers of the First Amendment. An investigation of Washington's thought, however, reveals that significant differences existed among the leading founding fathers on the meaning and limitations of the right to religious liberty. Washington would not "strictly separate" religion from politics or recognize a right to religious exemptions from neutral, but burdensome, laws. Judicial scholars and judges, accordingly, cannot claim that these interpretations represent "the founding fathers' understanding" of such matters. Washington, moreover, offers a theory of religious liberty capable of unifying the two religion clauses of the First Amendment. He teaches that both the ends and the means of government support and limitations of religious exercise must be defended in terms of public goods. His writings and actions offer a model of how a religiously diverse people can think and act in ways that safeguard both the individual's religious freedom and the community's legitimate concern for the common good. Although not the "Father of the Constitution," the father of our country stands ready to inform our deliberations on the meaning of religious freedom should we choose to enlist him.

NOTES

1. Max Farrand, ed. *The Records of the Federal Convention of 1787* (New Haven, CT: Yale University Press, 1966), 2:666.

2. *Everson v. Board of Education*, 330 U.S. 1, 13 (1947).

3. For further discussion of this point, see Daniel L. Dreisbach, "A Lively and Fair Experiment: Religion and the American Constitutional Tradition," *Emory Law Journal* 49 (Winter 2000): 228–38.

4. John C. Fitzpatrick, ed. "George Washington to the Reformed German Congregation in the City of New York, November 27, 1783," *The Writings of George Washington* (Washington, D.C.: United States Government Printing Office, 1931–1944), 27:249 (hereafter *Writings of George Washington*).

5. Paul F. Boller, *George Washington and Religion* (Dallas, TX: Southern Methodist University Press, 1963), especially ch. 5. Boller also offers a review of the scholarly debate on Washington's personal religious opinions in ch. 1.

6. See, for example, Washington's letter to Dr. James Anderson, July 25, 1798, *Writings of George Washington*, 36:365; and Washington's letter to Governor George Trumbull, July 18, 1775, *Writings of George Washington*, 3:344.

7. Boller, *George Washington and Religion*, 107.

8. John G. West Jr., "George Washington and the Religious Impulse," in *Patriot Sage: George Washington and the American Political Tradition*, ed. Gary L. Gregg and Matthew Spalding (Wilmington, DE: ISI Books, 1999), 269.

9. George Washington to James Anderson, December 24, 1795, *Writings of George Washington*, 34:407.

10. George Washington to Colonel Burgess Ball, September 22, 1799, *Writings of George Washington*, 37:372.

11. Frank E. Gizzard Jr., *George Washington: A Biographical Companion* (Denver, CO: ABC-CLIO, 2002), 268.

12. Madison's "strict separationism" has been championed most passionately by Irving Brant, "Madison: On the Separation of Church and State," *William and Mary Quarterly* 3d ser., 8 (January 1951): 3–24. For a thorough reconsideration of Madison's thought, see Vincent Phillip Muñoz, "James Madison's Principle of Religious Liberty," *American Political Science Review* 97 (February 2003): 17–32.

13. George Washington to George Mason, October 3, 1785, *Writings of George Washington*, 28:285 (Washington's emphasis). Washington wrote to Mason on account of Mason's sending to Washington a copy of a memorial and remonstrance against Henry's bill. It is fair to assume that Mason sent Washington Madison's "Memorial and Remonstrance," although it is unclear from Washington's letter, which

refers only to "a memorial and remonstrance." Madison published his "Memorial and Remonstrance" anonymously, and several other petitions against the bill were also circulating at that time.

14. Washington to Mason, October 3, 1785, *Writings of George Washington*, 28:285.

15. Elizabeth Fleet, ed., "Madison's 'Detatched [*sic*] Memoranda,'" *William and Mary Quarterly* 3d ser., 3 (October 1946): 559–60.

16. George Washington to the President of Congress, December 31, 1775, *Writings of George Washington*, 4:197–98, requesting an increase in the salary of military chaplains to $33 a month. On July 29, 1775, the Continental Congress, in its first official act regarding army chaplains, passed a resolution providing for a salary of $20 a month, the same as captains. For a discussion of Washington's military requests and orders pertaining to religion, see Boller, *George Washington and Religion*, 49–60.

17. George Washington to Governor Jonathan Trumbull, December 15, 1775, *Writings of George Washington*, 4:162.

18. General Orders, July 4, 1775, *Writings of George Washington*, 3:309.

19. General Orders, March 22, 1783, *Writings of George Washington*, 26:250.

20. General Orders, July 4, 1775, *Writings of George Washington*, 3:309.

21. General Orders, May 5, 1778, *Writings of George Washington*, 11:354.

22. Fleet, "Madison's 'Detached Memoranda,'" 560–62.

23. Both proclamations marked significant events, the former the ratification of the Constitution and the latter the diminished prospect of another foreign war.

24. George Washington, "Proclamation. A National Thanksgiving," October 3, 1787, in James D. Richardson, *A Compilation of the Messages and Papers of the Presidents: 1789–1897* (Washington, D.C.: Government Printing Office, 1896), 1:64.

25. George Washington, "A Proclamation," January 1, 1795, in Richardson, *Compilation of the Messages and Papers*, 1:180.

26. George Washington, "First Inaugural Address," April 30, 1789, *Papers of George Washington*, Presidential Series, ed. Dorothy Twohig (Charlottesville: University Press of Virginia, 1987), 2:174 (hereafter *Papers of George Washington*).

27. Steven B. Epstein, "Rethinking the Constitutionality of Ceremonial Deism," *Columbia Law Review* 96 (December 1996): 2110.

28. Washington's Farewell Address was not a speech, but a long letter addressed "To the PEOPLE of the United States," first published in *American Daily Advisor*, Philadelphia's largest newspaper, on September 19, 1796. For a discussion of the drafting and publication of the Farewell Address, see Matthew Spalding and Patrick J. Garrity, *A Sacred Union of Citizens: George Washington's Farewell Address and the American Character* (Lanham, MD: Rowman & Littlefield Publishers, 1996), 45–61; Felix Gilbert, *To the Farewell Address: Ideas of Early American Foreign Policy* (Princeton, NJ: Princeton University Press, 1961), ch. 5.

29. George Washington, "Farewell Address," September 19, 1796, *Writings of George Washington*, 35:229.

30. Washington, "Farewell Address," *Writings of George Washington*, 35:229.

31. Montesquieu, *The Spirit of the Laws*, bk. 3, chs. 1–2.

32. Montesquieu, *The Spirit of the Laws*, bk. 3, ch. 2. For Montesquieu's clarification of what he means by virtue see *The Spirit of the Laws*, bk. 3, ch. 5, 9n, and bk. 5, ch. 2.

33. Washington, "Farewell Address," *Writings of George Washington*, 35:229 (Washington's emphasis).

34. Washington, "Farewell Address," *Writings of George Washington*, 35:229; cf. Montesquieu, *The Spirit of the Laws*, bk. 24, chs. 1 and 6.

35. James Madison, "A Memorial and Remonstrance against Religious Assessments," article 5, *The Writings of James Madison*, ed. Gaillard Hunt (New York: G.P. Putnam's Sons, 1900–1910), 2:187.

36. George Washington, "First Inaugural Address," April 30, 1789, *Papers of George Washington*, 2:173–77.

37. George Washington, "Proclamation. A National Thanksgiving," October 3, 1789, *Compilation of the Messages and Papers*, 1:64.

38. George Washington, "A Proclamation," January 1, 1795, *Compilation of the Messages and Papers*, 1:180.

39. George Washington to the President of Congress, June 8, 1777, *Writings of George Washington*, 8:203.

40. James Madison, "A Memorial and Remonstrance," article 3, *The Writings of James Madison*, 2:185–86.

41. Thomas G. West claims that the American founders in general maintained this position. I think it is more properly assigned to Washington and not to Madison or Jefferson. See Thomas G. West, "Religious Liberty: The View from the Founding," in *On Faith and Free Government*, ed. Daniel C. Palm (Lanham, MD: Rowman and Littlefield, 1997), 3–27.

42. James Madison, "Memorial and Remonstrance," Article 1. Michael McConnell, a leading scholar of the original intentions of the Free Exercise Clause, claims Article 1 of Madison's "Memorial" sets forth an argument consistent with the interpretation that finds in the Free Exercise Clause a constitutional right for religious citizens to exemptions from all laws that, in their effect, burden religious exercise. Michael W. McConnell, "The Origins and Historical Understanding of Free Exercise of Religion," *Harvard Law Review* 103 (1990): 1453. For a competing interpretation of the original intentions of the Free Exercise Clause, see Philip A. Hamburger, "A Constitutional Right of Religious Exemptions: An Historical Perspective," *George Washington Law Review* 60 (1992): 915–48. Hamburger, it should be noted, fails to address McConnell's interpretation of Madison. For a criticism of McConnell's interpretation, see Muñoz, "James Madison's Principle of Religious Liberty."

43. Harry V. Jaffa, *The American Founding as the Best Regime: The Bonding of Civil and Religious Liberty* (Claremont, CA: The Claremont Institute for the Study of Statesmanship and Political Philosophy, 1990), 25.

44. George Washington to the United Baptist Churches of Virginia, May 1789, *Papers of George Washington*, Presidential Series, 2:424.

45. George Washington to Robert Dinwiddie, June 25, 1756, *Writings of George Washington*, 1:394. Washington refused to discharge the six Quakers on account of their religious beliefs.

46. The Religious Society called Quakers, from their Yearly Meeting for Pennsylvania, New-Jersey, and the western Parts of Virginia and Maryland, September 28–October 3, 1789 to George Washington, *Papers of George Washington*, Presidential Series, 4:267.

47. George Washington to the Society of Quakers, October 1789, *Papers of George Washington*, Presidential Series, 4:266.

48. Ibid.

49. Cf. John West, "George Washington and the Religious Impulse," 285.

50. George Washington to the Roman Catholics in America, March 15, 1790, *Papers of George Washington*, Presidential Series, 5:299–300.

51. George Washington to the Hebrew Congregation in Newport, Rhode Island, August 18, 1790, *Papers of George Washington*, Presidential Series, 6:285.

52. George Washington to the Pennsylvania Council of Safety, January 19, 1777, *Writings of George Washington*, 7:35. Also see Washington's letter to the same dated, January 29, 1777.

53. Boller, "George Washington and the Quakers," 73.

54. George Washington to Governor William Livingston, May 11, 1777, *Writings of George Washington*, 8:44–45.

55. George Washington, Power to Officers to Collect Clothing, Etc., November 1777, *Writings of George Washington*, 10:124. See also Washington's commands to Colonel John Siegfried, October 6, 1777, *Writings of George Washington*, 9:318.

56. George Washington to Brigadier General John Lacy, Junior, March 20, 1778, *Writings of George Washington*, 11:114.

57. *Sherbert v. Verner*, 374 U.S. 398 (1963).

58. *Wisconsin v. Yoder*, 406 U.S. 205 (1972).

59. *Employment Division, Department of Human Resources of Oregon* v. *Smith*, 494 U.S. 872 (1990).

60. General Assembly of the Presbyterian Church to George Washington, May 30, 1789, *The Papers of George Washington*, Presidential Series, 2:422.

61. George Washington to the General Assembly of the Presbyterian Church, May 1789, *The Papers of George Washington*, Presidential Series, 2:420–21.

62. Ibid., 2:420.

63. George Washington, Circular to the States, June 8, 1783, in *The Writings of George Washington*, ed. John C. Fitzpatrick, 39 vols. (Washington, D.C.: U.S. Government Printing Office, 1931–1944) 26:484–85.

2

One Public Religion, Many Private Religions

John Adams and the 1780 Massachusetts Constitution*

John Witte Jr.

JOHN ADAMS: LIFE AND LITERATURE, RELIGION AND POLITICS

"Popularity was never my mistress," John Adams wrote glumly in 1787, "nor was I ever, or shall I ever be, a popular man."[1] Two decades later, Adams remained pessimistic, but stoic, about his legacy: "Mausoleums, statues, [and] monuments will never be erected to me. I wish them not. Panegyrical romances will never be written, nor flattering orations spoken, to transmit me to posterity in brilliant colors. No, nor in true colors."[2]

For a century and a half after his death in 1826, John Adams's fears about his legacy proved painfully prophetic. With some notable exceptions,[3] historians tended to treat Adams sparingly, even grudgingly, offering their dull pages about his life and work before moving on to more colorful accounts of Benjamin Franklin, George Washington, Thomas Jefferson, and James Madison. To be sure, no serious historian denied Adams his impressive political resume. Noteworthy were his roles as legal counsel in the 1761 writs of assistance case; as "colossus" and "atlas" of independence and revolution in the Continental Congress; as chair of the committee that drafted the 1776 Declaration of Independence; as drafter of the 1780 Massachusetts Constitution; and as

---

*Portions of this article are drawn from my "'A Most Mild and Equitable Establishment of Religion': John Adams and the Massachusetts Experiment," in *Religion and the New Republic: Faith in the Founding of America*, ed. James H. Hutson (Lanham, MD: Rowman & Littlefield, 2000), 1–40. I wish to thank Charles Hooker for his excellent research assistance.

first vice president and second president of the United States. Some biographers took further note of Adams's revealing correspondence with his beloved wife Abigail[4] and his late-life correspondence with Thomas Jefferson.[5] Adams was certainly known and portrayed in "true colors." But just not in "brilliant colors."

No longer. While "masoleums, monuments, and statues" of Adams might still be wanting, writings of "brilliant color" are now in ample supply. Building on new critical editions of Adams's autobiography, papers, and letters, several recent studies have brought Adams to brilliant new light and life.[6] A veritable Adams renaissance is now upon us, and Adams is emerging rapidly from the shadows of the other founders. David McCullough, Pulitzer Prize–winning biographer of Adams, offers a telling anecdote. Five years ago, McCullough had set out to write a joint biography of Adams and Jefferson, fearing that "Adams could not hold his own with Jefferson." By the end, McCullough worried that Jefferson could not hold his own with Adams. "[O]n virtually all points of comparison between the two men, Jefferson comes in second."[7]

In this spate of new writings, much has been made of John Adams's Puritan origins and republican views of religion and government. Adams was born in 1735 in Braintree, Massachusetts. His mother was a pious homemaker, his father a farmer, cordwainer, and deacon of the local Puritan Congregational Church. The Adams family sent their precocious first-born son to Harvard College in 1751 to prepare for a vocation as minister in the Congregational Church. During his college years, however, Adams grew disenchanted with theology and was drawn more to science and then to law. He was particularly put off by the caustic casuistry of some of the theologians and Congregational preachers of his day. He feared, as he later put it, "that the study of Theology and the pursuit of it as a Profession would involve me in endless altercations and make my life miserable, without any prospect of doing good to my fellow men."[8]

Undecided upon his vocation after graduation, Adams took a one-year appointment as a Latin master at a grammar school in Worcester, Massachusetts. He continued to read theology and philosophy that year, but was drawn increasingly to the voracious study of law, history, and politics. In 1756, he resolved to pursue a legal career and took a legal apprenticeship, as was typical for a budding lawyer of the day. As was typical for a Puritan at that time, Adams saw the law as a proper vocation for a Christian to pursue. "The Practice of the Law," he later wrote in his diary, "does not dissolve the obligations of morality or of Religion."[9] To the contrary, a good Christian lawyer must be doubly vigilant to cultivate the habits of piety, prudence, industry, integrity, and learning. He must be doubly resistant to the temptations to "cupidity . . . avidity, envy, revenge, jealousy," and other "more ungovernable passions."[10] These were Puritan virtues to which Adams remained fiercely loyal throughout his long career.

Adams's firm rejection of the vocation of ministry, however, was part and product of his growing detachment from the strict Puritan worship patterns of his youth. Already in the late 1750s and 1760s, to the dismay of family and friends, Adams began to wander regularly into the sanctuaries of other churches and to read the writings of sundry Protestant and Catholic divines, along with Hebrew materials. While in Philadelphia for the sessions of the Continental Congress, Adams attended services in Presbyterian, Anglican, Catholic, Quaker, Baptist, and Methodist churches alike.[11] After his ambassadorial tours of Europe, he wrote proudly to his friend Benjamin Rush, I have attended public worship in all countries and with all sects and believe them all much better than no religion, though I have not thought myself obliged to believe all I heard."[12] When Rush pressed him to be clear about his denominational affiliation, Adams preferred to describe himself generically as a "life-long church animal," who wandered freely among many religious pastures.[13] "Ask me not . . . whether I am a Catholic or Protestant, Calvinist or Arminian. As far as they are Christians, I wish to be a fellow-disciple with them all."[14]

Striking this balance between the right to wander in one's private religious worship and the duty to uphold the commonplaces of Christianity was axiomatic for Adams. It not only defined the essence of his personal theology; it also became the first principle of his political philosophy. For Adams, every state and society had to find a way to balance the freedom of many private religions with the establishment of one public Christian religion.[15]

On the one hand, Adams said, every state and society had to establish by law some form of public religion, some image and ideal of itself, some common values and beliefs to undergird and support the plurality of private religions that it embraced. The notion that a state and society could remain neutral and purged of any religion was, for Adams, a philosophical fiction. Absent a commonly adopted set of values and beliefs, politicians would invariably hold out their private convictions as public ones. It was thus essential for each community to define the basics of its public religion. And in Adams's day, the basics of this public religion were principally the commonplaces of the Christian religion.

In Adams's view, the creed of this public religion was honesty, diligence, devotion, obedience, virtue, and love of God, neighbor, and self.[16] Its icons were the Bible, the bells of liberty, the memorials of patriots, and the Constitution.[17] Its clergy were public-spirited ministers and religiously devout politicians.[18] Its liturgy was the public proclamation of oaths, prayers, songs, and election and thanksgiving day sermons.[19] Its policy was state appointment of chaplains for the legislature, military, and prison; state sanctions against blasphemy,[20] sacrilege, and iconoclasm; and state sponsorship of religious societies, schools, and charities.[21] For Adams, this was to be only a "mild and equitable establishment of religion."[22] "[I]t can no longer be called in question," he wrote, that "authority in magistrates and obedience of citizens can be grounded on reason, morality, and the Christian religion, without [succumbing to] the monkery of priests or the knavery of politicians"—or other forms of "ecclesiastical or civil tyranny."[23]

On the other hand, Adams argued, every state and society had to respect and protect a plurality of forms of religious exercise and association, whose rights could be limited only by the parallel rights of juxtaposed religions, the concerns for public peace and security, and the duties of the established public religion. "[A]ll men of all religions consistent with morals and property," Adams argued, must "enjoy equal liberty [and] security of property . . . and an equal chance for honors and power."[24] The notion that a state could coerce all persons into adherence to a single established religion alone was, for Adams, equally a philosophical fiction. Persons would make their own private judgments in matters of faith, for the rights of conscience are "indisputable, unalienable, indefeasible, [and] divine."[25]

Moreover, the maintenance of religious pluralism was essential for the protection of religious and other forms of liberty. As Adams put it in a letter to Thomas Jefferson:

> Roman Catholics, English Episcopalians, Scotch and American Presbyterians, Methodists, Moravians, Anbabtists [*sic*], German Lutherans, German Calvinists, Universalitists, Arians, Priestlyians, Socinians, Independents, Congregationalists, Horse Protestants and House Protestants, Deists and Atheists and Protestants qui ne croyent rien [who believe nothing] are . . . [n]ever the less all Educated in the general Principles of Christianity: and the general Principles of English and American liberty.[26]

"Checks and balances, Jefferson"—in the political as well as the religious sphere—Adams went on in another letter,

> are our only Security, for the progress of Mind, as well as the Security of Body. Every Species of these Christians would persecute Deists, as [much] as either Sect would persecute another, if it had unchecked and unballanced Power. Nay, the Deists would persecute Christians, and Atheists would persecute Deists, with as unrelenting Cruelty, as any Christians would persecute them or one another. Know thyself, Human nature![27]

While Adams developed these views of religion and politics in numerous writings and actions over his long career, his most forceful expression of them came in the 1780 Massachusetts Constitution. This was the first state constitution of Massachusetts, which Adams in large measure drafted. The constitution struck this balance between the establishment of one public religion and the freedom of all private religions. Its most controversial provisions on religious test oaths and tithes were outlawed by amendments in 1821 and 1833. The harder edges of religious establishment were further blunted by judicial interpretation and legislative innovation over time.[28] But Adams's basic model of establishing one public religion, while protecting many private freedoms, remained unchanged in its fundamentals until the twentieth century.

What follows is a summary of the development of the Massachusetts Constitution, and then a careful analysis of how its religion clauses reflect Adams's views.

RELIGION AND THE FORMATION OF THE MASSACHUSETTS CONSTITUTION

On September 1, 1779, 293 delegates gathered in Boston to draft a new constitution for the new state of Massachusetts.[29] On September 4 the constitutional convention elected a committee of twenty-seven members—later augmented by four others—to prepare a draft declaration of rights and a frame of government. This committee, in turn, delegated the drafting to a three-member subcommittee of James Bowdoin, Samuel Adams, and John Adams. John Adams, widely respected for his legal and political acumen, was selected to push the pen for the subcommittee. He completed his work in mid-October. First the three-member subcommittee, then the full drafting committee made some modest alterations to Adams's draft.[30] The committee's draft was submitted to the full convention for debate on October 28, 1779.[31] The convention debated the draft constitution until November 12; Adams participated in this session of the debate, but set sail immediately thereafter for France. The convention completed its deliberations from January 27 to March 1, 1780, now without Adams.

Adams's draft constitution had a preamble and two main parts. Part I was a declaration of rights divided into articles; part II was a frame of government divided into chapters. The convention chose to vote separately on each article of the declaration of rights, and each chapter of the frame of government. Ten provisions of Adams's draft constitution touched on matters of religion and religious liberty—the preamble, articles I, II, III, VII, and XVIII of the declaration of rights, and chapters I, II, V, and VI of the frame of government. Five of these ten provisions were approved without comment, controversy, or change.

Four of the remaining provisions on religion in Adams's draft garnered modest discussion and revision in the constitutional convention. In article II, Adams had written, "It is the Duty of all men in society, publickly, and at stated seasons to worship the SUPREME BEING, the great Creator and preserver of the Universe." After brief discussion, the convention amended this to say, "It is the *right as well as the* duty of all men" so to worship.[32] In chapter I of the frame of government, Adams had stipulated that no person was eligible to serve in the house of representatives "unless he be of the Christian religion." The convention struck this provision, although it left untouched the next chapter, where Adams imposed the same religious conditions upon the offices of governor and lieutenant governor.[33] In the same spirit, Adams had proposed in chapter VI that all state officials and appointees swear the same religious test oath: "that I believe and profess the Christian religion and have a firm persuasion of its truth." The convention insisted on a slightly reworded version of this oath that was to be applied only to elected executive and legislative officers. All other officials were required simply to declare their "true faith and allegiance to this Commonwealth." After several delegates argued for a more specifically Protestant test oath, the convention added to both oaths a transparently anti-Catholic provision, which Adams and others later protested without success:

I do renounce and abjure all allegiance, subjection and obedience to . . . every . . . foreign Power whatsoever: And that no foreign . . . Prelate . . . hath, or ought to have, any jurisdiction, superiority, pre-eminence, authority, dispensing, or other power, in any matter, civil, ecclesiastical or spiritual within this Commonwealth.[34]

Adams's draft oath had concluded: "So help me God," but had then made specific provision "that any person who has conscientious scruples relative to taking oaths, may be admitted to make solemn affirmation" by other means. After some delegates protested that so generic an exemption might be subject to abuse, the convention restricted the exemption to Quakers only.[35] An 1821 amendment to the Constitution expunged the religious test oath for political office altogether.[36]

Article III, stipulating the payment of religious taxes in support of congregational ministers, was by far "the most controversial one in the whole draft constitution," occupying more than a third of the convention debate.[37] Given the heat of the religious-liberty debate on the eve of the convention, the controversy was not unexpected. Adams chose not to draft article III himself. "I could not satisfy my own Judgment with any Article that I thought would be accepted," he later wrote. "Some of the Clergy, or older and graver Persons than myself would be more likely to hit the Taste of the Public."[38] Adams did, however, approve without reservation a draft that came out of the full drafting committee and, as we shall see, incorporated establishment provisions elsewhere in the constitution.

The first draft of article III, submitted to the convention on October 28, 1779, read thus:

> Good morals, being necessary for the preservation of civil society; and the knowledge and belief of the being of GOD, His providential government of the world, and of a future state of rewards and punishment, being the only true foundation of morality, the legislature hath, therefore, a right, and ought to provide, at the expense of the subject, if necessary, a suitable support for the public worship of GOD, and of the teachers of religion and morals; and to enjoin upon all the subjects an attendance upon these instructions, at stated times and seasons; provided there be any such teacher, on whose ministry they can conscientiously attend.
>
> All monies, paid by the subject of the public worship, and of the instructors in religion and morals, shall, if he requires it, be uniformly applied to the support of the teacher or teachers of his own religious denomination, provided there be any on whose instructions he attends; otherwise it may be paid towards the support of the teacher or teachers of the parish or precinct in which the said moneys are raised.[39]

The first paragraph of this draft article III, stipulating the necessity and utility of public worship and religious instruction, was a common sentiment and not particularly controversial. The second paragraph, however, mandating the collection of religious tithes to support the same, was a matter of great controversy.

It takes a bit of historical imagination and explication to appreciate the controversy over state collection of church tithes. Article III was designed to raise to constitutional status a colonial pattern of church–state relations, introduced by a 1692 law and amended several times thereafter.[40] This law blended church and state for purposes of taxation. It designated one territory as both a "parish" and a "township" under the authority of one city council. (In large townships that had more than one church, the multiple "parishes" were called "precincts," and each of these likewise was subject to the same council's authority.) To be a member of the township was automatically to be a member of a parish (or precinct). Each of the nearly 290 parishes/townships in Massachusetts was required to have at least one Congregationalist "teacher of religion and morality" (that is, a minister). This minister would lead the local community not only in public worship, but often in education and charity as well. The community was required to provide him with a salary, sanctuary, and parsonage. Funds for this came from special religious taxes (usually called tithes, sometimes called church, parish, or religious rates). These were collected from all subjects in the township, who were by statutory definition also members of the parish.[41]

This tithing system worked well enough when all subjects within the same township were also active members of the same church. It did not work so well for people who were religiously inactive or members of a non-Congregationalist church, whether Baptist, Quaker, Anglican, or Catholic (the principal "dissenting" faiths in the state at the time). As the number of such dissenting churches grew within the townships of Massachusetts, so did the protests to paying these mandatory taxes in support of the Congregationalist ministers and churches.

During the eighteenth century, colonial courts eventually carved out exceptions for some religious dissenters, allowing them to pay their tithes to support their own dissenting ministers and churches. Such dissenters, however, were required to register each church as a separate religious society (or corporation) and to demonstrate their own faithful attendance at the same. Not all dissenting churches were able or willing to meet the registration requirements, and not all townships cooperated in granting the registrations or tithe exemptions.[42] If the dissenting church was too small to have its own full-time minister, registration was routinely denied or rescinded. If the dissenting church was conscientiously opposed to legal incorporation and registration, as were Baptists after 1773, their members could not be exempt from taxation. If a member of a registered dissenting church was too lax in his attendance of public worship, he could still be denied exemption from the Congregationalist tithe. And if a town treasurer was too pressed for revenue or too prejudiced against a certain group, he could refuse to give dissenting ministers their share of the tithes. In many of these cases, the Massachusetts courts proved notably churlish in granting standing, let alone relief, to groups or individuals who protested such inequities.[43]

It was this century-long system of religious taxation that the cryptic second paragraph of article III was designed to perpetuate. And it was this feature of the inherited tradition of religious establishment that caused such controversy before and at the convention.[44] The initial reaction to the draft of article III was so heated that convention members voted to put off debate until November 1. They also voted to suspend the rule that no member could speak twice to the same issue without requesting special privilege from the chair. Rancorous debate over the article broke out immediately on November 1. Some condemned the provision as a "too pale an approximation of a proper establishment." Others called for abolition of the article altogether. Still others decried the insufficient recognition of the concessions that dissenters had arduously won over the years. When matters deadlocked on November 3, the delegates appointed a seven-member, ad hoc committee of distinguished delegates to redraft the controversial article III.[45]

On November 6 this ad hoc committee put a new draft article III before the convention that spelled out the prevailing religious tax system in more detail. This new draft was debated intermittently for the next four days, and modest word changes were approved.[46] On November 10 a motion to abolish the article altogether was defeated. A slightly amended draft of the article was passed the following day. The final text of article III reads thus:

> As the happiness of a people, and good order and preservation of civil government, essentially depend upon piety, religion, and morality; and as these cannot be generally diffused through a Community, but by the institution of publick Worship of God, and of public instructions in piety, religion, and morality: Therefore, to promote the happiness and to secure the good order and preservation of

their government, the people of this Commonwealth have a right to invest their legislature with power to authorize and require . . . the several Towns, Parishes precincts and other bodies politic, or religious societies, to make suitable provision, at their own Expence, for the institution of the Public worship of GOD, and for the support and maintenance of public Protestant teachers of piety, religion and morality, in all causes which provision shall not be made Voluntarily.—And the people of this Commonwealth have also a right to, and do, invest their legislature with authority to enjoin upon all the Subjects an attendance upon the instructions of the public teachers aforesaid, at stated times and seasons, if there be any on whose instructions they can Conscientiously and conveniently attend—PROVIDED, notwithstanding, that the several towns, parishes, precincts, and other bodies politic, or religious societies, shall, at times, have the exclusive right of electing their public Teachers, and of contracting with them for their support and maintenance.—And all monies, paid by the Subject of the support of the public teacher or teachers of his own religious sect or denomination, provided there be any on whose institution he attends; otherwise it may be paid towards the support of the teacher or teachers of the parish or precinct in which the said monies are raised—And every denomina[t]ion of Christians, demeaning themselves peaceably, and as good Subjects of the Commonwealth, shall be equally under the protection of the Law: And no subordination of any one sect or denomination to another shall ever be established by law.[47]

This final text routinized, and raised to constitutional status, the traditional tithing system, and outlawed some of the hard-fought concessions that Baptists, Anglicans, and other dissenters had secured through litigation in the prior two decades. As Samuel Eliot Morison writes,

Article III was even less liberal than [the colonial] system, for instead of exempting members of dissenting sects from religious taxation, it merely gave them the privilege of paying their taxes to their own pastors. Unbelievers, nonchurch goers, and dissenting minorities too small to maintain a minister had to contribute to Congregational worship. The whole Article was so loosely worded as to defeat the purpose of the fifth paragraph [guaranteeing the equality of all sects and denominations]. Every new denomination that entered the Commonwealth after 1780, notably the Universalists and Methodists, had to wage a long and expensive lawsuit to obtain recognition as a religious sect. . . . [A] subordination of sects existed in fact.[48]

Article III was not without its own concessions, however. The tithe collection system was now to be local and "voluntary," rather than statewide, allowing Boston and, later, other townships to forgo mandatory tithing and have churches muster their own support through tithes, tuitions, or pew rents. Religious societies could now contract individually with their own minister, presumptively allowing them to pay their tithes directly to their chosen minister rather than to a potentially capricious town treasurer. Local townships and religious societies could now participate in the choice of their community minister, rather than be automatically saddled with a Congregationalist minister. This provision "had some unexpected results. Several of the towns and parishes, which thereby were given the exclusive right to elect their ministers . . . were converted to Unitarianism and settled Unitarian pastors over old Calvinist churches."[49] And the provision that no religious sect or denomination was to be subordinated to another was the first formal statement in Massachusetts history of religious equality before the law, not only for individuals, but also for groups.

On March 2, 1780, the convention put the final draft of the constitution before the people for ratification. On June 16, 1780, James Bowdoin, the president of the convention, announced, without caveat, that the entire constitution had garnered the requisite two-thirds vote.[50] On October 25, 1780, the constitution went into effect, the first day after ratification on which the general court sat. Among its other first acts, the general court pledged its support for religious liberty:

> Deeply impressed with a sense of the importance of religion to the happiness of men in civil society to maintain its purity and promote this efficacy, we shall protect professors of all denominations, demeaning themselves peaceably and as good subjects of the Commonwealth, in the free exercise of the rights of conscience.[51]

JOHN ADAMS AND THE MASSACHUSETTS MODEL OF RELIGIOUS LIBERTY

John Adams was both eclectic and pragmatic in crafting the religion clauses of the Massachusetts Constitution. This was part of the reason for his success. Although a Christian believer of Puritan extraction, Adams eschewed rigorous denominational affiliation or rigid doctrinal formulation, as we saw. Although a fierce American patriot, Adams knew the value of history and comparative politics. Much of his three-volume *Defense of the Constitutions of Government in the United States of America* (1788), among his other political writings, was devoted to sifting ancient, medieval, and early modern Western polities for useful lessons on the best construction of authority and the best protection of liberty. Many of his letters and other informal writings are chock full of favorable references to Greek, Roman, Catholic, Protestant, and Enlightenment writers alike. Although a vigorous moralist,

Adams offered his constitutional formulations without "a pretence of miracle or mystery." Any people "employed in the service of forming a constitution," he wrote, cannot pretend that they "had interviews with the gods, or were in any degree under the inspiration of Heaven." "[G]overnments [are] contrived merely by the use of reason and the senses." Constitutions "are merely experiments made on human life and manners, society and government."[52] There will always be "a glorious uncertainty in the law."[53]

In his constitutional experiment, Adams chose to balance the establishment of one public religion with the freedom of many private religions. This was, in part, a pragmatic choice. Adams knew that the Congregationalists would insist on their establishment, and that the dissenters would insist on their freedom. He sought to respect and protect both interests by combining what he called a "tempered" religious freedom with a "slender" religious establishment.[54]

This was also, in part, a principled choice. Adams was convinced that the establishment of one common public religion among a plurality of freely competing private religions was essential to the survival of society and the state. We must certainly begin "by setting the conscience free," Adams wrote. For,

> when all men of all religions consistent with morals and property, shall enjoy equal liberty . . . and security of property, and an equal chance for honors and power . . . we may expect that improvements will be made in the human character, and the state of society.[55]

But we must just as certainly begin by "setting religion at the fore and floor of society and government," Adams wrote. "Statesmen may plan and speculate for liberty, but it is religion and morality alone which can establish the principles upon which freedom can securely stand."[56] A common "religion and virtue are the only foundation, not only of republicanism and of all free government, but of social felicity under all governments and in all the combinations of human society."[57] "Without religion, this world would be something not fit to be mentioned in polite company—I mean hell."[58]

THE LIBERTY OF PRIVATE RELIGION

In the 1780 Massachusetts Constitution, Adams dealt rather briefly with the liberty of conscience and the free exercise of religion. He had already stated several times his devotion to the protection of such private religious rights, calling them "indisputable, unalienable, indefeasible, [and] divine."[59] He had praised the sagacity and sacrifice of his Protestant forbearers in securing such rights for themselves and their posterity.[60] And he saw both the necessity and utility of the continued protection of these rights for all religious groups. As he wrote in the spring of 1780 when the new constitution was being planned:

> our honest and pious Attention to the unalienable Rights of Conscience is our best and most refined Policy, tending to conciliate the Good Will, of all the World, preparing an Asylum, which will be a sure Remedy against persecution in Europe, and drawing over to our Country Numbers of excellent Citizens.[61]

In the preamble to the 1780 Massachusetts Constitution, Adams spoke of "the power of the people of enjoying in safety and tranquility their natural rights, and the blessings of life" and "the right of the people to take measures necessary for their safety, prosperity and happiness." These words were largely repeated in article I of the declaration of rights: "All men are born free and equal, and have certain natural, essential, and unalienable rights; among which may be reckoned the right of enjoying and defending their Lives and Liberties; that of acquiring, possessing and protecting property; in fine, that of seeking and obtaining their safety and happiness."[62]

In article II, Adams tendered more specific protections of religious liberty.

> It is the [right as well as the] duty of all men in society, publickly, and at stated seasons to worship the SUPREME BEING, the great Creator and preserver of the Universe. No subject shall be hurt, molested, or restrained, in his person, Liberty, or Estate, for worshipping GOD in the manner and season most agreeable to the Dictates of his own conscience, or for his religious profession or sentiments; provided he doth not Disturb the public peace, or obstruct others in their religious Worship.

Article III, at least tacitly, recognized the right to form religious associations, to select one's own minister, and to pay tithes directly to him. Chapter VI included within the ambit of religious freedom the right of Quakers to claim an exemption from the swearing of oaths to which they were "conscientiously opposed."

The freedom of private religion, as Adams defined it, was thus rather closely circumscribed. It was, in effect, the right of each individual to discharge divine duties, which the constitution helped to define. "It is the right as well as the duty" of each person to worship, article II states. While a person could worship in "the manner and season most agreeable to the Dictates of his own conscience," such worship, per article II, had to be directed to God, defined as "the SUPREME BEING, the great Creator and preserver of the Universe." Moreover, such worship, per article III, had to include "conscientious and convenient" "attendance upon the instructions of ministers" "at stated times and seasons." If a person's conscience dictated another object, order, or organization of worship, it was by definition neither religious nor protected as a constitutional right.

This right to private religion was further limited by social demands. Neither the preamble nor article I lists religion among the "natural rights," those rights held prior to society in the state of nature. Instead, article II emphasized the social character of religious rights; they are held by "all men in society" and involve "public worship." Each individual's religious rights are limited by the needs of society, by the need for public peace and for protection of the worship of others, as article II put it. And each individual's religious rights are subject to the "rights" and "powers" of society—to mandate church attendance, tithe payments, Christian affiliation, and oath swearing, as article III and chapters II and VI specify.[63]

By comparison with other state constitutions of the day, the Massachusetts Constitution was rather restrained in its protection of private religious freedom. Other states defined liberty of conscience expansively to include the right to choose and change religion, to be free from all discrimination on the basis of religion, and to be exempt from a number of general laws that prohibited or mandated conduct to which a religious party or group had scruples of conscience. Many states also defined free-exercise rights expansively to include freedom to engage in religious assembly, worship, speech, publication, press, education, travel, parentage, and the like without political or ecclesiastical conditions or controls.[64] Few such protections appear in the 1780 Massachusetts Constitution.

Adams, reflecting in part his self-imposed limits on religious wandering, was convinced that a more "tempered" form of religious freedom would bring the best "improvements to the character of each citizen."[65] On the one hand, he believed, following conservative conventions of the day, that to grant too much freedom of religion would only encourage depravity in citizens.[66] One preacher put it,

Man is not to be trusted with his unbounded love of liberty, unless it is under some other restraint which arises from his own reason or the law of God—these in many instances would make a feeble resistance to his lust or avarice; and he would pursue his liberty to the destruction of his fellow-creature, if he was not restrained by human laws and punishment.[67]

The state was thus required to "take mild and parental measures" to educate, encourage, and emulate a right belief and conduct.[68]

On the other hand, Adams believed, following more liberal conventions of the day, that

Compulsion, instead of making men religious, generally has a contrary tendency, it works not conviction, but most naturally leads them into hypocrisy. If they are honest enquirers after truth; if their articles of belief differ from the creed of their civil superiors, compulsion will bring them into a sad dilemma of choosing between a feigned and firm faith.[69]

The state was thus required to refrain from dictating the exact doctrines, liturgies, and texts of a right religion. This was the balance of religious freedom that Adams struck in crafting the constitution.

THE ESTABLISHMENT OF PUBLIC RELIGION

Adams further balanced this "tempered" liberty of private religion with a "slender" establishment of public religion. Adams had nothing but contempt for the harsh establishments of earlier centuries—those featuring state prescriptions of religious doctrines, liturgies, and sacred texts; state controls of religious properties, polities, and personnel; and state persecution of religious heresy, blasphemy, and nonconformity. His 1774 *Dissertation on the Canon and Feudal Law* was a bitter invective against the "civil and ecclesiastical tyranny" of earlier Catholic and Protestant establishments. His 1788 *Defense of the American Constitutions* devoted several long chapters to digesting critically the horrors of religious wars, crusades, inquisitions, and pogroms and the sorry plight of some of his Protestant forbearers.

The established public religion that Adams had in mind was much more "slender," "mild," "moderate," and "equitable" in form, tempered by its own provisions and by the juxtaposed guarantees of private religious freedom for all. As Adams set out his views in the constitution, the public religion was to be established (1) ceremonially, (2) morally, and (3) institutionally. It was only the third dimension of the public religious establishment, its institutionalization, that drew controversy.

Ceremonial Establishment

The establishment of public religious ceremonies is reflected especially in the preamble to the Massachusetts Constitution that Adams drafted. The preamble refers to the constitution as "a covenant" or "compact" between the people and God: "[T]he whole people covenants with each Citizen, and each Citizen with the whole people, that all shall be governed by certain Laws for the Common good." And again,

> the people of Massachusetts, acknowledging, with grateful hearts, the goodness of the Great Legislator of the Universe, in affording us, in the course of his Providence, an opportunity, deliberately and peaceably, without fraud, violence, or surprize, o[f] entering into an Original, explicit, and Solemn Compact with each other; and of forming a New Constitution of Civil Government for ourselves and Posterity; and devoutly imploring His direction in so interesting a Design, DO agree upon, ordain and establish the following Declaration of Rights and Frame of Government.

This is a covenant ceremonial liturgy, rooted in the Hebrew Bible and in a New England tradition going back to the Mayflower Compact of 1620.[70] The nature of the constitution is made clear: it is a "solemn" covenant with God invoked as witness, judge, and participant. The purposes of the covenant are set forth—to create and confirm the identity of the people (the "peoples" and "citizens of Massachusetts"), their common morals and mores (a devotion to the "common good"), and their cardinal institutions (their rights and frame of government). The ethic of the covenant is defined: it featured "gratitude," "peacefulness," integrity ("without fraud, violence, or surprize"), and prayerful devotion ("devoutly imploring His direction in so interesting a Design").

A variant of this covenant ceremony was the oath-swearing ritual of state officials. Adams wrote into chapter VI of the frame of government the requirement that all state officials must swear a full oath to the constitution and the commonwealth—not just privately, but before the people and their representatives in full assembly. "I, A,B, do declare, that I believe the christian religion, and have a firm persuasion of its truth . . . and I do swear, that I will bear true faith and allegiance to the said Commonwealth . . . so help me God." Adams's insistence on such oaths reflected the conventional view that the oath was "a cement of society" and "one of the principal instruments of government" for it invoked and induced "the fear and reverence of God, and the terrors of eternity."[71] This provision also reflected Adams's view that the oath of office was a public confirmation of the covenant among God, the people, and their rulers.

These preambulary and oath-swearing provisions were not merely a bit of hortatory throat clearing that preceded the real business of constitutional government. They established favorite ceremonies of the traditional public religion of Massachusetts. In the minds of more conservative Puritan sermonizers and subjects of the day, they raised the traditional image of Massachusetts being "under a solemn divine Probation"[72] and the image of the magistrate as God's vice regent, called to exemplify and enforce a godly life. Traditionally, the New England Puritans stressed ambition, austerity, frugality, and other virtues because the covenant rendered them agents of God, instruments of God's providential plan. For them to be lax in zeal, loose in discipline, or sumptuous in living would be a disservice to God, a breach of their covenant with God. Such a breach would inevitably bring divine condemnation on the community in the form of war, pestilence, poverty, and other forms of force majeure. Traditionally, the New England Puritans' belief in a "solemn divine probation" also rendered the reformation of society a constant priority. They had to ensure that all institutions and all aspects of society comported with the covenantal ideal. Thus, Puritan sermonizers urged their listeners,

> Reform all places, all persons and all callings. Reform the benches of judgment, the inferior magistrates. . . . Reform the universities, reform the cities, reform the counties, reform inferior schools of learning, reform the Sabbath, reform the ordinances, the worship of God. Every plant which my Father hath not planted shall be rooted up.[73]

It was this tradition, albeit in a less denominationally and doctrinally rigorous form, that Adams established in the constitution.

Beyond the preamble and the provisions on oath swearing, the constitution had a few more scattered evidences of a ceremonial establishment. God is invoked, by name or pseudonym (the "Great Legislator of the Universe" and "Supreme Being"), a dozen times. References to the "common" or "public good" appear four more times, as do two further references to divine "blessings" and "privileges." These provisions establishing the public religious ceremonies of Massachusetts are more overt and detailed than those of any other state constitution of the day. All these provisions, save the oath provision, were passed without controversy or even recorded comment. And they remain unchanged to this day.

Moral Establishment

The moral dimensions of the public religious establishment, implicated by the use of covenant and oath-swearing ceremonies, are set out clearly elsewhere in the 1780 constitution. Article II of the declaration of rights, as Adams formulated it, states, "It is the Duty of all men in society, publickly, and at stated seasons to worship the SUPREME BEING, the great Creator and preserver of the Universe." Article III follows with the reason for this duty:

> [T]he happiness of a people, and good order and preservation of civil government, essentially depend upon piety, religion, and morality; and . . . these cannot be generally diffused through a Community, but by the institution of publick Worship of God, and of public instructions in piety, religion, and morality.

Adams did not consider these constitutional endorsements of religious morality to be mere platitudes. In article XVIII of the declaration of rights, he rendered adherence to these moral duties integral to the character of public offices and public officials:

> A frequent recurrence to the fundamental principles of the constitution, and a constant adherence to those of piety, justice, moderation, temperance, industry, and frugality, are absolutely necessary to preserve the advantages of liberty, and to maintain a free government. The people ought, consequently, to have a particular attention to all those principles, in the choice of their Officers and Representatives, and they have a right to require of their lawgivers and magistrates, an exact and constant observance of them, in the formation and execution of the laws necessary for the good administration of the Commonwealth.

As article VII of the declaration put it, "Government is instituted for the Common good; for the protection, safety, prosperity, and happiness of the people." Adams rendered these same moral qualities essential ingredients of education within the state. Chapter V of the frame of government provides, "Wisdom, and knowledge, as well as virtue, diffused generally among the body of the people, [is] necessary for the preservation of their rights and liberties." It is thus

> the duty of Legislatures and Magistrates in all future generations of the Commonwealth to cherish the interests of literature and sciences, and all seminaries

of them; . . . to encourage private societies and public institutions, rewards and immunities, for the promotion of [education] . . . to countenance and inculcate the principles of humanity and general benevolence, public and private charity, industry and frugality, honesty and punctuality in their dealings, sincerity, good humour, and all social affections, and generous sentiments among the people.

The same chapter V confirms and commends the incorporation of Harvard College, since "the encouragement of arts and sciences, and all good literature, tends to the honor of God, the advantage of the Christian religion, and the great benefit of this and other United States of America."

None of these provisions establishing a public religious morality triggered much debate during the constitutional convention, and none of these provisions was amended or emended thereafter. Indeed, the famous Eleventh Amendment of 1833 that purportedly "disestablished religion" in Massachusetts simply repeated the mantra of the moral establishment: that "the public worship of GOD and instructions in piety, religion and morality, promote the happiness and prosperity of a people and the security of a Republican Government."

To this day, the Massachusetts Constitution on its face establishes both religious ceremonies and religious morality. To be sure, this language has become largely a dead letter in recent generations, its legal revival stymied by a political climate that is indifferent, if not hostile, to public religion and by a First Amendment interpretation that discourages, if not prohibits, the state's implementation of these provisions. But even in this climate, the Massachusetts courts have recently used these provisions to uphold the constitutionality of state funding of legislative chaplains and of political oaths ending in "so help me God."[74]

Institutional Establishment

It was the third dimension of the established public religion—article III's establishment of specific religious institutions supported by public taxes—that drew fire in the convention and ratification debates and was eventually outlawed by the Eleventh Amendment in 1833. Here, critics charged, the balance between private religious freedom and a public religious establishment tilted too much toward the latter.

It was one thing for the constitution to establish general public religious ceremonies and to define basic public morals and mores—to encourage "piety, religion, and morality," to endorse the public worship of God, to list the "moral virtues" necessary in a good ruler, to commend schools and colleges that offered religious and moral education, and to limit breaches of the peace and interferences in another's religious right, all on the assumption that "the happiness of a people, and the good order and preservation of civil government" depended upon the same.[75] Such provisions at least left a good deal of religious expression and participation open to voluntary choice and individual accent. It was quite another thing, however, for the constitution to institute religious practices by law—to require persons to attend a preferred form of public worship, to compel them to pay tithes in support of ministers and teachers, to force them to incorporate themselves into state-registered religious societies, and to require them to be faithful in their attendance at worship lest their tithes be diverted or their societies dissolved. For many, such an establishment crossed the line from gentle patronage to odious persecution.

John Adams had not drafted the controversial article III. Although he voted for it in the convention, he offered little by way of apologia for it. A number of other theologians and jurists of the day, however, rose to the defense of article III, offering arguments that appear quite consistent with Adams's views.[76] The most sustained arguments came from Massachusetts lawyer and later chief justice Theophilus Parsons, whom Adams respected well enough to encourage his precocious son John Quincy to clerk in his legal chambers.[77]

Theophilus Parsons had been a member of the seven-member ad hoc committee that had redrafted article III during the heated convention debate in early November 1779. He was later appointed chief justice of the Massachusetts supreme juridical court and had several occasions to enforce its provisions against detractors. In the case of *Barnes v. Falmouth* (1810), he offered "a diligent examination" of the "motives which induced the people to introduce into the Constitution a religious establishment, the nature of the establishment introduced, and the rights and privileges it secured to the people, and to their teachers."[78]

Parsons first argued for the necessity and utility of maintaining religion in a civil society and government. In a nutshell, he argued that the happiness of citizens is the goal of government; morality and virtue are essential ingredients to the achievement of happiness; religion and faith are essential wellsprings of morality and virtue; thus, government must support religion and faith. "The object of a free civil government is the promotion and security of the happiness of the citizens," he wrote, invoking and discussing several provisions of the Constitution.

These effects cannot be produced but by the knowledge and practice of our moral duties, which comprehend all the social and civil obligations of man to man, and of the citizen to the state. If the civil magistrate in any state could procure by his regulations a uniform practice of these duties, the government of that state would be perfect. To obtain that perfection, it is not enough for the magistrate to define the rights of several citizens, as they are related to life, liberty, property, and reputation, and to punish those by whom they may be invaded. Wise laws, made to this end, and faithfully executed, may leave the people strangers to many of the enjoyments of civil and social life, without which their happiness will be extremely imperfect. Human laws cannot oblige to the performance of the duties of imperfect obligation; as the duties of charity and hospitality, benevolence and good neighborhood; as the duties resulting from the relation of husband and wife, parent and child; of man to man, as children of a common parent; and of real patriotism, by influencing every citizen to love his country, and to obey all of its laws. These are moral duties, flowing from the disposition of the heart, and not subject to the control of human legislation. Neither can the laws prevent, by temporal punishments, secret offences, committed without witness, to gratify malice, revenge, or any other passion by assailing the most inestimable rights of others. For human tribunals cannot proceed against any crimes, unless ascertained by evidence; and they are destitute of all power to prevent the commission of offences, unless by the feeble examples exhibited in the punishment of those who may be detected.

Civil government, therefore, availing itself only of its own power, is extremely defective; and unless it could derive assistance from some superior power, whose laws extend to the temper and disposition of the human heart, and before whom no offence is secret, wretched indeed would be the state of man under a civil constitution of any form. The most manifest truth has been felt by legislators in all ages; and as man is born, not only a social, but a religious being, so, in the pagan world, false and absurd systems of religion were adopted and patronized by the magistrate, to remedy the defects necessarily existing in a government merely civil.[79]

Having demonstrated the necessity and utility of religion generally for civil society and government, Parsons then turned to the reasons for state support of Christian institutions in particular.

[T]he people of Massachusetts, in the frame of their government, adopted and patronized a religion, which, by its benign and energetic influences, might cooperate with human institutions, to promote and secure the happiness of the citizens, so far as it might be consistent with the imperfections of man. In selecting a religion, the people were not exposed to the hazard of choosing a false and defective religious system. Christianity had long been promulgated, its pretensions and excellences well known, and its divine authority admitted. This religion was found to rest on the basis of immortal truth; to contain a system of morals adapted to man, in all possible ranks and conditions, situations and circumstances, by conforming to which he would be meliorated and improved in all the relations of human life; and to furnish the most efficacious sanctions, by bringing to light a future state of retribution. And this religion, as understood by Protestants, tending, by its effects, to make every man submitting to its influence, a better husband, parent, child, neighbor, citizen, and magistrate, was by the people established as a fundamental and essential part of their constitution.[80]

Parsons then moved to answer criticisms that the institutionalization of religion mandated by article III was "inconsistent, intolerant, and impious."[81] First, he argued,

the manner in which this establishment was made, is liberal, and consistent with the rights of conscience on religious subjects. As religious opinions, and time and manner of expressing the homage due to the Governor of the universe, are points depending on the sincerity and belief of each individual, and do not concern the public interest, . . . the second article . . . guards these points from the interference of the civil magistrate . . . for every man, whether Protestant or Catholic, Jew, Mahometan, or Pagan.[82]

It is perfectly consistent for the state to maintain these guarantees of liberty of conscience for all and to "provide for the public teaching of the precepts of Protestant Christians to all the people" by collecting tithes to support their ministers and churches. To object that this is a violation of conscience, Parsons wrote, is "to mistake a man's conscience for his money" and to deny the state the right of collecting taxes from those whom it represents.

But as every citizen derives the security of his property, and fruits of his industry, from the power of the state, so, as the price of this protection, he is bound to contribute, in common with his fellow-citizens, for such public uses, as the state shall direct. And if any individual can lawfully withhold his contribution, because he dislikes the appropriation, the authority of the state to levy taxes would be annihilated; and without money it would soon cease to have any authority. But all moneys raised and appropriated for public uses, by any corporation, pursuant to powers derived from the state, are raised and appropriated substantially by the authority of the state. And the people, in their constitution, instead of devolving the support of public teachers of on the corporations, by whom they should be elected, might have directed their support to be defrayed out of the public treasury, to be reimbursed by the levying and collection of state taxes. And against this mode of support, the objection of an individual, disapproving of the object of the public taxes, would have the same weight it can have against the mode of public support through the medium of corporate taxation. In either case, it can have no weight to maintain a charge of persecution for conscience' sake. The great error lies in not distinguishing between liberty of conscience in religious opinions and worship, and the right of appropriating money by the state. The former is an unalienable right; the latter is surrendered to the state, as the price of protection.[83]

Second, Parsons argued, the notion that support for religious institutions was intolerant of the nonreligious failed to recognize the great public benefits that support of religious institutions brings them.

> The object of public religious instruction is to teach, and to enforce by suitable arguments, that practice of a system of correct morals among the people, and form and cultivate reasonable and just habits and manners; by which every man's person and property are protected from outrage, and his personal and social enjoyments promoted and multiplied. From these effects every man enjoys the most important benefits; and whether he be, or be not, an auditor of any public teacher, he receives more solid and permanent advantages from the public instruction, than the administration of justice in courts of law can give him. The like objection may be made by any man to the support of public schools.[84]

Arguments such as these proved sufficient to defend article III for more than half a century after ratification of the Massachusetts Constitution. This was the balance that Adams's dialectical model of religious liberty seemed to demand. All faiths were free, and it was up to individuals to devise their own religious institutions and practices in a manner they found convenient. One faith was fixed, and it was up to the state to devise its religious institutions and practices in a manner it found expedient. To leave private religious faiths uncontrolled would only encourage human depravity. To leave the public religious faith unsupported would only encourage social fragmentation, hence the need to add to a ceremonial and a moral establishment a more robust institutional establishment of the public religion.

However convincing such arguments might have been in theory, they ultimately proved unworkable in practice. In the fifty-three years of its existence, article III "was fruitful in lawsuits, bad feeling, and petty prosecution."[85] Both the casuistry and the clumsiness of the tithing and registration system were exposed in litigation. Resentment toward article III only increased as the religions of Massachusetts liberalized and pluralized, and the former Congregational churches were splintered into an array of Trinitarian and Unitarian forms.[86] Eventually, detractors so outnumbered proponents that the Massachusetts Constitution was amended. In 1833, article XI outlawed the institutional establishment of a public religion, even while explicitly preserving the ceremonial and moral establishment:

> As the public worship of GOD and instructions in piety, religion and morality, promote the happiness and prosperity of a people and the security of a Republican Government;—Therefore, the several religious societies of the

Commonwealth, whether corporate or incorporate, at any meeting legally warned and holden for that purpose, shall ever have the right to elect their pastors of religious teachers, to contract with them for their support, to raise money for erecting and repairing houses for public worship, for the maintenance of religious instruction, and for the payment of necessary expenses: And all persons belonging to any religious society shall be taken and held to be members, until they shall file with the Clerk of such Society, a written notice declaring the dissolution of their membership, and thenceforth shall not be liable for any grant or contract, which may be thereafter made, and denominations demeaning themselves peaceably and as good citizens of the Commonwealth shall be equally under the protection of the law; and no subordination of one sect or denomination to another shall ever be established by law.

Subsequent amendments of 1855, 1917, and 1974 closed the door tightly against any form of state fiscal and material aid to religious institutions and endeavors.[87]

CONCLUSION

In the preface to his *Defense of the Constitutions of Government in the United States of America* of 1788, John Adams wrote boldly,

The people in America have now the best opportunity and the greatest trust in their hands, that Providence ever committed to so small a number, since the transgression of the first pair; if they betray their trust, their guilt will merit even greater punishment than other nations have suffered, and in the indignation of Heaven . . . The United States have exhibited, perhaps, the first example of governments erected on the simple principles of nature; and if men are now sufficiently enlightened to disabuse themselves of artifice, imposture, hypocrisy, and superstition, they will consider this event as a [new] era in history. Although the detail of the formation of the American governments is at present little known or regarded either in Europe or in America, it may hereafter become an object of curiosity.

For, it is "destined to spread over the northern part of that whole quarter of the globe." Indeed, "[t]he institutions now made in America will not wholly die out for thousands of years. It is of the last importance, then, that they should begin right. If they set out wrong, they will never be able to return, unless it be by accident to the right path."[88]

Two centuries later, such sentiments prove remarkably prescient. The American framers did begin on the right path of religious liberty, and today we enjoy a remarkable freedom of thought, conscience, and belief as a consequence. American models of religious liberty have had a profound influence around the globe, and their principles now figure prominently in a number of national constitutions and international human rights instruments.[89]

To be sure, as Adams predicated, there has always been "a glorious uncertainty" in the law of religious liberty and a noble diversity of understandings of its details. This was as true in Adams's day as it is in our own. In Adams's day, there were competing models of religious liberty more overtly theological than his, whether Puritan, Anglican, Evangelical, or Catholic in inspiration. There were also competing models more overtly philosophical than his, whether classical, republican, Enlightenmentarian, or Whig in inclination. Today, these and other models of religious liberty have born ample progeny, and the rivalries among them are fought out in the courts, legislatures, and academies throughout the land.

Prone as he was to a dialectical model of religious liberty and a federalist system of government, Adams would likely approve of our rigorous rivalries of principle—so long as all rivals remain committed to constitutional ideals of democracy, liberty, and the rule of law. But Adams would also likely insist that we reconsider his most cardinal insights about the dialectical nature of religious freedom and religious establishment. Too little religious freedom, Adams insisted, is a recipe for hypocrisy and impiety. But too much religious freedom is an invitation to depravity and license. Too firm a religious establishment breeds coercion and corruption. But too little religious establishment allows secular prejudices to become constitutional prerogatives. Somewhere between these extremes, Adams believed, a society must find its balance.

The balance that John Adams struck in favor of a "mild and equitable establishment" of Protestantism can no longer serve a nation so fully given to religious pluralism. But the balance that the Supreme Court has struck in favor of a complete disestablishment of religion can also no longer serve a people so widely devoted to a public religion and a religious public. Somewhere between these extremes, our society must now find a new constitutional balance—with Adams's efforts serving as a noble instruction.

NOTES

1. Letter to James Warren (January 9, 1787), quoted by David McCullough, *John Adams* (New York: Simon & Schuster, 2001), 373.

2. Letter to Benjamin Rush (March 23, 1809), in *The Spur of Fame: Dialogues of John Adams and Benjamin Rush 1805–1813*, eds. John A. Schutz and Douglass Adair (Indianapolis, IN: Liberty Fund, 1966), 151. See detailed discussion in Joseph J. Ellis, *Passionate Sage: The Character and Legacy of John Adams*, 2d ed. (New York: W.W. Norton, 2001), 19–83.

3. See, e.g., Catherine Drinker Bowen, *John Adams and the American Revolution* (Boston: Little, Brown and Co., 1950); Page Smith, *John Adams*, 2 vols. (New York: Doubleday, 1962); Gilbert Chinard, *Honest John Adams* (Boston: Little, Brown, 1933).

4. See collection in C. F. Adams, ed., *Familiar Letters of John Adams and His Wife Abigail during the Revolution* (New York: Hurd & Houghton, 1876); id., ed., *Letters of John Adams Addressed to His Wife*, 2 vols. (Boston: Little and Brown, 1841); Andrew Oliver, *Portraits of John and Abigail Adams* (Cambridge, MA: Belknap Press, 1967); Charles W. Aikers, *Abigail Adams: An American Woman* (Boston: Little, Brown, 1980).

5. See Paul Wilstach, ed., *Correspondence of John Adams and Thomas Jefferson* (Indianapolis, IN: Bobbs-Merrill Co., 1925); Lester J. Cappon, ed., *The Adams-Jefferson Letters*, 2 vols. (Chapel Hill: University of North Carolina Press, 1959).

6. For primary texts, see L. H. Butterfield, ed., *Diary and Autobiography of John Adams*, 4 vols. (Cambridge, MA: Belknap Press, 1961); L. Kinvin Wroth and Hiller B. Zobel, eds., *Legal Papers of John Adams*, 3 vols. (Cambridge, MA: Belknap Press, 1965); L. H. Butterfield et al., eds., *The Book of Abigail and John: Selected Letters of the Adams Family, 1762–1784* (Cambridge, MA: Harvard University Press, 1975). See also more recently Robert J. Taylor et al., eds., *Papers of John Adams*, 2 vols. (Cambridge, MA: Belknap Press, 1977); C. Bradley Thompson, ed., *The Revolutionary Writings of John Adams* (Indianapolis, IN: Liberty Fund, 2000).

For recent studies, see, e.g., McCullough, *John Adams;* Ellis, *Passionate Sage;* C. Bradley Thompson, *John Adams & the Spirit of Liberty* (Lawrenceville: University Press of Kansas, 1998); John Ferling, *John Adams: A Life* (New York: Henry Holt & Co., 1992); Peter Shaw, *The Character of John Adams* (Chapel Hill: University of North Carolina Press, 1976); John R. Howe, *The Changing Political Thought of John Adams* (Princeton, NJ: Princeton University Press, 1966).

7. Quoted in Pauline Maier, "Plain Speaking," *New York Times* (May 27, 2001).

8. Adams, *Diary and Autobiography*, 3:262–63.

9. Adams, *Diary and Autobiography*, 1:43.

10. Quoted in Bernard Bailyn, "Butterfield's Adams: Notes for a Sketch," *William & Mary Quarterly*, 3d ser., 19 (1962): 238–56, at 254–6.

11. J. F. Adams, ed., *The Works of John Adams*, 10 vols. (Boston: Little & Brown, 1850–1856), 2:364, 378, 380, 382, 392, 393, 395, 400, 401, 404.

12. Letter to Benjamin Rush (April 18, 1808), in *The Spur of Fame*, 106–7.

13. Letter to Benjamin Rush (August 28, 1811), in *The Spur of Fame*, 191–95, at 193.

14. Letter to Benjamin Rush (January 21, 1810), in *The Spur of Fame*, 9:626, 627.

15. On the prevalence, and plasticity, of this theme in American history, see especially Martin E. Marty, *The One and the Many: America's Struggle for the Common Good* (Cambridge, MA: Harvard University Press, 1997).

16. See, e.g., Letter to Zabdiel Adams (June 21, 1776), in Adams, *Works*, 4:194: "The only foundation of a free constitution is pure virtue." Letter to Benjamin Rush (February 2, 1807), in *The Spur of Fame*, 75–77, at 76: "I say then that national moral-

ity never was and never can be preserved without the utmost purity and chastity in women; and without national morality a republican government cannot be maintained." Letter to Benjamin Rush (August 28, 1811), in *The Spur of Fame*, 191–95, at 192: "I agree with you in sentiment that religion and virtue are the only foundations not only of republicanism and of all free government but of social felicity under all governments and in all the combinations of civil society." In the same letter, Adams defended the "inculcation of 'national, social, domestic, and religious virtues'," "fidelity to the marriage bed," "the sanctification of the Sabbath," prohibitions "against ardent spirits, the multiplication of taverns, retailers, dram shops, and tippling houses . . . idlers, thieves, sots, and consumptive patients made for the physicians in those infamous seminaries." *The Spur of Fame,*191–95, at 192.

17. See, e.g., Letter to Benjamin Rush (February 2, 1807), in *The Spur of Fame,* 75–76: "The Bible contains the most profound philosophy, the most perfect morality, and the most refined policy that ever was conceived upon earth. It is the most republican book in the world. and therefore I will still revere it." See also Letter to Mrs. Adams (July 3 1776), in Adams, *Works,* 9:419–20 regarding the celebration of national symbols and events.

18. See especially Massachusetts Constitution (1780), art. XVIII and notes thereon in Adams, *Works,* 4:227–28.

19. Adams, *Works,* 4:227–28. See also Letter to Benjamin Rush (June 12, 1812), in *Spur of Fame,* 224–26, at 224 on thanksgiving sermons.

20. Late in his life, Adams expressed regret about blasphemy laws. In a letter of January 23, 1825, to Jefferson, he wrote, "We think ourselves possessed, or, at least, we boast that we are so, of the liberty of conscience on all subjects, and of the right of free inquiry and private judgments in all cases, and yet how far are we from these exalted privileges in fact! There exists, I believe, throughout the whole Christian world, a law which makes it a blasphemy to deny or to doubt the divine inspiration of all the books of the Old and New Testament. . . . In America, it is not much better; even in our own Massachusetts, which I believe, upon the whole, is as temperate and moderate in religious zeal as most of the States, a law was made in the latter end of the last century, repealing the cruel punishments of the former laws, but substituting fine and imprisonment upon all blasphemers. . . . I think such laws a great embarrassment, great obstructions to the improvement of the human mind. . . . I wish they were repealed. The substance and essence of Christianity, as I understand it, is eternal and unchangeable, and will bear examination forever." Adams, *Works,* 10:415–16.

21. For Adams's earlier views on this, see especially *A Dissertation on the Canon and Feudal Law* (1774), in *Works,* 3:448–64; and *Thoughts on Government Applicable to the Present State of the Colonies* (1776), in *Works,* 4:193–209. For later formulations, see Howe, *Changing Political Thought of John Adams,* 227ff.

22. Adams, *Works,* 2:399.

23. John Adams, *A Defense of the Constitutions of Government in the United States of America* (1788), in Adams, *Works,* 4:290–97; and John Adams, *A Dissertation on the Canon and Feudal Law* (1774), in Adams, *Works,* 3:451.

24. Letter to Dr. Price (April 8, 1785), in Adams, *Works,* 8:232. In Letter to Adrian van der Kemp (October 2, 1818), Adams again praised "freedom of religion" so long as it was "consistent with morals and property." Quoted by Howe, *The Changing Political Thought of John Adams,* 227n.

25. Adams, *Works*, 3:452–56.

26. Letter to Thomas Jefferson (June 28, 1813), in *Adams-Jefferson Letters*, 338–40, at 339–40.

27. Letter to Thomas Jefferson (June 25, 1813), in *Adams-Jefferson Letters*, 333–35, at 334.

28. See William C. McLoughlin, *New England Dissent* 1630–1833, 2 vols. (Cambridge, MA: Harvard University Press, 1971); Jacob C. Meyer, *Church and State in Massachusetts from 1740–1833*, repr. ed. (New York: Russell & Russell, 1968).

29. The delegates did not attend all sessions; the highest recorded vote on any issue was 247. Samuel Eliot Morison, "The Struggle over the Adoption of the Constitution of Massachusetts," *1780, Massachusetts Historical Society Proceedings* 50 (1916–1917): 353–412, 356.

30. Letter to Edmund Jennings (June 7, 1780), in Adams, *Works*, 4:216.

31. The draft is reprinted in Adams, *Works*, 4:213–67.

32. Adams, *Works*, 4:221 (emphasis added).

33. Chapter I, section III. See chapter II, section II (requiring that the governor "shall be of the Christian religion"); section III (requiring that the lieutenant governor "shall be qualified, in point of religion"). Adams, *Works*, 4:241, 242, 245, 251.

34. See chapter VI, art. I and *Journal*, 97, 109–10 (summarizing debates on February 10, 14, and 15, 1780 about the same).

35. Chapter VI, article I, with drafts in Adams, *Works*, 4:260–66.

36. Amendment, art. VI (1821) required the following oath for all officers: "I A.B. do solemnly swear that I will bear true faith and allegiance to the Commonwealth of Massachusetts, and will support the Constitution thereof. So help me GOD." Quakers were again excused from the oath. Amendment, art. VII (1821) underscored this: "No oath, declaration or subscription, excepting the oath of the previous Article," was required of executive or legislative officers.

37. Robert J. Taylor, *Construction of the Massachusetts Constitution* (Worcester, MA: American Antiquarian Society, 1980), 331.

38. Letter to William D. Williamson (February 25, 1812), in Adams, *Works*, 4:222n.

39. Reprinted in Adams, *Works*, 4:221–22; a slightly reworded version appears in the *Journal*, Appendix II, at 193.

40. *Acts and Resolves, Public and Private, of the Province of Massachusetts Bay* (Boston: Government Printer, 1869–1922), 1:62–63.

41. See sources and discussion in my "Tax Exemption of Church Property: Historical Anomaly or Valid Constitutional Practice?" *Southern California Law Review* 64 (1991): 363–415, at 368–80.

42. Morison, "The Struggle," 370.

43. See details in John D. Cushing, "Notes on Disestablishment in Massachusetts, 1780–1833," *William & Mary Quarterly*, 3d ser., 26 (1969): 169–90; McLoughlin, *New England Dissent*, 547–65; Meyer, *Church and State in Massachusetts*, 32–89.

44. The objections beforehand are summarized in my "Mild and Equitable Establishment of Religion," 4–9.

45. *Journal*, 38–40. Included was Theophilus Parsons discussed infra.

46. *Journal*, 43.

47. *Journal*, 45.

48. Morison, "The Struggle," 371.

49. Morison, "The Struggle," 375.

50. On the controversy surrounding the voting, see sources in my "Mild and Equitable Establishment of Religion," 14–15.

51. Reprinted in Taylor, *Construction*, 162–65, at 164.

52. Adams, *Works*, 4:297.

53. Letter to Josiah Quincy (February 9, 1811), in Adams, *Works*, 9:629–32, at 630.

54. Quoted by McLoughlin, *New England Dissent*, 560.

55. Adams, *Works*, 8:232.

56. Letter to Abigail Adams (1775), quoted and discussed in Edwin S. Gaustad, *A Religious History of America* (New York: Harper & Row, 1966), 127.

57. Letter to Benjamin Rush (August 28, 1811), in Adams, *Works*, 9:635, 636.

58. Letter to Thomas Jefferson (April 19, 1817), in Adams, *Works*, 10:253 at 254.

59. Adams, *Works*, 3:452–56.

60. Adams, *Works*, 3:452–56. See also his long discussion of the rise of religious liberty among European Protestants, in the *Defense of the Constitutions*, bk. 2.

61. Letter to Isaac Smith, Sr. (May 16, 1780), quoted by Taylor, *Construction*, 333–34n32.

62. Amendment, art. CVI (1982) rendered "all men" as "all persons" and added, "Equality under the law shall not be denied or abridged because of . . . creed."

63. Ronald M. Peters Jr., *The Massachusetts Constitution of 1780: A Social Compact* (Amherst: The University of Massachusetts Press, 1978), 51–52.

64. See sources and discussion in my *Religion and the American Constitutional Experiment: Essential Rights and Liberties* (Boulder: Westview Press, 2000), 23–56, 87–100.

65. Adams, *Works*, 8:232.

66. This emphasis on human depravity and the need for its restraint is especially pronounced in Adams's earlier writings, notably in his 1788 *Defense of the Constitutions*. Later in his life, Adams tempered this view. See, e.g., Letter to Thomas Jefferson (April 19, 1817), in Adams, *Works*, 10:253–55, at 254: "So far from believing in the total and universal depravity of human nature, I believe there is no individual totally depraved. The most abandoned scoundrel that ever existence, never yet wholly extinguished his conscience, and while conscience remains, there is some religion."

67. Simeon Howard, *A Sermon Preached before the Honorable Council . . . of Massachusetts-Bay* (Boston: John Bill, 1780), reprinted in J. W. Thornton, *The Pulpit of the American Revolution* (Boston: Gould and Lincoln, 1860), 355–96, at 362–63.

68. *Worcestriensis IV*, in Charles S. Hynemann and Donald S. Lutz, eds., *American Political Writing during the Founding Era, 1760–1805*, 2 vols. (Indianapolis, IN: Liberty Fund, 1983), 1:452.

69. *Worcestriensis IV*, 450.

70. See especially Donald S. Lutz, *The Origins of American Constitutionalism* (Baton Rouge: Louisiana State University Press, 1988). See also my "How to Govern a City on a Hill: The Early Puritan Contribution to American Constitutionalism," *Emory Law Journal* 39 (1990): 41–64, and my "Blest Be the Ties That Bind: Covenant and Community in Puritan Thought," *Emory Law Journal* 36 (1987): 579–601.

71. See Phillips Payson, "Election Sermon of 1778," reprinted in *American Political Writing*, 523–38, at 529. This was also one reason that Adams wrote into his draft of chapters I and II that every official must be "of the Christian religion."

72. W. Stoughton, *New Englands True Interest: Not to Lie* (1670), in *The Puritans: A Sourcebook of their Writings*, eds. Perry Miller and Thomas H. Johnson (New York: Harper & Row, 1963), 243.

73. Quoted in Harold J. Berman, "Religious Foundations of Law in the West: An Historical Perspective," *Journal of Law and Religion* 1 (1983): 3–46, at 30.

74. *Colo v. Treasurer and Receiver General*, 392 N.E. 2d 1195 (1979), consistent with *Marsh v. Chambers*, 463 U.S. 783 (1983); *Commonwealth v. Callahan*, 401 Mass. 627 (1988). See also the reflections of an associate justice of the supreme juridical court of Massachusetts, Herbert P. Wilkins, "Judicial Treatment of the Massachusetts Declaration of Rights in Relation to Cognate Provisions of the United States Constitution," *Suffolk University Law Review* 14 (1980): 887–930, at 891–97, 929–30.

75. As Adams put it, "Happiness, whether in despotism or democracy, whether in slavery or liberty, can never be found without virtue. The best republics will be virtuous, and have been so; but we may hazard a conjecture, that the virtues have been the effect of the well-ordered constitution, rather than the cause. And, perhaps, it would be impossible to prove that a republic cannot exist even among highwaymen, by setting one rogue to watch another; and the knaves themselves may in time be made honest men by the struggle." Adams, *Works*, 6:219.

76. See summary of other arguments in my "A Most Mild and Equitable Establishment," 24–28.

77. Ferling, *John Adams*, 297. Cf. Letter to Benjamin Rush (May 14, 1812), in *Spur of Fame*, 238–40, at 239, where Adams grouped Parsons with such statesmen as Jefferson, Madison, Hutchinson, and Sewall as "equally honest, equally able, equally ambitious, and equally hurried away by their passions and prejudices."

78. *Barnes v. Falmouth*, 6 Mass. 401, 404 (1810) (Barnes, C. J.), reprinted with revisions as Theophilus Parsons, *Defence of the Third Article of the Massachusetts Declaration of Rights* (Worcester, MA: 1820).

79. *Barnes v. Falmouth*, 404–5.

80. *Barnes v. Falmouth*, 405.

81. *Barnes v. Falmouth*, 405, 408.

82. *Barnes v. Falmouth*, 405–6.

83. *Barnes v. Falmouth*, 407–8.

84. *Barnes v. Falmouth*, 408–9.

85. Morison, *Constitutional History*, 24–25.

86. See the careful sifting of this case law in McLoughlin, *New England Dissent*, 636–59, 1084–1106, 1189–1284, with summaries in William G. McLouglin, "The Balkcom Case (1782) and the Pietist Theory of Separation of Church and State," *William & Mary Quarterly*, 3d ser. 24 (1967): 267–83; Cushing, "Notes on Disestablishment in Massachusetts."

87. Amendment, art. XVIII (1855); Amendment, art. XLVI (1917); Amendment, art. CIII (1974). See Wilkins, "Judicial Treatment," 892–94.

88. Adams, *Works*, 4:290, 292–93, 298.

89. See, generally, John Witte Jr. and Johan D. van der Vyver, eds., *Religious Human Rights in Global Perspective*, 2 vols. (The Hague: Martinus Nijhoff, 1996); John T. Noonan Jr., *The Lustre of our Country: The American Experience of Religious Freedom* (Berkeley: University of California Press, 1998).

3

The Religious Rhetoric of Thomas Jefferson

Thomas E. Buckley, S.J.

Toward the end of his presidency, Jefferson wrote an appreciative letter to a political ally, DeWitt Clinton. The New York Republican had sent him a copy of *A Vindication of Thomas Jefferson*. Written during the battles of the election campaign of 1800, the anonymous author defended Jefferson against the charges made by Rev. William Linn. In a published pamphlet widely serialized in the Federalist press, Linn, a Dutch Reformed minister in New York, reported that Jefferson had privately stated a wish "to see a government in which no religious opinions are held and where the security for property and social order rested entirely upon the force of the laws." The accusation, Jefferson wrote Clinton, that he wanted "the government without religion" was a "lie" and a "slander," which he "thought it best to leave to the scourge of public opinion." Yet, it still rankled the president years later.[1]

In fact, the misunderstanding persists to the present day that Jefferson was personally irreligious and desired his fellow Americans liberated from the shackles of belief. For example, in a recent address to a distinguished gathering of historians, Daniel Walker Howe stated that "organized Christianity continued to play a much more active role in American life than Jefferson had expected." Frequently, in the nineteenth century, "religious freedom turned out to mean freedom for religion rather than freedom from religion."[2] Would that development have surprised Jefferson? Had he hoped to free Americans "from religion"? From the bench of the U.S. Supreme Court in 2002, Associate

Justice John Paul Stevens invoked Jefferson's wall-of-separation metaphor in his dissent in the school voucher case. Stevens concluded, "Whenever we remove a brick from the wall that was designed to separate religion and government, we increase the risk of religious strife and weaken the foundation of our democracy."[3] Did Jefferson intend his famous wall to separate not just church and state, but also religion and government? Or did he mean what he told Clinton in 1807?

From the beginning of Jefferson's political career, a passion for religious freedom marked his writing and speeches. His efforts to wall off the civil government from matters of conscience and the strong rhetoric with which he voiced his views led some of his contemporaries, as well as later historians and legal scholars, to consider Jefferson hostile, or at best indifferent, toward religion. Yet, if we take him at his word, Jefferson was not personally irreligious, and, more importantly, he did not envision or desire the removal of religion and its values from the arena of politics and government. His concerns and the issues that aroused them were more complex. To understand them and him, we need to consider his varied contexts and to pay close attention to the diverse ways he spoke about religion and the situations that occasioned the shifts in his rhetoric. This chapter will consider especially Jefferson's invocation of religious language, imagery, and allusion in the public documents he crafted and the addresses he gave as a political figure and statesman.

AN EIGHTEENTH-CENTURY EPISCOPALIAN

Something must first be said about Jefferson's personal religious faith and its public expression. A few years before his death, he penned a careful letter to Benjamin Holt Rice, a Presbyterian minister in Petersburg, Virginia. The clergyman had appealed to the sage of Monticello to contribute to a collection he was promoting, probably for a new church building. Jefferson declined. "The principle that every religious sect is to maintain it's [sic] own teachers and institutions is too well established in our country to need justification," he wrote. "I have been from my infancy a member of the Episcopalian church, and to that I owe and make my contribution."[4]

This claim to membership must be examined. Jefferson was born into the established Church of England in Virginia. His formal religious affiliation began the day Peter and Jane Randolph Jefferson presented their newborn son for baptism in 1743. Anglican clergymen provided him with his early education, and along with the classics, Jefferson read the Bible and imbibed the New Testament's moral teachings. Many years later he would praise the teachings of Jesus as "the purest system of morals ever before preached to man." Throughout his life he would equate religion with morality rather than doctrine. That outlook was normal for his time and place. As Edward Bond has argued so cogently, from the beginning of colonization, public behavior rather than private belief formally identified a member of the church. Morality, not creed, was the key to Virginian Anglicanism. Controversies over theological doctrines and devotional practices were to be avoided at all costs, lest they fragment colonial society, as had occurred in England, most notably during the English Civil War. External conduct, therefore, became the hallmark of adherence to the church established by law. Rev. James Maury was the principal instructor of Jefferson's youth, and on one occasion the young Jefferson stood as godfather for Maury's newborn son. On Sundays he joined in church services conducted according to the *Book of Common Prayer*.[5] Such public acts constituted him an Anglican.

In 1760 Jefferson entered the College of William and Mary, an Anglican establishment, where he would spend the next seven years. Dumas Malone, his foremost biographer, suggests that during this time or shortly thereafter Jefferson "would not have called himself a Christian."[6] That is, however, to impose a twentieth-century doctrinal standard upon an eighteenth-century figure. Raised in the Low Church tradition, Jefferson as he matured increasingly tended toward a strictly rationalist faith. But such rationalism did not place him outside the Church of England or the Protestant Episcopal Church in Virginia. Moreover, religious references were constituent elements of his private correspondence with his closest friends throughout his life. A stunning example of this may be found in a letter he wrote in 1763 to John Page. In it the young Jefferson urged classic Anglican sentiments: "a perfect resignation to the divine will . . . till we arrive at our journey's end, where we may deliver up our trust into the hands of him who gave it, and receive such reward as to him shall seem proportioned to our merit." Forty-five years later he concluded another letter to his old friend: "God bless you, and give you health of days, until he shall do better for you."[7]

Consider what Jefferson heard from the pulpits of his day. Anglican ministers and lay readers in colonial Virginia frequently depended upon the published sermons of English preachers either as texts to be read aloud on Sunday morning or, in the case of clergymen, for ideas and guidance in putting together their own sermons. By far the most popular ones in print came from the pen of John Tillotson, the Latitudinarian archbishop of Canterbury and close friend of John Locke. They emphasized moral virtues and practical Christian living rather than dogma or theology. One of his students later reported that Tillotson had opined that "Christianity . . . was nothing else but the religion of nature, or pure morality, save only praying and making all our addresses to God in the name, and through the mediation of our Saviour, and the use of the two sacraments of Baptism and the Lord's Supper." As should be expected, the emphasis on scientific method and rational discourse profoundly impacted theological discussion within the Church of England. Tillotson himself rejected the vigorously Trinitarian Athanasian Creed and, like Locke, favored a policy of religious toleration and a comprehensive church.[8] Jefferson fit easily into this mental frame and, as he later wrote of Locke, might well have said of the good bishop, "where Tillotson has stopped short, we may go on."

Eighteenth-century enlightened, rational Anglicanism did not require a confessional belief, but rather a mode of worship. This, coupled with a common moral code, held Virginians together, not a set of religious tenets to which all men and women rendered univocal adherence. The church did not command one how or what to think about God, and Jefferson made full use of that latitude. He took religion seriously enough to think about it for himself. As an adult, he read from his own edited version of the New Testament, attended Sunday worship with the local community, served as a vestryman in his local parish, contributed to the support of the ministry, and believed what his reason convinced him was the truth. In his later years he embraced something like a Unitarian faith, but he did not switch churches. Even as he quietly rejected standard Christian doctrines like the Trinity and the divinity of Christ, he considered himself a Christian and remained comfortably within the Episcopalian fold throughout his life.[9]

THE RHETORIC OF REVOLUTION

After completing college and his studies for the bar, Jefferson assumed management of the farms he had inherited from his father, while gradually developing an extensive legal practice. In 1769 he became a member of the House of Burgesses in Williamsburg. He was only in his first term when he helped to prepare a formal address to Governor Botetourt. It included an assurance of "Prayers" and a desire that "Providence" would guide "his Lordship."[10] Insignificant formalism? Perhaps. But like most Americans of his and succeeding generations, he grew up and moved within a religious worldview. When operating within a political framework, outside the immediate practical arrangements of government such as constitution making, and especially when he wanted to stir people's souls, he regularly drew upon religious language and biblical references to strengthen his argument.

The young politician recognized the power of religious motivation from the outset. He and his confederates set out to make a revolution. They faced formidable obstacles, not the least of which was the resistance of their own countrymen, who needed to be persuaded that their cause was right and just. Whether they regularly attended church services or not, the vast bulk of Americans held traditional Protestant religious beliefs and shared a common civic morality about submission to legitimate authority. Those who could read, read the Bible and interpreted it for themselves. Jefferson would therefore draw upon this communal religious heritage to enlist the deepest values and ideals of his hearers and readers and to rally popular support for the Revolution. As historian Gordon Wood has recently pointed out about the Revolutionary era, "religion was that aspect of the culture that gave the highest level of meaning, order, and value to people's experience."[11] Jefferson explicitly tapped into this religious culture in three ways.

First, Jefferson drew on this religious culture by invoking God in prayer. He was part of the small group of Virginia Burgesses, the "radicals" who concocted the idea of proclaiming a day of prayer and fasting to rouse people's attention to the threat that the Coercive Acts posed in 1774 not just to Boston and Massachusetts Bay, but to all the colonies.[12] Soon afterward he and his fellow Burgess from Albemarle County, John Walker, invited the members of their local parish to come to a Saturday prayer service "to implore the divine interposition in behalf of an injured and oppressed people."[13] He would return to this theme in 1775 in the resolutions he drafted for the Virginia House of Burgesses to counter Lord North's proposal in the House of Commons. After listing the objections to the British plan and all the failed efforts at reconciliation, Jefferson asked rhetorically, "What then remains to be done?" The answer: "That we commit our injuries to the even-handed justice of that being who doth no wrong, earnestly beseeching him to illuminate the Councils and prosper the endeavors of those to whom America hath confided her hopes."[14] The revised code of state laws that he helped draft during the Revolution contained a bill "for Appointing days of Public Fasting and Thanksgiving" right alongside his proposed bill for religious freedom. As governor, Jefferson issued such a proclamation in 1779. It assigned a date for "publick and solemn thanksgiving and prayer" and encouraged "the several Ministers of religion" to hold appropriate religious services for their congregations.[15]

Second, Jefferson invoked the religious culture by making God the origin of people's rights. In virtually every major document he composed or in which he had a hand during the early years of the Revolution, Jefferson never failed to assert that God had given his creatures their fundamental rights, and that no government, no human agency, could abridge or annul them. This first becomes evident in 1774 in his draft for a declaration of rights, a relatively short text that he drew up for the Virginia convention meeting in August.[16] That same theme reappeared that summer in a much longer piece that he proposed as instructions from the Virginia convention to its delegates at the first Continental Congress in Philadelphia. In printed form Jefferson entitled it *A Summary View of the Rights of British America*. A long document, it essentially charged that the British Parliament was trampling the rights that God had given them. "The god who gave us life, gave us liberty at the same time," he wrote in the peroration.[17]

Jefferson elaborated on that point the following year. After the battles of Lexington, Concord, and Bunker Hill, the second Continental Congress felt obliged in the summer of 1775 to justify its actions in fielding an army; hence, the Declaration of the Causes and Necessity for Taking Up Arms. Jefferson's draft recited the evils committed by the British in and around Boston and then declared the American determination to use "all those powers" given us by "our creator" to uphold the "Liberty which he committed to us in sacred deposit."[18] What God had given them, they were now obligated by God to protect. The revolutionaries were acting defensively to safeguard what was essentially God's design. This conviction led Jefferson in 1776 to embrace for himself and for his state the motto he attributed to Benjamin Franklin: "Rebellion to Tyrants is Obedience to God."[19]

Third, Jefferson argued that Americans must then certainly act with God's approbation. In his draft of the Declaration of Causes, Jefferson called on God to witness the rectitude with which the Americans were defending themselves. Those who take up arms must be "assured that their cause is approved before supreme reason," he wrote, and later that they made this declaration "most solemnly . . . before God & the world."[20] A favorite biblical theme, God's supporting presence with his people during the Exodus, inspired his suggestion in 1776 that the great seal of the United States include a picture of "the children of Israel in the wilderness, led by a cloud by day and a pillar of fire by night."[21]

All three religious themes come together most fully in the crowning work of Jefferson's early political career, the Declaration of Independence. His original draft opened with a reference to the "laws of nature and of nature's god." It endorses belief in a creator who creates "all men . . . equal & independent" and vests them with "rights inherent & inalienable." This was his own work. After consulting with other members of the writing committee and review by the other members of the Congress, the concluding paragraph of the final declaration contains two other references to God. It begins with an appeal "to the Supreme Judge of the world for the rectitude of our intentions" and ends by expressing "a firm reliance on the protection of divine Providence" to support them in their struggle. If their motives and actions were justified in God's eyes, the American revolutionaries could then rely on God's support to see them through this conflict. Some read these last statements as formulaic for eighteenth-century political writing. That may be true, but if so, it simply reinforces the reason for including them. If Americans were to be persuaded to support the Revolution, they must be convinced that God would judge that they acted rightly and somehow would uphold them.[22] Religion went hand in hand with the Revolution—it touched people's minds and hearts and bound the community together in a common purpose.

THE RHETORIC OF RELIGIOUS FREEDOM

Religion could not be coerced. Jefferson was in Philadelphia in May and June of 1776, when a Virginia convention approved a constitution for the independent commonwealth and, in the article XVI of the declaration of rights, guaranteed religious freedom for all. That fall he was back in Williamsburg as a member from Albemarle County to the house of delegates, the lower house in the new assembly, for its first legislative session. At that meeting Jefferson offered resolutions that would have immediately disestablished the Church of England and placed all religious groups on an equal footing. He later referred to the debates over these resolutions as "the severest contests in which I have ever been engaged." He did not exaggerate. As John Nelson has conclusively demonstrated, the Anglican establishment in colonial Virginia was not only part of the warp and woof of the Old Dominion's life, it was also a vigorous institution well supported by the rank and file. Moreover, the church's parishes formed crucial components of local civil government. Disestablishment threatened to upend the political order and force the reordering of society. During the 1776 convention, Virginia's political leaders explicitly repudiated any such intention. They planned to maintain the religious status quo while granting only the minimal concessions necessary to conciliate religious dissenters and ensure their support in the Revolution.[23]

For men like Patrick Henry, Edmund Pendleton, and Robert Carter Nicholas, the survival of their religious community was not the sole concern. If they disestablished Anglicanism, they would abdicate an authority and responsibility they had held all their lives. The Church of England in Virginia had never been a separate organization, separately administered. Those who ruled the state, ruled the church. From the beginning of the colonial period, public taxation and property grants supported the church, and the gentry class, operating principally through lay vestries, controlled it. Nominally Episcopal in polity, the church was congregational in day-to-day management. Although the bishop of London periodically sent out commissaries with supervisory powers, the Virginia clergy remained firmly under the thumb of the lay elite. Whenever the reverend gentlemen challenged this arrangement—for example, at the time of the Parson's Cause— they lost. At the same time, the established church served as a major prop to the social order. The gentry regarded it as their church; it belonged to them and the society they governed. These Virginia gentlemen were separatists, not revolutionaries. They desired freedom from Great Britain for the sake of maintaining life as it had always been. From this perspective, the church was important for maintaining virtue and public morality, vital qualities in a republic. Disagreeing about means, not ends, Jefferson thought those qualities were not inimical to a society that guaranteed complete religious freedom. His friends in Williamsburg did not concur. They refused to dissolve a bulwark of their prestige and a major instrument for the social and political control of the state.[24]

Jefferson, however, was not without allies. Not only was James Madison an able, although quiet, lieutenant in the house, but outside the door, vociferous dissenters were demanding the fulfillment of the promise of complete religious freedom held out by the declaration of rights. In particular, they wanted relief from tithes for the Episcopal Church, as the former Church of England had begun to style itself. The previous August, newly elected Gov. Patrick Henry, responding to a gracious letter from a Baptist association, had praised the "catholic spirit prevailing in our country" and rejoiced that "religious distinctions which formerly produced some heats are now forgotten." His optimism proved premature, as he discovered that autumn. The opposing forces met head on when Separate Baptists and Presbyterians insisted on "equal liberty." Establishment supporters struck back with forceful arguments for retaining the church–state alliance.[25]

The politician from Monticello respected his adversaries as "honest men, but zealous churchmen."[26] He determined to confront them. In support of his resolutions for complete religious freedom and disestablishment, he compiled from various sources an extensive list of arguments. These notes, which formed the basis for one or more speeches he delivered in the assembly that fall, provide proof positive that the thoughts embodied in the Bill for Establishing Religious Freedom, although not enacted into law for another decade, were already fully developed in 1776. Indeed, the wording of his notes is at times almost identical with that of the religious-liberty bill, which he drafted the next year. Moreover, both the debate notes and the bill bear a marked resemblance to another product of his facile pen. Several years later, while serving as American minister to France, Jefferson published his *Notes on the State of Virginia.* This book provided a further opportunity to present his views on religious liberty in his native state and to lobby for the passage of his Virginia statute, which he placed in an appendix to his book. We can take these three texts together as essentially expressing his convictions on religious freedom.

The work of previous ages was his first concern, for Jefferson thought and wrote from a historical perspective. In his prepared remarks for the legislative debates of 1776 as well as in his query on religion in Virginia in the *Notes*, he began his case against the Anglican establishment by explaining the legal history and judicial status of religion in the commonwealth. Having researched his subject extensively, he listed with characteristic thoroughness all the statutes of Great Britain and Virginia that restricted religious belief and practice, noting in particular the punishments available to the civil arm for dealing with such crimes as apostasy, heresy, recusancy, popery, and blasphemy—an impressive summation. Edmund Randolph later described Jefferson's rhetoric in the assembly:

> the severest persecutions in England were ransacked for colors in which to paint the burdens and scourges of freedom in religion; and antiquated laws in England, against the exercise of which the people would even there have recoiled, were summoned up as so many demons hovering over every scrupulous conscience not bending to the church.[27]

However dramatic Jefferson's legislative presentation may have appeared to Randolph, the Albemarle delegate was making a crucial point. He wanted his colleagues to appreciate not the actual conditions of toleration in Virginia—the bulk of these old statutes were unenforced—but the contemporary legal status of religious freedom. The laws on the books, he argued, were out of joint and should be changed to reflect the liberality of the Revolutionary age. Now, at the outset of the Republic, was the appropriate time to clean up the statutes, particularly those dealing with religion. Virginians had a right to live with the security of good laws, rather than simply to depend on the climate of opinion. Opinion can change.

Jefferson then turned to his most fundamental reason for supporting disestablishment: the nature of religious belief as an "unalienable right." He ranked religious freedom among the most important of natural rights. This was not self-evident to the legislators, however, and Jefferson would labor mightily to convince them. These were essentially the same men who had sat in the Virginia convention earlier that year. While embracing the Declaration of Independence, with its essentially Lockean political philosophy, many of his liberty-minded auditors could not accept Jefferson's argument that natural rights included complete freedom of religious belief and practice, required the disestablishment of the state church, and mandated the equality of all religious groups. In attempting to persuade his fellow legislators to these views, Jefferson began from the premise that in forming society, people surrendered only those rights necessary for civil government. All others they retained, especially the rights of conscience. "If [there] is [any] unalienable right," he wrote in his debate notes, "[it] is religious." The reason is that "God requires every act [to be done] according to belief." Founded as it is on a divine imperative, the core of Jefferson's argument is a theological statement: God requires belief. This is God's choice as creator. Human beings possess a correlative responsibility. In his prepared remarks for the assembly, Jefferson wrote that in the exercise of "religious rights," each person is "answerable to God." He would repeat this practically verbatim in his *Notes on Virginia*. Religious belief is the human response to a divine command. Thus, for Jefferson the most fundamental right an individual possesses is that of conscience—the right to one's belief and its expression.[28] A corollary to conscience as a natural right is the exclusion of civil government from the area of religious thought. A person cannot surrender the responsibility for his own conscience to anyone else, even the civil magistrate. Moreover, Jefferson went beyond Locke and other advocates of conscience rights in wishing that they extended to all, even nonbelievers. In his *Letter Concerning Toleration*, the English philosopher had argued that toleration could not be extended to atheists, to those whose religion involves allegiance to a foreign power (that is, Roman Catholics), or to those whose religious faith does not permit them to extend to others the toleration they demand for themselves. "It was a great thing," Jefferson wrote, that Locke had gone "so far . . . but where he stopped short, we may go on." He tried to do so in a bill proposed by Edmund Pendleton to facilitate the naturalization process of "foreign Protestants." Both in committee and on the floor, Jefferson spoke for broadening the license to include Jews, Catholics, and other non-Protestants, and the bill was changed to read just "foreigners," and then "persons." But it failed to pass the legislature.[29]

In the theological foundation Jefferson laid for religious freedom and its universal application, he surpassed the thought of his generation. In addition to his theological argument from the nature of the relationship between God and the human person, he saw the religious pluralism resulting from complete freedom as a positive good, and he praised the diversity of places such as Pennsylvania and New York. What Robert Carter Nicholas fussed over as the "Babel of Religions" did not bother Jefferson. The Virginia legislator advocated pluralism for numerous reasons, not the least of which was his supreme confidence in the power of uncoerced reason to uncover truth. In the 1776 debates, he stated that uniformity is neither desirable nor attainable. A state religion suppresses "free inquiry," the only sure path to improvement and human progress. Replacing civil government as teacher and enforcer, Jefferson would set up truth, reason, and open discussion and debate. Freedom of investigation destroys error, he argued. In one of his abstracts from Locke, Jefferson wrote, "[Tr]uth will do well enough if left to shift for herself. . . . [S]he has no need of force to procure entrance into the minds of men. Error indeed has often prevailed by the assistance of power or force." His statute echoes this judgment: "truth is great and will prevail if left to herself."[30]

Jefferson's fellow legislators were not so confident. The concern of the majority of the assembly, at least ostensibly, was for the protection and preservation of religion as they understood it. In his closing arguments for complete religious freedom and disestablishment, Jefferson argued that true religion would not suffer from such a policy. In this respect, he subscribed to the antiestablishment position of the dissenters when he pointed out that Christianity had not needed state support for the first three hundred years of its existence, that decline had set in after civil government had begun to favor it, and that the "gates of hell" would not prevail in a disestablished Virginia. Voluntary support for the clergy would only increase their quality and their zeal. Jefferson's debate notes conclude with a discussion of the problems and evils of forced contributions to the church. He called his fellow legislators to be consistent with their work of the previous summer. The declaration of rights means "freedom of Religion," he insisted. Compelling people to support a religion other than their own violated conscience and forced them to cooperate in "heresy." Later, in the Virginia Statute for Religious Freedom, he would call that practice "sinful and tyrannical."[31]

A largely unpersuaded assembly did not respond to Jefferson's rhetoric in 1776, although it did repeal the British heresy statutes, exempt dissenters from church taxes, and suspend tithes for Episcopalians. Despite these limited gains, Jefferson prepared to press the issue. His new position on the Committee of Revisors established by the legislature to bring Virginia's laws into conformity with republican principles provided a splendid opportunity. The result was the Bill for Establishing Religious Freedom, which he drafted early in 1777. It contained everything for which Jefferson had worked the year before. His Virginia Statute for Religious Freedom offers the preeminent statement of the American faith as Jefferson defined it: a belief in God-given natural rights, the most important being freedom of thought and its expression, and the precedence of this right over any claims of civil government to control or influence it. A lengthy preamble asserts the freedom of the human mind, the separate spheres of religious and civil rights, the errors inherent in compelling belief, religious practice, and church taxes, the fallacy of allowing government officials to meddle in religious matters, and the all-sufficiency of human reason to discover truth. But the statute is not neutral toward religion. The opening lines refer to "Almighty God" in terms of creation, and the next appeal is to "the plan of the holy author of our religion," who did not use "coercions" to spread it. This is not to say that Jefferson inhibited freedom of conscience for the nonbeliever, only that he expressed himself in terms acceptable to a Christian society. His rhetoric fit the context.[32]

A brief enabling clause stated that all were free to believe, to express their belief, and to worship as they chose without in any way affecting "their civil capacities." The final paragraph is pure Jefferson: "the rights hereby asserted are of the natural rights of mankind." Because these rights were being expressed only in statutory law, future legislatures might tamper with them; but if they diminished them, they would be violating "natural right." In the corpus of Jefferson's work, there is no equal in terms of binding future generations. But first he had to bind his own, and Jefferson's confreres refused to pass the bill when it came before them in 1779. Instead they elevated its author to the governorship of Virginia, an inglorious position, made even more so when British raiders forced the state's chief executive to flee Monticello for the safety of the western mountains.[33]

In the years immediately following his term as governor, Jefferson put together his *Notes on the State of Virginia*. We can glimpse the emotional depth of Jefferson's concern for the fate of his statute from the passionate tone with which he condemned the "religious slavery" that Virginians continued to accept. The political context in which he wrote explains his heated rhetorical pitch. After the legislators in 1779 had shelved the Bill for Establishing Religious Freedom, they had seriously considered another bill "concerning religion" that would have taken Virginia in the opposite direction. Modeled on a statute South Carolina had passed the year before, it provided for a general assessment or tax for the support of Protestant ministers. In effect, the proposed law would establish Protestant Christianity as the religion of the commonwealth, and it had the backing of some of the most influential figures in Virginia politics. After heated debates, the assembly postponed this measure, but it remained a potential threat. Meanwhile Jefferson's proposal had come under severe attack in the press and petitions to the legislature.[34]

Then, in 1780 Massachusetts voters ratified a new state constitution that provided tax support for "public Protestant teachers of piety, religion, and morality." The rationale for a state-supported ministry was simple to grasp, and the arguments had already been proffered in Virginia. Religion promoted the public virtue necessary in a republic. Because it served the welfare of the state, the state should see to its support, and it could do so while allowing complete freedom of conscience and worship. The Massachusetts law said nothing about modes of worship, religious polity, or church discipline. As he compiled his *Notes on Virginia*, Jefferson certainly knew what this influential state had just done. Connecticut and New Hampshire had similar arrangements. Strong momentum existed in Virginia to follow suit, particularly as people watched the precipitous decline in the fortunes of the old established church. By the early 1780s the Episcopal ministry had shrunk to perhaps a third of its pre-Revolutionary strength. The voluntary system of church support did not maintain the clergy, and momentum was building in conservative circles to come to their aid; hence, Jefferson's inflamed rhetoric in Query XVII in the *Notes*.[35]

He began by citing the "intolerance" of the colonial government toward Presbyterians and Quakers, accused the Anglican clergy of "indolence," and claimed that by the time of the Revolution "two-thirds of the people had become dissenters." That wildly exaggerated statistic demonstrated the lengths to which he was prepared to carry his argument. But a recital of the inhibitions to conscience rights within English common law and the colonial heresy statutes provided Jefferson with the opportunity to contrast the current state of "civil freedom" with "religious slavery." In pressing his case for change, he returned to the same arguments he had used in debating disestablishment in 1776:

> Our rulers can have authority over such natural rights only as we have submitted to them. The rights of conscience we never submitted, we could not submit. We are answerable for them to our God. The legitimate powers of government extend to such acts only as are injurious to others.

Then came the pithy sentence that would later cause him so much political grief. "But it does me no injury for my neighbour to say there are twenty gods, or no god. It neither picks my pocket nor breaks my leg."[36]

Jefferson was attempting to differentiate between the sphere of activity appropriate to civil government and that reserved to the individual, but his political enemies would seize upon his language and fling it back in his face, particularly during the election campaigns of 1796 and 1800. The lawyer in Jefferson wanted to draw a distinction between belief and action; the state can move against an individual only when his external activity violates law. To restrict "opinion or tendency of opinion" violates freedom of religious belief. The statute repeats this view: "to suffer the civil magistrate to intrude his powers into the field of opinion and to restrain the profession or propagation of principles on supposition of their ill tendency is a dangerous fallacy, which at once destroys all religious liberty." Officials are tempted to make their views normative for society when they should make no move until an "overt" offense takes place.[37] Jefferson was keenly aware of the fallibility of all human authority, whether civil or ecclesiastical. In his arguments before the assembly in 1776, he pointed out that magistrates are human instruments, capable of corruption. Wherever they had uniformity, hypocrisy or atheism had resulted.

But the lawmakers had not accepted Jefferson's viewpoint then, nor would they a decade later. The story of the ultimate passage of Jefferson's bill has already been told. What needs to be pointed out here is the way in which the legislature, in Madison's words, "somewhat defaced" the preamble. In amending the bill, the senate excised the statement that "the opinions of men are not the object of civil government, nor under its jurisdiction." Conservatives dominated the upper house of the general assembly, and while the senators could not initiate legislation, they could amend it. Initially, a small majority wanted to eliminate the entire preamble and substitute article XVI of the declaration of rights. When the house of delegates rejected that proposal, the senators contented themselves with whittling away the more rationalist features of the preamble. Religion for them was something more than the product of reason, but they eventually approved the Bill for Religious Freedom in January 1786.[38]

A RHETORICAL ANTICLERICALISM

The limited function Jefferson assigned to the churches and clergy in society set him apart from many of his contemporaries and also made him regard religious pluralism as a positive benefit for America. His Anglican upbringing and Enlightenment education had convinced him that for all important purposes, religion is reducible to morality and that the morality taught by all religious groups or churches is essentially the same. He expressed this position on the assembly floor in 1776 when he argued that the special status of the established church was unnecessary for the welfare of society because the "teachers [of] every sect inculcate [the] same moral principles." His *Notes on Virginia* compared the religious situation in New York and Pennsylvania with that in the Old Dominion and praised the freedom and diversity in those northern states. "They flourish infinitely," Jefferson wrote. "Religion is well supported; of various kinds, indeed, but all good enough; all sufficient to preserve peace and order."[39]

In his view, the clergy existed to provide moral teaching, and a major presupposition of his statute was that each individual selects a church based on the moral instruction and example of its ministry. To require a person to contribute "to support this or that teacher of his own religious persuasion, is depriving him of the comfortable liberty of giving his contribution to the particular pastor whose morals he would make his pattern, and whose powers he feels most persuasive to righteousness." In the Jeffersonian scheme of things, the religious dimension of personal belief was absolute. He repeated this in a multitude of ways. The statute's line is famous: "Our civil rights have no dependence on our religious opinions, any more than our opinions in physics or geometry." He advised others not to waste time in theological study, eliminated it (with the help of his friend, the future bishop James Madison) from the curriculum of the College of William and Mary when he was the state governor, and tried to keep it out of the University of Virginia.[40]

If theology was irrelevant, its clerical practitioners were suspect, particularly if they were Presbyterians, Jesuits, or Episcopalians with Tory or Federalist proclivities. Jefferson thought the ministry had violated "the pure and holy doctrines of their master" and placed them in the same class with "soothsayers and necromancers." But he reserved special scorn for a "ranting clergy" whose evangelical religion he likened to "fanaticism."[41] The origin of this intense dislike for the clergy as a group is unclear. Yet, he could distinguish among clergymen. His life-long friendship with Bishop James Madison, the cousin of the other James Madison, began in their boyhood at Maury's School, and the two men regularly exchanged letters and visits. The first Episcopal bishop of Virginia was among Jefferson's staunchest Republican allies. During the Revolution after Virginia ended taxation for the established church, Jefferson led the subscription list for his local clergyman, Charles Clay, whose religion he admired for its "harmony with the liberties of mankind." Samuel Miller, a Presbyterian minister who helped found Princeton Theological Seminary, was another of Jefferson's clerical correspondents and political supporters. There were numerous others.[42] Although he could become furious with clergymen who opposed him politically or interfered with his designs for his university, Jefferson maintained throughout his life close relations with friends in the ministry.

In all the great struggles of his life—the move toward independence, the battle for religious liberty in Virginia, the political contests between Federalists and Republicans that culminated in the election of 1800—ministers could be found on all sides of a question and Jefferson knew it.

He seems to have trusted individual ministers, but not the office. In the Revolutionary period, he criticized the lack of American patriotism displayed by the bulk of the Anglican clergy and later commented on the "fangs" of the Episcopalians. Certainly, he feared the influence of preachers and for many years favored their exclusion from the state legislature. They should keep politics out of the pulpit and confine themselves to "lessons in the religion they profess." When John Holt Rice successfully united Presbyterian and other religious sentiment against Jefferson's choice of Thomas Cooper as a professor at the University of Virginia, the university's father could hardly contain his anger.[43] Truth could stand by itself, he thought, if the clergy were not so powerful. Religious pluralism helped keep them divided.

Much of Jefferson's anticlericalism derived from the election campaigns of 1796 and 1800 and was particularly directed against certain northern ministers, whom he considered enemies of religious freedom. They were Federalists like William Linn, who used Jefferson's rhetorical defense of the inviolability of conscience to attack the Republican candidate on religious grounds. For example, in a lengthy pamphlet published in 1796, William Loughton Smith contrasted Jefferson's attitude toward religion as exemplified in his *Notes on Virginia* with the sentiments expressed by George Washington's in his farewell address. Washington had urged "the *cultivation of religion.*" Jefferson treated it as unimportant. The Virginia statute had produced "a total disregard to *public worship*, an absolute *indifference to all religion whatever.*" Under the guise of religious freedom, Jefferson actually favored "freedom from religion." A boon companion of unbelieving Thomas Paine, the Virginia politician had "by *example* and *precept, discountenanced public worship.*"[44]

The tone grew even more vitriolic in 1800 as various writers labeled him an "infidel," an "atheist," and a "deist."[45] In a sermon attacking the Republican candidate for his lack of religion, James Ambercrombie, the Episcopal minister of Christ Church and St. Peter's in Philadelphia, invited other clergy "to aid me in support of our great and common cause." It would be horrible, the preacher added, for "a Christian community, *voluntarily*, to place at their head, as their *ruler* and *guide*, an acknowledged *unbeliever*, and of course, an *enemy* to their faith."[46] Federalist clergy such as Ambercrombie charged that Jefferson would head a government that had no regard for religion. A few years later his *Notes on Virginia* was called an "instrument of infidelity."[47] One wag even turned to verse:

> Some say our Chief regards religion
> No more than wild-goose, or a pigeon;
> But I'll maintain what seems an oddity,
> He's overstocked with that commodity.
> That man must have religion plenty,
> Who soars from "*no God*," up to "twenty,"—
> No doubt, of common folks the odds,
> As, "*no God*" is to "*twenty Gods.*"[48]

Others might joke, but Jefferson was not amused. Although his friends gave back in print as good as he got, and despite his election victory, he never forgave those clergymen for their efforts to defeat him. In the midst of the campaign heat, he wrote Benjamin Rush that some ministers, particularly "the Episcopalians and Congregationalists," hoped to establish "a particular form of Christianity through the United States." He thought their opposition to him was based on a correct knowledge that Jefferson would oppose their efforts. "I have sworn upon the altar of god," he wrote, "eternal hostility against every form of tyranny over the mind of man."[49]

Their charges of irreligion stung deeply. When a year or so later the opportunity presented itself to strike back, Jefferson seized it. That occasion was the famous letter from the Danbury Baptist Association in Connecticut. He replied with his even more famous statement that interpreted the no-establishment phrase of the religion clause in the

First Amendment in terms of "a wall of separation between church and state."[50] Overtly, he was explaining his refusal to order public days of prayer, but the publication of that letter only added fuel to the charges of irreligion and religious indifferentism, which he denied in his letter to DeWitt Clinton.

RELIGIOUS RHETORIC IN THE SERVICE OF NATIONAL UNITY

An even better denial, however, rests in his own presidential addresses and statements, which were designed to foster national unity. His name has become so attached to church–state separation and the privatization of religion in American public life that we have lost an appreciation of how much Jefferson identified the religious beliefs of the founding generation with the impetus toward revolution and the establishment of the new nation. If we exclude the work of the revolutionary clergy in their pulpits and tracts, few if any of the so-called founding fathers exceeded him in their use of religious language in those rhetorical moments that made the Revolution and bound us together as one people. At the outset of the Revolution, as we have seen, Jefferson was called upon to draft statements that would rally support for the American cause. In his writings then, he used religious affirmation as an effective rhetorical device to rally his fellow citizens to understand the justification for the Revolution and to support its prosecution. Later, as president, he sought to encourage national unity in the face of party divisions and to draw Americans together to work harmoniously toward building a new nation. We can trace that process.

When Jefferson came to the presidency in 1801 it marked the first time that control of the executive office had passed from one political party to another. The campaign, as noted earlier, was marked by bitter attacks that revolved around Jefferson's character, values, and religious beliefs. It was a searing experience for an intensely private man. The country was seriously divided along Federalist–Republican lines. Yet, while he watched this acrimonious political division, he had also observed a pluralism of a different kind, lived and acted out, without the spite and animosity that marked contemporary politics. Religion was flourishing. He and James Madison had been right. Religious diversity had not ended in fratricide. The churches were getting along. Ministers were competing against one another, but the competition did not create enmity.

The great revival at Cane Ridge with its mixture, among others, of Baptists, Methodists, and Presbyterians, was only five months away when Jefferson stood to take the oath of office and give his first inaugural address. He took as his theme the need for political tolerance and cooperation, and he made religious diversity the paradigm for political diversity. "Political intolerance" should go the route of "religious intolerance," he urged. "Every difference of opinion is not a difference of principle. We have called by different names brethren of the same principle. We are all Republicans, we are all Federalists." Religious pluralism could model the way in which the nation should find unity amid diversity, however that diversity might express itself. He pushed his point further. When he enumerated the "blessings" that had fallen upon the nation, the new president included "a benign religion." In all its diverse manifestations, American religions "inculcat[ed] honesty, truth, temperance, gratitude, and the love of man; acknowledging and adoring an overruling Providence, which by all its dispensations proves that it delights in the happiness of man here and his greater happiness hereafter." After a brief renewal of commitment to religious freedom along with other First Amendment rights, Jefferson ended his address with an invocation to "that Infinite Power which rules the destinies of the universe."[51]

In his religious references Jefferson was searching for common ground, for a language which his fellow citizens could understand and accept, whatever their political differences. A century before Teddy Roosevelt, Jefferson found the presidency a bully pulpit in the fullest extent of that term. People might take what he said on their own terms, but his intentions were clear. At least one serious Christian thought that the address "united" the people and reported to a correspondent in London, "Our new President is said to [be] unfriendly to religion. His inaugural address contradicts that insinuation. . . . [H]e believes in the divine mission of our Saviour, in the resurrection of the body by his power, and in a future state of rewards and punishments." Jefferson had not actually said all that, but the implications of the civic faith he presented were sufficient to satisfy Benjamin Rush.[52]

Despite continuing attacks on his personal religion, conciliation marked his presidency. As he told Clinton, he trusted "public opinion" to discover the truth. Religious references designed to unite his countrymen appeared throughout his writings. His annual messages to Congress were matter-of-fact statements that he sent down to the capital rather than delivering orally. In them he analyzed the condition of foreign relations, trade, the federal debt, Indian relations, and various domestic affairs. But often within his message he would place a reference to God's "goodness" and "bounty" in his providential care for the country. When the new Congress assembled in Washington in the December following his inauguration, Jefferson began his message by noting that the European wars had ended without American involvement. "[W]e are bound, with peculiar gratitude," he wrote, "to be thankful to Him that our own peace has been preserved." The next December, he elaborated, "Another year has come round, and finds us still blessed with peace and friendship abroad, law, order and religion at home, good affection and harmony with our Indian neighbours, our burthens lightened." All this had occurred "under the smiles of Providence" to whom "we owe" a "large measure of thankfulness." The old world returned to war in 1803. As he struggled for a middle course between France and Great Britain, Jefferson asked his fellow citizens to be grateful to "kind Providence" for keeping them out of the conflict. Two years later, after the yellow fever had struck two cities, he publicly thanked "Providence" for ending it.[53]

His second inaugural address pulled out all the stops, as he reached back into the Hebrew scriptures to enunciate his own vision of the nation.

> I shall need, too, the favor of that Being in whose hands we are, who led our fathers, as Israel of old, from their native land and planted them in a country flowing with all the necessaries and comforts of life; who has covered our infancy with His Providence and our riper years with His wisdom and power.[54]

As he had suggested almost three decades earlier in his proposal for the great seal, here, too, the Exodus event foreshadowed the experience of the American people. In 1808 he anticipated his retirement from the presidency: "I carry with me," he wrote, "the consolation of a firm persuasion that Heaven has in store for our beloved country long ages to come of prosperity and happiness."[55]

Among his earliest political acts had been the proposal of a day of prayer and fasting. During the Revolution, as a member of the select committee to revise the state's laws, he had drawn up a proposed bill to provide for such days. As president, however, he refused to proclaim them, that is to issue an executive order requiring them, out of the belief that the First Amendment interdicted such a command from the chief executive. In the federal system of government prescribed by the Constitution, that authority belonged to state governments and to the churches. Yet, in his second inaugural address, he invited his fellow citizens to "join in supplications with me" to God to bless the Republic. It was an invitation, not a command, in the area of church and state about whose boundaries Jefferson was scrupulously exact.[56]

Jefferson did not separate religion from government. Far from it. For Jefferson, religious belief could be placed at the service of national unity. He drew upon it in that fashion, first in the early formative years of the Revolution, especially in the great documents that expressed the intentions and self-understanding of the American Revolution. Similarly, he drew upon it in his years as president of the young republic. In both these important moments, one quality in his religious references merits our particular attention. Jefferson's religious language in the political arena was as inclusive as possible. Virtually all believers of whatever religious persuasion could embrace it.[57]

His public statements after leaving office always eschewed religious controversy and praised religious freedom. In 1820 a Jewish rabbi sent him a copy of the talk he had given at the dedication of a synagogue in Savannah. In reply, Jefferson thanked him and reported his gratitude "that his own country had been the first to prove to the world two truths, the most salutary to human society, that man can govern himself and that religious freedom is the most effectual anodyne against religious dissension."[58] At the outset of the Revolution, it had fallen to Jefferson to enunciate the principles that underlay the Revolution, first in Virginia and then for the new nation. He never forgot that he spoke for his generation, that his task was to bind his countrymen together for the cause. His religious rhetoric then and later during his presidency touched a common chord that virtually all Americans could hear. Far from being personally irreligious or attempting to wall government off from religion, Jefferson bears conspicuous responsibility for the development of an American civil religion, a complex of ideas, images, and symbols related to and dependent upon a transcendent reality we call God. Through his public writings and statements, he deliberately crafted this civic faith to bind the nation together.[59]

His final expression of this civic faith occurred at his death. John Adams died the same day—on the fiftieth anniversary of the promulgation of the Declaration of Independence. Understandably the nation viewed their deaths together on this day as a providential sign from God that validated the work of their lives and the nation they helped found. Speaker after speaker talked in religious terms of their meaning for America. Daniel Webster read in these events "a Divinity which shapes our ends." The work of Jefferson and Adams had become a "sacred trust." In Charleston, South Carolina, a southern orator found in Jefferson a wonderful model of "republican virtue," although he also noted, possibly with tongue in cheek, the occasion Jefferson had provided for others to practice virtue.[60]

But perhaps William Wirt, a Virginian, attorney general of the United States, and evangelical Christian, best capitalized on the coincidence. Speaking in the nation's capital, Wirt pointed out that Jefferson and Adams had died on "the great Jubilee of the nation." Americans should recognize "the voice of Heaven in this wonderful dispensation." In Wirt's flights of oratory, Jefferson and Adams became "Apostles of human liberty," whose passing displayed the hand of "Providence."[61] Like other clerical and lay speakers on this occasion, Wirt proposed that God had a hand in these events. Thus, even the timing of Jefferson's death, together with the death of Adams, served a religiously rhetorical purpose and bound the nation more closely together. Perhaps the sage of Monticello planned it that way.

APPENDIX: A BILL FOR
ESTABLISHING RELIGIOUS FREEDOM[62]

WELL aware that the opinions and belief of men depend not on their own will, but follow involuntarily the evidence proposed to their minds; that[63] Almighty God hath created the mind free, *and manifested his supreme will that free it shall remain by making it altogether insusceptible of restraint;* that all attempts to influence it by temporal punishments, or burthens, or by civil incapacitations, tend only to beget habits of hypocrisy and meanness, and are a departure from the plan of the holy author of our religion, who being lord both of body and mind, yet chose not to propagate it by coercions on either, as was in his Almighty power to do, *but to extend it by its influence on reason alone;* that the impious presumption of legislators and rulers, civil as well as ecclesiastical, who, being themselves but fallible and uninspired men, have assumed dominion over the faith of others, setting up their own opinions and modes of thinking as the only true and infallible, and as such endeavoring to impose them on others, hath established and maintained false religions over the greatest part of the world and through all time: That to compel a man to furnish contributions of money for the propagation of opinions which he disbelieves *and abhors,* is sinful and tyrannical; that even the forcing him to support this or that teacher of his own religious persuasion, is depriving him of the comfortable liberty of giving his contributions to the particular pastor whose morals he would make his pattern, and whose powers he feels most persuasive to righteousness; and is withdrawing from the ministry those temporary [temporal] rewards, which proceeding from an approbation of their personal conduct, are an additional incitement to earnest and unremitting labours for the instruction of mankind; that our civil rights have no dependence on our religious opinions, any more than [on] our opinions in physics or geometry; that therefore the proscribing any citizen as unworthy the public confidence by laying upon him an incapacity of being called to offices of trust and emolument, unless he profess or renounce this or that religious opinion, is depriving him injuriously of those privileges and advantages to which, in common with his fellow citizens, he has a natural right; that it tends also[64] to corrupt the principles of that very religion it is meant to encourage, by bribing, with a monopoly of worldly honours and emoluments, those who will externally profess and conform to it; that though indeed these are criminal who do not withstand such temptation, yet neither are those innocent who lay the bait in their way; *that the opinions of men are not the object of civil government, nor under its jurisdiction*; that to suffer the civil magistrate to intrude his powers into the field of opinion and to restrain the profession or propagation of principles on supposition of their ill tendency is a dangerous fallacy, which at once destroys all religious liberty, because he being of course judge of that tendency will make his opinions the rule of judgment, and approve or condemn the sentiments of others only as they shall square with or differ from his own; that it is time enough for the rightful purposes of civil government for its officers to interfere when principles break out into overt acts against peace and good order; and finally, that truth is great and will prevail if left to herself; that she is the proper and sufficient antagonist to error, and has nothing to fear from the conflict unless by human interposition disarmed of her natural weapons, free argument and debate; errors ceasing to be dangerous when it is permitted freely to contradict them.

WE the General Assembly of Virginia do enact[65] that no man shall be compelled to frequent or support any religious worship, place, or ministry whatsoever, nor shall be enforced, restrained, molested, or burthened in his body or goods, nor shall otherwise suffer, on account of his religious opinions or belief; but that all men shall be free to profess, and by argument to maintain, their opinions in matters of religion, and that the same shall in no wise diminish, enlarge, or affect their civil capacities.

AND though we well know that this Assembly, elected by the people for the ordinary purposes of legislation only, have no power to restrain the acts of succeeding Assemblies, constituted with powers equal to our own, and that therefore to declare this act [to be] irrevocable would be of no effect in law; yet we are free to declare, and do declare, that the rights hereby asserted are of the natural rights of mankind, and that if any act shall be hereafter passed to repeal the present or to narrow its operation, such act will be an infringement of natural right.

NOTES

1. Thomas Jefferson to DeWitt Clinton, May 24, 1807, in Paul Leicester Ford, *The Works of Jefferson*, 12 vols. (New York, 1904–1905), 10:404–5; [William Linn], *Serious Considerations on the Election of a President, Addressed to the Citizens of the United States* (New York, 1800), 18. Portions of this essay appeared earlier as "The Political Theology of Thomas Jefferson," in Merrill D. Peterson and Robert C. Vaughan, eds., *The Virginia Statute for Religious Freedom: Its Evolution and Consequence in American History* (Cambridge, 1988), 75–108. These are reprinted with the permission of Cambridge University Press.

2. Daniel Walker Howe, "Church, State, and Education in the Young American Republic," *Journal of the Early Republic* 22 (2002), 2.

3. *Zelman v. Simmons-Harris*, in *Daily Appellate Report*, June 28, 2002, 7308.

4. Thomas Jefferson to [Benjamin Holt Rice], August 10, 1823, xerox of original in the Pierpont Morgan Library, New York, NY.

5. Thomas Jefferson to William Baldwin, January 19, 1810, in Dickinson W. Adams, ed., *Jefferson's Extracts from the Gospels: "The Philosophy of Jesus" and "The Life and Morals of Jesus." The Papers of Thomas Jefferson*. Second series (Princeton, NJ, 1983), 345. Edward L. Bond, *Damned Souls in a Tobacco Colony: Religion in Seventeenth-Century Virginia* (Macon, GA, 2000), 39–92. The most detailed account of Jefferson's early life is in Dumas Malone, *Jefferson and His Time*, 6 vols. (Boston, 1948–1981), 27–48. For baptismal practice in colonial Virginia, see John K. Nelson, *A Blessed Company: Parishes, Parsons, and Parishioner in Anglican Virginia, 1690–1776* (Chapel Hill, NC, 2002), 211–17.

6. Malone, *Jefferson*, 1:109.

7. Jefferson to John Page, July 15, 1763, Julian P. Boyd, ed., *The Papers of Thomas Jefferson*, 29 vols. (Princeton, NJ, 1950–2002) 1:10; Jefferson to Page, September 6, 1808, Jefferson Papers, University of Virginia, Series 3, Roll 6, microfilm.

8. Thomas Birch, *The Life of the Most Reverend Dr. John Tillotson, Lord Archbishop of Canterbury* (London, 1752), 427. For Tillotson's popularity in Virginia and the content and style of sermons, see Bond, *Damned Souls*, 247, 248, 255, 297; and Nelson, *Blessed Company*, 200–10. There is abundant revisionist literature on eighteenth-century Anglican theological developments and the growth of Latitudinarian thought in England during this period. See, for example, William Gibson, *The Church of England, 1688–1832: Unity and Accord* (London, 2001); J. C. D. Clark, *English Society, 1688–1831: Religion, Ideology and Politics during the Ancient Regime*, 2nd ed. (Cambridge, 2000); John Walsh and Stephen Taylor, "Introduction: The Church and Anglicanism in the 'Long' Eighteenth Century," in *The Church of England, c. 1689–c.1833: From Toleration to Tractarianism*, eds. John Walsh, Colin Haydon, and Stephen Taylor (Cambridge, 1993), 35–48; Martin Fitzpatrick, "Latitudinarianism

at the Parting of the Ways: A Suggestion," in *The Church of England*, 209–27; John Gascoigne, *Cambridge in the Age of the Enlightenment* (Cambridge, 1989); and Brian Young, "A History of Variations: The Identity of the Eighteenth-Century Church of England," in *Protestantism and National Identity: Britain and Ireland, c.1650–c.1850*, eds. Tony Claydon and Ian McBride (Cambridge, 1998), 105–28. For the cultural shifts in late seventeenth-century Anglicanism, see Isabel Rivers, *Reason, Grace, and Sentiment, vol. 1: Whichcote to Wesley* (Cambridge, 1991), 53–59.

9. For contemporary Anglican faith and practice in Virginia, see Nelson, *Blessed Company*, 196–97, 205–7. The literature on Jefferson's religion is voluminous, but see especially Eugene R. Sheridan's "Introduction," in Adams, ed., *Jefferson's Extracts*, reprinted as *Jefferson and Religion* ([Charlottesville, VA], 1998); and "Liberty and Virtue: Religion and Republicanism in Jeffersonian Thought," in *Thomas Jefferson and the Education of a Citizen,* ed. James Gilreath (Washington, DC, 1999), 242–63; Charles B. Sanford, *The Religious Life of Thomas Jefferson* (Charlottesville, VA, 1984); Paul K. Conkin, "The Religious Pilgrimage of Thomas Jefferson," in *Jeffersonian Legacies*, ed. Peter S. Onuf (Charlottesville, VA, 1993), 19–49; and Edwin S. Gaustad, *Sworn on the Altar of God: A Religious Biography of Thomas Jefferson* (Grand Rapids, MI., 1996).

10. "Resolutions for an Answer to Governor Botetourt's Speech," Boyd, *Papers of Jefferson*, 1:27.

11. Gordon S. Wood, "Religion and the American Revolution," in *New Directions in American Religious History*, eds. Harry S. Stout and D. G. Hart (New York, 1997), 181. For Jefferson as rhetorician, see Jay Fliegelman, *Declaring Independence: Jefferson, Natural Language, and the Culture of Performance* (Stanford, CA, 1993); and Stephen E. Lucas, "Justifying America: The Declaration of Independence as a Rhetorical Document," in *American Rhetoric: Context and Criticism,* ed. Thomas W. Benson (Carbondale and Edwardsville, Ill., 1989), 67–130. For the domestic challenge facing the revolutionaries, see Pauline Maier, *From Resistance to Revolution: Colonial Radicals and the Development of American Opposition to Britain, 1765–1776* (New York, 1972), 228–96; and Lucas, "Justifying America," 80–81, 118–20.

12. "Resolution of the House of Burgesses Designating a Day of Fasting and Prayer," Boyd, *Papers of Jefferson*, 1:105–7.

13. "Thomas Jefferson and John Walker to the Inhabitants of the Parish of St. Anne," Boyd, *Papers of Jefferson*, 1:116.

14. "Virginia Resolutions on Lord North's Conciliatory Proposal," Boyd, *Papers of Jefferson*, 1:170–74 (quote on 173); see also 1:203.

15. Boyd, *Papers of Jefferson*, 2:556; 3:177–79, quotes on 177–78. As Daniel Dreisbach has pointed out, Jefferson bore conspicuous responsibility for drafting the section of the revised code that dealt with religion. In addition to the religious liberty and public prayer bills, this included statutes for preserving the established church's property, requiring Sabbath observance, and forbidding marriage within kinship degrees forbidden in the Bible. In evaluating his position on church–state relations, this entire corpus of work must be taken into account. See Daniel L. Dreisbach, "A New Perspective on Jefferson's Views on Church–State Relations: The Virginia Statute for Establishing Religious Freedom in its Legislative Context," *The American Journal of Legal History* 35 (1991): 172–204; and "Thomas Jefferson and Bills Number 82–86 of the Revision of the Laws of Virginia, 1776–1786: New Light on the Jeffersonian Model of Church–State Relations," *The North Carolina Law Review* 69 (1990): 159–211.

16. Boyd, *Papers of Jefferson*, 1:119.

17. Boyd, *Papers of Jefferson*, 1:121–35, quote on 135.

18. Boyd, *Papers of Jefferson*, 1, 197.

19. Boyd, *Papers of Jefferson*, 1:494–97, 677–79.

20. Boyd, *Papers of Jefferson*, 1:193, 197.

21. John Adams to Abigail Adams, August 14, 1776, in *Adams Family Correspondence*, ed. L. H. Butterfield. 6 vols. (Cambridge, MA, 1963), 2:96.

22. Boyd, *Papers of Jefferson*, 1:423, 432; Lucas, "Justifying America," 114–15. The evolution of the text is developed with photographs in Julian P. Boyd, *The Declaration of Independence* (Princeton, NJ, 1945).

23. "Rough Draft of Jefferson's Resolutions for Disestablishing the Church of England and for Repealing Laws Interfering with Freedom of Worship," in Boyd, *Papers of Jefferson*, 1:530–31; Ford, *Works of Jefferson*, 1:62; Nelson, *Blessed Company*, 13–16; Edmund Randolph, *History of Virginia*, ed. Arthur H. Shaffer (Charlottesville, VA, 1970), 263. For these debates, see Thomas E. Buckley, S.J., *Church and State in Revolutionary Virginia, 1776–1787* (Charlottesville, VA, 1977), 30–37.

24. David John Mays, *Edmund Pendleton, 1721–1803: A Biography* (Cambridge, MA, 1952), 2:132; Nelson, *Blessed Company*, 33–42.

25. Henry to Baptist Association meeting in Louisa County, August 13, 1776, in the *Virginia Gazette* (Dixon and Hunter), August 24, 1776; Religious Petitions, 1774–1802, Presented to the General Assembly of Virginia, October 16, 1776, microfilm, the Library of Virginia, Richmond.

26. Ford, *Works of Jefferson*, 1:62.

27. Boyd, *Papers of Jefferson*, 1:535–36; Randolph, *History of Virginia*, 264. For a helpful elaboration of Jefferson's 1776 debate notes, see Bernhard Fabian, "Jefferson's *Notes on Virginia*: The Genesis of Query xvii, *The different religions received into that State?*," *William and Mary Quarterly* (hereafter *WMQ*), 3rd ser., 12 (1955): 124–38.

28. "Jefferson's Outline of Argument," Boyd, *Papers of Jefferson*, 1:535–44, 555–58; Fabian, "Jefferson's *Notes on Virginia*," quotes on 129.

29. John Locke, *A Letter Concerning Toleration*, ed. Patrick Romanell (Indianapolis, IN, 1955), 50–2; Boyd, *Papers of Jefferson*, 1:548, 558–59.

30. *Virginia Gazette* (Purdie and Dixon), June 3, 1773; Boyd, *Papers of Jefferson*, 1:537, 547–48, 557; 2:546.

31. Boyd, *Papers of Jefferson*, 1:539; 2:545. See also George F. Sensabaugh, "Jefferson's Use of Milton in the Ecclesiastical Controversies of 1776," *American Literature* 26 (1955): 552–59.

32. Boyd, *Papers of Jefferson*, 2:545. The phrase "holy author of our religion" is ambiguous and could have been understood as a reference to Jesus Christ. Much later both Jefferson and Madison, although in slightly different versions, denied this intention and made the point that an amendment to insert the words "Jesus Christ" after this phrase had been rejected. For a discussion of this point, see Buckley, *Church and State*, 157–58, especially n45.

33. Boyd, *Papers of Jefferson*, 2:546, 546–47. For the fate of Jefferson's statute in 1779, see Buckley, *Church and State*, 48–56. For Jefferson's unhappy tenure as governor, see Malone, *Jefferson*, 1:301–69.

34. Thomas Jefferson, *Notes on the State of Virginia*, ed., William Peden (Chapel Hill, NC, 1954), 159; Buckley, *Church and State*, 49–60.

35. Anson Phelps Stokes, *Church and State in the United States* (New York, 1950), 1:424. See also C. Conrad Wright, "Piety, Morality, and the Commonwealth," *Crane Review* 9 (1967): 90–106; John Witte Jr., "'A Most Mild and Equitable Establishment of Religion': John Adams and the Massachusetts Experiment," *Journal of Church and State* 41 (1999): 213–52.

36. Jefferson, *Notes on Virginia*, 157–59.

37. Boyd, *Papers of Jefferson*, 1:537; 2:546.

38. Madison to Jefferson, January 22, 1786, Boyd, *Papers of Jefferson*, 9:196; Buckley, *Church and State*, 163.

39. Boyd, *Papers of Jefferson*, 1:538; Jefferson, *Notes on Virginia*, 161.

40. Boyd, *Papers of Jefferson*, 2:545; Buckley, *Church and State*, 61–3; Jefferson to Thomas Cooper, October 7, 1814, in *The Writings of Thomas Jefferson*, eds. Andrew A. Lipscomb and Albert Ellery Bergh. 20 vols. (Washington, DC, 1903), 14:200.

41. Jefferson to Charles Clay, January 29, 1815, Adams, *Jefferson's Extracts*, 363; Jefferson to [William Cabell Rives], September 18, 1811, copy made by William Cabell Rives, Hugh Blair Grigsby Paper, 1745–1944, Virginia Historical Society, Richmond, VA; Jefferson to Thomas Cooper, November 2, 1822, Ford, *Works of Jefferson*, 12:271

42. Boyd, *Papers of Jefferson*, 2:6; Miller to Jefferson, March 4, 1800, HM 5959, Henry E. Huntington Library, San Marino, CA. See also William Arthur to Thomas Jefferson, January 8, 1801, Coolidge Collection of Thomas Jefferson Manuscripts at the Massachusetts Historical Society, 1705–1826, Reel 5, microfilm, Library of Congress, Washington DC (hereafter LDC); Jefferson to James Ogilvie, January 31, 1806, Ford, *Works of Jefferson*, 8:417–19.

43. Jefferson to Madison, December 8, 1784; Jefferson to Chastellux, September 2, 1785, Boyd, *Papers of Jefferson*, 7:558; 8:470; Jefferson to P. H. Wendover, March 13, 1815 (endorsed as "not sent") Lipscomb and Bergh, *Writings of Jefferson*, 14:280; David E. Swift, "Thomas Jefferson, John Holt Rice and Education in Virginia, 1815–25," *Journal of Presbyterian History* 49 (1971): 32–58.

44. [William Loughton Smith], *The Pretensions of Thomas Jefferson to the Presidency Examined; and the Charges against John Adams Refuted. Addressed to the Citizens of America in General; and Particularly to the Electors of the President* (United States, 1796), 36–40 (quotes on 37, 39, and 40).

45. "The Jeffersoniad" No III, *Gazette of the United States and Daily Advertiser* [Philadelphia], July 12, 1800; [Linn], *Serious Considerations*. For studies of this issue in the election, see Charles O. Lerche Jr., "Jefferson and the Election of 1800: A Case Study in the Political Smear," *WMQ*, 3rd ser., 5 (1948), 467–91; Fred C. Luebke, "The Origins of Thomas Jefferson's Anticlericalism," *Church History* 32 (1963), 344–56; and Constance Bartlett Schulz, "Of Bigotry in Politics and Religion: Jefferson's Religion, the Federalist Press, and the Syllabus," *Virginia Magazine of History and Biography* 91 (1983), 73–91.

46. *Gazette of the United States and Daily Advertiser* [Philadelphia], August 30, 1800.

47. Clement Clarke Moore, *Observations upon Certain Passages in Mr. Jefferson's Notes on Virginia, Which Appear to Have a Tendency to Subvert Religion, and Establish a False Philosophy* (New York, 1804), 29.

48. "Canto IV: The Jeffersonian," in [Thomas Green Fessenden], *Democracy Unveiled; or, Tyranny Stripped of the Garb of Patriotism*, by Christopher Caustic (Boston, 1805), 102.

49. Jefferson to Rush, September 23, 1800, Lipscomb and Bergh, *Writings of Jefferson*, 10:175.

50. For a full discussion of this letter, its circumstances, and interpretation, see "Forum," *WMQ*, 3rd ser. 56 (1999), 775–824. See also Daniel L. Dreisbach, *Thomas Jefferson and the Wall of Separation between Church and State* (New York, 2002).

51. Thomas Jefferson, First Inaugural Address, March 4, 1801, in *Compilation of the Messages and Papers*, ed. James D. Richardson. 10 vols. (Washington, DC, 1896–99), 1:310, 311, 312.

52. Benjamin Rush to Granville Sharp, March 31, 1801, in John A. Woods, ed., "Correspondence of Benjamin Rush and Granville Sharp, 1773–1809," *Journal of American Studies* 1 (1967), 34.

53. Thomas Jefferson, First Annual Message, December 8, 1801; Second Annual Message, December 15, 1802; Third Annual Message, October 17, 1803; Fifth Annual Message, December 3, 1805, Richardson, *Compilation of the Messages and Papers*, 1:314, 330, 349, 370, 371. See also Robert M. Johnston, *Jefferson and the Presidency: Leadership in the Young Republic* (Ithaca, NY, 1978).

54. Thomas Jefferson, Second Inaugural Address, Richardson, *Compilation of the Messages and Papers*, 2:367–68, 370.

55. Thomas Jefferson, Eighth Annual Message, November 8, 1808, in Richardson, *Compilation of the Messages and Papers*, 1:371.

56. Richardson, *Compilation of the Messages and Papers* 370. For Jefferson's explanation see his letter to Samuel Miller, January 23, 1808, Lipscomb and Bergh, *Writings of Jefferson*, 11:428–30.

57. Allen Jayne offers a very different view in *Jefferson's Declaration of Independence: Origins, Philosophy and Theology* (Lexington, KY, 1998), but he seriously misunderstands the religious context in Revolutionary America when he states that "colonial American religions stultified individual determinations of morality, religious opinion, and politics on the part of their own members and followers.

"The concepts of God, man, and the source of religious truth common to the theologies of colonial Christian groups at the time of the Declaration of Independence, and their resultant authority over the individual, were not only antithetical to the political theory but also the heterodox theology of that document." (18) Jayne's reliance on Forrest G. Wood's *The Arrogance of Faith* (New York, 1990), may have contributed to his errors.

58. Jefferson to Dr. de la Motta, September 1, 1820, Jefferson Papers, ser. 10, microfilm, LDC. This letter was published in the *Richmond Enquirer*, March 13, 1821.

59. On civil religion, see Robert Bellah, "Civil Religion in America," in *American Civil Religion*, eds. Russell E. Richey and Donald R. Jones (New York, 1974). Bellah further clarified his interpretation of civil religion in *The Broken Covenant: American Civil Religion in Time of Trial* (New York, 1975) and "The Revolution and Civil Religion," in *Religion and the American Revolution*, ed. Jerald C. Brauer (Philadelphia, 1976). Also helpful are Sidney E. Mead, *The Nation with the Soul of a Church* (New York, 1975); and Ellis M. West, "A Proposed Neutral Definition of Civil Religion," *Journal of Church and State* 22 (1980): 23–40.

60. Daniel Webster, *A Discourse in Commemoration of the Lives and Services of John Adams and Thomas Jefferson Delivered in Faneuil Hall, Boston* (Boston, 1826), 38, 60; William Johnson, *Eulogy on Thomas Jefferson, delivered August 3d, 1826 in the First Presbyterian Church . . . of Charleston* (Charleston, SC, 1826), 27.

61. William Wirt, *A Discourse on the Lives and Characters of Thomas Jefferson and John Adams, Who Both Died on the Fourth of July, 1826. Delivered, at the Request of the Citizens of Washington, in the Hall of Representatives of the United States, on the Nineteenth October, 1826* (Washington, DC, 1826), 67, 68, 9; Johnson, *Eulogy*, 5.

62. Report of the Committee of Revisors Appointed by the General Assembly of Virginia in MDCCLXXVI (Richmond, VA: Dixon and Holt, 1784), 58–59; William Waller Hening, ed., *The Statutes at Large; Being a Collection of all the Laws of Virginia* (Richmond, VA: J. and G. Cochran, 1823), 12:84–86.

63. The italicized words in this document were deleted by amendments during the October 1785 session of the Virginia general assembly. The act as adopted begins: "WHEREAS, Almighty God . . ."

64. The act replaced "also" with "only."

65. The wording here was changed to "Be it enacted by the General Assembly. . ."

4

Religion and Politics in the Thought of James Madison

Garrett Ward Sheldon

[T]here could not be a stronger testimony in favor of Religion . . . than for men who occupy the most honorable and gainful departments and are rising in reputation and wealth, publicly to declare their unsatisfactoriness by becoming fervent Advocates in the cause of Christ.

—James Madison, 1773

James Madison is recognized as the "Father of the U.S. Constitution" for his pivotal role in the writing and adoption of that founding document of American democracy. He is less well recognized as a person of deep Christian faith, who integrated his religious beliefs and perspectives with his political thought and views of society and government. But Madison's public philosophy cannot be understood apart from his religious tenets, for his politics are premised in his theology. This chapter will show how James Madison's education and Christian experience informed his political theory and his practical involvement in the early American republic.[1]

The scholarly treatment of Madison's political ideas has largely neglected the religious dimension of his thought. Some have even denied this pervasive theological influence on Madison's political theory (and, by extension, the whole American constitutional system); but his education, writings, and actions clearly reveal the presence of an all-pervading Christian perspective in his worldview. This makes much of the twentieth-century scholarship on Madisonian democratic theory incomplete or inaccurate.[2] This chapter, within the context of this entire volume, seeks to correct that imbalance. By tracing the religious content of Madison's education and experience, along with its expression in his private and public writings, his personal character and demeanor, and his policies and public philosophy, I demonstrate that this major architect of American constitutional government operated from a Christian perspective and commitment.

THE LIFE OF JAMES MADISON

Almost all of James Madison's adult life was spent in public service. He was elected to the Virginia legislature immediately upon the national break with Great Britain, where he wrestled with the details of forming an independent commonwealth apart from England. He served on the Virginia Governor's Council, an executive body that implemented many state reforms. Madison was elected to the Continental Congress during the American Revolution and witnessed personally the trials of forging a national policy without a truly centralized government. After the successful completion of the War of Independence, Madison was instrumental in calling for revision of the Articles of Confederation and was elected as a Virginia delegate to the Constitutional Convention in Philadelphia (where he was the most influential advocate for the new U.S. Constitution). He served with distinction as secretary of state under President Thomas Jefferson (1801–1809) when that office was truly "second-in-command" to the chief executive (as it encompassed both domestic and international politics). Madison succeeded Jefferson as a two-term president during the tumultuous period of European wars (culminating in the Anglo-American War of 1812) and American expansion westward. Retiring to his Virginia estate, Montpelier, Madison continued in politics through his frequent advice to President James Monroe, his writings on federalism, and his participation in the Virginia Constitutional Convention of 1829.

During this entire active political life, Madison remained a scholar, political philosopher, and writer. He, among the American founders, came closest to embodying Plato's ideal of a "Philosopher King," both actively involved in day-to-day government and intellectually alive in the highest sense. His policy papers always drew upon perennial philosophy and principles. His *Federalist Papers* were excellent political journalism, but they were built upon the depths of Christian theology, classics of philosophy, and historical scholarship. Madison's writing on religious liberty (most notably his "Memorial and Remonstrance," included in the appendix to this chapter) drew upon the truths of scripture and the lessons of logic and history. Even mundane policy papers on money or territorial matters involved discussions of the great underlying questions of human nature, the realities of society, and God's providence. His public religious proclamations reveal a keen sensitivity to biblical truth, illuminated by the Divine Spirit. So, Madison's practical political activity and reflective intellectual life were fully integrated during his long public service to America. And both were led by his commitment to Christian principles, such as the innate sinfulness of humanity, the need for redemption, the persistence of human pride and selfishness (even among the faithful), and God's ultimate sovereignty. This Christian perspective on the world was also evident in Madison's personal character and demeanor: a devotion to duty that saw even worldly occupations as divine callings, a care and diligence in every task he undertook, a faithfulness to family and friends, and a personal humility, kindness, and self-control. Madison's family background, education, and writing and the reflections of others on his ideas and behavior show the underlying ethical and religious foundations of his life.

FAMILY AND EDUCATION

James Madison grew up on a four-thousand-acre plantation in the central Piedmont region of Virginia. He was the oldest of the twelve children of James and Nelly (Conway) Madison. In this rich natural setting of rolling hills and wooded mountains, James was raised amid not only the wealth of flora and wildlife, but also, as Douglass Adair wrote, "in an atmosphere of books and study."[3]

From one of the earliest families to arrive in colonial Virginia, Madison's ancestors rose from near obscurity to landed gentry. His great-grandfather, James Taylor II, was a royal surveyor of the Blue Ridge Mountain region in 1716. He was able to accumulate a thirteen-thousand-acre estate in Orange County, which he passed on to his daughter Frances, who married Ambrose Madison, son of a ship's carpenter who had settled in Virginia in the mid–1600s. Madison was thus born into an established family of wealth and prestige. He was baptized on March 31, 1751 in the local Anglican church, where his father was a vestryman. His education grew out of this family and church setting. Much of his primary education seems to have been under the tutelage of his paternal grandmother, remembered as a pious Christian woman who was also an intellectual and who drew upon an eighty-five-volume personal library of classics for her grandson's education. Madison particularly remembered her eight-volume collection of the British literary magazine *The Spectator*, edited by Joseph Addison, which he praised for advancing "truth, innocence, honor and virtue as the chief ornaments of life."[4]

At the age of twelve, Madison was sent to a boarding school run by a clergyman. Rev. Donald Robertson, a Scottish minister from the Universities of Aberdeen and Edinburgh, tutored Madison in the classics of Latin, Greek, French, literature, and theology and the sciences of mathematics and geography. Reverend Robertson represented the firm Christian Calvinism of his native Scotland (James Madison later said of him, "all that I have been in life I owe largely to that man.")[5] He kept notebooks on Plato, Euclid, Locke, and Fontenelle. His lessons were usually couched in Christian terminology, as in the following logical syllogism:

1. No sinners are happy.
2. Angels are happy,
   therefore;
3. Angels are not sinners.[6]

Reverend Robertson's curriculum included Thomas a Kempis's *Imitation of Christ*, Montesquieu's *Spirit of the Laws*, Justinian's *Institutes*, and the doctrinal masterpiece of English Calvinism, *The Westminster Confession*. He wrote in his tuition account book at the conclusion of Madison's studies, "Deo Gratia and Gloria."[7]

After four years of study at Robertson's boarding school, Madison returned to his home parish to continue his education with Rev. Thomas Martin. Also a Scotsman, Reverend Martin had recently graduated from the evangelical Calvinist college at Princeton, "the academic citadel of Presbyterianism in the New World."[8] It was probably Martin's influence that caused Madison's parents to send him to Princeton rather than the closer Anglican College of William and Mary. By the late 1760s the college in Williamsburg had a reputation for moral decadence and religious skepticism, while the New Jersey school was a lively and orthodox Christian college. As a friend of Madison's family wrote, "Mr. Madison was sent to Princeton College—perhaps through fear of the skeptical principles so prevalent at William and Mary. During his stay at Princeton a great revival took place, and it was believed that he partook of its spirit."[9]

Indeed, the Princeton that James Madison attended was born in revival, the eighteenth-century Christian revival known as the Great Awakening. This was a series of mass religious movements associated with the "New Light" Presbyterians, the New England divine Jonathan Edwards, and the Anglican preacher George Whitefield. Between 1730 and 1770, large outdoor revival services resulted in numerous conversions and reformed morals.[10] The College of New Jersey (Princeton) that Madison attended was founded as a New Light college to train evangelical ministers in this revivalist mode. Emphasizing the New Birth in the spirit that Jesus commended to Nicodemus (John 3: 5–8), the Princeton of Madison's day encouraged a personal experience of God and total commitment of one's life to Christ. Professors counseled students on their spiritual development, the college community met together twice daily to pray, and teachers lectured continually on the Bible and encouraged students' private devotion and commitment to Christ. As one scholar put it,

> The education that James Madison . . . received at [Princeton] . . . encouraged—but never demanded—a personal commitment of the student to Jesus Christ as Savior and Lord . . . the curriculum was not narrow, but was taught from the Christian perspective . . . a framework of absolutes . . . the Sovereignty of God. . . . His providence . . . the sinful nature of man . . . yet the great possibilities for good that man possesses when he is guided by his Maker.[11]

Madison tested out of the first two years at Princeton, passing examinations in English, Latin, Greek, and New Testament Bible. He finished the entire college course in two years and studied an additional six months of graduate work in Hebrew and theology, suggesting that he was considering a career as a minister in the church. His mentor and the college president, Rev. Dr. John Witherspoon, was the archetypical Scots Presbyterian Calvinist—firm in his commitment to the scriptures and to evangelical Christianity. Madison helped found the American Whig Society at Princeton, then signifying "a Scotch Presbyterian or a Dissenting American Presbyterian."[12] Princeton's evangelical Protestantism at this time meshed comfortably with Whig or democratic politics. As Mark Noll noted, "At Princeton . . . religious considerations were always central to the working out of republican theory."[13] Madison, following Dr. Witherspoon, combined Christian theology with republican political theory.

Among other things that Madison took from his Princeton education with John Witherspoon was the Calvinist notion of work as a divine calling. In Reformed theology, every individual is equipped and called by God for a particular vocation, which should be done for His glory. According to John Calvin, Christian "work" is not confined to the "religious" callings of church ministry, missionary travels, and the like, but includes any useful labor conducted for the glory of God and carried on in the spirit of Christ (according to God's laws and Jesus' teachings). So, the occupations of law, medicine, architecture, engineering, teaching, science, politics (or any useful occupation) could be a godly ministry, if done with devotion to Christ and the glory of God. Calvin especially considered service in government to be a high, divine calling (so much so that he ranked political work as equivalent service to God as church ministry). In Calvinist political theory, the best state would involve cooperation between the church (and its ministers) and the state (and its Christian rulers). Politics was not just about sin and corruption, power and influence, but infusing godly principles into the daily life of society. Madison shows that he conceived of his service in government in this Calvinist way, as a divine calling, with God-given gifts of intellect, communication, and administration, and with the great responsibility to use those gifts for the honor and glory of God, to Whom everyone would have to answer someday.

This Calvinist view of vocation is revealed in several of Madison's notes on William Burkitt's commentary on the Bible or on the Bible itself, while he was a student at Princeton. From *Acts* 23, Madison recorded, "Magistrates are not to be treated with ill words. . . . Titles of civil Honor and Respect given to persons in place and power are agreeable to the Mind and Will of God." From *Proverbs*, Madison notes that "not all our religion that's in our brains and tongue, and nothing in our heart and life, [because] it is not the talking but the walking and working person that is the true Christian." Noting from *The Acts of the Apostles* that Paul describes the Bereans as "more noble . . . in that they received the Word with all readiness of mind, and searched the Scriptures daily," Madison commends their actions as "as a noble example for all succeeding Christians to imitate and follow." In the passage of the Gospel of St. John describing Mary Magdalene looking into the holy sepulcher and seeing two angels in white, one at the head, the other at the foot of where the savior's body had lain, Madison reflects that "Angels [are] to be desired at our feet as well as at our head—not an angelical understanding and a diabolical conversation—not all our religion in our brains and tongue, and nothing in our heart and life." Similarly, commenting on the voice of Jesus telling the stricken Saul, "Arise and go into the city, and it shall be told thee what thou shalt do," Madison writes, "It is not the talking but the walking and working person that is the true Christian."[14] Such an emphasis on work as a Christian duty reflects the so-called Protestant work ethic and may explain why Madison could view his political career as a divine calling and equivalent to ministry in the church.

This view of the noble calling of political life was reinforced by his studies in political philosophy at Princeton. Under the title "Lectures on Moral Philosophy," Dr. Witherspoon taught law, politics, ethics, and philosophy from a Christian perspective, always subordinating the truths of pagan thinkers to the truth of Christ. From these lectures, Madison learned the classics of political theory, but always in the context of biblical doctrine. For example, the British liberalism of John Locke, with its social contract view of government and ideas of natural rights, were subordinated, for Witherspoon, to God's law:

> The natural [human] states may be enunciated thus: (1.) His state with regard to God . . . (2.) To his fellow creatures. (3.) Solitude or society. (4.) Peace or war. . . . (5.) His outward provision, plenty or want [i.e., economics]. . . . All men, and at all times, are related to God. They are made by him, and live by his providence.[15]

Man does have certain rights by nature, but these are always subordinate to God's law and will. Private property is a right, as is self-government, but both are to be held in stewardship to the God who gave those blessings and enjoyed in accordance with his law and dominion.

Similarly, Madison studied the classical republican theories of the ancient philosophers Aristotle and Cicero, with their emphasis on man's social nature, reason, and democratic participation; but these too were to be understood within the context of Christian truth. The public virtues and political activity of classical Greek culture are grounded in "(1.) The will of God. (2.) The reason and nature of things. (3.) The public interest. (4.) Private interest." Consequently, as Witherspoon taught,

The result of the whole is, that we ought to take the rule of duty from conscience enlightened by reason, experience, and every way by which we can be
supposed to learn the will of our Maker. . . . And we ought to believe that it is
as deeply founded as the nature of God himself, being a transcript of his moral
excellence, and that it is productive of the greatest good.[16]

Non-Christian knowledge is valuable because it reveals an aspect of
divine truth, but it is always subordinate to the whole of revealed
Christian truth. As Witherspoon notes, "There is nothing certain or
valuable in moral philosophy, but what is perfectly coincident with
the Scripture, where the glory of God is the First principle of action."[17]
For him, "The divine will is so perfect and excellent, that all virtue is
reduced to conformity to it—and . . . we ought not to judge of good
and evil by any other rule." The "moral perfections of good are holiness, justice, truth, goodness, and mercy," so the good person is "to
obey Him and submit to Him in all things . . . considering every good
action as an act of obedience to God."[18]

The nature of human evil and sin, then, is mankind's habitual dis-
obedience to God's law, his selfish and willful rebellion against God.
The Bible, for Witherspoon, gives "a clear and consistent account of
human depravity . . . opposition to the nature, and a transgression of
the law of God." Only surrender to Christ, acceptance of God's love
and forgiveness in Jesus Christ, and the indwelling of the Holy Spirit
leading to goodness can remedy this human evil. "I am none of
those," Witherspoon writes, "who either deny or conceal the depravity of human nature til it is purified by the light of truth, and renewed
by the Spirit of the living God."[19]

The political manifestation of human sin takes the form of lust for
power, control, domination, and oppression of others, using the instrument of the state. Expressions of private interest and prideful ambition will always plague political life. Religion will never be entirely
able to prevent this political manifestation of human sin because (1)
many people in government, even in a predominantly Christian nation, will not be redeemed and, therefore, are not led by the Spirit of
Christ, and (2) even the "saved" or truly "elect" believers will continue
to be tempted by and succumb to worldly power, wealth, and prestige and are, therefore, unreliable in moral virtue. This reality of the
persistence of sin and oppression in human politics commends a system that is large and complex enough to check ambition with ambition, the aggression of some being canceled out by the interest of others. Dr. Witherspoon writes that a republic should "be so complex so

that one principle may check the other. . . . They must be so balanced, that when everyone draws to his own interest or inclination there must be an even poise upon the whole."[20] He commends an "enlarged system" of federalism that will provide a "balance of power" to ensure tranquility and prevent oppression.[21] Madison echoes this formula in his famous *Federalist Paper* No. 10 when he states,

> The greater the number of citizens and extent of territory . . . renders factious combinations less dreaded. . . . Extend the sphere and you take in greater varieties of parties and interests; you make it less probable that a majority of the whole will have a common motive to invade the rights of other citizens . . . more difficult for all who feel it to discover their own strength and to act in unison with each other.

The government's "overlapping influence" can make power "divided and balanced" so that interests are "effectually checked and restrained by the others." In the just state, Madison insists, "ambition [political sin] must be made to counteract ambition."[22] This follows from Madison's Calvinist Christian view of human nature as sinful, which teaches us that "there is a degree of depravity in mankind," a "love of preeminence" causing endless "quarrels, jealousies, and envy," resulting from our "wounded pride."[23] Describing human nature as characterized by moral "depravity" or an inability to do good even when wishing to do so is distinctively Calvinist (or Augustinian, or Pauline—see Rom. 7: 18–19) and recognizes that the seeds of political evil are, in Madison's phrase, "sown in the nature of man."[24] Throughout his writings Madison adopts this Christian language of the innate sinfulness of mankind: his "imperfections and weaknesses," "follies . . . vanity" and "vices," "pride and parsimony" and desire for "personal glory."[25] The sad truth of fallen human nature is revealed abundantly in the Bible for Madison; it is that "wherever there is an interest and power to do wrong, wrong will generally be done."[26] This applies to all people: rich or poor, black or white, male or female, educated or ignorant, liberal or conservative; no human is immune from the inherent sin of Adam. Therefore, no group or race or class can be wholly trusted with absolute political power; only a pluralistic political system of checks and balances (like that created by the U.S. Constitution) can protect against the sinful tyranny of one individual or group over others. Personal repentance and political realism are the only remedies for human sin and cruelty. This Christian perspective is the only constant in the American political system. The

United States is a "Christian nation" not in having an official church or specific religious doctrines imbedded in the Constitution, but in this underlying Christian perspective that forms the premises of our political and social structure.

But James Madison's Christianity shows itself in more than his general approach to understanding human nature and politics and his commendation of a federal constitutional system of "checks and balances." His shifts in political philosophy between the historiographic categories of Lockean liberalism and classical republicanism, over his long political career; his advocacy of religious liberty; his arguments for the justice of the American political structure; and his continual rhetorical references to this Christian perspective all prove his adherence to that religious viewpoint.

MOVEMENT BETWEEN LOCKEAN LIBERALISM AND CLASSICAL REPUBLICANISM

Scholars have noted that Madison's use of secular political philosophies (Lockean and classical) shift over time, suggesting a possible inconsistency or confusion. But, when seen through his underlying Christian perspective, these shifts in Madison's ideology become clear and coherent. At one point, during his presidency, when Madison seemed to be shifting between different (and inconsistent) ideological positions, he noted, from this underlying Christian perspective, that only a stubborn pride would dogmatically adhere to a single theoretical perspective when circumstances commended another.[27]

As mentioned earlier, the British liberal political theory of John Locke, so prevalent in Revolutionary America, conceived of mankind as "free, equal and independent" individuals, possessing natural rights to "Life, Liberty and Property" and creating a government through a social contract to protect those individual natural rights against criminals, a majority of the community, or even the state itself. This ideology, so concisely articulated in Thomas Jefferson's Declaration of Independence, also formed the basis of Madison's arguments for a strong national government to protect individual rights (especially of private property) against the majority communities in the states. However, after the U.S. Constitution was formed to guarantee those individual rights, a new threat to justice arose from high Federalist control of the national regime (especially under President John

Adams) that used state power to violate civil liberties (particularly freedom of speech and press via the Alien and Sedition Acts), causing Madison to appeal to the other dominant ideology in the founding period, classical republicanism. This political philosophy, drawn from the ancient Greek and Roman thinkers, conceived of mankind as naturally social, requiring close, participatory, democratic communities to realize individuals' unique humanity and a just polity. In America, this ideology was expressed through the anti-Federalists or states' rights activists, who advocated limiting the power of the federal government. Madison employed classical republicanism in defense of constitutional liberties violated by the national government and remedied by coordinated state action (as in his Virginia Resolutions of 1798). During his years as secretary of state under President Jefferson and his own two-term presidency, Madison often shifted between these seemingly contradictory ideological stances. Finally, he evinced similar inconsistency in his political statements during a long retirement from public life.

Is James Madison confused or paradoxical? No, this leading intellectual of the founding generation is simply employing popular political paradigms and rhetoric (as his teacher Dr. Witherspoon taught him in the "Lectures on Moral Philosophy" at Princeton) to address contemporary problems understood from a Christian perspective on human nature and society. The coherence underlying his shifts in secular philosophy comes from his grounding in a biblical faith. Ultimately, Madison sees the value of American federalism in its balancing of local states' rights communitarianism (classical republicanism), whose potential evil lies in the impoverished majority's oppressing, and robbing, the wealthy minority, with the protection of individual rights through the national constitution with (Lockean) centralized state power, which remedies the former potential evil, but whose own wicked tendency is the concentration of power and consequent financial corruption and political tyranny, in turn remedied by appeals to local sovereignty. This balancing of centralized and decentralized political institutions and the practices, philosophies, and the values they contain ensures, for Madison, the tempering of sinful human nature's continual attempts to use political power to advance selfish interests and oppress other people. This separation of power into federal and state regimes, combined with the dividing of political authority between overlapping governmental branches (legislative, executive, and judicial) solves the persistent problem of political corruption and oppression. By recognizing, from a Christian perspective, the reality of sin, Madisonian pluralism pits "ambition against ambition" to ameliorate the total domination of one evil dictator or group over everyone else. It may mean that there are many "petty" dictators or competing interests, but they will, over time, cancel one another out, preventing any one from permanently tyrannizing over all.

So, depending on where he saw the greatest threat to justice or the greatest source of injustice (democracy's tendency to oppress the minority or concentrated national power's tendency towards tyranny), Madison appealed to the other component to check and neutralize that evil.[28]

For example, as a delegate to the national Continental Congress during the American Revolution, Madison experienced the difficulty of conducting a unified war effort without true centralized authority. The states' jealousy toward each other and stinginess toward the central government threatened to destroy the war effort and doom the colonies to renewed domination by Britain. Inadequate provisions for the army, irregular regulation of currency and the economy, social disorder and interstate conflict all resulted from state leaders' greed, envy, and penuriousness. Even before independence was won, the states were quarreling over land claims in the western territory. Madison wrote in 1782 that "the territorial claims . . . of Virginia are opposed by Rhode Island, New Jersey, Pennsylvania, Delaware and Maryland . . . by envy and jealousy naturally excited by superior resources and importance."[29] The origin of this policy problem was human sin; the political remedy was a central government strong enough to impose order on chaotic state claims (eventually, through the federal courts). This led Madison to critique the chaotic Articles of Confederation in an essay entitled "Vices of the Political System of the United States," notably (1) failure of the states to comply with legal requisitions (and the central government having no power to compel compliance); (2) encroachment by the states on the federal authority (especially in international affairs); (3) state violations of laws and treaties; (4) trespasses by states on the rights of each other "adverse to the spirit of union [and] vexatious in themselves"; (5) want of consent in matters of common national interest (defense policy, trade and currency regulation, uniform naturalization policy, patent law and internal public utilities); (6) inadequate protection of individual rights to property against "internal violence" and illegal rebellion; (7) absence of legal sanctions at the national level; and (8) "insecurity of private rights."[30] We see Madison's appeal to Lockean liberalism and a strong national government to secure individual natural rights against the chaos and democratic communities of the Articles of Confederation and the sins that express themselves through such states rights' policies. His arguments, developed fully during the Constitutional Convention and in his *Federalist Papers,* effectively underlie the Constitution's structure in America.

However, when that constitutional republic was established with its strong, independent national government to protect Lockean rights, Madison witnessed the abuse of that national power under the Federalist president John Adams, causing him to draw upon classical republican or anti-Federalist ideology as a remedy. Now the greatest threat to justice and political stability emerged from the concentration of power in the central government used to serve the vanity and pride of Federalist leaders. Adams's arrogance led to his support of the Alien and Sedition Acts, which unconstitutionally expanded his executive power and violated the individual freedoms of speech and press. Madison (and Jefferson) invoked states' rights aspects of federalism to preserve civil liberties in the Virginia and Kentucky resolutions (1798–1799). The origin of the political crisis for Madison was human sin hiding behind constitutional principle; the remedy was appealing to an alternative ideology serving America federalism (classical republicanism).

President John Adams was the quintessential sinner in Madison's eyes. He was proud, vain, overly sensitive to slights, constantly seeking praise, and harsh towards his critics. As Jefferson described him, "He hates Franklin, he hates Jay, he hates the French, he hates the English."[31] Madison observed Adams's "pompous vanity" which soon displayed itself in "a scene of ambition" and "violent passions," and found the president's political speeches "abominable and degrading," leading to "artful and wicked" schemes.[32] The most wicked of Adams's political schemes turned out to be the Alien and Sedition Acts. After a newspaper article critical of the Adams administration characterized the president as "old, querulous, bald, blind, crippled, [and] toothless," the Federalist Congress passed a law making criticism of the government a federal crime.[33] Republican newspaper editors were fined and imprisoned for criticizing Federalist officials. This violation of the constitutional right of free speech and press enforced by the national government caused Madison to argue for classical republican states rights in defense of liberty. In classical language, Madison attacked this "monster" of "alarming infractions of the Constitution" and recommended that the states "who are parties" to the U.S. Constitution "have the right and are duty bound to interpose for arresting the progress of [this] evil."[34] If the central government's "usurpation" and "criminal degeneracy" was not stopped by the states, the Adams's administration and Federalist Party could effectively establish a monarchy by suppressing "the right of freely examining public characters and measures, and . . . free communication among the people . . . which has ever been justly deemed the only effectual guardian of every other right."[35] Madison's arguments in the Virginia Resolutions and especially his lengthy "Report on the Resolutions" (1799) are credited with not only destroying the Alien and Sedition Acts, but also the Adams presidency when he lost the election to Thomas Jefferson in 1800. Madison's skillful use of classical republican language against a sinful, dictatorial, national regime resonated with the American populace.

Once again in national government (as secretary of state from 1801–1809 and as president from 1809–1817), Madison shifted between Lockean liberal federalism and classical republican states' rights, but was always motivated by his Calvinist Christian sense of where the greatest evil (or manifestation of human sin and ambition) appeared: the disorder of "confederacy" or the authoritarianism of centralized government. As when he was a member of the Revolutionary Continental Congress, Madison saw the need for strong national power in foreign affairs (the Louisiana Purchase and Embargo Act) and American economics (the National Bank). Yet, as he saw centralized power encroaching on more and more domestic legislation (the proper purview of the states), he endorsed strict constructionism of the Constitution's limits on national power. Rejecting a federal law on internal improvements at the end of his presidency, Madison wrote, "The legislative powers vested in Congress are specified and enumerated [and] . . . [t]o refer the power in question to the clause 'to promote for the common defense and general welfare' would be contrary to the established and consistent rules of interpretation."[36]

In retirement, Madison wrote on numerous public issues, again drawing upon Lockean or classical perspectives, depending on where he saw the greatest need to balance the power and the excesses of human sin and ambition. He pushed for extending the right to vote during the second Virginia Constitutional Convention, saying that given the "selfish" nature of man and the human tendency for a minority in government to exploit and oppress others, it is best if the largest number of citizens participate in elections.[37] He responded to John C. Calhoun's anti-Federalist nullification thesis by reminding the public that the Constitution balanced national and regional authority, while

> those who have denied or doubted the supremacy of the Judicial power of the United States and denounce at the same time a nullifying power in a State, seem not to have sufficiently averted to the utter inefficiency of a supremacy in a law of the Land, without a supremacy in the exposition and execution of the law; nor the destruction of all equipoise between Federal Government and the State Governments [if no authority for universal national law exists.]

Yet, he viewed with suspicion Chief Justice John Marshall's expansion of national power in *Cohens v. Virginia* as an "apparent disposition to amplify the authority of the Union at the expense of the States."[38] Calhoun's principle that any single state could nullify federal law was an "absurdity" for Madison, in its most "naked and suicidal form," which could result in a "fatal inlet to anarchy."[39] Sensing at the end of his life that the "extravagant presumption" of this confederate heresy was the severest threat to the United States, Madison penned a last testament entitled "Advice to My Country," in which he states his hope that "the Union of the States be cherished and perpetuated. Let the open enemy to it be regarded as a Pandora with her box opened; and the disguised one, as the Serpent creeping with his deadly wiles into Paradise."[40] Had more Americans taken this advice, the Civil War might have been averted.

So, Madison's historical shifts between the Lockean liberal and classical republican ideologies can be attributed to his underlying Christian perspective, a consistent Christian worldview that allowed shifts in alternative ideologies.

RELIGIOUS LIBERTY

James Madison reveals his Christian approach to human nature and society in his attitude towards church–state relations. Religious freedom for Madison was primarily to serve the cause of Christian evangelism. Without liberty of conscience and religious belief, the spreading of the Gospel is hampered. This was true, for Madison, where non-Christian governments persecuted Christian believers; but it was even truer, as in early Virginia, where an official state church limited the preaching of the Bible. In colonial Virginia, as in Great Britain, single-church denomination (the Anglican or Church of England), aligned with the government and supported by mandatory taxes, discriminated against "unofficial" churches and ministers (such as Baptist, Presbyterian, and the like). These policies restricted the spread of the Christian faith and led to a worldly and corrupt "official" church. So, Madison's advocacy of religious freedom in Virginia (and then in the whole United States through the Constitution's First Amendment) was primarily to help evangelize America, creating a healthy, vibrant Christian culture. Social virtue was dependent on religious morals, and true religion was best spread through religious freedom.

James Madison never forgot the sight of a Baptist minister, jailed in Culpepper, Virginia, for preaching the Gospel, addressing his flock through the bars of his prison cell. The established church that persecuted "dissenting sects" of Christians was worse, in some ways, than the Roman Empire that openly killed Christians because it attacked Christians from a supposedly religious motive, discrediting both religion and the church. Madison described such state-sponsored persecution of Christians as a "diabolical Hell."[41] Official status rendered the church wealthy and proud, infected with worldliness and moral corruption. It had none of the inspiring examples of the early church. It was pompous and boring. Such an official institutionalized church was not effective in teaching the truths of Jesus or enhancing the spread of the Holy Spirit. Only the unofficial evangelical churches in Virginia (Methodist, Presbyterian, Baptist, Brethren) were lively and attractive, drawing souls to Christ with the message of God's love. The official Anglican church was cold and dead, officious and decadent. Madison insisted that "Ecclesiastical Establishments tend to great ignorance and Corruption."[42] A wealthy, socially prominent official church aligned with the state appealed to human pride, arrogance, and sin. Instead of humbly glorifying God, these proud priests and bishops gloried in their own grand cathedrals and gaudy vestments, their proud titles and large salaries. They became like the Pharisees: outwardly religious, but inwardly evil and dead. The picture they presented of Christianity was not of the meek and lowly Jesus, but of high worldly honor and riches. The poor, common people especially, could not relate to such a proud religious institution. And being connected to the state made these churchmen "mischievous . . . [in] politics," considering themselves above the law.[43] The church became an official department of the state, an interest group hogging at the public trough. Christianity in this setting had become characterized, for Madison, by "Pride, ignorance and Knavery among the Priesthood and Vice and Wickedness among the Laity."[44] Having personally witnessed lively Christian revivals at Princeton, Madison was horrified by the sight in his native state of Christian ministers in prison "for publishing their Religious Sentiments which in the main are very orthodox."[45] He wrote to a Princeton classmate that the dignified Anglican clergy denounced the evangelical preachers and their lively worship services as wild "enthusiasm" and used "incredible and extravagant" stories to discredit these evangelicals, when their real concern was the rival preachers' potential to "endanger their livings and security."[46] Such "religious bondage," Madison insisted, echoing his mentor Dr. Witherspoon, "shackles and debilitates the mind and unfits it for every noble enterprise."[47] A democratic society needed a free religious environment; the ethics of Christ flourished in freedom and fostered a virtuous republic. Given human sin, it was safest to have competing denominations; as Madison put it, "Industry and Virtue have been promoted by mutual emulation and mutual inspection."[48] As Witherspoon had taught, "Liberty put in motion all the human powers. . . . [I]t promotes industry, and in this respect happiness—it produces every latent quality, and improves the human mind,—Liberty is the nurse of riches, literature and heroism."[49] Madison, expressing the same idea, wrote that "Commerce and Arts have flourished" where religious liberty existed (as in Pennsylvania).

James Madison's classic exposition on religious freedom and its advantages to Christian evangelism was his famous "Memorial and Remonstrance" against a proposed Virginia law assessing public taxes to finance the churches (see the full text in the appendix to this chapter). In it, Madison gave the Reformed Christian (Westminster Confession) view of the necessity for religious freedom. First, he stated that religious belief is a matter of individual conscience; it cannot be externally coerced or forced by law or violence. God has given humans free will to accept or reject him; only a voluntary submission to Christ is pleasing to God. A state religion violates this divine freedom and perverts the true faith. The best means for converting the population to Christianity is the free preaching of the Gospel of Jesus Christ, the witness and example of ordinary Christians, and reliance on the Holy Spirit to convict people of their sins and accept God's forgiveness and redemption through Christ; not the "unhallowed perversion of the means of salvation" in an official religion's coercion and persecution.[50] Historically, Madison notes, the true church has flourished without the support of state laws (and even under persecution by the government) relying only on God's care and providence. Restricted state churches, "instead of maintaining the purity and efficacy of religion," for Madison, "have had a contrary operation."[51] Instead of advancing the faith, corrupt state churches have retarded it because, given human vanity and pride, government sanction of a single church has produced, for Madison, the "fruit" of "pride and indolence in the Clergy, ignorance and servility in the Laity."[52] The light of Christ shone "in its greatest luster," for Madison, "prior to its incorporation with Civil policy."[53] Worse, the corrupt, worldly official church was prostituted to support unjust governments, "upholding the thrones of political tyranny," further damaging the mission of the church to bring people to Christ.[54]

Madison's "Memorial and Remonstrance" rallied the free Christian sentiments in Virginia, defeated the religious assessment bill, and paved the way for the Virginia Bill for Establishing Religious Freedom, and later the religious-freedom clause of the First Amendment to the U.S. Constitution. His belief that Christianity would spread in a free environment was confirmed: the faith grew and deepened in Virginia. Forty years later, Madison wrote that "there has been an increase of religious instruction since [then]. . . . Religious instruction is now diffused throughout the community by preachers of every sect with almost equal zeal." In a disestablished society, ministers will attract others to Christianity by "the purity of their lives and the attention of the people on their instructions."[55] As he wrote to Jasper Adams at age eighty-three, Madison believed that Christianity is "the best and purist religion," and its spread is best accomplished by Christian means: prayer, persuasion, and reliance upon God's grace and spirit, rather than by the civil government.[56]

RELIGIOUS PERSPECTIVE IN *THE FEDERALIST PAPERS*

After serving as the most persuasive delegate to the federal Constitutional Convention and its most assiduous chronicler, Madison became its most articulate advocate through his tightly reasoned arguments in his *Federalist Papers*. Originally newspaper essays to persuade the New York ratifying convention to approve the proposed constitution, these papers became the classic exposition of the principles of American republicanism. Throughout Madison's articles, his Christian perspective—on the sinful nature of man, the dangers of prideful ambition and political oppression, and the need for institutional checks and balances to ameliorate those sins—are amply evident. For example, in *Federalist Paper No. 40*, Madison answers the anti-Federalists' attacks on the new Constitution by reminding them that "a faultless plan was not to be expected [due to] . . . the fallibility to which . . . a body of men [is] liable."[57] However, given the regional and ideological conflicts at the convention, Madison concluded that "it is impossible to consider the degree of concord which ultimately prevailed as less than a miracle."[58]

In *Federalist Paper No. 10*, Madison expressed the view that a constitutional federal republic is best because it will "break and control the violence of faction," the "mortal disease" of democratic governments. Factions, for Madison, are groups motivated by selfish interests who use political power to violate the rights of individuals (such as freedom of religion) or oppress the whole community. Such political factions "are sown in the nature of man," causing people to "vex and oppress each other." Madison holds that this sinful "propensity of mankind" towards continual "mutual animosities" displays itself through "the most frivolous and fanciful distinctions" of class or dress or manners, prompting envy, hatred, and anger "sufficient to kindle their unfriendly passions and excite their most violent conflicts."[59]

For example, Madison notes individuals are given different natural abilities, gifts, and talents, which lead to different occupations and economic and social accomplishments and benefits (compare the Bible's description of different gifts in the church at 1 Cor. 12:20–31). But sinful humanity, because each man wants everything and resents others' gifts or the acclaim and attention they get, feels jealousy, and conflict results. Such human jealousy of others' abilities or accomplishments can lead men to try to use the government to suppress those capacities or take away others' status or property. Government's proper role is to protect these God-given gifts and the fruits thereof. The best way to accomplish this, for Madison, is to create a constitutional republic that divides power, preventing any single faction from dominating the whole state and harming others. "The greater the number of citizens and extent of territory . . . renders factious combinations less dreaded."[60] The disorganized system of American government under the Articles of Confederation, whose independent sovereign states encouraged regional, religious, and economic factions, exacerbated this human tendency to pride, envy, and conflict. As with all historical confederacies (Greek, German, Dutch, etc.), "Domestic vicissitudes, convulsions and carnage" resulted from the inevitable "mutual jealousies, fears, hatreds and injuries" of competing egos and factions. Without a strong central regime unifying and balancing these conflicting interests, the nation becomes "a nerveless body incapable of regulating its own members, insecure against external dangers, and agitated with unceasing fermentations in its own bowels." Besides this social indigestion, Madison finds that the "jealousies, pride [and] clashing pretensions" of this "political monster" produce "general imbecility, confusion and misery" of the sort Madison experienced in the Continental Congress.[61] Even more disturbing, for Madison, is the historical tendency of such confederate anarchy to lead to dictatorial tyranny, which is "oftener grown out of the assumptions of power called for, by a defective constitution, than out of the full exercise of the largest constitutional authority." An orderly, lawful society, therefore, remains "among the chief blessings of civil society" for Madison.[62]

He asks the political opponents of the new Constitution to "keep in mind that they themselves also are but men and ought not to assume an infallibility in prejudging the fallible opinions of others."[63] The weakness of human nature being what it is, Jesus' precept "Judge not, less ye be judged" might be a good one to follow. Human minds being so naturally blind, even holy scripture is often misunderstood; Madison notes that "When the Almighty himself condescends to address mankind in their own language, his meaning, luminous as it must be, is rendered dim and doubtful by the cloudy medium through which it is communicated."[64] Critics of the Constitution, Madison implores in *Federalist Paper* No. 41, should realize that "the purist of human blessings must have a portion of alloy in them" and "the choice must always be made, if not of the lesser evil, at least of the GREATER, not the PERFECT good."[65] Imperfect men expecting perfection are inevitably disappointed, Madison concludes from his Christian realism. "If men were angels," he states in his famous phrase from *Federalist Paper* No. 51, "no government would be necessary," for angels ceaselessly worship and obey God; men do not. "If angels were to govern men, neither external nor internal controls on government would be necessary" because angels, unlike humans, have no sin.[66] But humans are tainted by ever sinful motives, even when these are masked by virtuous rhetoric, so the political system must recognize that and install checks and balances to pit "ambition against ambition," securing a general peace and justice. The goal "of every political constitution" Madison writes, is "to obtain for rulers men who possess most wisdom to discern and most virtue to pursue, the common good of society . . . and . . . to take the most effectual precautions for keeping them virtuous while they continue to hold their public trust." One remedy for the tendency of power to corrupt was, for Madison, the constitutional provision for limited terms and frequent elections ("the greater the power is, the shorter ought to be its duration"). Still, even the best constitution is "insufficient" to control the "wickedness of men."[67] Even the "elect," the chosen and called of God who are devout Christians, can be corrupted by power and money; a system of government is needed that protects the nation even from them, in Madison's Augustinian Christian view of the persistence of human pride and sin.

CHRISTIAN LANGUAGE IN MADISON'S POLITICAL WRITINGS

Finally, throughout Madison's life, his writings contained Christian language, terminology, and rhetoric, showing his appreciation of the biblical view of man as sinful and rebellious towards God, redeemed and made righteous only through Christ, and of a world under God's ultimate grace and providence. These were not rhetorical flourishes, but reflective of a deep, consistent Christian faith and worldview. Madison saw events and people in the world through the lens of the Christian faith. A few examples will demonstrate this Madisonian religious perspective on life.

Madison wrote of the "follies of mankind," of the "vanity" of city life and the "vices" encouraged by the Articles of Confederation. He found the Frenchman Lafayette motivated by "personal glory" and saw his own refusal to supply free liquor at campaign rallies attributed to "pride or parsimony." State territorial conflicts were grounded in "envy and jealousy," while a rumor that Dr. Benjamin Franklin had become an American traitor prompted Madison to write, "little did I ever expect to hear that Jeremiah's doctrine that 'the heart of man is deceitful above all things and desperately wicked,'" would apply to the Philadelphian. But, the reality of human sin for Madison meant that even the most trusted friend could betray you;: "wherever there is an interest and power to do wrong, wrong will generally be done." And sadly, for Madison, "human conscience . . . is known to be inadequate in individuals" to overcome their evil actions, even among Christians, for "religion itself may become a motive to persecution and oppression."[68] Madison warned his friend William Bradford of the "emptiness of Earthly Happiness," of the world's "allurements and vanities," and urged his Princeton classmate to keep "a watchful eye" lest "while we are building ideal monuments of Renown and bliss here we neglect to have our names enrolled in the Annuls of Heaven." In old age, Madison eschewed giving too much political advice, fearing the charge of senility. Drawing on the biblical standard of a lifespan, Madison wrote, "a man whose years have but reached the canonical three-score-and-ten (and mine are much beyond the number) should distrust himself, whether distrusted by his friends or not, and should never forget that his arguments . . . will be answered by allusions to the date of his birth."[69]

Madison's Pauline advice to his friend was echoed in his recommendations to Thomas Jefferson on the theology collection for the new University of Virginia library, including many classics of the early church (St. Clement, Tertullian, Iranaeus, Augustine) and the Reformation (Luther, Calvin, Wesley, Edwards, Mather).[70] This Protestant perspective led Madison to urge everyone "to practice Christian forbearance, love, and charity towards each other."[71] It led him to characterize even the boundary negotiations over the Mississippi River as bound by "nature and providence," and to find a medieval Catholic Spanish empire's "government, religion and manners unfit them, of all nations in Christendom for a coalition with" the United States.[72] From his Christian realist perspective, he was not surprised, during the War of Independence, by French allies' intrigue and dishonesty or by English barbarity and duplicity. Ambassador John Adams's "vanity," Benjamin Franklin's moral lapses in Paris, and Robert Morris's financial corruption (as American finance director) did not surprise Madison.[73] Where temptations existed for prideful egoism, sexual immorality, or financial corruption, many men would fall.

The frequent moral and ethical lapses of his colleagues did not lead Madison to a Machiavellian cynicism or casual acceptance of human wrongs. The high moral precepts of the Bible must be upheld. The national debts incurred during the war must be repaid as a moral duty. For Madison, gratitude to the "blessings" of God required that His standards of "justice, good faith, honor, gratitude and all other qualities which enable the character of a nation" must be respected as America's "cardinal and essential virtues." To disregard those Judeo-Christian standards of morality threatened, in Madison's covenant theology, the loss of the Almighty's blessings.[74] A recognition of the reality of human sin did not excuse moral lapses, but demanded a more dedicated commitment to Christ.

Contrasting the principles of the American government with those of the British, Madison based the constitutional limits of the U.S. government in an Augustinian view of man's sinful, fallible nature, while the unlimited power of the English state assumed infallibility in the monarch.[75] Madison was fearful during negotiations with France for the Louisiana Purchase that requesting all of the western territory would appear to be "greedy ambition" on America's part. Still, he found Spain "obstinate and wicked" in their policies, northeasterners were marked by "depravity and stupidity" in their opposition to the Embargo Act, and Great Britain committed the "original sin" of violating American shipping prior to the War of 1812. Madison used that Calvinist reference to "original sin" also to describe "the dreadful fruit" of the institution of slavery in America. He described those attempting to destroy the Union as a "Serpent" in "Paradise."[76] Quoting liberally from the Bible, Madison expressed faith in God's goodness and providence for the United States, especially as we sought the Lord's guidance in personal and public life, obeyed his moral precepts, and honored him with humble and noble deeds. After the War of 1812, President Madison proclaimed,

> No People ought to feel greater obligations to celebrate the goodness of the Great Disposer of Events of the Destiny of Nations than the people of the United States. . . . He protected and cherished them under all their difficulties and trials. . . . And to the same Divine Author of Every Good and perfect Gift, we are indebted for all those privileges and advantages, religious as well as civil; which are so richly enjoyed in this land.

In his State of the Union address of 1813, Madison expressed thanks for "the numerous blessings with which our beloved Country continues to be favored in, above all for the light of divine truth."[77] Madison, it should be noted, followed the precedent of Washington and Adams, and rejected that of Jefferson, in issuing presidential proclamations calling for national days of prayer and thanksgiving.[78] As well, he regularly attended worship services as president, both in local congregations and in the U.S. House of Representatives.

Finally, late in his life, during a contemplative retirement, Madison looked toward the future social development in the United States. Already in the mid-nineteenth century, the socialist principles of Robert Owen's communal economics were appearing in America. The utopian socialism and economic liberalism that claimed to overcome human selfishness with equal property distribution caused Madison to warn Americans from a Calvinist Christian view not to forget pridefully the reality of sin. He warned of "the impossibility of banishing evil altogether from human society" and against deceiving oneself that the curse of work could be "relished" in an egalitarian society. Madison's Christian realism of the persistence of sin in all social systems warned against the socialist illusion that "love of equality will supercede the [human] desire of distinction" or that technology-induced leisure would elevate man rather than create "the vicious resorts for the envy of idleness."[79] All human social attempts to create virtuous citizens or a heaven on earth were a vain, prideful illusion. Only a recognition of the biblical image of man as fallen and sinful, redeemed, and made good through Christ and his Holy Spirit would promise a relatively peaceful, prosperous, and virtuous America.

APPENDIX: A MEMORIAL AND REMONSTRANCE AGAINST RELIGIOUS ASSESSMENTS[80]

We the subscribers, citizens of the said Commonwealth, having taken into serious consideration, a Bill printed by order of the last Session of General Assembly, entitled "A Bill establishing a provision for Teachers of the Christian Religion," and conceiving that the same if finally armed with the sanctions of a law, will be a dangerous abuse of power, are bound as faithful members of a free State to remonstrate against it, and to declare the reasons by which we are determined. We remonstrate against the said Bill,

1. Because we hold it for a fundamental and undeniable truth, "that Religion or the duty which we owe to our Creator and the manner of discharging it, can be directed only by reason and conviction, not by force or violence." The Religion then of every man must be left to the conviction and conscience of every man; and it is the right of every man to

exercise it as these may dictate. This right is in its nature an unalienable right. It is unalienable, because the opinions of men, depending only on the evidence contemplated by their own minds cannot follow the dictates of other men: It is unalienable also, because what is here a right towards men, is a duty towards the Creator. It is the duty of every man to render to the Creator such homage and such only as he believes to be acceptable to him. This duty is precedent, both in order of time and in degree of obligation, to the claims of Civil Society. Before any man can be considered as a member of Civil Society, he must be considered as a subject of the Governour of the Universe: And if a member of Civil Society, who enters into any subordinate Association, must always do it with a reservation of his duty to the General Authority; much more must every man who becomes a member of a particular Civil Society, do it with a saving of his allegiance to the Universal Sovereign. We maintain therefore that in matters of Religion, no man's right is abridged by the institution of Civil Society and that Religion is wholly exempt from its cognizance. True it is, that no other rule exists, by which any question which may divide a society, can be ultimately determined, but the will of the majority; but it is also true that the majority may trespass on the rights of the minority.

2. Because if Religion be exempt from the authority of the Society at large, still less can it be subject to that of the Legislative Body. The latter are but the creatures and vicegerents of the former. Their jurisdiction is both derivative and limited: it is limited with regard to the co-ordinate departments, more necessarily is it limited with regard to the constituents. The preservation of a free Government requires not merely, that the metes and bounds which separate each department of power be invariably maintained; but more especially that neither of them be suffered to overleap the great Barrier which defends the rights of the people. The Rulers who are guilty of such an encroachment, exceed the commission from which they derive their authority, and are Tyrants. The People who submit to it are governed by laws made neither by themselves nor by an authority derived from them, and are slaves.

3. Because it is proper to take alarm at the first experiment on our liberties. We hold this prudent jealousy to be the first duty of Citizens, and one of the noblest characteristics of the late Revolution. The free men of America did not wait till usurped power had strengthened itself by exercise, and entangled the question in precedents. They saw all the consequences in the principle, and they avoided the consequences by denying the principle. We revere this lesson too much soon to forget it. Who does not see that the same authority which can establish Christianity, in exclusion of all other Religions, may establish with the same

ease any particular sect of Christians, in exclusion of all other Sects? that the same authority which can force a citizen to contribute three pence only of his property for the support of any one establishment, may force him to conform to any other establishment in all cases whatsoever?

4. Because the Bill violates that equality which ought to be the basis of every law, and which is more indispensable, in proportion as the validity or expediency of any law is more liable to be impeached. If "all men are by nature equally free and independent," all men are to be considered as entering into Society on equal conditions; as relinquishing no more, and therefore retaining no less, one than another, of their natural rights. Above all are they to be considered as retaining an "*equal* title to the free exercise of Religion according to the dictates of Conscience." Whilst we assert for ourselves a freedom to embrace, to profess and to observe the Religion which we believe to be of divine origin, we cannot deny an equal freedom to those whose minds have not yet yielded to the evidence which has convinced us. If this freedom be abused, it is an offence against God, not against man: To God, therefore, not to man, must an account of it be rendered. As the Bill violates equality by subjecting some to peculiar burdens, so it violates the same principle, by granting to others peculiar exemptions. Are the Quakers and Mennonites the only sects who think a compulsive support of their Religions unnecessary and unwarrantable? Can their piety alone be entrusted with the care of public worship? Ought their Religions to be endowed above all others with extraordinary privileges by which proselytes may be enticed from all others? We think too favorably of the justice and good sense of these denominations to believe that they either covet pre-eminences over their fellow citizens or that they will be seduced by them from the common opposition to the measure.

5. Because the Bill implies either that the Civil Magistrate is a competent Judge of Religious truth; or that he may employ Religion as an engine of Civil policy. The first is an arrogant pretension falsified by the contradictory opinions of Rulers in all ages, and throughout the world: the second an unhallowed perversion of the means of salvation.

6. Because the establishment proposed by the Bill is not requisite for the support of the Christian Religion. To say that it is, is a contradiction to the Christian Religion itself, for every page of it disavows a dependence on the powers of this world: it is a contradiction to fact; for it is known that this Religion both existed and flourished, not only without the support of human laws, but in spite of every opposition from it had

been left to its own evidence and the ordinary care of Providence. Nay, it is a contradiction in terms; for a Religion not invented by human policy, must have pre-existed and been supported, before it was established by human policy. It is moreover to weaken in those who profess this Religion a pious confidence in its innate excellence and the patronage of its Author; and to foster in those who still reject it to its own merits.

7. Because experience witnesseth that ecclesiastical establishments, instead of maintaining the purity and efficacy of Religion, have had a contrary operation. During almost fifteen centuries has the legal establishment of Christianity been on trial. What have been its fruits? More or less in all places, pride and indolence in the Clergy, ignorance and servility in the laity, in both, superstition, bigotry and persecution. Enquire of the Teachers of Christianity for the ages in which it appeared in its greatest luster; those of every sect, point to the ages prior to its incorporation with Civil policy. Propose a restoration of this primitive State in which its Teachers depended on the voluntary rewards of their flocks, many of them predict its downfall. On which Side ought their testimony to have greatest weight, when for or when against their interest?

8. Because the establishment in question is not necessary for the support of Civil Government. If it be urged as necessary for the support of Civil Government only as it is a means of supporting Religion, and it be not necessary for the latter purpose, it cannot be necessary for the former. If Religion be not within the cognizance of Civil Government how can its legal establishment be necessary to Civil Government? What influence in fact have ecclesiastical establishments had on Civil Society? In some instances they have been seen to erect a spiritual tyranny on the ruins of the Civil authority; in many instances they have been seen upholding the thrones of political tyranny: in no instance have they been seen the guardians of the liberties of the people. Rulers who wished to subvert the public liberty, may have found an established Clergy convenient auxiliaries. A just Government instituted to secure & perpetuate it needs them not. Such a Government will be best supported by protecting every Citizen in the enjoyment of his Religion with the same equal hand which protects his person and his property; by neither invading the equal rights of any Sect, nor suffering any Sect to invade those of another.

9. Because the proposed establishment is a departure from that generous policy, which, offering an Asylum to the persecuted and oppressed of every Nation and Religion, promised a luster to our country, and an accession to the number of its citizens. What a melancholy mark is the Bill

of sudden degeneracy? Instead of holding forth an Asylum to the persecuted, it is itself a signal of persecution. It degrades from the equal rank of Citizens all those whose opinions in Religion do not bend to those of the Legislative authority. Distant as it may be in its present form from the Inquisition, it differs from it only in degree. The one is the first step, the other the last in the career of intolerance. The magnanimous sufferer under this cruel scourge in foreign Regions, must view the Bill as a Beacon on our Coast, warning him to seek some other haven, where liberty and philanthropy in their due extent, may offer a more certain repose from his Troubles.

10. Because it will have a like tendency to banish our Citizens. The allurements presented by other situations are every day thinning their number. To superadd a fresh motive to emigration by revoking the liberty which they now enjoy, would be the same species of folly which has dishonoured and depopulated flourishing kingdoms.

11. Because it will destroy that moderation and harmony which the forbearance of our laws to intermeddle with Religion has produced among its several sects. Torrents of blood have been spilt in the old world, by vain attempts of the secular arm, to extinguish Religious discord, by proscribing all difference in Religious opinion. Time has at length revealed the true remedy. Every relaxation of narrow and rigorous policy, wherever it has been tried, has been found to assuage the disease. The American Theatre has exhibited proofs that equal and compleat liberty, if it does not wholly eradicate it, sufficiently destroys its malignant influence on the health and prosperity of the State. If with the salutary effects of this system under our own eyes, we begin to contract the bounds of Religious freedom, we know no name that will too severely reproach our folly. At least let warning be taken at the first fruits of the threatened innovation. The very appearance of the Bill has transformed "that Christian forbearance, love and charity," which of late mutually prevailed, into animosities and jealousies, which may not soon be appeased. What mischiefs may not be dreaded, should this enemy to the public quiet be armed with the force of a law?

12. Because the policy of the Bill is adverse to the diffusion of the light of Christianity. The first wish of those who enjoy this precious gift ought to be that it may be imparted to the whole race of mankind. Compare the number of those who have as yet received it with the number still remaining under the dominion of false Religions; and how small is the former! Does the policy of the Bill tend to lessen the disproportion? No; it at once discourages those who are strangers to the light of revelation from coming into the Region of it; and countenances by ex-

ample the nations who continue in darkness, in shutting out those who might convey it to them. Instead of Levelling as far as possible, every obstacle to the victorious progress of Truth, the Bill with an ignoble and unchristian timidity would circumscribe it with a wall of defence against the encroachments of error.

13. Because attempts to enforce by legal sanctions, acts obnoxious to so great a proportion of Citizens, tend to enervate the laws in general, and to slacken the bands of Society. If it be difficult to execute any law which is not generally deemed necessary or salutary, what must be the case, where it is deemed invalid and dangerous? And what may be the effect of so striking an example of impotency in the Government, on its general authority?

14. Because a measure of such singular magnitude and delicacy ought not to be imposed, without the clearest evidence that it is called for by a majority of citizens, and no satisfactory method is yet proposed by which the voice of the majority in this case may be determined, or its influence secured. "The people of the respective counties are indeed requested to signify their opinion respecting the adoption of the Bill to the next Session of Assembly." But the representation must be made equal, before the voice either of the Representatives or of the Counties will be that of the people. Our hope is that neither of the former will, after due consideration, espouse the dangerous principle of the Bill. Should the event disappoint us, it will still leave us in full confidence, that a fair appeal to the latter will reverse the sentence against our liberties.

15. Because finally, "the equal right of every citizen to the free exercise of his Religion according to the dictates of conscience" is held to be the same tenure with all our other rights. If we recur to its origin, it is equally the gift of nature; if we weigh its importance, it cannot be less dear to us; if we consult the "Declaration of those rights which pertain to the good people of Virginia, as the basis and foundation of Government," it is enumerated with equal solemnity, or rather studied emphasis. Either then, we must say, that the Will of the Legislature is the only measure of their authority; and that in the plenitude of this authority, they may sweep away all our fundamental rights; or, that they are bound to leave this particular right untouched and sacred: Either we must say, that they may control the freedom of the press, may abolish the Trial by Jury, may swallow up the Executive and Judiciary Powers of the State; nay that they may despoil us of our very right of suffrage, and erect themselves into an independent and hereditary Assembly or, we must say, that they have no authority to enact into law the Bill under consideration. We the Subscribers say,

that the General Assembly of this Commonwealth have no such authority: And that no effort may be omitted on our part against so dangerous an usurpation, we oppose to it, this remonstrance; earnestly praying, as we are in duty bound, that the Supreme Lawgiver of the Universe, by illuminating those to whom it is addressed, may on the one hand, turn their Councils from every act which would affront his holy prerogative, or violate the trust committed to them: and on the other, guide them into every measure which may be worthy of his [blessing, may re]dound to their own praise, and may establish more firmly the liberties, the prosperity and the happiness of the Commonwealth.

NOTES

1. This approach to Madison's political thought is developed in my book, *The Political Philosophy of James Madison* (Baltimore: The Johns Hopkins University Press, 2001), especially, xi–xvi and 6–37.

2. This deficiency is especially pronounced in the major biography of Madison by Irving Brant, *James Madison* (Indianapolis, IN: Bobbs-Merrill, 1941) and numerous other studies (e.g., essays in Robert S. Alley, ed., *James Madison on Religious Liberty* [Buffalo, NY: Prometheus Books, 1985]; Lance Banning, *The Sacred Fire of Liberty* [Ithaca, NY: Cornell University Press, 1995]; Thomas Lindsay, "James Madison on Religion and Politics: Rhetoric and Reality," *American Political Science Review* 85 (December 1991): 1321–1337). Notable exceptions to these trends include the excellent biography by Ralph Ketcham, *James Madison* (Charlottesville: University Press of Virginia, 1990), James Hutson's *Religion and the New Republic* (Lanham, MD: Rowman & Littlefield, 2000); and the classic essay by James Smylie, "Madison and Witherspoon: Theological Roots of American Political Thought," *Princeton University Library Chronicle* 22 (Spring 1961).

3. Douglass Adair, "Notes and Documents, James Madison's Autobiography," *William and Mary Quarterly*, 3d ser. 2 (April 1945): 195.

4. Quoted in Mary-Elaine Swanson, *The Education of James Madison* (Montgomery, AL: Hoffman Center, 1992), 2. For this entire section on James Madison's education, I am indebted to Anita Rivera Simpkins's doctoral dissertation, "James Madison on Education" (Charlottesville, University of Virginia, 1998), on which I served as an outside reader.

5. In Brant, *James Madison*, 62.

6. Brant, *James Madison*, 62.

7. Brant, *James Madison*, 58.

8. Merrill D. Peterson, ed., *James Madison* (New York: Harper & Row, 1974), 17.

9. Brant, *James Madison*, 73, 77.

10. See Alan Heimert and Perry Miller, *The Great Awakening* (Indianapolis, IN: Bobbs-Merrill, 1967).

11. Swanson, *Education of James Madison*, 107.

12. Brant, *James Madison*, 84.

13. Mark Noll, *Princeton and the Republic, 1768–1872* (Princeton, NJ: Princeton University Press, 1989), 8–9.

14. James Madison, "Commentary on the Bible," 1770. *The Papers of James Madison I*, eds. William T. Hutchinson and William M. E. Rachel (Chicago: University of Chicago Press, 1962), 58.

15. John Witherspoon, *Lectures on Moral Philosophy*, ed. Jack Scott (Newark, DE: University of Delaware Press, 1982), 123.

16. Witherspoon, *Lectures on Moral Philosophy*, 87.

17. Witherspoon, *Lectures on Moral Philosophy*, 64.

18. Witherspoon, *Lectures on Moral Philosophy*, 85, 102, 103.

19. John Witherspoon "Lectures on Divinity," in Smylie, "Madison and Witherspoon," 121; John Witherspoon, "Part of a Speech in Congress," in *The Works of John Witherspoon*, 9 vols. (Edinburgh: Ogle and Aikman, 1804–5), 4:350.

20. Witherspoon, *Works*, 3:435.

21. Witherspoon, *Works*, 4:351; 349.

22. James Madison, *Federalist Papers*, ed. Isaac Kramnick (New York: Penguin, 1987), 308, 311, 319.

23. *Federalist Papers*, 339, 124, 242, 245, 319, 266, 344–45.

24. John Calvin, *Institutes of the Christian Religion*, ed. John McNeill (Philadelphia: Westmister Press, 1960), I.1.i. See also *Federalist Papers* 339, 124, 165.

25. Quoted in Peterson, *James Madison*, 57, 74; Ketcham, *James Madison*, 65.

26. Quoted in Peterson, *James Madison*, 164.

27. For an extended discussion of Lockean liberal and classical republican ideologies in early-American historiography, see my appendix in Garrett Ward Sheldon, *The Political Philosophy of Thomas Jefferson* (Baltimore: Johns Hopkins University Press, 1991). See also Sheldon, *The Political Philosophy of James Madison*, 110.

28. For a full discussion of this, see Sheldon, *The Political Philosophy of James Madison*.

29. Peterson, *James Madison*, 94.

30. Peterson, *James Madison*, 103–6.

31. Ketcham, *James Madison*, 93.

32. Ketcham, *James Madison*, 391–92.

33. Ketcham, *James Madison*, 393.

34. Gaillard Hunt, ed. *The Writings of James Madison* (New York: Putnams, 1906), 6:327–28.

35. Hunt, *The Writings of James Madison*, 6:328–29.

36. Peterson, *James Madison*, 363.

37. Peterson, *James Madison*, 390.

38. Ketcham, *James Madison*, 632.

39. Marvin Meyers, ed. *The Mind of the Founder* (Hanover, N.H.: University Press of New England, 1981), 420, 427.

40. Peterson, *James Madison*, 407.

41. Peterson, *James Madison*, 29.

42. Peterson, *James Madison*, 29.

43. Peterson, *James Madison*, 29.

44. Peterson, *James Madison*, 29.

45. Peterson, *James Madison*, 29.
46. Peterson, *James Madison*, 30.
47. Peterson, *James Madison*, 30.
48. Peterson, *James Madison*, 30.
49. Witherspoon, *Lectures on Moral Philosophy*, 147.
50. Peterson, *James Madison*, 93.
51. Peterson, *James Madison*, 93.
52. Peterson, *James Madison*, 93.
53. Peterson, *James Madison*, 93.
54. Peterson, *James Madison*, 94.
55. Ketcham, *James Madison*, 167.
56. Daniel Dreisbach, *Religion and Politics in the Early Republic* (Lexington, KY: University Press of Kentucky, 1996), 117. Space limitations make it impossible to consider Madison's role in framing the First Amendment or the way judges, attorneys, and scholars have used Madison's views to shed light on this amendment. With respect to the establishment clause, Madison has been appealed to as an advocate of both strict separation and neutrality, as well as other views. With respect to the free exercise clause, his views have been used to argue that legislatures and courts must, or, alternatively, may not, exempt religious citizens from generally applicable laws. For a recent treatment of much of this literature, as well as an innovative approach to Madison's view of church–state relations, see Vincent Phillip Muñoz, "James Madison's Principle of Religious Liberty," *American Political Science Review* 97 (February 2003), 17–32.
57. *Federalist Papers*, 266.
58. Peterson, *James Madison*, 144.
59. *Federalist Papers*, 124.
60. *Federalist Papers*, 127.
61. *Federalist Papers*, 160–61, 165–66.
62. *Federalist Papers*, 171, 243.
63. *Federalist Papers*, 242.
64. *Federalist Papers*, 245.
65. *Federalist Papers*, 266.
66. *Federalist Papers*, 319.
67. Ketcham, *James Madison*, 65.
68. Peterson, *James Madison*, 23–24, 103–6, 87, 42, 57, 74.
69. Peterson, *James Madison*, 23–24; Meyers, *Mind of the Founder*, 389.
70. Ketcham, *James Madison*, 652–53.
71. Peterson, *James Madison*, 73.
72. Peterson, *James Madison*, 101.
73. Ketcham, *James Madison*, 93, 122–23.
74. Peterson, *James Madison*, 76–78.
75. Hunt, *Writings of James Madison*, 6:388.
76. Peterson, *James Madison*, 245; Ketcham, *James Madison*, 418, 431.
77. Swanson, *Education of James Madison*, 263–64.
78. Some scholars argue that Madison only issued the calls in response to a request by Congress, and, as evidence, cite his criticism of such proclamations in his "De-

tached Memoranda" (e.g., Muñoz, "James Madison's Principle of Religious Liberty," 28–29). I believe that any hesitation Madison had with respect to issuing such proclamations was grounded in his respect for the voluntary exercise of religion, not the fear of religion.

79. Peterson, *James Madison*, 387–88.

80. From Robert Rutland et al., eds. *The Papers of James Madison*. Vol. 8 (Chicago: University of Chicago Press, 1973), 298–304.

5

John Witherspoon's Revolutionary Religion*

Jeffry H. Morrison

The practice of true and undefiled religion . . . is the great foundation of public prosperity and national happiness.

—John Witherspoon for the Second Continental Congress[1]

In America it is religion which leads to enlightenment and the observance of divine laws which leads men to liberty.

—Alexis de Tocqueville[2]

In the portentous year 1776, Edward Gibbon published the first volume of his *Decline and Fall of the Roman Empire,* in which he had little good to say about Christianity and even less about clerics. "The influence of the clergy," he wrote, "might be usefully employed to assert the rights of mankind; but so intimate is the connection between the throne and the altar, that the banner of the church has very seldom been seen on the side of the people."[3] But Gibbon was wrong about that, as even the editors of his magnificent history note,[4] and as the career of his contemporary the Rev. John Witherspoon illustrates. In 1776 Gibbon himself was a member of Parliament, implacably opposed to the American Revolution, while Witherspoon was sitting in the American Continental Congress pushing for independence from Gibbon's King George III. Reverend Witherspoon was a member of

---

*A different version of this chapter was published as "John Witherspoon and 'The Public Interest of Religion,'" *Journal of Church and State* 41 (1999): 551–73.

the so-called Black Regiment, American clergy who agitated and sometimes even fought for independence.[5]

There was no abler advocate for American independence or better representative of the intertwining of religion and politics in early America than John Witherspoon. In 1774 John Adams, who had no patience for fools or innocents, called Witherspoon a "clear, sensible" preacher and "as high a Son of Liberty, as any Man in America."[6] Although something of a forgotten founder today, in fact Witherspoon was a "colossus" in his day[7]: nationally reputed as a politician and signer of the Declaration of Independence, arguably the most influential clergyman in America, and president of the College of New Jersey at Princeton during one of the most important quarter-centuries in the whole of American history. In each of these roles Witherspoon was outstanding; taken together they mark him as "an incredible . . . figure in the growth of America," in Ralph Ketcham's words.[8]

Given Witherspoon's unique status among the founders as a political clergyman, this chapter briefly rehearses his careers in politics and religion, then reconstructs his views on the public role of religion, or what can be called his political theology. The discussion of political theology centers around two political sermons from the voluminous *Works of John Witherspoon*,[9] "The Dominion of Providence over the Passions of Men" (1776) and the "Sermon Delivered at a Public Thanksgiving after Peace" (1782), along with three religious proclamations (1776, 1781, 1782) drafted by Witherspoon for the Continental Congress.

POLITICS AND RELIGION

John Witherspoon, D.D., LL.D.,[10] lived an eventful life that spanned the last three quarters of the eighteenth century. Born in Scotland in the same year as Adam Smith at the dawning of the Scottish Enlightenment, Witherspoon was educated in its heart at the University of Edinburgh. After graduation and ordination, Witherspoon emerged as the leader of the more evangelical Popular Party in the Scottish Presbyterian Church. His witty and sometimes caustic pen, coupled with shrewdness and genuine piety, earned him an international reputation by the 1760s and an invitation to fill the presidency of the de facto Presbyterian College of New Jersey at Princeton. At the urging of Benjamin Rush, the trustees of the college, and George Whitefield,[11] the Anglican evangelist who helped touched off the First Great Awakening, Witherspoon emigrated to Princeton in 1768 to become the sixth president of the college. He remained at Princeton until his death in 1794.

Witherspoon's formal political career was spent in the founding's epicenter around Philadelphia over fifteen crucial years. He served periodically in the New Jersey provincial and state legislatures (1774–1789), in the Continental and Confederation congresses throughout the Revolution (1776–1782),[12] and in the New Jersey convention that ratified the federal Constitution (1787). Witherspoon made a lasting mark on the Congress during his six-year career. He argued for declaring independence at a critical juncture,[13] and he was the only practicing clergyman and college president to sign the Declaration. He served on a staggering 126 committees (Presbyterians are great ones for committees), and drafted the instructions to the American peace commissioners in France in 1781. He also drafted three religious proclamations for the Congress, a full third of those Congress issued during his tenure. Between signing the Declaration of Independence and ratifying the Constitution,[14] Witherspoon had a direct hand in passing the two most celebrated documents of the American founding. And if we include the Articles of Confederation, which he also signed, Witherspoon was instrumental in passing three of the four Organic Laws of the United States.[15]

Witherspoon's political influence continued long after his own retirement from elective politics in 1789. The list of his Princeton students who went on to significant positions in public affairs during the founding period is long and distinguished, and includes twelve members of the Continental Congress; five delegates to the Constitutional Convention; one U.S. president (James Madison, who stayed on six months after his 1771 graduation to study Hebrew under Witherspoon)[16]; a vice president (Aaron Burr, class of 1772); forty-nine U.S. representatives; twenty-eight senators; three Supreme Court justices; eight district judges; one secretary of state; three attorneys general; and two foreign ministers. Twenty-six of Witherspoon's graduates were state judges, seventeen were members of their state constitutional conventions, and fourteen were members of the state conventions that ratified the federal Constitution.[17] Garry Wills has accordingly tagged Witherspoon "probably the most influential teacher in the entire history of American education."[18]

Witherspoon also had a formidable ministerial career and was among the most influential clergymen in America during the last quarter of the eighteenth century. He came from a distinguished line of Presbyterian pastors: his great-grandfather had signed the Solemn League and Covenant (1648) aligning Scotland with the Parliamentary forces in the English Civil War in exchange for preserving the Reformed (i.e. Calvinist) religion in Scotland, and his mother claimed lineal descent from John Knox. His international reputation was quickly transferred to America. Early on he formed powerful connections throughout the colonies with pastors like Ezra Stiles and Timothy Dwight in New England, as well as other ministers in the deep South, including a distinguished clerical son-in-law. One daughter married Madison's friend the Rev. Samuel Stanhope Smith, founder of what became Hampden-Sydney College in Virginia and later the seventh president of Princeton. Witherspoon was also a fixture in the Congregational-Presbyterian Confederation that met between 1766 and 1775. That confederation linked Congregationalists from the General Association of Connecticut with Presbyterians to oppose a potential Anglican establishment,[19] that perennial bugaboo of American dissenters. In those joint conventions Witherspoon solidified his relationship with Reverend Stiles, the Congregationalist president of Yale College, who found Witherspoon "a very learned divine," but complained privately that he was too much of a politician.[20]

By 1776 Presbyterians had nearly 600 congregations in America, mostly in the middle and southern colonies[21]; this put them second to their close Reformed cousins the Congregationalists. Presbyterians were a potent force among the Reformed churches, which included the Congregationalists as well as Dutch and German Reformed, and were collectively "the largest religious sector of the United States" at the time.[22] From 1785 through 1789, Witherspoon was the leading figure in organizing the Presbyterian synods into a national body. Out of that national movement came catechisms, confessions, a directory of worship, and a "Form of the Government" of the church that bore strong marks of Witherspoon's influence. His introduction to the "Form of the Government" set out the denomination's first principles of church polity, including a strongly worded section on nonestablishment of religion. Being the most prominent Presbyterian clergyman of the late eighteenth century[23] put Witherspoon near the top, and perhaps at the very top, of the ministerial heap in founding-era America.

His status as a minister and a magistrate inevitably led Witherspoon to the crossroads of religion and politics in the founding period and gave his messages heft. On the congressional fast day of May 17, 1776,

Witherspoon preached what became his most famous sermon, "The Dominion of Providence over the Passions of Men."[24] That sermon, by his own admission the first overtly political one from his pulpit, was dedicated to the "Honourable JOHN HANCOCK, Esq., President of the Congress of the United States of America." It turned out to be one of the most important political sermons of the Revolutionary era, and it helped vault Witherspoon into the Continental Congress less than two months later. "The Dominion of Providence" was a predictable Calvinist discourse on the general sovereignty of God, inspired by Psalm 76:10: "surely the wrath of man shall praise thee; the remainder of wrath shall thou restrain."[25] But the sermon also contained a large section that Witherspoon called an "improvement" on the biblical text, in which he applied the general scriptural teaching to the particulars of the American situation and laid out some of his own thoughts on the proper relationship between religion and government. (Like the "plain-style" Puritan sermons of old and New England, Witherspoon's sermons typically comprised three parts, the last of which applied the biblical text to the lives and immediate circumstances of his listeners.)[26]

Late that same year, Witherspoon was tapped to draft a proclamation for the Congress recommending a "day of solemn fasting and humiliation." Issued on December 11, 1776, it was the first of three religious proclamations composed by Witherspoon between 1776 and 1782. It urged all the United States "to implore of Almighty God the forgiveness of the many sins prevailing among the ranks, and to beg the countenance and assistance of his Providence in the prosecution of the present just and necessary war." And it recommended to both civil and military officers "the exercise of repentance and reformation."[27]

Witherspoon also wrote thanksgiving day proclamations that were issued on October 26, 1781, and October 11, 1782, in keeping with Congress's practice of issuing thanksgiving day proclamations each October throughout the war.[28] These days of fasting, prayer, and thanksgiving were sometimes recommended to the states in strong language. Witherspoon's Fast Day Proclamation of 1776, for example, recommended that a fast be appointed "as soon as possible" and advised "in the most earnest manner" that persons in authority encourage repentance and reformation and discourage immorality in those under them. These proclamations employed the language of the covenant theology held by Witherspoon and other Reformed Protestants, which taught that God had made a covenant with the people of the United States to bless them as long as they were holy and to curse them when they were sinful. As the country was engaged in a desperate war with Great Britain, Witherspoon and the Congress urged all the American people, "public bodies, as well as private persons, to reverence the Providence of God, and look up to him as the supreme disposer of all events."[29] Even on days of thanksgiving, the people were

> to confess our manifold sins; to offer up our most fervent supplications to the God of all grace, that it may please Him to pardon our offences, and incline our hearts for the future to keep all his laws . . . and cause the knowledge of God to cover the earth, as the water covers the seas.[30]

In September 1782, Witherspoon was a member of a three-man congressional committee appointed to consider a petition of support for Philadelphia printer Robert Aitken's translation and printing of the Bible.[31] The committee returned a resolution on September 12, drafted by Witherspoon and approved substantially unchanged by the Congress, which said,

> The United States in Congress assembled, highly approve the pious and laudable undertaking of Mr. Aitken, as subservient to the interest of religion . . . and being satisfied . . . of his care and accuracy in the execution of the work, they recommend this edition of the Bible to the inhabitants of the United States.[32]

Aitken's work thus became the first English bible published in North America.[33] Apparently, Witherspoon and his colleagues believed that the ready availability of bibles was an important prerequisite not only to personal, but also to public, happiness: "[M]ake us a holy, that so we may be an happy[,] people," Congress prayed (there is no other word for it) in a fast day proclamation of March 19, 1782.[34]

That autumn Witherspoon also delivered what has erroneously been called the "Sermon Delivered at a Public Thanksgiving after Peace,"[35] a sermon that, like "The Dominion of Providence," expresses Witherspoon's thinking on the proper relationship between religion and American politics. This sermon is peculiarly interesting: Witherspoon preached it in his capacity as a minister just weeks after he retired from the Continental Congress in obedience to a congressional thanksgiving day proclamation he had written himself in his capacity as a congressman. The proclamation asked the states to "command" those citizens under their authority to observe a day of "solemn thanksgiving to God for all his mercies" and recommended a "cheerful obedience to his [God's] laws, and . . . the practice of true and undefiled religion, which is the great foundation of public prosperity and national happiness."[36] Witherspoon accordingly began his sermon by thanking God for "the goodness of his providence to the United States of America, in the course of a war, which has now lasted seven years," then suggested that "[t]hose who are vested with civil authority ought also, with much care, to promote religion and good morals among all under their government."[37]

We can see from these few examples just how visible a symbol Witherspoon was of the intermingling of religion and politics during the American founding. In fact, if we wished to invent a figure who at once represented America's early commitments to religion and politics, we could hardly do better than to invent the parson-politician from New Jersey. Certainly Witherspoon never shrank from this dual role. He conspicuously wore his clerical outfit (including a large Geneva collar) to sessions of the Congress,[38] and he ridiculed a provision in the new Georgia Constitution of 1789 that stated, "No clergyman of any denomination shall be a member of the general assembly."[39] Posing as a confused parson, Witherspoon suggested in a newspaper editorial that the following section be substituted to clear up "ambiguities" in the Georgia constitution.

> No clergyman, of any denomination, shall be capable of being elected a member of the Senate or House of Representatives, because [here insert the grounds of offensive disqualification, which I have not been able to discover] Provided always, and it is the true intent and meaning of this part of the constitution, that if at any time he shall be completely deprived of the clerical character by those by whom he was invested with it, as by deposition for cursing and swearing, drunkenness or uncleanness, he shall then be fully restored to all the privileges of a free citizen; his offence shall no more be remembered against him; but he may be chosen either to the Senate or House of Representatives, and shall be treated with all the respect due to his *brethren*, the other members of Assembly.[40]

Witherspoon was able to move deftly, sometimes even comically, between his sacred and secular roles because his beliefs about religion and civil government were perfectly synchronized with those of nearly all the founders, even less-than-orthodox founders like Benjamin Franklin, John Adams, and George Washington.

POLITICAL THEOLOGY

How did John Witherspoon, this most visible symbol of both church and state during the founding, conceive of the public role of religion, and what did he think was the proper interaction between church and state in the young American republic he helped create? In other words, what was his political theology? To begin with, Witherspoon's public religion was not the sort of thing that the young Abraham Lincoln wanted a half century later when he recommended that "reverence for the laws" become the "political religion" of the land.[41] Lincoln's political religion was, if it can be put this way, a purely secular affair: It was a religion without a god. But to Witherspoon this kind of political religion would not do. In order to be most useful in public affairs, religion had to be rooted in sincere belief in, and worship of, God. Witherspoon did occasionally refer to the cause of independence as "sacred,"[42] but that is as close as he ever came to Lincoln's political religion. He sometimes spoke of "visible religion,"[43] or "the public credit of religion," as he did in "On the Religious Education of Children," a sermon preached in New York in 1789.[44] But most often Witherspoon used the phrase "the public interest of religion."

Just what sort of religion was in "the public interest"? That is not a trivial question because, as Gibbon noted, regardless of whether a religion were true or even sincerely believed,

> a prudent magistrate might observe with pleasure and eventually support the progress of a religion which diffused among the people a pure, benevolent, and universal system of ethics, adapted to every duty and every condition of life, recommended as the will and reason of the supreme Deity, and enforced by the sanction of eternal rewards and punishments.[45]

Because Witherspoon was a magistrate and a minister, we ought perhaps to ask how he defined religion's public interest and whether it mattered to him if the religion were true or if its practitioners really believed it.

The only kind of religion that could be in the public interest for Witherspoon was what he habitually called "true religion." He preferred compound terms like "true religion" or "true and undefiled religion"[46] to the naked word "religion," and he supplied a precise definition of what true religion meant to him. First (and we would expect nothing less from a minister of the gospel), true religion had to be Christian. "There can be no true religion," he said, "till there be a discovery of your lost state by nature and practice and an unfeigned acceptance of Christ Jesus as he is offered in the gospel."[47] Second, "True religion is nothing else but an inward temper and outward conduct suited to your state and circumstances in providence at any time."[48] True religion thus had both inward and outward components, the inward being the soul's "temper" and the outward the expression of that temper in personal conduct. This understanding of true religion was consistent with the New Light theology of the day that stressed personal regeneration and holy conduct as a necessary accompaniment of saving faith. By true religion Witherspoon meant something like genuine or sincere religion, the kind of Christianity that was marked by genuine conversion and that changed a person inside and out. However, while Witherspoon always emphasized the importance of right living, it is not clear how closely he identified with all expressions of New Light piety. According to the memoirs of Aaron Burr (no New Light, he), Witherspoon passed off the revival that swept the Princeton campus during his presidency as "not true and rational religion, but fanaticism."[49] Ebenezer Bradford, a student during the Princeton revival of 1772, wrote to Joseph Bellamy that Witherspoon and Rev. Elihu Spencer were

> great enemies to what they call Eastward, or New Divinity. . . . The Dr. has lately been conversed with upon these things since they have made such progress in the College, and declares that he is neither for nor against them; however, he both preaches and converses in contradistinction to them.[50]

Bellamy, a Connecticut New Light revivalist and associate of Jonathan Edwards, had written a well-known booklet, *The Nature of True Religion Delineated* (1750), which Witherspoon owned and appears to have read closely. Bellamy wrote that part of being made in the image of God included having a "temper of mind or frame of heart perfectly answerable to the moral law; the moral law being, as it were, a transcript of the moral perfections of God."[51] In his fourth lecture on moral philosophy, Witherspoon concluded,

> The result of the whole is, that we ought to take the rule of duty from conscience enlightened by reason, experience, and every way by which we can be supposed to learn the will of our Maker, and his intention in creating us such as we are. And we ought to believe that it is as deeply founded as the nature of God himself, being a transcript of his moral excellence, and that it is productive of the greatest good.[52]

While his posture may have been noncommittal or even skeptical toward the New Divinity enthusiasm of Edwards and Bellamy, Witherspoon was solidly in their camp regarding Christian doctrines such as the moral law and the moral attributes of God.

When he spoke of "true religion," and especially when his topic had to do with public life, Witherspoon meant nonsectarian orthodox Christianity as expressed, for example, in the Nicene Creed. Witherspoon was a staunch Calvinist, and it is tempting to read Reformed Protestantism back into his language, but his works do not necessarily demand such a reading, and other factors suggest a broader, catholic meaning, chiefly his manifest Christian ecumenism. Witherspoon was on good terms with individual Anglicans like George Whitefield, whom he considered a minister of "great zeal and discernment." He complimented Roman Catholic sects like the Jansenists, whose "admirable practical treatises" he commended to his Protestant divinity students—and this in an age of anti-Catholic bigotry.[53] True, he sometimes used prejudicial language—he referred to "papists" and "Popery"—but then, what colonial Protestant did not? Witherspoon was more tolerant than most, and he hinted at increased religious liberty for Catholics: "we ought in general to guard against persecution on a religious account as much as possible. . . . Papists are tolerated in Holland without danger to liberty. And though not properly tolerated, they are now connived at in Britain."[54]

Surprisingly, Witherspoon did not seem to use the word "true" to emphasize the truth of Christianity in contrast to other religions, although he certainly assumed its truth, especially in his sermons. When defining true religion he focused more on Christian behavior than on the "peculiar distinctions" of doctrine that divide sects. Put differently, Witherspoon stressed universal Christian practice rather than the deep and frequently divisive fine points of faith.

> Do not suppose, my brethren, that I mean to recommend a furious and angry zeal for the circumstantials of religion, or the contentions of one sect with another about their peculiar distinctions. I do not wish you to oppose anybody's religion, but everybody's wickedness. Perhaps there are few surer marks of the reality of religion than when a man feels himself more joined in spirit to a true holy person of a different denomination, than to an irregular liver of his own.[55]

From this we should not infer that Witherspoon ranked faith or doctrine lower than practice or that he had a merely instrumental view of Christianity. This kind of recommendation was simply his way of encouraging Christian unity on the New Testament model. In fact, one gets the overall impression that Witherspoon felt brotherly affection for any Christian who was sincere and a "regular liver," regardless of denomination.

To be sure, Witherspoon did think true religion was useful: On one occasion he told an audience, "Be assured that true religion is the way to health, peace, opulence and public esteem."[56] And he could sound rather like his pragmatic but unorthodox colleague Benjamin Franklin at times. Franklin, although he counted Witherspoon among his many friends, was an unconcealed skeptic when it came to Reformed doctrine and only valued the Christian religion for the good behavior it produced. In his *Autobiography* Franklin used language nearly identical to Witherspoon's about "peculiar doctrines" and sects to record his disgust at a Presbyterian's preaching because "his discourses were chiefly either polemic arguments, or explications of the peculiar doctrines of our sect, and were all to me very dry, uninteresting, and unedifying, since not a single moral principle was inculcated or enforced, their aim seeming to be rather to make us Presbyterians than good citizens."[57]

But unlike Franklin, Witherspoon continually brought his audiences back to the state of their own souls, despite his emphasis on Christian behavior. Even in "The Dominion of Providence," preached on an explicitly political occasion, Witherspoon reminded his listeners that the eternal state of their souls was to be their crucial concern. Important as the political questions of the day were (and in May of 1776 they were important indeed), still Witherspoon had to ask, "is it of less moment my brethren whether you shall be the heirs of glory or the heirs of hell?"[58] In less political settings Witherspoon was even more emphatic about the centrality of salvation. Lecturing his divinity students, President Witherspoon insisted, "Religion is the grand concern to us all, as we are men;—whatever be our calling and profession, the salvation of our souls is the one thing needful."[59] From first to last Witherspoon comes across as a sincere, pious, and orthodox Christian. Throughout his pastoral career he was unwavering in his commitment to Reformed Protestantism, even though he was also committed (in qualified ways) to some tenets of the Enlightenment, such as confidence in the methods of natural science and in human reason.[60] And he was consistent in defining true religion: sincere, orthodox Christianity that results in virtuous behavior.

Witherspoon supplied an equally explicit definition of the public interest of religion in "The Dominion of Providence."

Suffer me to recommend to you, an attention to the public interest of religion, or in other words, zeal for the glory of God and the good of others. I have already endeavored to exhort sinners to repentance; what I have here in view is to point out to you the concern which every good man ought to take in the national character and manners, and the means which he ought to use for promoting public virtue; and bearing down impiety and vice.[61]

Here again Witherspoon emphasized the public or "visible" nature of religion, by recasting the two tablets of the Decalogue as "the glory of God and the good of others." Having exhorted his listeners to attend to the private component of religion, that is, to the state of their own souls, he turned to the public or corporate component, the "public interest" of religion. True religion must have a keen interest in "the national character and manners," and its role must be nothing less than the promotion of public virtue and the prevention of public vice. Profanity, impiety, and "immorality of every kind" must be ridden down for the political good of the Republic.

Nothing is more certain than that a general profligacy and corruption of manners make a people ripe for destruction. A good form of government may hold the rotten materials together for some time, but beyond a certain pitch, even the best constitution will be ineffectual, and slavery must ensue. On the other hand, when the manners of a nation are pure, when true religion and internal principles maintain their vigour, the attempts of the most powerful enemies to oppress them are commonly baffled and disappointed.[62]

For Witherspoon (and indeed for nearly all the founders) virtue, and therefore religion, was a necessary condition for successful republican government because virtue was necessary for maintaining republican liberty, and religion in turn was necessary for virtue. "[I]f we go to the history of mankind," Witherspoon said, "we shall find that . . . the knowledge of divine truth . . . certainly is the way to virtue."[63] In a protracted section of the "Thanksgiving Day Sermon" (1782), Witherspoon elaborated on what he had said in "The Dominion of Providence" concerning the place that virtue and religion had in holding a republic together.

[I]n free states, where the body of the people have the supreme power properly in their own hands, and must be ultimately resorted to on all great matters, if there be a general corruption of manners, there can be nothing but confusion. So true is this, that civil liberty cannot be long preserved without virtue. A monarchy may subsist for ages, and be better or worse under a good or bad prince, but a republic once equally poised, must either preserve its virtue or lose its liberty.[64]

It was religion, and especially the virtues that flow from true religion, that gave vigor to the Republic.

Let us endeavour to bring into, and keep in credit and reputation, everything that may serve to give vigour to an equal republican constitution. Let us cherish a love of piety, order, industry, frugality. Let us check every disposition to luxury, effeminacy, and the pleasures of a dissipated life. . . . And in our families let us do the best by religious instruction, to sow the seeds which may bear fruit in the next generation. We are one of the body of confederated States. For many reasons I shall avoid making any comparisons at present, but may venture to predict, that whatsoever State among us shall continue to make piety and virtue the standard of public honour, will enjoy the greatest inward peace, the greatest national happiness, and in every outward conflict will discover the greatest constitutional strength.[65]

"Piety, order, industry, frugality": here is a long-hand version of what has been called, ever since Max Weber, the Protestant work ethic.[66] But Witherspoon was not playing a lone hand among the founders when he linked these virtues together. John Adams, who was heir to a long line of Puritans and continued to adhere to the Protestant social ethic despite his own move toward Unitarianism, proposed the following thought experiment:

Suppose a nation in some distant region should take the Bible for their only law-book, and every member should regulate his conduct by the precepts there exhibited! Every member would be obliged, in conscience, to temperance and frugality and industry; to justice and kindness and charity toward his fellow men; and to piety, love, and reverence, towards Almighty God. In this commonwealth, no man would impair his health by gluttony, drunkenness, or lust; no man would sacrifice his most precious time to cards or any other trifling and mean amusement.[67]

Like Adams and so many other founders, Witherspoon's formulation of the relationship between religion and republicanism reduced to this truism: no republic without liberty, no liberty without virtue, and no virtue without religion.

By insisting that religion was a necessary condition for healthy republican government, Witherspoon was swimming in the mainstream of eighteenth-century American political thought. We can again turn to John Adams for support. "Statesmen," he wrote, "may plan and speculate for liberty, but it is religion and morality alone, which can establish the principles upon which freedom can securely stand. The only foundation of a free constitution is pure virtue."[68] George Washington was more explicit still in connecting virtue to religion. In a familiar section of his Farewell Address, Washington said, "Of all the dispositions and habits which lead to political prosperity, Religion and morality are indispensable supports. . . . And let us with caution indulge the supposition, that morality can be maintained without religion."[69] (Historian Fred Hood has even written that an "amazing similarity" of language between Hamilton's draft of the Farewell Address and Witherspoon's "Lectures on Moral Philosophy" makes the influence of the lectures on that address "immediately apparent.")[70] In this regard Witherspoon was typical not only of the political founders, but of American Presbyterians as well. The Presbytery of Hanover, Virginia, acknowledged in 1784 that

> it is absolutely necessary to the existence and welfare of every political combination of men in society, to have the support of religion and its solemn institutions, as affecting the conduct of rational beings more than human laws can possibly do. On this account it is wise policy in legislators to seek its alliance and solicit aid in a civil view, because of its happy influence upon the morality of its citizens.[71]

The Continental Congress itself thought it was appropriate "humbly to approach the throne of Almighty God" to ask "that he would establish the independence of these United States upon the basis of religion and virtue."[72] Still, by insisting that "true religion" meant orthodox Christianity, Witherspoon was nearer the right bank of the mainstream, to push that watery metaphor a bit farther, than American political elites like Adams and Washington. On this particular point Witherspoon was closer to the anti-Federalist Charles Turner, who claimed that "without the prevalence of *Christian piety and morals,* the best republican Constitution can never save us from slavery and ruin."[73]

Religion was not only a necessary support of republican government, for Witherspoon it, or at least its reputation, was more important even than acts of the legislature. The public credit of religion was "more powerful than the most sanguinary laws."[74] Moreover, he thought, "Magistrates . . . are called to use their authority and influence for the glory of God and the good of others."[75] Those public officials who "would have their authority both respected and useful, should begin at the source, and reform or restrain that impiety towards God, which is the true and proper cause of every disorder among men."[76] In fact, so important was religion in Witherspoon's estimation that he could say, "Whoever is an avowed enemy to God, I scruple not to call him an enemy to his country."[77] Such a conclusion shocks the modern ear, but it is logical given the premise with which Witherspoon began, namely that religion is a necessary support of republican government. Even George Washington came to a similar conclusion in his Farewell Address, warning, "In vain would that man claim the tribute of Patriotism, who should labor to subvert these great Pillars of human happiness [religion and morality], these firmest props of the duties of Men and citizens."[78] Little wonder then that Witherspoon was willing to grant civil authorities a hand in promoting piety or preventing impiety.

This was his conclusion in "Jurisprudence," the fourteenth of his "Lectures on Moral Philosophy," in which he took up the thorny issue of church–state interaction. Witherspoon's first preliminary remark on jurisprudence was that "a constitution is excellent, when the spirit of the civil laws is such as to have a tendency to prevent offences and make men good, as much as to punish them when they do evil." This in turn raises the question, "what can be done by law to make the people of any state virtuous?" (Here is one instance in which Witherspoon sounded a clear note from the ancient political theorists, who, as Rousseau reminds us, "spoke incessantly about mores and virtue.")[79] Because "virtue and piety are inseparably connected, then to promote true religion is the best and most effectual way of making a virtuous and regular people," Witherspoon said. "Love to God, and love to man, is the substance of religion; when these prevail, civil laws will have little to do." But this is too easy: It sidesteps "a very important disquisition, how far the magistrate ought to interfere in matters of religion." That disquisition is supremely important because "[r]eligious sentiments are very various—and we have given it as one of the perfect rights in natural liberty, and which ought not to be alienated even in society, that every one should judge for himself in matters of religion."[80] Like the authors of the Westminster Confession before him, and James Madison after him,[81] Witherspoon always argued that the conscience must be left free. The Westminster divines had written that "God alone is Lord of the conscience,"[82] and Witherspoon reproduced that language when he drafted the introduction to the "Form of the Government" of the Presbyterian Church in the United States. The "Form of the Government" (1788) read as follows:

The Synod of New-York and Philadelphia are unanimously of opinion I. That "God alone is Lord of the conscience; and" . . . they consider the rights of private judgement, in all matters that respect religion, as universal and alienable [*sic*]: They do not even wish to see any religious constitution aided by the civil power, further than may be necessary for protection and security, and, at the same time, equal and common to all others.[83]

Witherspoon had no desire to see any particular Christian denomination, even his own, formally established as an official religion because such an establishment would violate dissenter's rights of conscience. He did not take this to mean, however, that the state could play no role whatever in promoting true religion.

Nonestablishment and liberty of conscience still left room for civil magistrates to promote religion and even to "make public provision for the worship of God." There were three "particulars" that civil magistrates were free to do without violating the conscience. The first two included the following:

> (1.) The magistrate (or ruling part of any society) ought to encourage piety by his own example, and by endeavoring to make it an object of public esteem.
> . . . Magistrates may promote and encourage men of piety and virtue, and they may discountenance those whom it would be improper to punish. (2.) The magistrate ought to defend the rights of conscience, and tolerate all in their religious sentiments that are not injurious to their neighbors.

As if to underscore the point, Witherspoon even argued for toleration of a sect (like Catholics) that was thought to hold "tenets subversive of society and inconsistent with the rights of others" because such sects perhaps "are never dangerous, but when they are oppressed."[84] But freedom of conscience did not mean that sects or individuals were free to act any way they pleased: "(3.) The magistrate may enact laws for the punishment of acts of profanity and impiety. The different sentiments of men in religion, ought not by any means to encourage or give a sanction to such acts as any of them count profane." Then, smuggled in between two enumerated points about toleration, came the most accommodationist statement Witherspoon ever made, although even this was rather mild.

> Many are of the opinion, that besides all this, the magistrate ought to make public provision for the worship of God, in such manner as is agreeable to the great body of the society; though at the same time all who dissent from it are fully tolerated. And indeed there seems to be a good deal of reason for it, that so [sic] instruction may be provided for the bulk of common people, who would, many of them, neither support nor employ teachers, unless they were obliged. The magistrate[']s right in this case seems to be something like that of a parent, they have a right to instruct, but not to constrain.[85]

This was a subtle position, neither wholly separationist nor wholly accommodationist. For Witherspoon the relationship between civil government and religious piety was crucial, and the two could be balanced so that the demands of public order and individual conscience could both be satisfied without doing violence to either. His stress on the importance of piety helps explain why Witherspoon objected so vigorously to John Adams's nomination of Thomas Paine for secretary of the congressional Committee on Foreign Affairs in 1777. Witherspoon, a member of the committee, accused Paine, who had mocked original sin and other commonly held Christian doctrines in *Common Sense*, of having "bad character" and questionable patriotism. This was not the mere prejudice of a sanctimonious cleric; Paine had in fact struck out several pro-colonial passages from Witherspoon's political essays when he was editor of the *Pennsylvania Magazine*, claiming they were "too free." And Witherspoon had, despite its anti-Christian passages, defended the political arguments of *Common Sense*, showing that he, for one, knew how to separate his religious from his political opinions.[86] (Besides, by 1805 Adams had come around to Witherspoon's opinion of Paine with a vengeance: "Tom Paine . . . such a mongrel between pig and puppy, begotten by a wild boar on a bitch wolf, never before in any age of the world was suffered by the poltroonery of mankind, to run through such a career of mischief.")[87]

But for all of his recommendations that magistrates "use their authority for the glory of God" and "reform and restrain impiety," Witherspoon was no theocrat. Nor does his talk of making "public provision for the worship of God" prove that he advocated "active state support of Protestant Christianity," as one commentator has claimed,[88] let alone any sort of establishment. To begin with the obvious, Witherspoon did not stipulate "Protestant Christianity," only public worship that was agreeable to the "great body of the people." Presumably, this could have meant Roman Catholicism in Maryland, or other traditions at more local levels such as counties or townships. Furthermore, "public provision for the worship of God" could admit of any number of government actions, all short of promoting Protestantism, sectarian Christianity, or even what are called today "Judeo-Christian" values. After all, Witherspoon himself wrote three recommendations for days of prayer and thanksgiving on behalf of the Continental Congress that were so general that they did not mention Christ at all. This sort of public provision for worship through religious proclamations is a far cry from establishment and was in fact engaged in by Thomas Jefferson and James Madison at the state level and by Madison at the federal level.[89]

Witherspoon, as we have seen, held the axiomatic view of his day that republican government and civil liberty (as he said in the "Thanksgiving Day Sermon") relied on religion for their very existence. But then he turned the proposition back on itself and argued that religion relied on civil liberty as well. The two had in fact been so closely related throughout history that they were nearly inseparable.

> The knowledge of God and his truths have from the beginning of the world been chiefly, if not entirely, confined to those parts of the earth where some degree of liberty and political justice were to be seen. . . . There is not a single instance in history in which civil liberty was lost, and religious liberty preserved entire.[90]

When we examine history, Witherspoon insisted, we find that "knowledge of divine truth . . . has been spread by liberty."[91] The two liberties, in other words, are not so easy to separate in practice as they may be in theory. That is why Witherspoon ended "The Dominion of Providence" with a prayer that "God grant that in America true religion and civil liberty may be inseparable, and that the unjust attempts to destroy the one, may in the issue tend to the support and establishment of both."[92] To Witherspoon, religious and civil liberty were theoretically distinct, but practically indistinguishable. Put slightly differently, civil and religious liberty were to be treated as formally distinct, but informally indistinguishable.

For Witherspoon religion was most powerful as a prepolitical, or more properly, a subpolitical force. Although subpolitical and informal, true religion was more powerful than either the laws or the form of government, or what is the same thing, the constitution. True religion was to act as a sort of leaven, working its healthy influence throughout the political body without benefit of formal establishment, but with equitable aid and protection from the state. Witherspoon's devotion to the American Revolution, in which he was far in advance of the rest of New Jersey's leadership, becomes easier to understand once this close relationship in his mind between civil and religious liberty is noted. To Witherspoon, independence was a sort of "sacred" cause because nothing less than the interest of the gospel was at stake. "If therefore we yield up our temporal property," he argued, "we at the same time deliver the conscience into bondage."[93] And all history seemed to teach that the progress of the gospel and true religion would be slow indeed if the conscience were so bound. On the other hand, in an environment of civil and religious liberty like America's, the gospel could progress relatively unimpeded.

Witherspoon, like other Reformed Americans, saw himself as the inheritor of a sturdy tradition of Protestant resistance to the divine right of kings and civil tyranny that predated Locke and Sydney (two thinkers named by Jefferson as influences on the Declaration of Independence)[94] by a century. True, a limited principle of popular sovereignty can be detected in the early medieval period, and a more radical statement of the doctrine was made by Marsilius of Padua in the late Middle Ages.[95] But of the modern constitutionalists, the English, French, Scottish, and Swiss reformers developed a sophisticated body of literature arguing against the divine right of kings, and more important to Witherspoon, articulating a case for resistance to arbitrary or tyrannical government. The resistance literature that arose during the later stages of the Protestant Reformation built on the work of John Calvin, but went far beyond the limited right of resistance articulated in his *Institutes of the Christian Religion*. Even that archpredestinarian, who generally emphasized the obligation of individual Christians to obey their earthly rulers in the *Institutes*, had to admit, "[N]othing is more desirable than liberty."[96] Calvin accordingly left the door to resistance slightly ajar by recognizing a right of "magistrates of the people, appointed to restrain the willfulness of kings" to disobey oppressive rulers. These magistrates were to be appointed by the people in extraordinary circumstances to restrain the "fierce licentiousness of kings" who "betray the freedom of the people."[97]

Witherspoon appears to have considered the Continental Congress just such a magistracy of the people, appointed to restrain a willful British ministry and Parliament. (Like Calvin, he believed that "[a]ll persons, young and old, love liberty.")[98] Especially to Reformed audiences, he repeatedly emphasized that the Revolution was a popular movement and that the Congress was composed of the legitimate representatives of the people, and he rejected the notion that a small group of political elites engineered the war over the wishes of the people. In the "Thanksgiving Day Sermon" of 1782, Witherspoon reminded the congregation, "[T]he truth is, the American Congress owes its existence and its influence to the people at large. I might easily shew, that there has hardly any great or important step been taken, but the public opinion has gone before the resolutions of that body."[99] The "Pastoral Letter" to the Presbyterian ministers of the Synod of New York and Philadelphia in 1775 emphasized that Congress had been appointed by the people under extraordinary circumstances.

In particular, as the Continental Congress, now sitting at Philadelphia, consist of delegates chosen in the most free and unbiased manner, by the body of the people, let them not only be treated with respect, and encouraged in their difficult service . . . but adhere firmly to their resolutions.[100]

In a personal letter from 1778 Witherspoon related,

Another mistake, into which the ministry and parliament of England fell, was, that this was a deep-laid scheme of a few artful and designing men, who stirred up the multitude for their own ends; that the sentiments in favour of America, were by no means general; but that the artful leaders imposed upon them. . . . Alas! they know nothing of the matter.[101]

Two years later Witherspoon wrote to a friend in Scotland, "There is no instance in the whole contest, in which the public opinion did not go before their [Congress's] resolutions. To go back to the very beginning—the declaration of independence was forced upon the majority of the then Congress, by the people in general."[102] Even a public document like his "Thoughts on American Liberty" (1774) contained an analysis of the Congress that sounded remarkably similar to Calvin's magistracy:

The Congress is, properly speaking, the representative of the great body of the people of North America. Their election is for a particular purpose, and a particular season only. . . . It is an interruption or suspension of the usual forms, and an appeal to the great law of reason, the first principles of the social union, and the multitude collectively, for whose benefit all the particular laws and customs of a constituted state, are supposed to have been originally established.[103]

There is even an oral tradition that Witherspoon urged the adoption of the Calvinistic-sounding phrase "with a firm Reliance on the Protection of divine Providence" toward the end of the Declaration. Although there is no contemporary written record of Witherspoon making such a suggestion, either in the scanty records of the Continental Congress from July 1776 or elsewhere, that tradition has found its way into the musical *1776* and polemical books like *Christianity and the Constitution*.[104] However, the providential language does not appear in Jefferson's so-called Original Rough Draft (which includes the changes made by Jefferson himself and the Committee of Five)[105]; that language was, by Jefferson's own account, suggested by someone else from the floor of the Congress.[106]

Whether that someone was Witherspoon, no one knows. Such a suggestion is consistent with Witherspoon's political theology, and "divine Providence" was his preferred way of referring to God's active superintendence over creation. What matters is that Witherspoon had a clearly defined and not uncharacteristic view of public religion during the founding, which fit nicely with the latter religious references in the Declaration of Independence. Witherspoon was of course more explicit than the Congress had been in the Declaration. To him orthodox Christianity was a necessary condition for successful republican government, and civil and religious liberty were mutually dependent. Religion was not only compatible with liberal principles or with what the founders called a "republican form of government," it was literally indispensable to them. Yet, for all this, Witherspoon was not a theocrat: church and state were to be kept separate to the extent that no particular denomination was to be established by law, and the state could have no power over any ecclesiastical body. However, civil magistrates could encourage religion by their own example or by religious proclamations and could punish profanity and impiety. Although civil liberty and religious liberty could be separated conceptually, in reality the interests of the one were bound to the interests of the other. There was, to use Jefferson's well-worn phrase, a "wall of separation" between church and state, but for Witherspoon that wall was not "high and impregnable," as the Supreme Court has since held,[107] but low and permeable. In short, John Witherspoon subscribed to a sort of political-theological creed in which there could be no civic happiness without holiness, and according to which there was a very definite "public interest of religion."[108]

APPENDIX: FAST DAY PROCLAMATION OF DECEMBER 11, 1776[109]

Whereas, the war in which the United States are engaged with Great Britain, has not only been prolonged, but is likely to be carried to the greatest extremity; and whereas, it becomes all public bodies, as well as private persons, to reverence the Providence of God, and look up to him as the supreme disposer of all events, and the arbiter of the fate of nations; therefore,

Resolved, That it be recommended to all the United States, as soon as possible, to appoint a day of solemn fasting and humiliation; to implore of Almighty God the forgiveness of the many sins prevailing among all ranks, and to beg the countenance and assistance of his Providence in the prosecution of the present just and necessary war.

The Congress do also, in the most earnest manner, recommend to all the members of the United States, and particularly the officers civil and military under them, the exercise of repentance and reformation; and further, require of them the strict observation of the articles of war, and particularly, that part of the said articles, which forbids profane swearing, and all immorality, of which all such officers are desired to take notice.

It is left to each State to issue out proclamations fixing the days that appear most proper within their several bounds.

Thanksgiving Day Proclamation of October 26, 1781[110]

Whereas, it hath pleased Almighty God, the father of mercies, remarkably to assist and support the United States of America in their important struggle for liberty, against the long continued efforts of a powerful nation: it is the duty of all ranks to observe and thankfully acknowledge the interpositions of his Providence in their behalf. Through the whole of the contest, from its first rise to this time, the influence of Divine Providence may be clearly perceived in many signal instances, of which we mention but a few.

In revealing the councils of our enemies, when the discoveries were seasonable and important, and the means seemingly inadequate or fortuitous; in preserving and even improving the union of the several States, on the breach of which our enemies placed their greatest dependence; in increasing the number and adding to the zeal and attachment of the friends of Liberty; in granting remarkable deliverances, and blessing us with the most signal success, when affairs seemed to have the most discouraging appearance; in raising up for us a powerful and generous ally, in one of the first of the European powers; in confounding the councils of our enemies, and suffering them to pursue such measures as have most directly contributed to frustrate their own desires and expectations; above all, in making their extreme cruelty to the inhabitants of these States, when in their power, and their savage devastation of property, the very means of cementing our union, and adding vigor to every effort in opposition to them.

And as we cannot help leading the good people of these States to a retrospect on the events which have taken place since the beginning of the war, so we recommend in a particular manner to their observation, the goodness of God in the year now drawing to a conclusion; in which the Confederation of the United States has been completed, in which there have been so many instances of prowess and success in our armies; particularly in the Southern States, where, notwithstanding the difficulties with which they had to struggle, they have recovered the whole country which the enemy had overrun, leaving them only a post or two on or near the sea; in which we have been so powerfully and effectually assisted by our allies, while in all the conjunct operations the most perfect harmony has subsisted in the allied army; in which there has been so plentiful a harvest, and so great abundance of the fruits of the earth of every kind, as not only enables us easily to supply the wants of the army, but gives comfort and happiness to the whole people; and in which, after the success of our allies by sea, a General of the first Rank, with his whole army, has been captured by the allied forces under the direction of our Commander in Chief.

It is therefore recommended to the several states to set apart the thirteenth day of December next, to be religiously observed as a Day of Thanksgiving and Prayer; that all the people may assemble on that day, with grateful hearts, to celebrate the praise of our gracious Benefactor; to confess our manifold sins; to offer up our most fervent supplications to the God of all grace, that it may please Him to pardon our offences, and incline our hearts for the future to keep all his laws; to comfort and relieve all our brethren who are in distress or captivity; to prosper all husbandmen, and give success to all engaged in lawful commerce; to impart wisdom and integrity to our counsellors, judgment and fortitude to our officers and soldiers; to protect and prosper our illustrious ally, and favor our united exertions for the speedy establishment of a safe, honorable and lasting peace; and bless all seminaries of learning; and cause the knowledge of God to cover the earth, as the water covers the seas.

Thanksgiving Day Proclamation of October 11, 1782[111]

It being the indispensable duty of all nations, not only to offer up their supplications to Almighty God, the giver of all good, for his gracious assistance in a time of distress, but also in a solemn and public manner to give him praise for his goodness in general, and especially for great and signal interpositions of his Providence in their behalf; therefore the United States in Congress assembled, taking into their consideration the many instances of divine goodness to these States, in the course of the important conflict in which they have been so long engaged; the present happy and promising state of public affairs; and the events of the war in the course of the year now drawing to a close, particularly the harmony of the public councils, which is so necessary to the success of the public cause; the perfect union and good understanding which has hitherto subsisted between them and their allies, notwithstanding the artful and unwearied attempts of the common enemy to divide them; the success of the armies of the United States and those of their allies, and the acknowledgment of their independence by another European power, whose friendship and commerce must be of great and lasting advantage to these States; do hereby recommend it to the inhabitants of these States in general, to observe, and request the several States to interpose their authority in appointing and commanding the observation of Thursday, the twenty-eighth day of November next, as a day of solemn thanksgiving to

God for all his mercies; and they do further recommend to all ranks and testify their gratitude of God for his goodness, by a cheerful obedience to his laws, and by protecting, each in his station, and by his influence, the practice of true and undefiled religion, which is the great foundation of public prosperity and national happiness.

NOTES

1. John Witherspoon, Congressional Thanksgiving Day Proclamation, October 11, 1782, in *The Journals of the Continental Congress, 1774–1789*, ed. Worthington C. Ford et al. (Washington, DC: U.S. Government Printing Office, 1904–37), 23:647.

2. Alexis de Tocqueville, *Democracy in America*, trans. George Lawrence, ed. J. P. Mayer (New York: Harper & Row, 1988), 45.

3. Edward Gibbon, *The History of the Decline and Fall of the Roman Empire*, 3 vols. (New York: Modern Library, n.d. [1776–88]), ch. 3, 1:52–53.

4. Gibbon, *Decline and Fall*, 1:53n.

5. An example of a fighting parson of the Black Regiment was Rev. John Peter Gabriel Muhlenberg, who eventually rose to the rank of major general in the Continental army. See Edward Frank Humphrey, *Nationalism and Religion in America, 1774–1789* (New York: Russell & Russell, 1965), 114–15; and James H. Hutson, *Religion and the Founding of the American Republic* (Washington, DC: Library of Congress, 1998), 44–45.

6. John Adams, diary entry of August 27, 1774, in *The Diary and Autobiography of John Adams*, ed. Lyman H. Butterfield, 4 vols. (Cambridge, MA: Harvard University Press, 1961), 2:112.

7. Hutson, *Religion and the Founding of the American Republic*, 47. The best biography of Witherspoon remains Varnum Lansing Collins's *President Witherspoon: A Biography*, 2 vols. (Princeton, NJ: Princeton University Press, 1925; repr., New York: Arno Press, 1969).

8. Ralph Ketcham, "James Madison's Religion," in *James Madison on Religious Liberty*, ed. Robert S. Alley (Buffalo, NY: Prometheus Books, 1985), 179.

9. See, generally, *The Works of John Witherspoon*, 9 vols. (Edinburgh: Ogle & Aikman et al., 1804–5) [hereinafter *Works*].

10. Witherspoon earned an M.A. and studied divinity at Edinburgh, and was awarded an honorary doctorate in divinity from St. Andrews and an honorary doctor of laws from Yale College. (St. Andrews and Yale conferred honorary degrees on another American patriot, Benjamin Franklin.)

11. See, generally, L. H. Butterfield, ed., *John Witherspoon Comes to America: A Documentary Account Based Largely on New Materials* (Princeton, NJ: Princeton University Library, 1953); Collins, *President Witherspoon*, 1:98; and Iain H. Murray, *Revival and Revivalism* (Edinburgh: Banner of Truth Trust, 1994), 41–42.

12. For stylistic reasons, the term "Continental Congress" will be used to designate the Congress from 1781–1782, even though the second Continental Congress technically became the Confederation Congress after the adoption of the Articles of Confederation in 1781.

13. On or about the first of July 1776, Witherspoon apparently argued down the conservative party in Congress led by John Dickinson of Pennsylvania, who claimed that the colonies were not yet ripe for independence. Witherspoon shot back that in his judgment they were not only ripe, but "in danger of becoming rotten for the want of it." See Ashbel Green, *The Life of the Revd. John Witherspoon*, ed. Henry Lyttleton Savage (Princeton, NJ: Princeton University Press, 1973), 159–60.

14. Witherspoon signed the Form of Ratification of the Constitution on behalf of Somerset County, New Jersey, on December 18, 1787.

15. The Organic Laws of the United States, as they appear in the first volume of the United States Code are the Declaration of Independence (1776), the Articles of Confederation (1777), the Northwest Ordinance (1787), and the Constitution (1787). See "The Organic Laws of the United States of America," in *United States Code: Containing the General and Permanent Laws of the United States, in Force on January 4, 1994*, 35 vols. (Washington, DC: U.S. Government Printing Office, 1995), 1:xxxix–lxix.

16. "After graduating from the College of New Jersey in 1771, Madison spent an extra year at Princeton studying Hebrew under President John Witherspoon, a commitment that suggests he was contemplating the ministry." John Murrin, "Religion and Politics in America from the First Settlements to the Civil War," in *Religion and American Politics: From the Colonial Period to the 1980s*, ed. Mark A. Noll (New York: Oxford University Press, 1990), 41–42n.

17. See generally, James McLachlan et al., eds., *Princetonians: A Biographical Dictionary*, 5 vols. (Princeton, NJ: Princeton University Press, 1976–91). Past scholarship has always undercounted the number of Witherspoon's graduates in public affairs.

18. Garry Wills, *Explaining America: The Federalist* (Garden City, NY: Doubleday, 1981), 18.

19. See Collins, *President Witherspoon*, 1:139; and Humphrey, *Nationalism and Religion in America, 1774–1789*, 446–47.

20. Collins, *President Witherspoon*, 1:138, 155. Yale conferred the honorary doctor of laws on Witherspoon in 1785 just as Princeton had on Stiles the prior year. See Collins, *President Witherspoon*, 2:145.

21. See Roger Finke and Rodney Stark, *The Churching of America, 1776–1990: Winners and Losers in Our Religious Economy* (New Brunswick, NJ: Rutgers University Press, 1992), 25, noting that Presbyterians had 588 congregations in 1776. See also Edwin Scott Gaustad and Philip L. Barlow, *New Historical Atlas of Religion in America* (New York: Oxford University Press, 2001), 38; and James H. Smylie, "Introduction," *Journal of Presbyterian History* 52 (1974): 304.

22. Fred J. Hood, *Reformed America: The Middle and Southern States, 1783–1837* (Tuscaloosa: University of Alabama Press, 1980), 2.

23. Witherspoon was "the most influential spokesman for colonial Presbyterianism" and "the premier of American Presbyterianism." See Ned C. Landsman, "Presbyterians and Provincial Society: The Evangelical Enlightenment in the West of Scotland, 1740–1775," *Eighteenth-Century Life* 15 (1991): 205; and Humphrey, *Nationalism and Religion in America*, 441.

24. For the text and commentaries on the sermon, see William Safire, ed., *Lend Me Your Ears: Great Speeches in History* (New York: W. W. Norton & Co., 1992), 425–30 (abridged); Ellis Sandoz, ed., *Political Sermons of the American Founding Era*,

1730–1805 (Indianapolis, IN: Liberty Press, 1991), 529–58; John Witherspoon, *The Selected Writings of John Witherspoon*, ed. Thomas Miller (Carbondale: Southern Illinois University Press, 1990), 126–47 [hereinafter *Selected Writings*]; and Witherspoon, *Works*, 5:176–236.

25. Witherspoon, "The Dominion of Providence Over the Passions of Men," in *Works*, 5:176 [emphasis in original]. Witherspoon had an honorary degree conferred on Hancock at the Princeton commencement of 1769.

26. On Puritan sermons in the "plain style," see Daniel J. Boorstin, *The Americans: The Colonial Experience* (New York: Random House, 1958), 11.

27. *Journals of the Continental Congress,* 6:1022.

28. Hutson, *Religion and the Founding of the American Republic,* 53.

29. Fast Day Proclamation of December 11, 1776, in *Journals of the Continental Congress*, 6:1022.

30. Thanksgiving Day Proclamation of October 26, 1781, in *Journals of the Continental Congress*, 21:1076.

31. Aitken (1734–1802), an elder in the Presbyterian church, had published Witherspoon's "Dominion of Providence" in the spring of 1776.

32. *Journals of the Continental Congress,* 19:118. A copy of the draft of the resolution in Witherspoon's handwriting is part of the Witherspoon Collection, Manuscripts Division, Department of Rare Books & Special Collections, Princeton University Library.

33. Hutson, *Religion and the Founding of the American Republic,* 57.

34. Fast Day Proclamation of March 19, 1782, in *Journals of the Continental Congress*, 22:138. (This proclamation was not written by Witherspoon.)

35. In *Works*, 5:237–70. This sermon was preached in late 1782, not on April 19, 1783 as V. L. Collins and the editor of Witherspoon's *Works* thought. Internal and external evidence points to November 28, 1782, declared by Congress a day of fasting and thanksgiving in a proclamation written by Witherspoon himself, as the date of delivery. For a fuller discussion, see my "John Witherspoon and 'The Public Interest of Religion,'" *Journal of Church and State* 41 (Summer 1999): 557–58n.

36. Thanksgiving Day Proclamation of October 11, 1782, in *Journals of the Continental Congress*, 23:647.

37. Witherspoon, "Sermon Delivered at a Public Thanksgiving After Peace," in *Works*, 5:237, 265.

38. Ashbel Green records that Witherspoon would never "consent, as some other clerical members of Congress did, to change, in any particular, the dress which distinguished his order." See Green, *Life of the Revd. John Witherspoon*, 161.

39. Article I, section 18 of the proposed Georgia constitution of 1789, in William F. Swindler, ed., *Sources and Documents of United States Constitutions*, 10 vols. (Dobbs Ferry, NY: Oceana Publications, 1973–79), 2:453.

40. Witherspoon, "On the Georgia Constitution" (1789), in *Works*, 9:223.

41. Abraham Lincoln, "Address before the Young Men's Lyceum of Springfield, Illinois," January 27, 1838, in *The Collected Works of Abraham Lincoln*, ed. Roy P. Basler, 9 vols. (New Brunswick, NJ: Rutgers University Press, 1953–55), 1:112.

42. "The cause [independence] is sacred, and the champions for it ought to be holy." See "Dominion of Providence," in *Selected Writings*, 146.

43. See, for example, "The Nature and Extent of Visible Religion," in *Works*, 2:323–51.

44. "[B]e not wanting in your endeavours and prayers for the *public interest of religion*, and the prosperity of the Redeemer's kingdom. Support, by your conduct and conversation, the *public credit of religion*. What is more powerful over the minds of men and the manners of the age, than public opinion? It is more powerful than the most sanguinary laws." Witherspoon, "On the Religious Education of Children" (1789), in *Works*, 4:144 [emphasis added]. Witherspoon had been sounding this theme before he ever went to America. See, for example, his "Prayer for National Prosperity" (1758) in *Works*, 5:57–89, and "Seasonable Advice to Young Persons" (1762), in *Works*, 5:123, which recommended a concern for "the public interest of religion."

45. Gibbon, *Decline and Fall*, 1:639.

46. In addition to his congressional Thanksgiving Day Proclamation from October 1782, Witherspoon also used the phrase "true and undefiled religion" in a sermon titled "Christian Magnanimity" and in "The Dominion of Providence." See "Sermon XXIV: Christian Magnanimity" (1775), in *Works*, 5:273 ("as magnanimity is an amiable and noble quality, one of the greatest ornaments of our nature, so I affirm that it belongs only to true and undefiled religion, and that every appearance of the one, without the other, is not only defective but false"); and "The Dominion of Providence over the Passions of Men" (1776) in *Selected Writings*, 144 ("he is the best friend to American liberty who is most sincere and active in promoting true and undefiled religion, and who sets himself with the greatest firmness to bear down profanity and immorality of every kind").

47. Witherspoon, "Dominion of Providence," in *Selected Writings*, 137.

48. Witherspoon, "Dominion of Providence," in *Selected Writings*, 147.

49. In Matthew L. Davis, ed., *Memoirs of Aaron Burr*, 2 vols. (New York: Harper & Bros., 1836), 1:28.

50. See Ebenezer Bradford to Joseph Bellamy, April 18, 1772, in Mark A. Noll, *Princeton and the Republic, 1768–1822* (Princeton, NJ: Princeton University Press, 1989), 44.

51. Joseph Bellamy, "True Religion Delineated" (1750), in *The Works of Joseph Bellamy*, 2 vols. (Boston: Doctrinal Tract and Book Society, 1853; repr. New York: Garland Publishing, 1987), 1:135.

52. Witherspoon, "Lecture IV," in *An Annotated Edition of Lectures on Moral Philosophy by John Witherspoon*, ed. Jack Scott (Newark: University of Delaware Press, 1982), 87 [hereinafter *Lectures on Moral Philosophy*].

53. On Whitefield, see Iain H. Murray, *Revival and Revivalism* (Carlisle, PA: Banner of Truth Trust, 1994), 41; on the Jansenists, see Witherspoon, "Lectures on Divinity II," in *Works*, 8:25.

54. Witherspoon, "Lecture XIV: Jurisprudence," in *Lectures on Moral Philosophy*, 160.

55. Witherspoon, "Dominion of Providence," in *Selected Writings*, 144.

56. Witherspoon, "Seasonable Advice to Young Persons" (1762), in *Works*, 5:116.

57. Benjamin Franklin, "Autobiography II," in *Benjamin Franklin's Autobiographical Writings*, ed. Carl Van Doren (New York: Viking Press, 1945), 624–25.

58. Witherspoon, "Dominion of Providence," in *Selected Writings*, 137.

59. Witherspoon, "Lectures on Divinity I," in *Works*, 8:12.

60. "Enlightenment" is a notoriously slippery word, and I am using it here in a nontechnical way.

61. Witherspoon, "Dominion of Providence," in *Selected Writings*, 144 [emphasis added].

62. Witherspoon, "Dominion of Providence," in *Selected Writings*, 144.

63. Witherspoon, "Dialogue on Civil Liberty; delivered at a Public Exhibition in Nassau-Hall, January 1776," in *Pennsylvania Magazine* (April 1776), 165.

64. Witherspoon, "Sermon Delivered at a Public Thanksgiving," in *Works*, 5:266.

65. Witherspoon, "Sermon Delivered at a Public Thanksgiving," in *Works*, 5:269–70.

66. See generally, Max Weber, *The Protestant Ethic and the Spirit of Capitalism*, trans. Talcott Parsons (London: HarperCollins, 1991 [1930]).

67. John Adams, diary entry of February 22, 1756, in *The Selected Writings of John and John Quincy Adams*, ed. Adrienne Koch and William Peden (New York: Alfred A. Knopf, 1946), 5.

68. John Adams to Zabdiel Adams, June 21, 1776, in *The Works of John Adams*, ed. Charles Francis Adams, 10 vols. (Boston: Little, Brown, and Co., 1850–56), 9:401.

69. Washington, Farewell Address, September 19, 1796, in *The Writings of George Washington*, ed. John C. Fitzpatrick, 37 vols. (Washington, DC: U.S. Government Printing Office, 1931–40), 35:229.

70. See Hood, *Reformed America*, 10, 17. Hood provides no documentary support for this assertion.

71. In William Henry Foote, ed., *Sketches of Virginia: Historical and Biographical* (Philadelphia: William S. Martien, 1850; repr. Richmond: John Knox Press, 1966), 337.

72. Witherspoon, Thanksgiving Day Proclamation of October 20, 1779, in *Journals of the Continental Congress*, 15:1191–92.

73. In Herbert J. Storing, ed., *The Complete Anti-Federalist*, 7 vols. (Chicago: University of Chicago Press, 1981), 1:23 [emphasis in original].

74. Witherspoon, "On the Religious Education of Children," in *Works*, 4:144.

75. Witherspoon, "Dominion of Providence," in *Selected Writings*, 145.

76. Witherspoon, "Sermon Delivered at a Public Thanksgiving," in *Works*, 5:269.

77. Witherspoon, "Dominion of Providence," in *Selected Writings*, 144.

78. George Washington, Farewell Address, in *Writings of George Washington*, 35:229.

79. Jean-Jacques Rousseau, "Discourse on the Sciences and the Arts [First Discourse]," in *Basic Political Writings*, trans. and ed. Donald A. Cress (Indianapolis, IN: Hackett Publishing Co., 1987), 12.

80. Witherspoon, "Lecture XIV: Jurisprudence," in *Lectures on Moral Philosophy*, 159–60.

81. In his famous "Memorial and Remonstrance" of 1785, Madison wrote that the "Religion then of every man must be left to the conviction and conscience of every man; and it is the right of every man to exercise it as these may dictate." See Madison, "Memorial and Remonstrance against Religious Establishments," article 1, in *James Madison: Writings*, ed. Jack N. Rakove (New York: Library of America, 1999), 30.

82. The Westminster Confession of Faith (1647), chap. XX, art. II, in Philip Schaff, ed., *The Creeds of Christendom*, 3 vols. (Grand Rapids, MI: Baker Book House, 1990), 3:644.

83. "Introduction, The Form of the Government and Discipline of the Presbyterian Church in the United States of America," *op. cit.*, cxxxiii–cxxxiv. The Constitution of the Presbyterian Church was drafted in 1787 and ratified in 1788. (The description of liberty of conscience as an "alienable" right is probably a typographical error; the context dictates that it read "inalienable.")

84. Witherspoon, "Lecture XIV: Jurisprudence," in *Lectures on Moral Philosophy*, 160.

85. Witherspoon, "Lecture XIV: Jurisprudence," in *Lectures on Moral Philosophy*, 161.

86. See Collins, *President Witherspoon*, 2:25.

87. In Paul Johnson, *A History of the American People* (New York: Harper Collins, 1997), 210.

88. "In fact, Witherspoon believed that a policy of toleration could have adverse effects if not offset by active state support of Protestant Christianity." Hood, *Reformed America*, 18.

89. For example, Virginia governor Thomas Jefferson issued a "Proclamation Appointing a Day of Thanksgiving and Prayer" on November 11, 1779, which appointed a day of "publick and solemn thanksgiving and prayer to Almighty God." See *The Papers of Thomas Jefferson*, ed. Julian P. Boyd et al., 30 vols. to date (Princeton, NJ: Princeton University Press, 1950–), 3:177–79. On October 31, 1785, James Madison introduced "A Bill for Appointing Days of Public Fasting and Thanksgiving" in the Virginia general assembly that authorized religious proclamations and required ministers to "attend and perform divine service and preach a sermon" on days of public fasting and thanksgiving "on pain of forfeiting fifty pounds for every failure." The bill was endorsed by Jefferson. See *Papers of Thomas Jefferson*, 2:556. Years later as president, Madison issued religious proclamations that were criticized, according to his own account in the "Detached Memoranda" for "using general terms" and "for not inserting particulars according with the faith of certain Xn sects." See Madison, "Detached Memoranda" (ca. 1819?), in "Madison's 'Detatched [*sic*] Memoranda,'" ed. Elizabeth Fleet, *William and Mary Quarterly*, 3d. ser., 3 (1946): 560–61.

90. Witherspoon, "Dominion of Providence," in *Selected Writings*, 140–41.

91. Witherspoon, "Dialogue on Civil Liberty," in *Selected Writings*, 165.

92. Witherspoon, "Dominion of Providence," in *Selected Writings*, 147.

93. Witherspoon, "Dominion of Providence," in *Selected Writings*, 141.

94. "All its [the Declaration's] authority rests then on the harmonizing sentiments of the day, whether expressed in conversation, in letters, printed essays, or in the elementary books of public right, as Aristotle, Cicero, Locke, Sidney, &c." Thomas Jefferson to Henry Lee, May 8, 1825, in *Thomas Jefferson: Writings*, ed. Merrill D. Peterson (New York: Library of America, 1984), 1501.

95. See Julian H. Franklin, ed., "Introduction," in *Constitutionalism and Resistance in the Sixteenth Century: Three Treatises by Hotman, Beza, and Mornay* (New York: Pegasus, 1969), 11–12.

96. See John Calvin, "Commentary on Genesis 39:2," in *Institutes of the Christian Religion*, trans. Ford Lewis Battles, ed. John T. McNeill, 2 vols. (Philadelphia: Westminster Press, 1960), 2:1494n.

97. *Institutes*, bk. IV, ch. XX, 2:1519.

98. Witherspoon, "Letters on Education" (1775), in *Works*, 8:170.

99. Witherspoon, "Sermon Delivered at a Public Thanksgiving" (1782), in *Works*, 5:254–55.

100. Witherspoon, "Pastoral Letter" (1775), in *Works* 5:171–73.

101. "On the Contest Between Great Britain and America," Witherspoon to unnamed correspondent, September 3, 1778, in *Works*, 9:169–70.

102. "On the Affairs of the United States," Witherspoon to unnamed Scottish correspondent, March 20, 1780, in *Works*, 9:174–75.

103. Witherspoon, "Thoughts on American Liberty" (1774), in *Works*, 9:73–74.

104. "Some believe the phrase 'with a firm Reliance on the protection of Divine Providence' in the final sentence [of the Declaration] was his [Witherspoon's] contribution." John Eidsmoe, *Christianity and the Constitution: The Faith of Our Founding Fathers* (Grand Rapids, MI: Baker Book House, 1987), 86.

105. *Papers of Thomas Jefferson*, 1:427.

106. See the version of the Declaration in Jefferson's "Notes of Proceedings in the Continental Congress," in *Papers of Thomas Jefferson*, 1:315, 319. At 319 Jefferson represents the "Original Rough Draft" and the congressional additions in parallel columns.

107. *Everson v. Board of Education*, 330 U.S. 1, 18 (1947). For the Court's use of Jefferson's metaphor, see Daniel L. Dreisbach, *Thomas Jefferson and the Wall of Separation between Church and State* (New York: New York University Press, 2002).

108. James Hutson says that the conviction that "holiness was prerequisite for secular happiness" was a legacy of the Confederation as a whole from 1774 to 1789, which perhaps not coincidentally were the exact years of Witherspoon's political career. See Hutson, *Religion and the Founding of the American Republic*, 58.

109. *Journals of the Continental Congress*, 6:1022.

110. *Journals of the Continental Congress*, 21:1074–1076.

111. *Journals of the Continental Congress*, 23:647.

6

Benjamin Franklin and the Role of Religion in Governing Democracy

Howard L. Lubert

In 1773, Benjamin Franklin wrote a letter to the French physician and botanist Jacques Barbeu-Dubourg, acknowledging Dubourg's "observations on the causes of death, and the experiments which you propose for recalling to life those who appear to be killed by lightning." To Franklin, Dubourg's experiments demonstrated "sagacity" and "humanity" and resembled experiments that years earlier Franklin had conducted in an effort to cure paralysis. He recalled that once, while living in London, he and a friend had discovered three drowned flies in a newly opened bottle of Virginia wine. Franklin had heard stories about drowned flies "being revived by the rays of the sun" and, true to his nature, he proposed an experiment. The flies were placed on a sieve and exposed to the sun. In less than three hours, two of the flies began to show signs of life. "At length," he wrote, they recovered and "began to fly, finding themselves in Old England, without knowing how they came thither."[1] Already nearly seventy years old, Franklin concluded the letter with his "wish" that

> it were possible, from this instance, to invent a method of embalming drowned persons, in such a manner that they may be recalled to life at any period, however distant; for having a very ardent desire to see and observe the state of America a hundred years hence, I should prefer to any ordinary death the being immersed in a cask of Madeira wine, with a few friends, till that time, to be then recalled to life by the solar warmth of my dear country! But since in all probability we live in an age too early and too near the infancy of science, to hope to see such an art brought in our time to its perfection, I must for the present content

myself with the treat, which you are so kind as to promise me, of the resurrection of a fowl or a turkey cock.[2]

The letter is quintessential Franklin: jovial, inquisitive, ingenious. It also tells us something about how he viewed the world. In this letter we discern his faith in science and scientific progress; we sense the optimism that defined his character; and we glimpse the central role that friendship and sociability played in his life.

We might well wonder where God has gone, too, for in Franklin's vision of the future, physical laws no longer bind: Man has seemingly mastered nature. He is a time traveler whose explorations extend beyond the spatial to the temporal. He evades death and perhaps divine judgment itself. In short, Franklin's suggestion that man wields his destiny—a central component of Franklin's political and philosophic thought—inevitably raises questions about the role, if any, he perceived for religion in political life.

Franklin's intellectual prowess was turned decidedly toward the practical. He had little patience for what he called "metaphysics" and dismissed most theological assertions as hopelessly speculative. That skepticism led him to embrace the principle of religious liberty. He also associated religious dogmatism with self-love and believed that ambitious and avaricious religious leaders were often the cause of religious intolerance. He was especially critical of religious leaders for habituating their parishioners to be disputatious, a habit he found to be at odds with private and public felicity. For Franklin, the personal friendships and sense of common purpose that he deemed essential to republican government were less likely to take root among a disputatious populace.

Franklin also believed that religious dogmatism fostered public cynicism by placing religious leaders and sects in situations that forced them to stake out positions that conflicted (or seemed to conflict) with their theological beliefs or the public good. Such cynicism could have broad civic consequences, for if citizens grew too distrustful, they would come to assume that all public leaders were hypocrites and that claims made on behalf of the public good were masquerades for private interests.

Still, Franklin believed that religion could play a vital role in shaping and preserving the modern republic because he believed religion to be uniquely capable of educating a citizenry for democracy. Religion could reaffirm faith in the public good and habituate citizens to identify their private happiness with publicly spirited acts. Similarly, religious faith could help temper the selfish passions of community leaders. In order for religion to play these beneficial roles, however, it had to be recast. Franklin found sectarian religion dogmatic and divisive. In its stead, Franklin sought to propagate core religious principles on which most religious faiths were based. Moreover, he sought to redirect the teachings of sectarian religion, which he believed fostered excessively introverted citizens focused inordinately on traditional forms of piety, by promulgating the belief that public service was the highest moral duty owed to God.

A BRIEF SKETCH OF FRANKLIN'S LIFE[3]

Franklin was born in Boston, Massachusetts, on January 17, 1706. He was one of ten children born to Josiah Franklin and his second wife, Abiah Folger. (Josiah had seven children by his first wife.) When Franklin was eight years old, his father sent him to the Boston Grammar School in preparation for life in the church. The school proved expensive, and within a year Franklin was sent to George Brownell's school. At age ten he was removed from school altogether and began to apprentice for his father's candle- and soap-making business. Franklin chafed at this work and, at age twelve, signed apprenticeship papers with his half-brother James, a printer who in 1721 would begin publishing the *New England Courant*.

Newspaper work was more to Franklin's liking. Although he did not have much formal schooling, he learned to read at an early age and was a voracious reader. As a child he read Bunyan, Plutarch, Defoe, Mather, and others. He improved his writing by reading, briefly outlining and then later rewriting in his own words essays he found in a volume of Addison's *The Spectator*. By the time he turned sixteen he was reading Locke, Xenophon, and Shaftesbury. In 1722 he wrote a series of "letters" to his brother's newspaper, disguising his authorship under the pseudonym "Silence Dogood." The *Courant* ran fourteen letters in all.

In October 1723, after continual disputes with James that seemed to worsen after he revealed his authorship of the Dogood letters, Franklin fled to Philadelphia. Arriving destitute, he quickly obtained work in Samuel Keimer's print shop. There he came to the attention of the colony's governor, William Keith, who promised to back him financially and encouraged him to travel to London to purchase equipment for a print shop of his own. Franklin arrived in London in 1724 only to discover that Keith had failed to provide letters of credit. He obtained work at Palmer's, a printing house where he read and set the type for William Wollaston's *The Religion of Nature Delineated* (1725), to which he wrote a refutation entitled *A Dissertation on Liberty and Necessity, Pleasure and Pain* (1725), one of his few theological tracts and a publication that he later declared an erratum.

In 1726, Franklin returned to Philadelphia, where he again took up work as a printer in Keimer's shop. By 1730 he owned his own business and was publisher of the *Pennsylvania Gazette*. In 1732 he began writing and publishing *Poor Richard's Almanack*. The *Almanack* was immensely successful, helping to make Franklin rich and spreading his name worldwide. (The introduction to the last *Almanack*, popularly known as "The Way to Wealth," has been reprinted hundreds of times and in numerous languages.) By 1748 Franklin had retired from active work as a printer, turning the daily operations of his business over to David Hall and drawing an annual salary of £1,000.

Retired from business, Franklin turned to his first love, science, and to projects of a more public nature. He already had helped found the first circulating library in America (1731), the first fire company in America (1739), and the American Philosophical Society (1743). He was instrumental in the creation of a city hospital (1751) and the Academy for the Education of Youth (incorporated in 1753, it later became the University of Pennsylvania). He initiated projects for establishing a city police force and for lighting, paving, and cleaning the streets of Philadelphia. His scientific curiosity, combined with his desire to improve the lives of those around him, led Franklin to invent and then refuse a patent for the Franklin stove (1744). His other inventions included bifocals, a flexible metal catheter, an improved clock, an improved design for street lamps, and a musical instrument he called the Armonica.

Well before his "retirement" Franklin was writing pieces on earthquakes and leading discussions on scientific topics in his Junto, a debating club he established in 1727. In 1737 he discovered that northeast storms (so-called northeasters) move toward the southwest. He was instrumental in charting the Gulf Stream, and he was the first to measure how color affected the absorption of heat. His most substantial discoveries involved electricity. Franklin demonstrated that lightning was electrical. Even more revolutionary were his theoretical observations about the properties of electricity. Franklin was the first person to offer a unified theory of electrical action. His "one-fluid theory" was a rejection of medieval mysticism, paved the way for future research, and was, in the estimation of one modern physicist, a precursor to the electron theory. His experiments and theoretical observations on electricity won him international fame and recognition, including the Copley Medal of the Royal Society of London (1753).[4]

Franklin's scientific pursuits were interrupted by public demands for his service and by a series of political crises. He was a member of the Pennsylvania Assembly (1751–1764) and in 1754 represented Pennsylvania at the Albany Congress, where he authored a plan of union designed to unite the colonies against the French and Indians. In 1757 the Pennsylvania Assembly sent him to England as its representative in an ongoing dispute with the colony's proprietors. He went back to Philadelphia in 1762, only to return shortly thereafter to London, where he would remain until 1775. During this latter stay Franklin's reputation soared as he defended the colonies against claims of parliamentary sovereignty, writing scores of letters to London newspapers under a variety of pseudonyms, defending the colonies before the House of Commons (copies of Franklin's famous "examination" in February 1766 were quickly published and widely read), and serving as agent to Parliament for the colonies of Pennsylvania, New Jersey, Georgia, and Massachusetts.

Franklin returned to Philadelphia in May 1775 and was immediately chosen a delegate to the second Continental Congress, where he wrote a plan of union, organized the post office (Franklin was the first postmaster general of the United States), served on a commission to Canada, and was one of the representatives sent to listen to Lord Howe's last-minute proposal for peace. He was one of five members on the committee appointed to write the Declaration of Independence and was made part of the diplomatic mission sent to obtain French assistance. His superior diplomatic skills, his unparalleled fame and popularity among the French people, and the vanity and unpleasantness of his fellow diplomats led Congress to confer sole diplomatic power on Franklin. Franklin served as a commissioner in peace negotiations with Great Britain and, upon returning to Philadelphia in September 1785, was chosen president of the executive council of Pennsylvania. In 1787 he was a delegate to the Constitutional Convention. In his last public act, he signed a petition to Congress advocating the abolition of slavery. He died on April 17, 1790.

FRANKLIN'S RELIGIOUS VIEWS

Even during his lifetime, Franklin's religious beliefs were a subject of controversy. John Adams denounced Franklin as an atheist in his diary.[5] Yet, elsewhere Adams admitted, "While [Franklin] had the singular felicity to enjoy the entire esteem and affection of all the philosophers of every denomination, he was not less regarded by all the sects and denominations of Christians."[6] Scholars have not settled the issue. Some scholars argue that Franklin was irreligious.[7] Some find in Franklin's thought a Quaker influence, while numerous others point to a strong Puritan influence.[8] Some scholars reject the Puritan hypothesis, but maintain that Franklin was a Christian.[9] To others, Franklin was a deist.[10] Alfred Owen Aldridge has argued that Franklin embraced polytheism.[11] And recently, Kerry Walters has argued that Franklin adopted a principle of "theistic perspectivism."[12]

The differing scholarly assessments reflect Franklin's shifting theological commitments, his reluctance to criticize any particular religious sect, his reticence to discuss his own religious convictions, and the ambiguity that characterizes much of his religious commentary. Franklin's religious thought underwent profound change during his life. "My Parents had early given me religious Impressions, and brought me through my Childhood piously in the Dissenting Way," Franklin writes in the *Autobiography*. "But I was scarce 15 when, after doubting by turns of several Points as I found them disputed in the different Books I read, I began to doubt of Revelation itself."[13] By his mid-teens Franklin had rejected the theology of his Reformed Protestant ancestors. "I had been religiously educated as a Presbyterian," Franklin explains, but "some of the Dogmas of that Persuasion, such as the Eternal Decrees of God, Election, Reprobation, etc. appear'd to me unintelligible, others doubtful, and I early absented myself from the Public Assemblies of the Sect, Sunday being my Studying-Day."[14] By rejecting these core doctrines of Puritan theology—providence, election, and original sin—Franklin in effect renounced Puritanism.

Furthermore, the general orientation of Franklin's thought was at odds with Puritanism. For example, like Cotton Mather, Franklin preached good works; unlike Franklin, however, Mather insisted that "no *good works* can be done by any man until he be *justified*."[15] By linking good works to justification, Mather articulated the Puritan concept of the "double calling." For Puritans, one's "outward calling" in good works was necessarily a product of one's "inward calling," or one's calling unto Christ. Doing good to man presupposed that one's heart had first been infused by grace and that one's actions were motivated by a desire to glorify God. Franklin, however, emphasized the works themselves.[16] In fact, he wrote, "it would not be quite absurd if a Man were to thank God for his Vanity" because vanity "is often productive of Good to the Possessor and to others that are within his Sphere of Action."[17] Any Puritan worth his salt would reject Franklin's remark as apostasy. Conversion of the heart to Christ was possible only after experiencing the profound humiliation that comes with recognizing one's inability to free oneself from sin.[18] Puritans emphasized piety, preached man's depravity, and were often plagued by doubt about the state of their souls. Franklin emphasized morality, rejected original sin, and insisted that "doing Good to Man" is the primary human obligation.[19]

Franklin also questioned Christ's divinity and thus the core Christian belief. His most famous expression of skepticism regarding Christ's divinity came in a letter he wrote to Ezra Stiles in which he confessed that he had "some doubts as to his [Jesus'] Divinity."[20] Elsewhere, Franklin likewise questioned what he saw as the human inclination to ascribe attributes, including divine ones, to beloved religious leaders. Writing in the *Autobiography* about Rev. George Whitefield, Franklin observed that Whitefield might have attracted many more adherents had it not been for his practice of publishing his religious doctrines. Such writings provided an easy target for his enemies. "Unguarded Expressions and even erroneous Opinions delivered in Preaching might have been afterwards explain'd," Franklin wrote, "or qualified by supposing others that might have accompanied them; or they might have been denied; but *litera scripta manet* [the written word remains]."[21] By attacking his writings, Whitefield's critics greatly curtailed his influence. Franklin continues, had Whitefield,

> never written anything … he would have left behind him a much more numerous and important Sect. And his Reputation might in that case have been still growing, even after his Death; as there being nothing of his Writing on which to found a Censure; and give him a lower Character, his Proselytes would be left at Liberty to feign for him as great a Variety of Excellencies, as their enthusiastic Admiration might wish him to have possessed.[22]

Contextually, Franklin's remark applies to Whitefield, but his remark might apply to all historical religious figures. Zealots often embellish the character of their religious leaders. Under the right conditions, in particular, when a religious leader leaves little traceable record, his followers might even create his character out of whole cloth. Their creativity is bounded only by their enthusiasm and presumably might include the elevation of the human to the divine.

There are other, perhaps more valuable, reasons why religious principles are better left unpublished. Franklin notes that religious doctrine put into writing tends over time to assume the appearance of unquestionable truth. According to Franklin, however, claims about the nature of God are inherently speculative. What may be thought true today may prove untrue tomorrow. Accordingly, Franklin applauds the "singular . . . Modesty" of the Dunkers, who resisted publishing their beliefs for

> fear that if we should once print our Confession of Faith, we should feel ourselves as if bound and confin'd by it, and perhaps be unwilling to receive farther Improvement; and our Successors still more so, as conceiving what we their Elders and Founders had done, to be something sacred, never to be departed from.[23]

Committing beliefs to writing transforms them into scripture; but if, as the Dunkers believed, theological knowledge is in a state of constant progression, then no profession of belief can be sacred because this progression has not reached its end. Franklin's point rings clear: Christian scripture itself ought not to be taken as the final, literal word of God.

Although Franklin suggests that men cannot definitively assert the divine nature of Christ and scripture, he does not conclude that Christ's teachings are untrue or without value. Nor does questioning Christ's divinity preclude him from declaring, "As to Jesus of Nazareth . . . I think the System of Morals and his Religion, as he left them to us, the best the World ever saw or is likely to see." Indeed, while Franklin questioned Christ's divinity, he saw "no harm . . . in its being believed, if that Belief has the good Consequence, as probably it has, of making his Doctrines more respected and better observed."[24]

What moral doctrine did Christ preach? Benevolence. Franklin's moral philosophy is based on what he viewed as the core elements of true Christian benevolence: a strong commitment to social action, a sense of moral obligation to assist others and promote the public good, and a view of human nature as fully capable of meeting that moral calling. Franklin roots Christianity in a theology of good works, portraying Christ as a compassionate figure dedicated chiefly to improving the temporal lives of those around him. Regrettably, over time the benevolence or love that Christ preached had "received various corrupting Changes."[25] New doctrines like original sin and preordination promoted introversion, anxiety, and intolerance. They also led to moral relativism and fatalism.

Consider, for example, Franklin's mature assessment of his *Dissertation on Liberty and Necessity, Pleasure and Pain* (1725), his rebuttal to Wollaston's *Religion of Nature Delineated*. Wollaston's book is a fairly standard argument for natural religion, which posits that virtue and vice are based in nature and that a benevolent God who rewards virtue and punishes vice in an afterlife must therefore exist.[26] In the *Dissertation*, Franklin challenged the premise that morality exists in nature. Beginning instead with the premise that God is infinite in his "Wisdom, Goodness and Power," Franklin deduced that "there can be nothing either existing or acting in the Universe against or without his Consent; and what He consents to must be good, because He is good; therefore EVIL doth not exist."[27] Furthermore, if by definition all human conduct aims toward some preordained good, it follows that there is neither merit nor demerit in human conduct; "therefore every Creature must be equally esteem'd by the Creator."[28] Like many of his contemporaries, Franklin pointed to a perceived moral dilemma inherent in predestinarian thought. If all is preordained and if nature or God is inherently good, then the notions of good and evil are mere human constructions, nomenclatures that people use to place values on certain conduct, even though all behavior is equally good in the eyes of God.

Eventually, Franklin determined that assertions about God's nature are hopelessly speculative. People cannot ultimately know what God perceives to be good. Yet, rather than reject the notions of good and evil, Franklin argued that people can make moral distinctions based on the consequences that human conduct has in human affairs. Moral distinctions are meaningful when measured in light of their impact on human felicity. This seems to be the lesson he learned from his youthful, exuberant embrace of deism. In the *Autobiography* he writes that his early advocacy of deism "perverted" some of his friends, who in turn "wrong'd me greatly without the least Compunction." Recalling "[Governor] Keith's Conduct towards me, (who was another Freethinker) and my own towards Vernon and Miss Read which at Times gave me great Trouble," Franklin continues, "I began to suspect that this Doctrine tho' it might be true, was not very useful." The doctrine that "Vice and Virtue were empty Distinctions," Franklin muses,

> appear'd now not so clever a Performance as I once thought it; and I doubted whether some Error had not insinuated itself unperceiv'd into my Argument, so as to infect all that follow'd, as is common in metaphysical Reasonings. I grew convinc'd that *Truth, Sincerity* and *Integrity* in Dealings between Man and Man, were of the utmost Importance to the Felicity of Life, and I form'd written Resolutions, (which still remain in my Journal Book) to practice them ever while I lived. Revelation had indeed no weight with me as such; but I entertain'd an Opinion, that tho' certain Actions might not be bad *because* they were forbidden by it, or good *because* it commanded them; yet probably those Actions might be forbidden *because* they were bad for us, or commanded *because* they were beneficial to us, in their own Natures, all the Circumstances of things considered.[29]

While Franklin never expressly renounced the deistic creed he preached as a young man, he did, however, come to believe that separating moral arguments from traditional theological beliefs would prove socially harmful. And, while he never argued that utility is truth, he did maintain "that utility is, in my opinion the test of value in matters of invention, and that a discovery which can be applied to no use, or is not good for something, is good for nothing."[30]

While Franklin personally emphasized morality and good works, he perceived that piety remained essential to human felicity. He maintained that the only theological truth men could possess was that God existed. Yet, he came to recognize that conceiving of God as a mere First Cause would prove disastrous because most people need to believe in a benevolent God who watches over us and who intervenes in the world for our good. This conception of God is a critical source of meaning and hope in human lives.

Furthermore, this belief is necessary to direct human conduct in beneficial ways. For Franklin, the virtuous life is the well-lived life, but few people pursue it for its own sake. Religion, with its appeals to love, hope, and fear, is the most reliable inducer of virtuous behavior. "You yourself may find it easy to live a virtuous Life without the Assistance afforded by Religion," Franklin admonished an anonymous correspondent,

> But think how great a Proportion of Mankind consists of weak and ignorant Men and Women, and of inexperienc'd and inconsiderate Youth of both Sexes, who have need of the Motives of Religion to restrain them from Vice, to support their Virtue, and retain them in the Practice of it till it becomes *habitual*, which is the great Point for its Security.[31]

Accordingly, Franklin invoked religious language and ritual in order to promote socially beneficial behavior, arguing that the most acceptable form of worship is to do good works and going so far as to suggest that good works, not piety, are the path to salvation. "I think vital religion has always suffered when orthodoxy is more regarded than virtue," Franklin wrote in a letter to his father. "And the Scripture assures me, that at the last Day, we shall not be examin'd [by] what we *thought*, but what we *did*; and our Recommendation will not be that we said *Lord, Lord*, but that we did GOOD to our Fellow Creatures."[32]

This emphasis on good works remained one of the five bedrock articles in Franklin's religious creed. Franklin described that creed in the *Autobiography*. "I never doubted," he wrote, "the Existence of the Deity, that he made the World, and govern'd it by his Providence; that our Souls are immortal; and that all Crime will be punished and Virtue rewarded either here or hereafter."[33] Yet, even in his creed Franklin's religious beliefs remain elusive. One might infer from it that Franklin's deism allowed for a special providence, an interpretation that seems to be illustrated in his essay "On the Providence of God in the Government of the World" (1732) and in his famous speech at the Constitutional Convention, in which he implored fellow delegates to call on the guidance of an intervening God.[34]

At the same time, however, there are compelling reasons to interpret Franklin as a deist who believed only in a general providence. For example, while "On the Providence of God" offers a prima facie argument for a deity that "sometimes interferes by his particular Providence, and sets aside the Events which would otherwise have been produc'd in the Course of Nature, or by the Free Agency of Men," it is one of the few metaphysical pieces Franklin wrote as a young man, works he later rejected.[35] More pointedly, in his "Articles of Belief and Acts of Religion" (1728), Franklin depicted a "Supreme most perfect Being" who is "infinite and incomprehensible" to men, "INFINITELY ABOVE . . . [their] Worship or Praise," and who does not pay "the least regard [to] such an inconsiderable Nothing as Man."[36] In general, one looks in vain among Franklin's voluminous writings for explicit expressions of belief in a god who intervenes in human affairs.

Similarly, Franklin's 1787 speech in which he called upon fellow delegates to pray for divine assistance may merely reflect his long-held belief in the social utility of prayer. For example, in late 1747 (during King George's War) Franklin launched a voluntary association for the defense of the colony and, "Calling in the Aid of Religion," he proposed "the Proclaiming a Fast, to promote Reformation, and implore the Blessings of Heaven on our Undertaking." He then drafted a proclamation "in the accustomed Style." Franklin's motive, however, appears more pragmatic than spiritual. He did not act from a belief that prayer and fasting would elicit an act of special providence. Rather, he perceived an official fast to be an effective way to solicit adequate manpower. Accordingly, Franklin had the proclamation printed in both English and German and disseminated throughout the colony in order to give "the Clergy of the different Sects an Opportunity of Influencing their Congregations to join in the Association."[37] Indeed, less than two years earlier, during the attack on Louisbourg, Franklin lampooned the public call for "a fast and prayer day" as a weapon for victory. He calculated that in the months following the approval for the mission, "forty-five millions of prayers" had been offered, "which, set against the prayers of a few priests in the garrison, to the Virgin Mary, give a vast balance in [the colonists'] favor." Failure in the mission would reflect poorly on the power of prayer to elicit God's favor. "If you do not succeed," Franklin concluded sarcastically, "I shall have but an indifferent opinion of Presbyterian prayers in such cases, as long as I live. Indeed, in attacking strong towns I should have more dependence on *works*, than on *faith*."[38]

Franklin's creed reflects his faith in human agency as well as his recognition of the value of religion for human felicity. Indeed, his creed is consistent with deism, for while the term *providential* in the seventeenth century clearly referred to forces outside of nature, in Franklin's America it had also come to refer to the normal workings of nature itself. Furthermore, he does not say that vice will necessarily receive divine punishment. Rather, vice may bring about its own punishment due to the inherent ill effects it has on individuals; or, it may be punished by a community because of the social ills it produces.[39] This was the doctrine Franklin planned to "explain and enforce" in his proposed book *The Art of Virtue*. "[V]icious Actions are not hurtful because they are forbidden, but forbidden because they are hurtful, *the Nature of Man alone consider'd*: That it was therefore every one's Interest to be virtuous, who wish'd to be happy even in this World."[40] For Franklin, virtue is necessary for anyone, even one who disavows the doctrine of divine judgment, who wishes to live the happy life. "A vicious Man could not properly be called a Man of Sense," Franklin argued in a Socratic dialogue because a life without virtue cannot be a truly happy one.[41]

For Franklin, then, human felicity is the product of human effort. Rejecting the doctrine of special providence, Franklin maintained that man was responsible for his own happiness, a lesson he intimates when recollecting his near-shipwreck in 1757. The ship on which he took passage to London nearly crashed on the rocks near Falmouth, England. Only the warning from a lighthouse, along with quick action by the captain, saved the ship. "This Deliverance," Franklin writes, "impress'd me strongly with the Utility of Lighthouses, and made me resolve to encourage the building more of them in America, if I should live to return there."[42] Franklin's use of "deliverance" here is deliberate and layered in meaning. Read superficially, Franklin seems to assert special providence, literally a deliverance from the jaws of death by divine intervention. But read more carefully, we see again that Franklin's faith rests with man. It is the lighthouse—literally, man-made light, and not God's light—that has delivered them. The way to felicity is not through a search for God's light, but rather through man shining his own light on the world.[43] It is the lighthouse, not prayer, that proves useful. Indeed, the escape from shipwreck is providential not in the sense of divine intervention, but rather in the sense of human foresight.

THE INFLUENCE OF FRANKLIN'S
RELIGIOUS BELIEFS ON HIS POLITICAL THEORY

Franklin's religious beliefs informed his political theory in various ways. His assumptions about the limits to human understanding led him to advocate religious liberty. Because humans could not achieve certainty regarding God's nature, religious intolerance could not be based on sectarian claims to theological truth. The most that one could say about religious creeds and their leaders was that they were more or less useful in promoting human well-being. Thus, Franklin embraced religion generally, being of the "Opinion of its Propriety, and of its Utility when rightly conducted."[44] Religion "rightly conducted" would promote benevolence and toleration toward others, encourage good works, and thereby promote the public good. Such attitudes, Franklin advertised, invoking a religious argument to promote a moral and civic goal, were not merely useful, but divine in origin. "The Divine Being seems to have manifested his Approbation of the mutual Forbearance and Kindness with which the different Sects treat each other," he wrote in his *Information to Those Who Would Remove to America* (1784), "by the remarkable Prosperity with which He has been pleased to favour the whole Country."[45] And in a quintessentially Franklinesque act, he wrote "A Parable against Persecution" (1755), penned in the King James style, which told a story of Abraham's abuse of a passerby who did not worship God and of God's subsequent anger toward Abraham and which Franklin had bound into his Bible for unsuspecting readers to discover.[46]

Like many of his contemporaries, Franklin held that faith could not be willed. In fact, Franklin possessed an almost visceral distaste for physical compulsion, an attitude derived at least in part from childhood experience. Early in the *Autobiography*, when he explains how and why he fled Boston, Franklin thrice expresses the resentment he felt toward his brother James "for the Blows his Passion too often urg'd him to bestow upon me."[47] James's "harsh and tyrannical Treatment of me," Franklin notes, might have been "a means of impressing me with that Aversion to arbitrary Power that has stuck to me thro' my whole life."[48] For Franklin, physical force was counterproductive in religious and civic matters, producing only resentment, anger, and enmity. Political and religious repression, he wrote caustically in his *Rules by Which a Great Empire May Be Reduced to a Small One* (1773), were reliable methods for inciting disaffection and rebellion among a population.[49]

Franklin's religious skepticism also predisposed him to avoid speculation and dogmatism in politics. His political arguments were characteristically grounded in the experiential, and he rejected metaphysical reasoning in politics as he did in religious matters. When the delegates to the 1787 Constitutional Convention deadlocked over the issue of representation in Congress, Franklin pronounced the debates "a melancholy proof of the imperfection of the Human Understanding" and likened them to "groping as it were in the dark to find political truth."[50] When it became clear that the delegates would not unanimously endorse the draft constitution, Franklin beseeched the few objectors to sign the document. Franklin acknowledged that the document contained provisions that he disapproved. Still, he would sign it.

[H]aving lived long, I have experienced many instances of being obliged, by better information or fuller consideration, to change my opinions even on important subjects, which I once thought right, but found to be otherwise. It is therefore that the older I grow, the more apt I am to doubt my own judgment, and to pay more respect to the judgment of others. Most men indeed as well as most sects in Religion, think themselves in possession of all truth, and that wherever others differ from them it is so far error.[51]

Franklin's political theory was related to his religious beliefs, then, insofar as they both evolved from an epistemological assumption about human understanding. People are capable of discerning certain elemental truths, truths such as the existence of God and natural rights, that are self-evident to human reason. Absolute knowledge in politics and religion, however, exceeds human knowledge, and personal and public felicity suffers when people act otherwise.

Moreover, human reason is often corrupted by self-love. Experience proved that parsons and proprietors alike were often driven by self-love and tended to divide communities into sects or parties. As early as 1731 Franklin arrived at the following political maxims:

> That the great Affairs of the World, the Wars, Revolutions, etc. are carried on and effected by Parties.
>
> That the View of these Parties is their present general Interest, or what they take to be such.
>
> That while a Party is carrying on a general Design, each Man has his particular private Interest in View.

Franklin believed that political actors were almost always motivated by self-interest. "[F]ew in Public Affairs act from a mere View of the Good of their Country, whatever they may pretend," he argued. Even when their actions "bring real Good to their Country . . . Men primarily consider'd that their own and their Country's Interest was united, and did not act from a Principle of Benevolence."[52]

Recall that for Franklin vanity is not necessarily a socially destructive force. When Franklin spoke of vanity as a positive force, however, he conceived it as the desire to be esteemed or well regarded by one's compatriots. Underlying this desire was a genuine desire to serve the public good. In other words, vanity that coexisted with an ethic of social benevolence could be socially constructive. Too often, however, seemingly public-spirited acts mask baser motives. Most men, governed by self-love and the desire for glory, simply associate the public good with their private interest; or, they ignore the public interest altogether. Franklin singled out two passions in particular that reflect this self-love and that "have a powerful influence in the affairs of men. These are ambition and avarice; the love of power and the love of money." These two great forces, Franklin remarked at the 1787 convention, when united in the view of the same object . . . have in many minds the most violent effects. Place before the eyes of such men a post of *honour* that shall at the same time be a place of *profit*, and they will move heaven and earth to obtain it.[53]

Franklin's battles with the proprietary government in Pennsylvania, along with his experience with ministry officials in the decade prior to independence, confirmed his beliefs about ambition and avarice and sowed in him a deep distrust of executive power. For example, at the 1787 convention Franklin objected to the executive veto, stating, "He had had some experience of this check in the Executive on the Legislature, under the proprietary Government of [Pennsylvania]. The negative of the Governor was constantly made use of to extort money." The executive would in turn use the extorted money to "bribe the Legislature into a compleat subjection to the will of the Executive."[54] Similarly, he worried about the appointment power, noting that control over "all profitable offices" would permit the executive to buy dominance (as was the case with the British monarch). The executive, Franklin asserted ruefully, "will be always increasing here, as elsewhere, till it ends in monarchy."[55] Consequently, Franklin endorsed the plural executive. An executive council "would not only be a check on a bad President but be a relief to a good one."[56]

Franklin's concern about avarice and the influence of money in politics also made him wary of attaching salaries to public office. Combining positions of power and honor with positions of financial gain, salaried offices would attract men driven by self-love rather than a genuine regard for the public good. "And of what kind are the men that will strive for this profitable pre-eminence, through all the bustle of cabal, the heat of contention, the infinite mutual abuse of parties, tearing to pieces the best of characters," Franklin asked rhetorically as he argued that the executive should receive no salary. "It will not be the wise and moderate, the lovers of peace and good order, the men fittest for the trust. It will be the bold and the violent, the men of strong passions and indefatigable activity in their selfish pursuits."[57] Alternatively, by denying public officers salary and remunerating only their necessary expenses, men "more desirous of obtaining the Esteem of their Countrymen—than avaricious or eager, in the pursuit of wealth" would be attracted to political leadership.[58] He insisted that his proposal was not hopelessly utopian. He pointed out that Quakers, prohibited by faith from litigating, resolve disputes through arbitration at their meetings. "Committees of these sit with patience to hear the parties . . . supported [only] by a sense of duty, and the respect paid to usefulness." Similarly, General Washington led "our armies . . . for eight years together without the smallest salary." Franklin was confident that "we shall never be without a sufficient number of wise and good men to undertake and execute well and faithfully the Office[s] in question."[59]

At the core of these statements was a fundamental belief about the potential conflict between wealth and republican government. We will "sow the seeds of contention, faction & tumult," Franklin urged, "by making our posts of honor, places of profit."[60] Party conflict between those who capture political office and "their vanquished competitors of the same spirit" was inevitable.[61] Conflict and distrust between avaricious rulers and the people was also certain. It was critical to structure political institutions to discourage scoundrels from political life while encouraging virtue among the populace. "In free Governments the rulers are the servants and the people their superiors & sovereigns," Franklin said in defense of a provision making the executive ineligible for reelection. "For the former therefore to return among the latter was not to *degrade* but to *promote* them."[62] It was important that the delegates avoid constructing institutions that would "depress the virtue & public spirit of our common people; of which they displayed a great deal during the war."[63] He thus objected to a proposal to establish a property qualification for the suffrage. He likewise opposed property qualifications for holding office. Virtue and wealth often went hand in hand, but the relationship was not a necessary one.

> If honesty was often the companion of wealth, and if poverty was exposed to peculiar temptation, it was not less true that the possession of property increased the desire of more property—Some of the greatest rogues he was ever acquainted with, were the richest rogues. We should remember the character which the Scripture requires in Rulers, that they should be men hating covetousness.[64]

Scripture might command that rulers not be covetous, but to Franklin experience proved that men often view politics as an instrument for obtaining wealth and preeminence. Indeed, Franklin suggested that even religious convictions rarely impede self-love, for even the truly pious are likely to use politics for selfish gain. "'Tis not inconsistent with Charity to distrust a Religious Man in Power, tho' he may be a good Man," Franklin wrote in one of his Dogood essays. "[H]e has many Temptations 'to propagate *publick Destruction* for

Personal Advantages and Security': And if his Natural Temper be covetous, and his Actions often contradict his pious Discourse, we may with great Reason conclude, that he has some other Design in his Religion besides barely getting to Heaven."[65] Years later, Franklin objected when the convention took up a provision to provide "liberal" legislative salaries. He agreed that the salaries ought to be

> as fixed as possible; but disliked the word "*liberal.*" He remarked the tendency of abuses in every case, to grow of themselves when once begun, and related very pleasantly the progression in ecclesiastical benefices, from the first departure from the gratuitous provision for the Apostles, to the establishment of the papal system.[66]

In fact, Franklin grew increasingly critical of the legal bonds that defined church–state relations in Anglo-American society. Like other founders, Franklin concluded that mixing church and state would corrupt religious as well as political institutions. He thus opposed religious tests for political office. He likewise opposed state support of religious sects, writing that when the "Professors" of a given sect "are oblig'd to call for the help of the Civil Power, it is a sign, I apprehend, of its being a bad one."[67]

But Franklin focused his most piercing criticism of religious leaders on their habit of disputatiousness. Franklin traced his own disputatious habits to his early education when, as a young boy, he read most of his father's "Books in polemic Divinity." Recollecting the fondness that he and his boyhood friend John Collins had for "Argument," Franklin observes in the *Autobiography* that this

> disputatious Turn . . . is apt to become a very bad Habit, making People often extremely disagreeable in Company, by the Contradiction that is necessary to bring it into Practice, and thence, besides souring and spoiling the Conversation, is productive of Disgusts and perhaps Enmities where you may have occasion for Friendship. *I had caught it by reading my Father's Books of Dispute about Religion.*[68]

Reflecting on his youth, Franklin regrets "that at a time when I had such a Thirst for Knowledge, more proper Books had not fallen in my Way."[69] In what sense were these books improper? Franklin tells us that argumentativeness spoils the conversation, creates ill will, and kills potential friendships. For Franklin, conversation and friendship are sources of private felicity. The argumentative man is inevitably the lonely, and hence the unhappy, man. Because these books undermine these sources of private felicity, Franklin concludes that they are unhealthy.

A key assumption in Franklin's political thought is the notion that disputatiousness is a learned trait, that it undermines civility, and that it is inculcated by ambitious sectarian leaders. "[N]ow a days," Franklin complained, "we have scarce a little Parson, that does not think it the Duty of every Man within his Reach to sit under his petty Ministrations, and that whoever omits them offends God."[70] Clerical vanity fostered competition for parishioners and sowed the seeds for division within the community. Rather than preaching to "inspire, promote or confirm Morality," clergy instead preached sermons that "serv'd principally to divide us and make us unfriendly to one another."[71]

Thus, disputatiousness is incompatible with public felicity, too. Franklin repeatedly indicted sectarian leaders for harming the public interest, a charge he spelled out in his defense of the Revs. Samuel Hemphill and George Whitefield. Hemphill came to Philadelphia from Ireland in 1734 to assist the Rev. Jedediah Andrews, a highly influential Presbyterian clergyman in the Philadelphia synod. Andrews was a strict Calvinist, a man whose sermons Franklin found to be "chiefly either polemic Arguments, or Explications of the peculiar Doctrines of our Sect." During his sermons, Franklin wrote critically, "not a single moral Principle was inculcated and enforc'd, their Aim seeming to be rather to make us Presbyterians than good Citizens."[72] Hemphill was different and quickly grew popular. Even Franklin, who regularly avoided church, "became one of [Hemphill's] constant Hearers, his Sermons pleasing me as they had little of the dogmatical kind, but inculcated strongly the Practice of Virtue, or what in the religious Style are called Good Works."[73] Within a few months, however, Andrews formally accused Hemphill of preaching heterodoxy, and in late 1735 Hemphill was found guilty by the synod.[74]

Whitefield arrived in Philadelphia in November 1739 and was the leading figure in the Great Awakening. Unlike Hemphill, Whitefield adhered to the orthodox tenets of Calvinist thought. He preached original sin and saving grace and, as Kerry Walters points out, saw little difference between liberal religion and atheism.[75] While Franklin did not find his sermons spiritually appealing, others did. "The Multitudes of all Sects and Denominations that attended his Sermons were enormous," Franklin wrote, calculating the audience at times to be in the tens of thousands. Despite Whitefield's fundamental orthodoxy, however, "the Clergy taking a Dislike to him, soon refus'd him their Pulpits and he was oblig'd to preach in the Fields."[76]

Whatever their theological differences, both clergymen shared two characteristics that Franklin identified as essential to all useful religions. First, both men were capable of drawing "together considerable Numbers of *different Persuasions.*" Their ability to affect change in people's behavior, regardless of denomination, was profound. "It was wonderful to see the Change soon made in the Manners of our Inhabitants," Franklin recalled of Whitefield's arrival. "[F]rom being thoughtless or indifferent about Religion, it seem'd as if all the World were growing Religious; so that one could not walk thro' the Town in an Evening without Hearing Psalms sung in different Families of every Street."[77] Second, both Hemphill and Whitefield focused on the "outward state." Even Whitefield, who maintained the strict Calvinist view of human depravity, spent considerable time and energy promoting public projects. At least, it is this public-spirited man that Franklin portrays in the *Autobiography*. It was Whitefield's "benevolent Heart" that led him to propose establishing an orphanage in Georgia. Franklin's explicit recognition of Whitefield's benevolence is informative. It is Whitefield's love for others and his desire to improve their lives in tangible, outward ways that attracts Franklin and earns his respect.

Conversely, the tendency of most religious leaders to place their own self-interest above that of the public (or their parishioners) was manifest in their reactions to Whitefield and Hemphill. The local clergy must have seen Whitefield's extraordinary popularity and the vast sums of money he was able to raise as a threat to their ministries and, thus, to their status in the community. In addition to being banned from the pulpits, Whitefield became the target of rumors by some of his "Enemies . . . that he would apply these Collections to his own private Emolument," a charge that Franklin rebuts, declaring that "[I] am to this day decidedly of Opinion that he was in all his Conduct, a perfectly *honest Man.*"[78]

By emphasizing Whitefield's fundamental decency, Franklin may have been implying that most religious leaders are self-interested and dishonest. This assessment certainly permeates the pamphlets he wrote in Hemphill's defense. When Hemphill was charged, Franklin "became his zealous Partisan, and contributed all I could to raise a party in his Favor."[79] Franklin claimed that personal vanity explained the clergy's hostility, whose motives he questioned by attacking some of the trial procedures. He called the accusers dishonest and malicious, and when it became known that the sermons Hemphill had been preaching were not his own, Franklin defended him, charging that the clergy deliberately chose the dullest material for their sermons. Were the clergy to serve their flock or parade their erudition? Only vainglory could prevent the clergy from using popular and effective sermons simply because they were not the authors.[80]

Certainly, the local clergy found Hemphill and Whitefield theologically objectionable. Franklin recognized that theological clashes were in play, but theological differences were precisely the problem. Sectarianism fosters division and hostility and, ironically, interferes with private felicity by impeding friendships that enrich life. Franklin took care to note that despite their fundamental religious differences, he and Whitefield retained "a mere civil Friendship, sincere on both sides, [that] lasted to his Death." Likewise, Franklin believed that by fostering ill will, sectarianism interfered with public felicity. Franklin's ability to transcend religious differences enabled him to promote the public good. Thus, he observed, when one of the trustees of the academy died and a dispute among the board arose over what denomination the new trustee should represent, "At length one mention'd me, with the Observation that I was merely an honest Man, and of no Sect at all; which prevail'd with them to choose me."[81]

RELATION OF RELIGIOUS TRUTH TO GOVERNMENT AUTHORITY

Although Franklin remained critical of religious dogmatism and wary of doctrinaire religious leaders, throughout much of his life he actively supported religious institutions. Indeed, in Philadelphia Franklin supported various churches, including Christ Church, where he rented a pew, and reportedly contributed to every religious society in the city. Franklin understood that religion remained a potent social force that political leaders must respect. Political leaders would be foolish to attempt to govern without acknowledging a role for religion in public life or, worse, to question religion itself. Franklin learned this lesson as a young man in Boston, where his "indiscreet Disputations about Religion began to make me pointed at with Horror by good People, as an Infidel or Atheist."[82]

Franklin again experienced religion's profound influence when the Rev. Whitefield solicited funds for his orphanage. Franklin had endorsed Whitefield's plan to build an orphanage for children in Georgia; however, the two men disagreed on where to build it. When Whitefield refused to alter his plan, Franklin decided not to contribute. But when Whitefield began to preach, Franklin "began to soften," and he decided to contribute the copper he had in his pocket. Whitefield's oratory soon shamed Franklin into giving his silver dollars, too; "and he finish'd so admirably, that I emptied my Pocket wholly into the Collector's Dish, Gold and all." A friend of Franklin's, a fellow member of the Junto, was also at the sermon. Like Franklin, he had determined not to give.

> Suspecting a Collection might be intended, [he] had by Precaution emptied his Pockets before he came from home; towards the Conclusion of the Discourse however, he felt a strong Desire to give, and apply'd to a Neighbor who stood near him to borrow some Money for the Purpose. The Application was unfortunately to perhaps the only Man in the Company who had the firmness not to be affected by the Preacher. His Answer was, *At any other time, Friend Hopkinson, I would lend to thee freely; but not now; for thee seems to be out of thy right Senses.*[83]

One does not sense here any regret on Franklin's part. Whitefield's project was the type that Franklin regularly endorsed, and despite his disapproval of its location, the orphanage might achieve some good. Yet, the larger point still holds: religion and religious appeals can be tremendously powerful, overcoming even the determination of men of reason. Whitefield's "Eloquence had a wonderful Power over the Hearts and Purses of his Hearers," Franklin recalls.[84] Twice in the *Autobiography* he describes Whitefield's effect on people as wonderful, denoting his admiration for and astonishment at—and his wariness of—the power of religion and its leaders. And while that power might be harnessed for good, it was also susceptible to abuse.

Moreover, Franklin worried that religious zealotry could breed public cynicism toward religion generally and in turn could corrupt public faith in government. For Franklin, the civic consequences from the tension between religious dogmatism on the one hand, and common sense and human inclination on the other, were nowhere better represented than in the Quakers' struggle with pacifism. "The Quakers suffer'd from having establish'd and publish'd it as one of their Principles, that no kind of War was lawful, and which being once published, they could not afterwards, however they might change their minds, easily get rid of." Having stated publicly their opposition to war, the Quakers found themselves pulled in opposite directions by faith and necessity. Franklin recalls that the Quakers, reluctant to offend the king by directly refusing his request for a military appropriation, and equally reluctant to offend "their Friends the Body of Quakers on the other, by a Compliance contrary to their Principles," employed "a Variety of Evasions to avoid Complying, and Modes of disguising the Compliance when it became unavoidable." They could not grant money for gunpowder because it was a component of war. Rather than refuse the aid, they "voted an Aid . . . of Three Thousand Pounds . . . and appropriated it for the Purchasing of Bread, Flour, Wheat, *or other Grain*."[85]

The dilemma in this tension between faith and necessity embarrassed the Quakers in two ways. First, necessity (the threat of imminent attack) led some followers to question the tenet of absolute pacifism.[86] Second, as the controlling party in the assembly, the Quakers had to choose a course. The distress they experienced is evidenced by the machinations they used to reconcile necessity with principle. In this case, necessity and principle seemed irreconcilable, and the Quakers appeared hypocritical.

Franklin recalls a similar incident involving the Moravians. In 1755 Franklin was part of a three-member commission charged with securing the population of Lehightown, Pennsylvania. "I was surprised to find it in so good a Posture of Defense," Franklin recalls.

> I mention'd . . . my Surprise [to Bishop Spangenberg]; for knowing they had obtain'd an Act of Parliament exempting them from military Duties in the Colonies, I had suppos'd they were conscientiously scrupulous of bearing Arms. He answer'd me, "That it was not one of their establish'd Principles; but that at the time of their obtaining that Act, it was thought to be a Principle with many of their People. On this Occasion, however, they to their Surprise found it adopted by but a few." It seems they were either deceiv'd in themselves, or deceiv'd the Parliament. But Common Sense aided by present Danger, will sometimes be too strong for *whimsical* Opinions.[87]

As with the Quakers, the Moravians' behavior elicited public suspicion. Their actions belied their earlier professions. Either they misled Parliament, or they were unsettled about their own beliefs. If they deliberately misled Parliament, they appeared hypocritical and self-serving. If they had a change of heart, it suggested that no sect possessed absolute truth. Theological claims would thus devolve into mere whimsical opinions, perceived as baseless and capricious.

They would become the mere objects of fashion, attractive today and out of style tomorrow.

Such incidents could undermine political as well as religious authority. A sect might find itself faced with a choice between holding strictly to its beliefs and active participation in politics. "To avoid this kind of Embarrassment the Quakers have of late Years been gradually declining the public Service in the Assembly and in the Magistracy," Franklin explained, "Choosing rather to quit their Power than their Principle."[88] If the sect's participation in public affairs had been beneficial, as Franklin believed of the Quakers, then the withdrawal would leave the polity a bit more impoverished.[89] Alternatively, if the sect yielded on principle, or seemed to yield on principle, then it would appear evasive, unprincipled, and hypocritical. Viewing it as insincere or opportunist, people would become cynical about moral and political authority.[90]

According to Franklin, the inclination toward dogmatism and disputatiousness, if left unreformed, would raise public doubts concerning the motivations of public leaders. For that reason, Franklin sought to establish social norms, particularly among political leaders, compatible with the democratic polity he saw emerging in America.[91] Too often men lessened "their Power of doing Good by a Positive assuming Manner that seldom fails to disgust [and which] tends to create Opposition," Franklin repeatedly warned.[92] The consequences of this habit were alarmingly evident at the convention, where, he claimed, the delegates' attitudes led unnecessarily to stalemate.

> [Declarations] of a fixed opinion, and of determined resolution, never to change it, neither enlighten nor convince us. Positiveness and warmth on one side, naturally beget their like on the other; and tend to create and augment discord & division in a great concern, wherein harmony & Union are extremely necessary to give weight to our Councils, and render them effectual in promoting & securing the common good.[93]

Dogmatism in politics undermines the public good by producing ill will between people and thus rendering agreement more difficult. Furthermore, discord weakens the public's faith in its leaders. In the above case, Franklin was concerned that the delegates' stubbornness on the issue of representation would saddle them with a reputation for incessant dispute, leading the public to perceive them as motivated by parochial interests rather than the common good and, thereby, jeopardizing popular support for the Constitution.

It was this concern about the public's perception of the convention, combined with his concern about the mood among the delegates, that led Franklin to propose opening each morning session with a prayer "imploring the assistance of Heaven."[94] Franklin knew how religion might promote the public good. It could help foster a sense of communal purpose among the citizenry; it could help temper the influence of self-interest and provincialism among political leaders; and it could increase public confidence in those leaders. In short, Franklin sought to use religion to counteract the effects of dogmatism among the delegates.

Franklin expected that daily prayer would have two beneficial effects. First, a daily ritual of prayer would reaffirm public confidence in the delegates. Specifically, the daily invocation of God's blessing would inject humility into the convention. Humility, or at least the appearance of it, is important for avoiding public ridicule, and democratic leadership requires humility.

This is the subtext of Franklin's self-deprecating anecdote about his "bold and arduous Project of arriving at moral Perfection." While he boasts of modest success in improving some of his virtues, he notes that "My Scheme of Order . . . vex'd me so much, and I made so little Progress in Amendment, and had such frequent Relapses, that I was almost ready to give up the Attempt, and content myself with a faulty Character in that respect." Franklin humorously likens his struggle to a man "who in buying an Axe of a Smith my Neighbor, desired to have the whole of its Surface as bright as the Edge." The smith, Franklin explains, "consented to grind it bright for him if he would turn the Wheel," a task that proved "very fatiguing." After laboring at the wheel for some time, the man decided to "take his Axe as it was without farther grinding. No, says the Smith, Turn on, turn on; we shall have it bright by and by; as yet 'tis only speckled. Yes, says the Man; but—*I think I like a speckled Axe best.*"[95] Franklin here pokes fun at man's capacity to rationalize. But significantly, Franklin also concludes that a speckled axe *is* best:

> For something that pretended to be Reason was every now and then suggesting to me, that such extreme Nicety as I exacted of myself might be a kind of Foppery in Morals, which if it were known would make me ridiculous; that a perfect Character might be attended with the Inconvenience of being envied and hated; and that a benevolent Man should allow a few Faults in himself, to keep his Friends in Countenance.[96]

This long, closing line is the key to the entire passage. Man's self-delusion comes not merely in his ability to rationalize, but also in his capacity to believe that human nature is perfectible and that perfection is desirable. The attempt to achieve moral perfection would render a person the object of ridicule. Franklin chooses his words carefully. Such a person literally would be ridiculous, the subject of contemptuous laughter. Moreover, the effort would constitute a "Foppery in Morals." Again, diction is key. Foppery derives from "fop," a man who is excessively vain and concerned about his manners and appearance. It is akin to "fob," which implies an act of deception.[97] Franklin's point grows clear. Because humans are inherently imperfect, a man who is perceived to be pursuing perfection (and certainly the man who claims to have achieved it) will be considered a fraud and excessively vain. Posturing of this type, Franklin suggests, leads only to ridicule, envy, and hatred. And one cannot lead in a democracy when one is ridiculed, envied, and hated.

Second, Franklin believed that daily prayer would actually affect the delegates' attitudes and behavior. Franklin was a "sincere lover of social worship" and was "deeply sensible of its usefulness to society."[98] The ritual of social prayer could inculcate an ethic of civic duty, habituating men to the virtue of social benevolence. The desire to serve the public, the inclination to subvert one's private interests and opinions to the public weal, could be taught. Religious rituals were particularly effective at inculcating the virtue of public-spiritedness because appeals to divinity served to remind individuals of a greater good beyond their own self-interest or the interests of their constituents. Even if the participants in a ritual initially seemed merely to be going through the motions, the social and repetitious nature of the ritual could alter attitudes over time, thereby transforming labored practice into a love of virtue.[99]

In short, Franklin called on prayer as a rhetorical device to achieve a political outcome. A lifetime of experience had taught him the power that religious appeals can have over men, and he sought to invoke one now, as had Whitefield and other clergy—indeed, as he had previously done—to alter people's attitudes and conduct. But for the ritual to work, it had to resonate with its audience. Only an invocation of special providence could humble the delegates and succeed where appeals to reason and fairness had failed. Once more Franklin drew on his Presbyterian upbringing as a guide. Using language typically absent in his private correspondence, Franklin called on his fellow delegates to "humbly [apply] to the Father of Lights to illuminate" their deliberations. He reminded them of the "Superintending providence in our favor" that had seen them through the war and of their special charge to complete the work that had begun with independence. "[O]ur future national felicity," Franklin argued, depended on God's "concurring aid." Without the "assistance of Heaven," he added, invoking the missionary tone of his Puritan ancestors,

> [W]e shall succeed in this political building no better than the Builders of Babel: We shall be divided by our little partial local interests; our projects will be confounded, and we ourselves shall become a reproach and bye word down to future ages. And what is worse, mankind may hereafter from this unfortunate instance, despair of establishing Governments by Human Wisdom and leave it to chance, war and conquest.[100]

By continuously suggesting that the American experiment had thus far succeeded only through divine providence, prayer would humble the delegates and, in turn, cause them to be more receptive to the opinions of their fellow delegates, more suspect of their own, and more inclined to cooperate through a conviction that they were charged with promoting the public good, even where it might conflict with their particular local interest.

CONCLUSION

Franklin came to believe that religious faith is beneficial to the polity. When "rightly conducted," religion serves a critical public function by fostering civic-minded citizens. It molds them to be charitable and kind, infuses them with fellow feeling, and teaches them to identify their private felicity with the public good. Dogmatic religion has the opposite effect. It teaches people to be judgmental and unmerciful. It is divisive and fosters oppression, cynicism, and distrust. In short, it molds citizens unfit for democracy.

Franklin's ideal was to promote religion generally, while modifying the dogmatism that characterized sectarian religion. In the last decades of his life, he sporadically took up this challenge, attempting to promote religion, while rescuing it from its self-destructive tendencies. His effort to revise the Book of Common Prayer, in which he aimed to encourage more widespread worship, while redirecting its message, was just such an attempt. Eliminating repetition and shortening the length of the morning and evening services would "procure a more general attendance." At the same time, Franklin proposed changing the Catechism, which he deemed "not so well adapted to the capacities of children as might be wished"[101] and unsuitable for "the Christian doctrine of forgiveness of injuries, and doing good to enemies."[102] Franklin thus conceived a role for religion in shaping democratic values: tolerance, benevolence, and public-spiritedness.

Franklin also sought to mold men capable of leading that citizenry. Franklin had this purpose in mind when he contemplated the creation of the Society of the Free and Easy. Once again, religious faith was central to his plan. At the heart of this "party" was a creed that included the "Essentials of every known Religion" and that was stripped "free of everything that might shock the Professors of any Religion," thereby ensuring that the society did not alienate potential members or public trust through the expression of controversial theological views. Moreover, the creed's doctrines of divine judgment and good works would help constrain self-love, while promoting the virtue of public service. The society's members, habituated to public service as the highest virtue and "being by the general Practice and Habit of the Virtues, free from the Dominion of Vice, and particularly by the Practice of Industry and Frugality, free from Debt," would turn their attention to public affairs, thereby serving the public, while exemplifying a genuine regard for public service.[103]

Finally, the creed would promote humility and, thus, assist in teaching the society's members how to govern in a democracy. Democratic leaders govern by persuasion rather than by force. They must solicit the respect and affection, not the fear, of the people. Similarly, they have to understand the power of envy in democratic society. The habit of "modest diffidence" that these men of virtue would acquire— avoiding an air of certainty; leaving undeclared, at least temporarily, one's authorship of a good idea; in short, maintaining at least the appearance of humility—was vital to Franklin's idea of democratic leadership. Habituated to tolerance and the practice of humility, moderate in tastes and of independent means, these men, free from the dogmatism and appetites that often corrupt and dedicated to serving the public, would act as models of democratic citizenship.

Indeed, Franklin ultimately conceived the society as a training ground for democratic citizens. He assumed that the society's members would search for additional "ingenuous well-disposed Youths" to admit into their ranks. While the society was initially to remain secret and open only to young, single men (in order to "prevent Solicitations for the Admission of improper Persons"), Franklin's plan was consistent with his democratic sensibilities. For he assumed that its numbers would become "considerable"—at which time it would become public—thus, "very useful, by forming a great Number of good Citizens." As the number of temperate, benevolent, civic-minded citizens grew, democracy would flourish. But Franklin was not "discourag'd by the seeming Magnitude of the Undertaking." Always confident in man's ability to improve his world, Franklin wrote,

> I have always thought that one Man of tolerable Abilities may work great Changes, and accomplish great Affairs among Mankind, if he first forms a good Plan, and, cutting off all Amusements or other Employments that would divert his Attention, makes the Execution of that same Plan his sole Study and Business.[104]

APPENDIX: BENJAMIN FRANKLIN TO JOSEPH HUEY, JUNE 6, 1753[105]

". . . The faith you mention has doubtless its use in the world; I do not desire to see it diminished, nor would I endeavour to lessen it in any man. But I wish it were more productive of good works than I have generally seen it: I mean real good works, works of kindness, charity, mercy, and publick spirit; not holiday-keeping, sermon-reading or hearing, performing church ceremonies, or making long prayers, filled with flatteries or compliments, despised even by wise men, and much less capable of pleasing the deity. The worship of God is a duty, the hearing and reading of sermons may be useful; but if men rest in hearing and praying, as too many do, it is as if a tree should value itself on being watered and putting forth leaves, though it never produced any fruit.

Your great Master thought much less of these outward appearances and professions than many of his modern disciples. He preferred the doers of the word to the mere hearers; the son that seemingly refused to obey his Father and yet performed his commands, to him that professed his readiness but neglected the works; the heretical but charitable Samaritan, to the uncharitable though orthodox priest and sanctified Levite; and those who gave food to the hungry, drink to the thirsty, raiment to the naked, entertainment to the stranger, and relief to the sick, etc. though they never heard of his name, he declares shall in the last day be accepted, when those who cry Lord, Lord; who value themselves on their faith though great enough to perform miracles but have neglected good works shall be rejected. . . ."

NOTES

1. Benjamin Franklin to Jacques Barbeu-Dubourg, [April?] 1773, in *The Writings of Benjamin Franklin*, ed. Albert H. Smyth (New York: The Macmillan Co., 1907), 6:43.

2. Franklin to Jacques Barbeu-Dubourg, *Writings of Benjamin Franklin*, 6:43–44.

3. See generally, Carl Becker, *Benjamin Franklin: A Biographical Sketch* (Ithaca, NY: Cornell University Press, 1946).

4. Franklin was also elected to the French Academy of Sciences (1773), received the honorary master of arts degree from Harvard and Yale (1753) and William and Mary (1756), the LL.D. from St. Andrews (1759), and the D.C.L. from Oxford (1762). For the claim that Franklin anticipated the modern electron theory, see Robert A. Millikan, "Benjamin Franklin as a Scientist," in *Meet Dr. Franklin*, ed. Roy N. Lokken (Philadelphia: The Franklin Institute, 1981), 33–46.

5. L. H. Butterfield, ed., *Diary and Autobiography of John Adams* (Cambridge, MA: Harvard University Press, 1961), 2:391.

6. Charles Francis Adams, ed., *The Works of John Adams* (Boston: Little, Brown and Co., 1850–56), 1:661.

7. J. A. Leo Lemay, "Franklin and the *Autobiography*: An Essay on Recent Scholarship," *Eighteenth Century Studies* 1 (Winter 1967): 210. See also Kenneth Murdock, "Jonathan Edwards and Benjamin Franklin," in *The Literature of the American People: An Historical and Critical Survey*, ed. Arthur Hobson Quinn (New York: Appleton-Century-Crofts, 1951), 116–23; Ralph L. Ketcham, *Benjamin Franklin* (New York: Washington Square Press, 1965).

8. For the Quaker influence, see Henry Seidel Canby, *Classic Americans: A Study of Eminent American Writers from Irving to Whitman* (New York: Harcourt Brace & Co., 1931), 34–45. For the Puritan influence, see William Pencak, "*Benjamin Franklin's Autobiography*, Cotton Mather, and a Puritan God," *Pennsylvania History* 53 (January 1986): 1–25; Charles L. Sanford, "An American *Pilgrim's Progress*," *American Quarterly* 6 (Winter 1954): 297–310; David Levin, "The Autobiography of Benjamin Franklin: The Puritan Experimenter in Life and Art," *The Yale Review* 53 (Winter 1963): 258–75.

9. Mason Locke Weems, *Life of Benjamin Franklin* (Hagerstown, MD: Printed by the author, 1818); James Parton, *Life and Times of Benjamin Franklin* (New York: Mason Brothers, 1864); James M. Stifler, "The Religion of Benjamin Franklin," *Benjamin Franklin Gazette* 3 (May 1940): 11–14; Albert Hyma, *The Religious Views of Benjamin Franklin* (Ann Arbor, MI: George Wahr Publishing Co., 1958).

10. James Turner, *Without God, without Creed: The Origins of Unbelief in America* (Baltimore: The Johns Hopkins University Press, 1985); Cecil B. Currey, "Ben Franklin's Religion," *Mankind* 5 (August 1975): 22–27; Daniel Walden, "Benjamin Franklin's Deism: A Phase," *The Historian* 26 (May 1964): 350–61; Harold E. Taussig, "Deism in Philadelphia during the Age of Franklin," *Pennsylvania History* 37 (July 1970): 217–36; Bernard Fay, *Franklin, The Apostle of Modern Times* (Boston: Little,

Brown and Co., 1929); Leonard W. Labaree, "Franklin and the Presbyterians," *Journal of the Presbyterian Historical Society* 35 (December 1957): 217–28.

11. Alfred Owen Aldridge, *Benjamin Franklin and Nature's God* (Durham, NC: Duke University Press, 1967).

12. Kerry S. Walter, *Benjamin Franklin and His Gods* (Urbana: University of Illinois Press, 1999).

13. Benjamin Franklin, *Benjamin Franklin's Autobiography: An Authoritative Text*, ed. J. A. Leo Lemay and P. M. Zall (New York: W. W. Norton & Co., 1986), 45.

14. Franklin, *Autobiography*, 65.

15. Cotton Mather, *Bonifacius: An Essay Upon the Good*, ed. David Levin (Cambridge: Cambridge University Press, 1966), 27; quoted in Campbell Tatham, "Benjamin Franklin, Cotton Mather, and The Outward State," *Early American Literature* 6 (Winter 1971–1972), 224. Tatham rejects the Puritan hypothesis. See also Norman S. Fiering, "Benjamin Franklin and the Way to Virtue," *American Quarterly* 30 (Summer 1978): 199–223.

16. Mather writes, "Until a man be united unto the glorious Christ, who is *our life*, he is a *dead man*. And, I pray, what *good works* to be expected from such a man? They will all be *dead works*." *Bonifacius*, 27; quoted in Tatham, "The Outward State," 224. Conversely, Franklin wrote that "one of the Apostles" claimed that "*Faith without Works is dead*; and, *shew me your Faith without Works, and I will shew you mine by my Works*." Benjamin Franklin, "Dialogue Between Two Presbyterians," *The Papers of Benjamin Franklin*, ed. Leonard W. Labaree et al. (New Haven, CT: Yale University Press, 1959–), 2:30.

17. Franklin, *Autobiography*, 2.

18. For a discussion of the Puritan conversion experience and claims placing Franklin in it, see David L. Parker, "From Sound Believer to Practical Preparationist: Some Puritan Harmonics in Franklin's *Autobiography*," in *The Oldest Revolutionary: Essays on Benjamin Franklin*, ed. J. A. Leo Lemay (Philadelphia: University of Pennsylvania Press, 1976), 67–75; William Breitenbach, "Religious Afflictions and Religious Affections: Antinomianism and Hypocrisy in the Writings of Edwards and Franklin," in *Benjamin Franklin, Jonathan Edwards, and the Representation of American Culture*, eds. Barbara B. Oberg and Harry S. Stout (New York: Oxford University Press, 1993), 13–26; Karl T. Weintraub, "The Puritan Ethic and Benjamin Franklin," *Journal of Religion* 56 (July 1976): 223–37.

19. Franklin called the doctrine of original sin an "Opinion every whit as ridiculous as that of imputed Righteousness." See Franklin, "A Defence of the Rev. Mr. Hemphill's Observations" (1735), *Papers*, 2:114.

20. Letter to Ezra Stiles, March 9, 1790, in *Benjamin Franklin: Writings*, ed. J. A. Leo Lemay (New York: The Library of America, 1987), 1179.

21. Franklin, *Autobiography*, 90.

22. Franklin, *Autobiography*, 90–91.

23. Franklin, *Autobiography*, 97.

24. Letter to Ezra Stiles, March 9, 1790, *Franklin: Writings*, 1179–80.

25. Letter to Stiles, *Franklin: Writings*, 1179. See his letter to Joseph Huey, June 6, 1753, *Papers*, 4:505–6.

26. For a succinct summary of Wollaston's argument, see Walters, *Franklin and His Gods*, 45–48.

27. *Papers*, 1:59.

28. *Papers*, 1:63. Franklin also denies the soul's immortality. *Papers* 1:66, 71.

29. Franklin, *Autobiography*, 45–46.

30. "An Economical Project: To the Authors of *The Journal of Paris*" (April 26, 1784), *Franklin: Writings*, 985.

31. Letter from Benjamin Franklin to ———— [ ], December 13, 1757, *Papers*, 7:294.

32. Letter to Josiah and Abiah Franklin, April 13, 1738, *Papers*, 2:204. See also his letter to Joseph Huey, June 6, 1753, *Papers*, 4:505–6.

33. Franklin, *Autobiography*, 65.

34. "I have lived, Sir, a long time," Franklin said, "and the longer I live, the more convincing proofs I see of this truth—*that God governs in the affairs of men.*" Speech of June 28, 1787, in Max Farrand, ed., *The Records of the Federal Convention* (New Haven, CT: Yale University Press, 1966), 1:451.

35. *Papers*, 1:268. Franklin drafted the essay for the Junto and perhaps simply presented it in the same "sincere Spirit of Enquiry after Truth" that marked discourse in the Junto generally. Franklin, *Autobiography*, 48. For Franklin's rejection of metaphysics, see his letters to [Thomas Hopkinson?], October 16, 1746, *Papers*, 3:88–89, and to Benjamin Vaughan, November 9, 1779, *Papers*, 31:58–59.

36. *Papers*, 1:102. After depicting God as a mere First Cause, Franklin adds that because of the human inclination to "pay Divine Regards to SOMETHING," the deity created inferior gods to whom people can pray. *Papers*, 1:102–3. According to Walters, Franklin believed that these lesser gods—the objects of sectarian religions—are human constructs that are nonetheless necessary and valuable to human felicity. *Franklin and His Gods*, 82–87.

37. Franklin, *Autobiography*, 93. Franklin proposed the association after the Quaker assembly refused to appropriate funds for the colony's defense. Franklin, *Autobiography*, 92. See *Plain Truth; or, Serious Considerations on the Present State of the City of Philadelphia and Province of Pennsylvania* (1747), *Papers*, 3:188–204.

38. Letter to John Franklin, [May?] 1745, *Papers*, 3:26–27. Years later Franklin wrote "I rather suspect, from certain circumstances, that though the general government of the universe is well administered, our particular little affairs are perhaps below notice, and left to take the chance of human prudence or imprudence, as either may happen to be uppermost." Letter to George Whitefield, [before September 2, 1769], *Papers*, 16:192.

39. When Franklin states *his* "religious Principles," he writes that "*Crime* will be punished and Virtue rewarded either here or hereafter." When he describes the creed he wrote for the "Society of the *Free and Easy*," the doctrine becomes "God will certainly reward Virtue and punish Vice either here or hereafter." Franklin, *Autobiography*, 65, 75. In the former there is no explicit agent.

40. Franklin, *Autobiography*, 75 [emphasis mine].

41. Franklin, *Autobiography*, 80. "A Man of Sense," February 11, 1734/35, *Papers*, 2:15–19.

42. Franklin, *Autobiography*, 142.

43. In contrast with his 1787 convention speech, in this passage Franklin does not expressly refer to "providence" or to an intervening God. Nevertheless, his use of "deliverance" would have conjured up notions of divine intervention. See *The Oxford English Dictionary*, 2d ed., s.v. "deliverance."

44. Franklin, *Autobiography*, 65.

45. *Franklin: Writings*, 983.
46. Franklin, *Papers*, 6:114–24.
47. Franklin, *Autobiography*, 17.
48. Franklin, *Autobiography*, 16.
49. *Papers*, 20:389–99.
50. Farrand, *Records*, 1:451.
51. Farrand, *Records*, 2:641–42. See also Franklin, *Autobiography*, 97.
52. Franklin, *Autobiography*, 77.
53. Farrand, *Records*, 1:82.
54. Farrand, *Records*, 1:99.
55. Farrand, *Records*, 1:103.
56. Farrand, *Records*, 2:542.
57. Farrand, *Records*, 1:82.
58. Farrand, *Records*, 1:91–92.
59. Farrand, *Records*, 1:84–85.
60. Farrand, *Records*, 1:83.
61. Farrand, *Records*, 1:82.
62. Farrand, *Records*, 2:120.
63. Farrand, *Records*, 2:204.
64. Farrand, *Records*, 2:249.
65. Silence Dogood, No. 9 (July 23, 1722), *Papers*, 1:30–31. In this essay Franklin quotes liberally from Cato's Letter No. 31 (May 27, 1721), and its influence on him is evident. See Ronald Hamowy, ed., *Cato's Letters: Or, Essays on Liberty, Civil and Religious, and other Important Subjects* (Indianapolis, IN: Liberty Fund, 1995), 1:227.
66. Farrand, *Records*, 1:216.
67. Letter to Richard Price, October 9, 1780, *Papers*, 33:390. See also his letter to Samuel Cooper, May 15, 1781, *Papers*, 35:68–69.
68. Franklin, *Autobiography*, 9, 11 [emphasis mine].
69. Franklin, *Autobiography*, 9.
70. Letter to Joseph Huey, June 6, 1753, *Papers*, 4:506.
71. Franklin, *Autobiography*, 65.
72. Franklin, *Autobiography*, 66.
73. Franklin, *Autobiography*, 81.
74. On the Hemphill affair, see Merton A. Christensen, "Franklin on the Hemphill Trial: Deism Versus Presbyterian Orthodoxy," *William and Mary Quarterly*, 3rd ser., vol. 10 (July 1953): 422–40; Walters, *Franklin and His Gods*, 136–40.
75. Walters, *Franklin and His Gods*, 142.
76. Franklin, *Autobiography*, 89–90, 87.
77. Franklin, *Autobiography*, 81, 87 [emphasis mine].
78. Franklin, *Autobiography*, 89.
79. Franklin, *Autobiography*, 81.
80. See generally, Christensen, "Franklin on the Hemphill Trial."
81. Franklin, *Autobiography*, 89, 99.
82. Franklin, *Autobiography*, 17.
83. Franklin, *Autobiography*, 88–89.
84. Franklin, *Autobiography*, 88.

85. Franklin, *Autobiography*, 96.

86. See Franklin, *Autobiography*, 94–95.

87. Franklin, *Autobiography*, 124 [emphasis mine].

88. Franklin, *Autobiography*, 97.

89. On Franklin's political relations with the Quakers, see William S. Hanna, *Benjamin Franklin and Pennsylvania Politics* (Palo Alto, CA: Stanford University Press, 1964); James H. Hutson, *Pennsylvania Politics, 1746–1770* (Princeton, NJ: Princeton University Press, 1974); Robert Middlekauff, *Benjamin Franklin and His Enemies* (Berkeley: University of California Press, 1996).

90. Franklin does not charge the Quakers with hypocrisy. In fact, he drafted a bill exempting conscientious objectors from military service. *Papers*, 6:266–73. But he suggests that the public might have perceived the Quakers to be hypocrites. See Franklin, *Autobiography*, 94–95.

91. For a thoughtful analysis of Franklin's efforts to shape social habits to an emerging democratic society, see Steven Forde, "Benjamin Franklin's *Autobiography* and the Education of America," *American Political Science Review* 86 (June 1992): 357–68.

92. Franklin, *Autobiography*, 14.

93. Farrand, *Records*, 1:197.

94. Farrand, *Records*, 1:452.

95. Franklin, *Autobiography*, 73.

96. Franklin, *Autobiography*, 73.

97. See *The Oxford English Dictionary*, 2d ed., s.v. "foppery," "fob."

98. "Preface to an Abridgement of the Book of Common Prayer" (before August 5, 1773), *Papers*, 20:346.

99. For a thoughtful discussion of this idea, see Fiering, "Franklin and the Way to Virtue."

100. Farrand, *Records*, 1:451–52.

101. "Franklin's Contribution to an Abridgment of the Book of Common Prayer" (before August 5, 1773), *Papers*, 20:346, 350. His version would retain only expressions of "our duty towards God, and our duty toward our neighbor."

102. Letter to Granville Sharp, July 5, 1785, in *Writings of Benjamin Franklin*, 9:358. Franklin also wrote an abridgment of the Lord's Prayer. "A New Version of the Lord's Prayer" (1768?), *Papers*, 15:299–303.

103. Franklin, *Autobiography*, 78.

104. Franklin, *Autobiography*, 78–79.

105. Benjamin Franklin to Joseph Huey, June 6, 1753, in *The Papers of Benjamin Franklin*, ed. Leonard W. Labaree et al. (New Haven: Yale University Press, 1959–), 4:504–6.

7

James Wilson

Presbyterian, Anglican, Thomist, or Deist?
Does It Matter?

Mark D. Hall

James Wilson is buried in America's Westminster Abby—Christ Church, Philadelphia. This Anglican church is only blocks away from the First Presbyterian church in Philadelphia, where Wilson rented a pew until the end of his life. Some scholars report that Wilson joined the Anglican Communion in 1778, perhaps at the behest of one his best friends, William White, the first Anglican bishop of Philadelphia. Others claim he that never abandoned the Presbyterianism of his native Scotland. Still others pay no attention to his denominational commitments, arguing that he was actually a Thomist or a deist. Finally, some scholars say nothing about his religious identification or beliefs, apparently concluding that these things are unrelated to his political and legal accomplishments.

It is a central thesis of this book, and of this chapter, that religion does matter. It matters for a number of reasons, but with respect to politics it is particularly significant because the most interesting political questions are ultimately moral questions, and most peoples' moral views are tied to their religious commitments. Even if political actors are not themselves religious (and many of them have been), they have been forced to take into account the religious sensibilities of the people they represent or govern. This is particularly true with respect to America, where religion—specifically, Christianity—has been central to our political tradition. It is certainly true in the case of James Wilson.

BIOGRAPHY

James Wilson was born in Carskerdo, Scotland, in 1742, the son of a lower-middle-class farmer. Dedicated to the ministry at birth, he received an uncommonly good classical education that enabled him to win a scholarship to the University of St. Andrews. Wilson studied there for four years before entering the university's divinity school, St. Mary's, in 1761. He was forced to withdraw in 1762 upon the death of his father, and for a few years served as a tutor to support his family. The life of a pedagogue did not suit Wilson, so as soon as his siblings were old enough to support their mother, he immigrated to America in search of greater opportunities. Arriving in Pennsylvania in 1765, Wilson taught Latin and Greek at the College of Philadelphia for a year before reading law under John Dickinson. He flourished as a lawyer and, as the Revolution approached, was drawn into politics.

Wilson achieved national recognition in 1774 with the publication of "Considerations on the Nature and Extent of the Legislative Authority of the British Parliament," the first essay to argue that Americans had absolutely no obligation to obey Parliament. He was able to put his theory of resistance into practice after he was appointed to the Continental Congress in 1775. He became an important participant in the debates over the controversy with Great Britain, and eventually cast the tie-breaking vote in the Pennsylvania delegation in favor of independence.

Wilson was one of the eight framers of the Declaration of Independence to attend the Constitutional Convention, and one of only six to sign both documents. Among the few delegates to attend the convention from start to finish, he participated in all of the most significant proceedings. He spoke more times (168) than any other member, save Gouverneur Morris, and was a member of the important Committee of Detail. His contributions have led scholars as diverse as James Bryce, Randolph G. Adams, Max Farrand, Ralph Ketcham, Adrienne Koch, Clinton Rossiter, Samuel Beer, and Paul Johnson to agree that Wilson was second only to James Madison, and was perhaps on a par with him, in terms of influence on the Constitution.[1]

Under Wilson's leadership, Pennsylvania became the second state, and the first large one, to ratify the Constitution. As the only member of the state's ratifying convention to have attended the federal convention, Wilson was in an excellent position to defend the Constitution. He began his defense with his "State House Yard Speech," an address that soon became, according to Gordon Wood, "the basis of all Federalist thinking."[2] By the end of 1787, the speech had been reprinted in thirty-four newspapers in twelve states, and it was circulated in pamphlet form throughout the former colonies.[3] According to Bernard Bailyn, "in the 'transient circumstances' of the time it was not so much the *Federalist* papers that captured most people's imaginations as James Wilson's speech of October 6, 1787, the most famous, to some the most notorious, federalist statement of the time."[4] Following the ratification of the U.S. Constitution, Wilson played a major role in the Pennsylvania constitutional convention of 1789–1790.[5]

Wilson was appointed associate justice of the U.S. Supreme Court in 1789. Although the Court heard relatively few cases during his tenure, he wrote notable opinions in *Hylton v. U.S.* (1796), *Ware v. Hylton* (1796), *Wiscart v. D'Auchy* (1796), and *Chisholm v. Georgia* (1793). His most significant opinion was issued while riding circuit in 1792. In *Hayburn's case*, Wilson led Justice John Blair and district court judge Richard Peters to declare Congress's Invalid Pension Act of 1792 to be unconstitutional. Because Congress rapidly altered the act to meet his objections, and because the Supreme Court never issued an opinion, the case is often overlooked as the first instance where a federal court declared an act of Congress to be unconstitutional.[6]

Wilson's most significant contribution to American jurisprudence took place off the Court. From 1790 to 1792 he gave a series of law lectures at the College of Philadelphia. Because he believed that law should be "studied and practised as a science founded in principle" not "followed as a trade depending merely upon precedent," many of his lectures are devoted to broad moral, epistemological, and political issues.[7] Consequently, they contain some of the most explicitly theoretical analysis of America's constitutional order by one who played a central role in its formation.[8]

Wilson was never able to revise his lectures into the definitive treatise on American law that he desired (they were, however, edited and published by his son, Bird Wilson, in 1804).[9] In 1798 an economic downturn devastated an overleveraged Wilson, who had begun speculating in western land in the early 1770s. Thrown into jail on two separate occasions, he spent his final days hiding from creditors in a tavern in Edenton, North Carolina. There, he contracted malaria and died on August 21, 1798. He was buried with little ceremony in Edenton, where his body remained until it was reburied at Christ Church in 1906.

THE LITERATURE

Throughout the twentieth century, scholars have had a tendency to dismiss many of the founders' religious claims as rhetorical flourish. In a similar manner, many recent students of Wilson ignore his clear, consistent, and systematic appeals to God, generally, and Christian natural law theory, more specifically. A good example of this is Roderick Hills's 1989 article "The Reconciliation of Law and Liberty in James Wilson," in which Hills argues that the primary purpose of Wilson's law lectures was to synthesize "Grotius's notion of natural liberty or perfect justice with the ancient Stoic notion of natural law or distributive justice."[10] This thesis is not patently unreasonable, but it is troubling that Hills refuses to defend his assertion that Wilson's conception of natural liberty or law was completely secular.[11] He simply ignores Wilson's clear statements that natural law is based on God. More significantly, given the thesis of his article, Hills does not even discuss Wilson's claim that Grotius weakened international law by removing it from its natural law foundation.[12]

Like Hills, other recent Wilson scholars, including Stephen Conrad, Jennifer Nedelsky, Shannon Stimson, and Samuel Beer, ignore his reliance on a traditional Christian conception of natural law.[13] In doing so, these authors neglect some of Wilson's most important and interesting views. For instance, none of them even refers to his claim that Congress is limited by "natural or revealed law" and his strong implication that the Supreme Court can strike down a statute on the basis of this law. It is possible, of course, to argue that Wilson was confused or not serious when he made these statements, but these scholars do not make this argument.[14]

Far more surprising, writers who believe that America had a "Christian Founding" and who claim that virtually every founder was an orthodox Christian have either ignored Wilson or have questioned his orthodoxy. For instance, John Eidsmoe provides a detailed treatment of thirteen founders in *Christianity and the Constitution*, where he classifies George Washington, Alexander Hamilton, and James Madison as "strong Christians," but does not even consider Wilson, even though the latter had more influence on the Constitution than any founder besides Madison.[15] More to the point, M. E. Bradford notes in *A Worthy Company* that fifty to fifty-three of the fifty-five authors of the Constitution were orthodox Christians, definitively leaving out only Hugh Williamson (a heterodox Presbyterian who speculated about unfallen men who lived on comets) and Wilson (who, he allows, might have been a deist, but "was probably a free thinker in the privacy of his study").[16]

Although recent scholars have tended to dismiss or ignore Wilson's religious language, this has not always been the case. Randolph G. Adams, in the preface to his 1930 collection of Wilson's writings, noted the similarities between Wilson and St. Thomas Aquinas and suggested that further study of this connection might prove fruitful.[17] This claim prompted a number of Catholic scholars to look at Wilson. Pioneering work in this regard was done by May G. O'Donnell, who published her findings in a 1937 book, *James Wilson and the Natural Law Basis of Positive Law.* More significant, and far more theoretically sophisticated, was William F. Obering's 1938 work, *The Philosophy of Law of James Wilson.* He contends that "Wilson was a convinced theist and bases the whole system of law on God, the Creator, an all-wise, and benevolent Providence of the universe."[18] Obering argues that this commitment provided Wilson with a "solid metaphysical foundation under his ethics in general and his jurisprudence in particular."[19] Once such a base was established, it was possible for Wilson to build a comprehensive theory of government and law. Obering ends his work with the conclusion that Wilson was effectively a Thomist.[20]

For thirty years after the publication of Father Obering's book, Neo-Scholastic scholars published an impressive number of doctoral dissertations, articles, and books arguing that Wilson was a serious natural law theorist.[21] Few of these works were theoretically sophisticated or added anything new to Obering's interpretation. One exception to this rule, Francis De Sales Powell's 1951 dissertation, "A Thomistic Evaluation of James Wilson and Thomas Reid," takes issue with Obering's attempt to reconcile Wilson's use of both Scottish moral-sense theory and Thomism. However, this work is never cited in the literature on Wilson.[22] In fact, other than Obering's book, it is rare to find any of these works cited by contemporary scholars. The main reason for this seems to be that Neo-Scholastic authors primarily wrote in Neo-Scholastic forums, where they could make assumptions that were unpopular in the general academy. Thus, they wrote primarily for themselves and had little influence on mainstream scholarship of the founding era, in general, or, more specifically, on Wilson scholarship.

One does not need to be a Thomist to conclude that Wilson embraced a Christian conception of natural law. For instance, Robert G.

McCloskey, the great student of American political thought and editor of Wilson's papers, noted,

> Among the several things that might be emphasized about this Wilsonian concept of natural law, perhaps the most important are its explicitly deistic origin and its normative quality. This is not the secularized natural law of some eighteenth century rationalists nor is it merely a morally indifferent rule of necessity like the "laws" of motion. It is God's ordainment, and it imposes ethical duties on men and on states.[23]

In my 1997 book, *The Political and Legal Philosophy of James Wilson*, I argue that both McCloskey and Neo-Scholastics were correct in recognizing the importance of Wilson's appeals to the Christian natural law tradition. No substantive claim of my book has been attacked by reviewers of the book as much as this one. Most notably, David Thomas Konig, Stephen Conrad, and Gary McDowell have criticized my interpretation in book reviews.[24] However, like the scholars mentioned above who reject the importance of Wilson's appeals to the Christian natural law tradition, they offer no arguments to support their criticism.[25] On the other hand, several scholars have suggested that a major strength of my book is that I take Wilson's Christian natural law teachings seriously.[26]

The only academic to publish a substantive critique of the idea that Wilson was a serious Christian natural law theorist, in both his review of my book and in his own article on Wilson, is Eduardo Velásquez.[27] He argues that sophisticated scholars can carefully read between the lines of Wilson's "Christian" rhetoric to find that for him, "human happiness or pleasure is the foundation of the natural law."[28] Moreover, Wilson's emphasis on self-preservation and acceptance of consent theory help to demonstrate that he does not adhere to the Christian natural law tradition. Instead, Velásquez argues that he embraced a modern theory of natural rights grounded primarily in self-interest, albeit one ameliorated by his affirmation of human sociability.[29]

Wilson clearly and consistently appealed to Christian principles throughout his works, something particularly evident and relevant with respect to his natural law theory. Given this reality, why do most contemporary students of Wilson ignore or refuse to take seriously his religious views? I believe that there are three major answers to this question. First, all too many academics remain convinced that intelligent people are not religious. Hence, it follows that the religious language of an obviously intelligent person like Wilson must be merely rhetorical. Second, some scholars who respect religion or are religious themselves believe modern liberalism is so antithetical to religion that when they conclude that Wilson is a liberal, they automatically dismiss his religious language as window dressing. Finally, some scholars are so desirous of finding a new, more interesting, interpretation of Wilson that they see little reason to resuscitate a seventy-year-old interpretation (even in part) and favor a new reading of Wilson more in accord with current scholarly trends.

Of course, few scholars would admit to adhering to the first or third reasons for neglecting Wilson's Christian theory of natural law, and I do not mean to question the good faith of any specific scholar I have mentioned. Moreover, I should make it clear that I believe a student of Wilson could legitimately conclude that he was not sincere about his religious/moral beliefs without fitting into any of the above three categories. However, as I argue below, there is a strong prima facie case that important elements of Wilson's political and legal philosophy rely on explicitly Christian principles. If scholars want to deny this, they should, at a minimum, provide arguments for their position.

RELIGIOUS BELIEFS AND DENOMINATION COMMITMENTS

Wilson was raised a Scottish Presbyterian, he studied to become a Presbyterian minister, and his best biographer, Page Smith, wrote that he "could never bring himself to abandon completely the forms and doctrines of his parents' church."[30] Similarly, William B. Miller, relying on church archives, documented that Wilson was a member of the governing board of the Presbyterian church of Carlisle in 1773 and that he made regular contributions to, and rented a pew from, the First Presbyterian Church of Philadelphia from 1778 until his death in 1798.[31] Nevertheless, it is not clear that Wilson remained an active member of the church of his youth throughout his entire life.

Shortly after arriving in America, Wilson became fast friends with William White, who later became the first Anglican bishop of Philadelphia. In 1768, the two friends wrote a series of newspaper articles for the *Pennsylvania Chronicle and Universal Advertiser*.[32] Around this time, Page Smith suggested that White had almost convinced Wilson to become an Anglican, but that he did not succeed.[33] However, L. J. Trinterud, in his book on early American Presbyterianism, claimed that Wilson left the Presbyterian Church in 1782.[34]

Moreover, several scholars have stated that Wilson became an Episcopalian, and Deborah Gough even specifies that he joined Christ Church in 1778.[35] However, none of these authors offer any evidence to support their claims.

To referee between these competing claims, I examined the pew rental records and other documents for Christ Church, Philadelphia. I found no mention of Wilson or his family until March 1794, where he is recorded as renting three seats on the front row of the church's gallery. The seats cost approximately seven pounds per year, and his accounts were paid in full until the end of his life. Interestingly, the account warden continued to charge Wilson's estate for the pew until 1801 when his son, Bird, paid the accumulated debt and took over the pew in his own name.[36]

Of course, renting a pew may say little about Wilson's actual commitments (after all, Wilson apparently rented pews at two different churches between 1794 and 1798, and founders like Benjamin Franklin rented a pew from Christ Church). Other evidence, however, suggests that Wilson's conversion was more than window dressing. For instance, his son, Bird, who later became an Episcopalian priest, noted in his biography of William White that he had been raised under White's "pastoral care."[37] As well, Wilson had his last son, Henry, baptized at Christ Church soon after his birth in 1796.[38] On balance, the evidence strongly suggests that James Wilson became an active Episcopalian in 1794.

Denominational commitments are not unimportant, but more significant for our purpose is the extent to which Wilson's Christian beliefs influenced his political philosophy and, hence, his contributions to the creation of the American republic. Rather than attempt to summarize all of his beliefs that influenced his political views and actions, I shall focus on his acceptance of Christian natural law theory. This focus is justified in light of the significance of natural law for Wilson's political theory and actions. It also allows me to document my claim in some detail, making it difficult for skeptics to claim that I am basing my argument on isolated or unimportant passages from Wilson's works.

WILSON'S THEORY OF NATURAL LAW

The Neo-Scholastic interest in Wilson discussed above is somewhat ironic as Wilson was a lifelong Protestant who never cited St. Thomas

Aquinas, and his references to the Catholic Church or, particularly, popes, were often negative.[39] However, throughout his works, and particularly in his law lectures, Wilson clearly, consistently, and systematically appealed to the Christian natural law tradition.

He began his law lectures by focusing on the theoretical basis of law, noting that "to direct the more important parts of our conduct, the bountiful Governour of the universe has been graciously pleased to provide us with a law; and that, to direct the less important parts of it, he has made us capable of providing a law for ourselves."[40] Following Richard Hooker, who in turn borrowed from St. Thomas Aquinas, he divided the first type of law, which he called "divine law," into four "species."[41]

The first species of divine law, "eternal law," concerns God's eternal plan for the universe.[42] Wilson's understanding of the second species of law, "celestial law," came directly from Richard Hooker's *Of the Laws of Ecclesiastical Polity*. Like Hooker, he believed that celestial law governs men and angels in the "celestial and perfect state." Accordingly, it is not clear to men in the present state because they can see it "but darkly, and as through a glass."[43] The third species of divine law is comprised of physical laws by which "the irrational and inanimate parts of the creation are governed." He explained that the "great Creator of all things has established general and fixed rules, according to which all the phenomena of the material universe are produced and regulated." The science whereby these laws may be known is called natural philosophy.[44]

The fourth type of divine law is "that law which God has made for man in his present state." There are several manifestations of this law:

> As promulgated by reason and the moral sense, it has been called natural; as promulgated by the holy scriptures, it has been called revealed law.
>
> As addressed to men, it has been denominated the law of nature; as addressed to political societies, it has been denominated the law of nations.
>
> But it should always be remembered, that this law, natural or revealed, made for men or for nations, flows from the same divine source: it is the law of God.[45]

Wilson contended that because God created the world and has "infinite power—infinite wisdom—and infinite goodness," he has "supreme right to prescribe a law for our conduct, and that we are under the most perfect obligation to obey that law."[46] Similarly, he stated several times that our obligation to obey natural law is rooted in the "will of God."[47]

Wilson argued that God's laws are always good. Negatively, they prevent "chaos and disorder."[48] Positively, they promote the happiness of men and women. He contended,

> Being infinitely and eternally happy in himself, his goodness alone could move him to create us, and give us the means of happiness. The same principle that moved his creating, moves his governing power. The rule of his government we shall find to be reduced to this one paternal command—Let man pursue his own perfection and happiness.[49]

Wilson's connection of God's laws to happiness have led some scholars to conclude that he was a utilitarian or a Hobbesian natural-rights theorist. Yet, in the context of his lectures, Wilson is no more a utilitarian or modern natural-right theorist than St. Thomas, who also connected God's natural law to human perfection and human happiness.[50]

God's moral laws may be known through the "reason, conscience, and the holy scriptures."[51] Because humans are made in the image of God, and because Wilson's view of the Fall was more Catholic than Calvinist, he did not see anything contradictory in arguing that natural law could be known through reflecting on one's nature. More than once he quoted St. Paul's claim that natural law is "engraven by God on the hearts of men."[52] Moreover, one can learn much about God's laws from studying nature. Sounding like St. Thomas, he noted,

> When we view the inanimate and irrational creation around and above us, and contemplate the beautiful order observed in all its motions and appearances; is it not the supposition unnatural and improbable—that the rational and moral world should be abandoned to the frolicks of chance, or to the ravage of disorder?[53]

Wilson believed that every human has a moral sense that provides knowledge of the first principles of morality. Such knowledge allows men and women to resolve most moral problems, but it is occasionally necessary to reason from first principles to solve particular problems. Moreover, one's moral sense, and even the moral sense of a society, may become corrupt through disuse, faulty education, or bad laws. Thus, it is not surprising that people have moral disagreements and that some cultures accept practices that are considered immoral by people in other cultures. Even so, careful consideration will show that people and cultures agree on moral issues far more often than they disagree. As people come to understand the requirements of natural law, it may be said to progress. In Wilson's words, "the law of nature, though immutable in its principles, will be progressive in its operations and effects." He was quite clear that it is only our knowledge of the natural law that changes, not the natural law itself.[54]

The second great class of law, human law, "must rest its authority, ultimately, upon the authority of that law which is divine."[55] It may be divided into two species: "1. That which a political society makes for itself. This is municipal law. 2. That which two or more, political societies make for themselves. This is the voluntary law of nations."[56] Municipal law includes the civil and criminal laws made by legislatures for the governing of society. In creating these laws, legislators must remain cognizant of "the very close and interesting connexion, which subsists between the law of nature and municipal law."[57] He emphasized that human laws should be "an emanation from the law of nature and morality." If they are not, they are void.[58]

The second species of human law is the "law of nature, when applied to states or political societies." Wilson examined this law, now commonly referred to as international law, in detail. In doing so he became, according to Randolph G. Adams, the first American to write systematically about the law of nations. He approached the subject by critiquing the views of two of the giants of international law, Hugo Grotius and Samuel von Pufendorf. Most significant for our purposes, Wilson was highly critical of Grotius for depriving the law of nations of the "greatest part of its obligatory force" by removing the idea that it is based on natural law, which is based upon "the will of God."[59]

NATURAL RIGHTS

According to Brian Tierney, thinkers in the Christian natural law tradition have derived natural rights from natural laws since at least the twelfth century.[60] Similarly, scholars such as Clinton Rossiter have argued that many of the founders relied on "natural law as the source of natural rights."[61] This is clearly the case with Wilson, who referred to the "rights, to which we are entitled by the supreme and uncontrollable laws of nature" and argued that natural rights are simply rights individuals are "entitled" to "by nature and nature's law."[62]

Over the last fifty years, a number of scholars, particularly those influenced by Leo Strauss, have argued that thinkers such as Thomas Hobbes and John Locke fundamentally altered traditional Christian natural law theory while retaining some of its language. Instead of relying on God as the source of natural law, they adopted a theory of natural rights based on self-interest. Many of these scholars agree that this theory was prevalent among American elites in the founding era. This tradition has encouraged some scholars to attribute such views to Wilson, in spite of his pervasive Christian natural law rhetoric.[63]

No one has made this case with respect for Wilson more clearly than Eduardo Velásquez. In doing so, he focuses much attention on Wilson's claim that "the defense of one's self, [is] justly called the primary law of nature."[64] While this quotation does have a Hobbesian flavor, in the context of all of Wilson's writings on natural law, it is more likely that Wilson's view of self-preservation and its place in his moral system was no more Hobbesian than similar views offered by St. Thomas in *Summa Theologica* (I, II, Q. 94, a. 2) or by Cicero in *Pro Milone*, which Wilson cited and quoted from in support of the above quotation.[65] In fact, Velásquez attempts to ameliorate his claim regarding Wilson's natural-rights theory by arguing that he borrowed from Scottish notions of human sociability.[66] But Wilson's view of rights is better understood in light of the Christian natural law tradition.

Wilson thought that because natural rights are based on natural law, they exist prior to government. Being ultimately grounded in God, they must always be respected. The protection of natural rights is the first task of government. Wilson rhetorically asked,

> What was the primary and principal object in the institution of government? Was it—I speak of the primary and principal object—was it to acquire new rights by a human establishment? Or was it, by a human establishment, to acquire a new security for the possession or the recovery of those rights, to the enjoyment or acquisition of which we were previously entitled by the immediate gift, or by the unerring law, of our all-wise and all-beneficent Creator?[67]

For him it was clearly the latter.

Wilson provided an extensive discussion of the nature and scope of natural rights in his law lecture entitled "Of the Natural Rights of Individuals." Among other things, he argued that an individual has a "natural right to his property, to his character, to liberty, and to safety."[68] Although all of these are worthy of discussion, I focus here on his view of the right to life and liberty as they most clearly demonstrate the close connection between natural law and natural rights.

When discussing liberty, Wilson rejected the extreme, individualistic brand of freedom envisioned by many modern liberals. Instead, he taught that liberty must always be understood within the limits placed on it by moral and civil law. He noted. "Without liberty, law loses its nature and its name, and becomes oppression. Without law, liberty also loses its nature and its name, and becomes licentiousness." This concept was so important to Wilson that he quoted a similar dictum from Cicero as the epigraph for his law lectures: *Lex fumamentum est libertatits, qua fruimur. Legum omnes servi sumus, ut liberi esse possimus.*[69]

In the state of nature, there is no civil law, so liberty is limited only by natural law. In civil society men and women are still required to obey the latter, but they are also bound by positive laws. Wilson conceded that "by the municipal law, some things may be prohibited, which are not prohibited by the law of nature."[70] Yet, restrictions may not violate the natural rights of a person, and they must clearly benefit the public. Although Wilson did not provide a detailed discussion regarding what sort of regulations would be acceptable, it seems clear that he was referring either to minor restrictions, such as requiring drivers to drive on the right side of the road, or more significant restrictions in times of extreme danger, such as conscription during times of war. It is evident, however, that he had confidence that under a just government, individuals would be freer than they were in a state of nature. There is no reason to doubt his sincerity when he claimed that

> under a government which is wise and good, every citizen will gain more liberty than he can lose by these prohibitions. He will gain more by the limitation of other men's freedom, than he can lose by the diminution of his own. He will gain more by the enlarged and undisturbed exercise of his natural liberty in innumerable instances, than he can lose by the restriction of it in a few.[71]

Wilson had a fairly expansive conception of the scope of liberty protected by natural law. This is best illustrated by his discussion of freedom of conscience, or, in his words, "rights of conscience inviolate."[72] He contended,

> The right of private judgment is one of the greatest advantages of mankind; and is always considered as such. To be deprived of it is insufferable. To enjoy it lays a foundation for that peace of mind, which the laws cannot give, and for the loss of which the laws can offer no compensation.[73]

Because individuals must be free to make their own choices, Wilson supported the general freedom of an individual to "act according to his own inclination" if he "does no injury to others" and if "more publick interests do not demand his labours."[74] It is not clear exactly how far Wilson was ready to extend this principle, but at a minimum he certainly meant that the government should not interfere with an individual's liberty to think and believe what he wants. This was particularly true in matters of religion.

Given the centrality of Christianity for Wilson's political theory, it is important to emphasize that he was a strong advocate of religious liberty. In his inaugural law lecture, for instance, after he praised Locke's work on religious toleration, he reminded his audience that a law in favor of freedom of religion had been passed in Maryland as early as 1649. He then noted with pride that when Lord Baltimore was urged to repeal the law, "with the enlightened principles of a man and a Christian, he had the fortitude to declare, that he never would assent to the repeal of a law, which protected the natural rights of men, by ensuring every one freedom of action and thought."[75] Moreover, Wilson did not restrict his conception of liberty to matters of the heart and mind. He fully supported the right of the people "to speak, to write, to print, and to publish freely." Yet, he believed each of these rights to have limits, as indicated by his support of laws against libel and slander.[76]

Wilson embraced a thoroughly Christian view of the right to life. He explained, with evident approval,

> With consistency, beautiful and undeviating, human life, from its commencement to its close, is protected by the common law. In the contemplation of the law, life begins when the infant is first able stir in the womb. By the law, life is protected not only from immediate destruction, but from every degree of actual violence, and in some cases, from every degree of danger.[77]

On the basis of this principle, Wilson criticized ancient societies, such as Sparta, Athens, China, and Rome, for the practice of exposing or killing unwanted infants. He also condemned the "gentle Hindoo" who "is laudably averse to the shedding of blood; but he carries his worn out friend and benefactor to perish on the banks of the Ganges."[78] He justified laws against crimes such as "assault," "battery," "rape," and "homicide" because these actions violate this right.[79]

The right to life was very important to Wilson. From the womb to one's natural death, it must be protected. The high value he placed on life came from his view of its origin. In his most famous Supreme Court opinion, he noted, "MAN, fearfully and wonderfully made, is the workmanship of his all perfect CREATOR."[80] The implications of this are significant. For instance, when writing on suicide, he explained that it was not by his own voluntary act that the man made his appearance upon the theatre of life; he cannot, therefore, plead the right of the nation, by his own voluntary act to make his exit. He did not make; therefore, he has no right to destroy himself. He alone, whose gift this state of existence is, has the right to say when and how it shall receive its termination.[81]

Life is a gift from God, and it must be protected. For this reason natural law prevents individuals from killing or attacking each other, although it allows for death as a punishment for particularly horrible crimes. If a person is sentenced to death, however, Wilson made it clear in a grand jury charge that "an interval should be permitted to elapse before [the sentence's] execution, as will render the language of political expediency consonant to the language of religion."[82]

Wilson's view of natural rights was firmly based upon his theory of natural law. Because rights are based upon God's universal and absolute law, they must always be respected. Such a theory helped Wilson to justify the colonies' revolt against England, and it played an important role in his contributions to the creation of the American republic.[83] Yet, the rights of individuals are limited by the natural law upon which they are founded. Wilson clearly rejected the extreme individualistic view of rights that would come to dominate American political theory and law.[84]

RELEVANCE AND IMPACT

Wilson's view of rights is relevant today as scholars attempt to understand the founders' views of the nature and limits of the rights protected by the Constitution and Bill of Rights. Although he was not immediately involved in writing or ratifying the Bill of Rights, given his significant role in writing, ratifying, and interpreting the U.S. Constitution and his influence on American law through his law lectures, Wilson's views are clearly worthy of consideration. Surely they are at least as relevant as those of Thomas Jefferson, whose 1802 letter to the Danbury Baptist Association has wielded such influence in American constitutional law (and, of course, Jefferson wasn't even in America when the Constitution or Bill of Rights were written or ratified).

More significantly, virtually all of Wilson's contributions to the creation of American political institutions were influenced by his belief that "the primary and the principle object in the institution of government" is "to acquire a new security for the possession or the recovery of those rights, to the enjoyment or acquisition of which we were previously entitled by the immediate gift, or by the unerring law, of our all-wise and all-beneficient Creator."[85] Because he thought every person could know natural law "by our conscience, by our reason, and by the Holy Scriptures" and because he had a relatively optimistic view of human nature, he was led to embrace democracy with more consistency than any other major founder.[86] He advocated, for instance, the direct, popular, and proportional election of representatives, senators, and the chief executive at both the federal and state levels. Also, he opposed property qualifications for voters and limitations on who could hold office.

Although Wilson was a consistent advocate of democratic institutions, he recognized that humans are corruptible; therefore, he did not rely uncritically on the goodwill of elected officials or the electorate. Accordingly, he supported the separation of powers and checks and balances. Significantly, he argued that legislatures are limited in what they can do by "natural and revealed law," and the context of this claim suggests that he believed courts could declare legislative acts that did so to be void.[87]

Although Wilson supported judicial review, he objected to the addition of a bill of rights to the U.S. Constitution because he thought Congress was already limited by its enumerated powers and, more significantly, that a bill of rights would be dangerous. He argued that if an "attempt to enumerate [natural rights] is made, it must be remembered that if the enumeration is not complete, everything not expressly mentioned will be presumed to be purposefully omitted."[88] To address this problem, Madison proposed, and the states eventually ratified, the Ninth Amendment to the U.S. Constitution.

Wilson's contributions at the federal convention and his view of judicial review and the Bill of Rights cannot be understood if one does not comprehend his theory of natural rights. The latter is best interpreted in light of the Christian natural law tradition. Because rights are based on a universal, transcendent conception of natural law, they must be protected against infringements from both minorities and majorities. The primary purpose of government is to protect these rights and to make positive law in accordance with natural law. Wilson's views on natural law and how it is known informed his many significant contributions to the creation of the American republic.

CONCLUSION

Space constraints prevent a more detailed discussion of the relationship between Wilson's religious faith and his political theory and actions. In my book on Wilson, I attempt to flesh these out in detail and consider them in their proper historical context. Even the limited discussion of Wilson in this chapter, however, should make it clear that a strong case can be made that he was a serious Christian thinker. This suggests that contemporary scholars who simply ignore Wilson's religious language do so at great risk. Although it is possible to argue that all of Wilson's religious language was mere rhetorical flourish, it is troubling that many contemporary Wilson scholars do not even feel compelled to make such an argument.

APPENDIX: OF LAWS

Of law there are different kinds. All, however, may be arranged in two different classes. 1. Divine. 2. Human laws. The descriptive epithets employed denote, that the former have God, the latter, man, for their author.

The laws of God may be divided into the following species.

1. That law, the book of which we are neither able nor worthy to open. Of this law, the author and observer is God. He is a law to himself, as well as to all created things. This law we may name the "law eternal."
2. That law, which is made for angels and the spirits of the just made perfect. This may be called the "law celestial." This law, and the glorious state for which it is adapted, we see, at present, but darkly and as through a glass: but hereafter we shall see even as we are seen; and shall know even as we are known. From the wisdom and the goodness of the adorable Author and Preserver of the universe, we are justified in concluding, that the celestial and perfect state is governed, as all other things are, by his established laws. What those laws are, it is not yet given us to know; but on one truth we may rely with sure and certain confidence—those laws are wise and good. For another truth we have infallible authority—those laws are strictly obeyed: "In heaven his will is done."
3. That law, by which the irrational and inanimate parts of the creation are governed. The great Creator of all things has established general and fixed rules, according to which all the phenomena of the material universe are produced and regulated. These rules are usually denominated laws of nature. The science, which has those laws for its object,

is distinguished by the name of natural philosophy. It is sometimes called, the philosophy of body. Of this science, there are numerous branches.

4. That law, which God has made for man in his present state; that law, which is communicated to us by reason and conscience, the divine monitors within us, and by the sacred oracles, the divine monitors without us. This law has undergone several subdivisions, and has been known by distinct appellations, according to the different ways in which it has been promulgated, and the different objects which it respects.

As promulgated by reason and the moral sense, it has been called natural; as promulgated by the holy scriptures, it has been called revealed law.

As addressed to men, it has been denominated the law of nature; as addressed to political societies, it has been denominated the law of nations.

But it should always be remembered, that this law, natural or revealed, made for men or for nations, flows from the same divine source: it is the law of God.

Nature, or, to speak more properly, the Author of nature, has done much for us; but it is his gracious appointment and will, that we should also do much for ourselves. What we do, indeed, must be founded on what he has done; and the deficiencies of our laws must be supplied by the perfections of his. Human law must rest its authority, ultimately, upon the authority of that law, which is divine.

Of that law, the following are maxims—that no injury should be done—that a lawful engagement, voluntarily made, should be faithfully fulfilled. We now see the deep and the solid foundations of human law.

It is of two species. 1. That which a political society makes for itself. This is municipal law. 2. That which two or more political societies make for themselves. This is the voluntary law of nations.

In all these species of law—the law eternal—the law celestial—the law natural—the divine law, as it respects men and nations—the human law, as it also respects men and nations—man is deeply and intimately concerned. Of all these species of law, therefore, the knowledge must be most important to man.

Those parts of natural philosophy, which more immediately relate to the human body, are appropriated to the profession of physick.

The law eternal, the law celestial, and the law divine, as they are disclosed by that revelation, which has brought life and immortality to light, are the more peculiar objects of the profession of divinity.

The law of nature, the law of nations, and the municipal law form the objects of the profession of law.

From this short, but plain and, I hope, just statement of things, we perceive a principle of connexion between all the learned professions; but especially between the two last mentioned. Far from being rivals or enemies, religion and law are twin sisters, friends, and mutual assistants. Indeed, these two sciences run into each other. The divine law, as discovered by reason and the moral sense, forms an essential part of both.

From this statement of things, we also perceive how important and dignified the profession of the law is, when traced to its sources, and viewed in its just extent.

The immediate objects of our attention are, the law of nature, the law of nations, and the municipal law. On the two first of these three great heads, I shall be very general. On the last, especially on those parts of it, which comprehend the constitutions and publick law, I shall be more particular and minute.

NOTES

1. James Bryce, "James Wilson: An Appreciation," *The Pennsylvania Magazine of History and Biography* (October 1936), 360; Randolph G. Adams, ed. *Selected Political Essays of James Wilson* (New York: Alfred Knopf), 20; Max Farrand, *The Framing of the Constitution of the United States* (New Haven, CT: Yale University Press, 1913), 197; Ralph Ketcham, *James Madison: A Biography* (Charlottesville: University Press of Virginia, 1971), 229; Adrienne Koch, "Introduction," in *Notes of the Debates in the Federal Convention of 1787* (New York: W.W. Norton, 1987), xii; Clinton Rossiter, *1787: The Grand Convention* (New York: W.W. Norton and Co., 1966), 247–48; Samuel Beer, *To Make A Nation* (Cambridge, MA: Harvard University Press, 1993), 360; Paul Johnson, *A History of the American People* (New York: HarperCollins, 1997), 193.

2. Gordon Wood, *The Creation of the American Republic* (Chapel Hill: University of North Carolina Press, 1969), 530, 539–40.

3. John P. Kaminski and Gaspare J. Saladino, eds. *The Documentary History of the Ratification of the Constitution* (Madison: State Historical Society of Wisconsin, 1981), 13:344.

4. Bernard Bailyn, *The Ideological Origins of the American Revolution.* Enlarged ed. (Cambridge, MA: Harvard University Press, 1992), 328.

5. See especially Robert Brunhouse, *The Counter-Revolution in Pennsylvania, 1776–1790* (New York: Octagon Books, 1972).

6. 2 U.S. (2 Dall.) 410 (1792); Max Farrand, "The First Hayburn case, 1792," *American Historical Review* (1907–1908), 281–85.

7. Robert McCloskey, ed. *The Works of James Wilson,* 2 vols. (Cambridge, MA: The Belknap Press of Harvard University Press, 1967), 564 (hereafter cited as *Works*).

8. Benjamin F. Wright, *American Interpretations of Natural Law* (Cambridge, MA: Harvard University Press, 1931), 281. The lectures were particularly influential in the nineteenth century. Joseph Story, for instance, refers to them throughout his *Commentaries on the Constitution of the United States,* 3rd ed. 2 vols. (Boston: Little, Brown, and Co., 1858).

9. On the text of the lectures, and Bird Wilson's changes, see Mark David Hall, "James Wilson's Law Lectures," *The Pennsylvania Magazine of History and Biography* CXXVIII (January 2004), 63–76.

10. Roderick M. Hills Jr., "The Reconciliation of Law and Liberty in James Wilson," *Harvard Journal of Law and Public Policy* 12 (1989), 891.

11. Hills suggests that Wilson's claim that "Order proportion and fitness pervade the universe" shows that he had a stoic view of natural law (*Works*, 67; Hills, "Reconciliation," 893). He does not attack, or even acknowledge, the possibility that this idea could have a Thomistic origin.

12. *Works*, 150.

13. Stephen A. Conrad, "Polite Foundation: Citizenship and Common Sense in James Wilson's Republican Theory," *1984 Supreme Court Review*, ed. Philip Kurland (Chicago: Chicago University Press, 1985); Stephen A. Conrad, "Metaphor and Imagination in James Wilson's Theory of Federal Union," *Law and Social Inquiry* 13 (1988): 1–70; Stephen A. Conrad, "James Wilson's 'Assimilation of the Common-Law Mind'," *Northwestern University Law Review* 84 (Fall 1989): 186–219; Jennifer Nedelsky, *Private Property and the Limits of American Constitutionalism* (Chicago: University of Chicago Press, 1990); Shannon Stimson, "'A Jury of the Country,' Common Sense Philosophy and the Jurisprudence of James Wilson," in Richard Sher and Jeffrey Smitten, eds., *Scotland and America in the Age of Enlightenment* (Princeton, NJ: Princeton University Press, 1990); Samuel Beer, *To Make a Nation*.

14. *Works*, 329.

15. John Eidsmoe, *Christianity and the Constitution: The Faith of Our Founding Fathers* (Grand Rapids, MI: Baker Book House, 1987). Similarly, see Norman Cousins, *In God We Trust: The Religious Beliefs and Ideas of the American Founding Fathers* (New York: Harper & Brothers, 1958).

16. M. E. Bradford, *A Worthy Company: Brief Lives of the Framers of the United States Constitution* (Marlborough, NH: Plymouth Rock Foundation, 1982), ix, 81–87. Tim LaHaye follows Bradford's analysis uncritically in *Faith of Our Founding Fathers* (Brentwood, TN: Wolgemuth and Hyatt, 1987).

17. Randolph G. Adams, *Selected Political Essays of James Wilson* (New York: Alfred A. Knopf, 1930), 7.

18. William F. Obering, *The Philosophy of Law of James Wilson: A Study in Comparative Jurisprudence* (Washington, DC: Catholic University of America, 1938), 50.

19. Obering, *The Philosophy of Law*, 19.

20. Obering, *The Philosophy of Law*, 186.

21. See for example, J. Moss Ives, "St. Thomas Aquinas and the Constitution," *Thought* 13 (December 1937): 567–87; and Mary T. Delahanty, *The Integralist Philosophy of James Wilson* (New York: Pageant Press, 1969).

22. Francis De Sales Powell, "A Thomistic Evaluation of James Wilson and Thomas Reid," Ph.D. dissertation, Georgetown University, 1951.

23. McCloskey, in *Works*, 38. Also see Hadley Arkes, *Beyond the Constitution* (Princeton, NJ: Princeton University Press, 1990), 64, and John West, *The Politics of Revelation and Reason: Religion and Civic Life in the New Nation* (Lawrence: University Press of Kansas, 1996), 41–45.

24. Reviews of my book include David Thomas Konig, *American Historical Review* (February 1999): 185–86; Stephen A. Conrad, *Journal of American History* (June 1998): 217–18; Gary McDowell, *Times Literary Supplement* (April 30, 1999): 12–13.

25. Unless one counts as an argument Stephen Conrad's implication that I am inclined toward a natural law interpretation because I am a cultural conservative, a claim

he supports by pointing out that I cite books by James Davison Hunter and James Q. Wilson in the conclusion to my book. Ironically, Hunter was not arguing for any sort of natural law theory, and I have criticized James Q. Wilson for not following through on the natural law implications in his book that I cite in my conclusion (Mark Hall, review of James Q. Wilson, *The Moral Sense, Southeastern Political Review* 23 [March 1995], 170–71). If Conrad wanted to show that I think natural law theory has much to offer contemporary theoretical debates, he might have cited my text in the conclusion, where I say that it does, or noted my praise of John Finnis and Robert George as being among the best contemporary natural law theorists. Mark Hall, *The Political and Legal Philosophy of James Wilson* (Columbia: University of Missouri Press, 1997), 199–201. Once he has demonstrated this point, however, it is still incumbent upon him to offer some reason why my claim that Wilson's commitment to the Christian natural law tradition was of primary (but not sole) importance is false.

26. See, for instance, George Carey, *American Political Science Review* 92 (March 1998): 203–4; Michael Novak, *On Two Wings: Humble Faith and Common Sense at the American Founding* (San Francisco: Encounter, 2002), 140; Garrett Ward Sheldon, *The Political Philosophy of James Madison* (Baltimore: Johns Hopkins University Press, 2001), 130.

27. Eduardo A. Velásquez, *Law and History Review* (Spring 1999): 184–87; Eduardo Velásquez, "Rethinking America's Modernity: Natural Law, Natural Rights and the Character of James Wilson's Liberal Republicanism," *Polity* 29 (Winter 1996), 193–220. Several authors assert that Wilson rejected Christian natural law theory in books dedicated to broader themes. Some, such as Wilson Carey McWilliams and Thomas Pangle, make short arguments to support their assertions. Their arguments are not unreasonable, but in the context of the whole of Wilson's treatment of natural law, they are not convincing. I address some of these claims in notes throughout this chapter. Wilson Carey McWilliams, *The Idea of Fraternity in America* (Berkeley: University of California Press, 1973), 193–99; Thomas Pangle, *The Spirit of Modern Republicanism: The Moral Vision of the American Founders and the Philosophy of Locke* (Chicago: University of Chicago Press, 1988), 122–23; Morton Horwitz, *The Transformation of American Law: 1780–1860* (Cambridge, MA: Harvard University Press, 1977), 8–20.

28. Velásquez, "Rethinking America's Modernity," 205.

29. Velásquez, "Rethinking America's Modernity," 205–20; and Velasquez, review of *The Political and Legal Philosophy of James Wilson*, 187.

30. Page Smith, *James Wilson: Founding Father, 1742–1798* (Chapel Hill: University of North Carolina Press, 1956), 28.

31. William B. Miller, "Presbyterian Signers of the Declaration of Independence," *Journal of the Presbyterian Historical Society* 36 (September 1958): 148–51.

32. Smith, *James Wilson*, 32–35.

33. Smith, *James Wilson*, 28–29.

34. L. J. Trinterud, *The Formation of an American Tradition: A Re-examination of Colonial Presbyterianism* (Philadelphia: Westminster Press, 1949), 256–57.

35. Deborah Gough, *Christ Church, Philadelphia* (Philadelphia: Barra Foundation, 1995), 137, 145; M. E. Bradford, *A Worth Company*, 83. Cf. Owen Ireland, *Religion, Ethnicity and Politics: Ratifying the Constitution in Pennsylvania* (University Park: The Pennsylvania State University Press, 1995), esp. 167, 259.

36. Pew Registers, Lists of Pew Holders, 1785–1800; Account Wardens, Pew Rent Records 1770–1801. Christ Church Archives Microfilm, reels 28–30. The pew rental records also show that Christ Church provided a pew for the "President of the United States" when the national government met in Philadelphia.

37. Bird Wilson, *Memoir of the Life of the Right Reverend William White, D.D.* (Philadelphia: James Kay, Jun. & Brother, 1839), 269.

38. Henry was Wilson's only child by his second wife, Hannah. Hannah Wilson was raised a Quaker, so there is no reason to believe that James had Henry baptized at Christ Church on her behalf. Smith, *James Wilson*, 380.

39. See, for instance, *Works*, 63, 120, 729–30.

40. *Works*, 126. Note that Wilson seems to depart from common practice by not capitalizing personal pronouns referring to God. In his lecture drafts, however, he follows traditional practices and capitalizes such pronouns. For some reason, his son, or the printer, changed these pronouns to the lower case. For further discussion see Mark David Hall, "James Wilson's Law Lectures," 70–71.

41. *Works*, 123.

42. *Works*, 123–24; Aquinas, *Summa Theologica*, Q.93. Art. 1–6

43. *Works*, 124; Richard Hooker, *Laws of Ecclesiastical Polity*, ed. John Keble (Oxford: The Clarendon Press, 1888), 1:204–5.

44. *Works*, 124.

45. *Works*.

46. *Works*, 128, 126, 132–33. In his discussion of the relationship between God's goodness and power, Wilson proposed and then immediately rejected the idea that "infinite goodness could be disjoined from almighty power." Wilson Carey McWilliams takes this to be a subtle hint that he rejected traditional Christian theology. However, I think it is more accurate to focus on Wilson's conclusion, which is best regarded as a first principle that people cannot help but believe. In other words, it is simply obvious, if not rationally provable, that God is omnipotent, omniscient, and good. Of course the modern reader might object that this notion of God is really a Judeo-Christian one, and that this is hardly a principle to which all people naturally gravitate (if such principles do in fact exist), but the correctness of Wilson's claim is not at issue here (*Works*, 128, McWilliams, *The Idea of Fraternity in America*, 194).

47. For example, *Works*, 132, 150, 153.

48. *Works*, 130.

49. *Works*, 129.

50. For instance, Cornelia Geer Le Boutillier asserted that Wilson's natural law ideas were "completely utilitarian," in *American Democracy and Natural Law* (New York, Columbia University Press, 1950), 115, 118. More recently, Eduardo Velásquez has argued that it is important that Wilson shifted his claim that God wants man to "pursue his own perfection and happiness" to God wanting man to "pursue his happiness and perfection" (Velásquez "Rethinking America's Modernity," 204–5; *Works* 129, 145). However, if one considers the context of both claims, a different picture emerges. I do this in the text for the first quote and would point out that the second one is followed by a discussion of the immutable and universal character of natural law (*Works* 129, 145). Moreover, Wilson later discussed men seeking their "perfection or happiness," although this time in the context of human government (*Works*, 579). Altogether, when Wilson's claims are taken in context, his teachings are thoroughly

compatible with a Christian conception of natural law, as is recognized by his Neo-Scholastic interpreters (e.g., Obering, *Philosophy of Law*, 51–57). Cf. Aristotle, *Ethics*, esp. bks. 1 and 10; St. Thomas Aquinas, *Summa Theologica*, II, I, Qs. 1–5.

51. *Works*, 144.

52. *Works*, 125, 133–34, 143–45, 200, 102, 136. Compare the last quote with Romans 2: 14–15: "For when the Gentiles, which have not the law, do by nature the things contained in the law, these, having not the law, are a law unto themselves: Which shew the work of the law *written in their hearts*, their conscience also bearing witness . . ." (emphasis added).

53. *Works*, 129. Compare this quote with St. Thomas Aquinas, *On Truth*, Q. 5, a. 2, c.; and *Summa Theologica*, Q. 94.

Unlike some of his contemporaries, Wilson did not think that the Bible was only a source of moral teaching. He seemed to take seriously its discussion of miracles such as the flood, the Tower of Babel, and the Resurrection. *Works*, 376, 711–12, 715. See also *Works*, 126, 130, 143, 399, 585. For a detailed discussion of Wilson's view of the Bible, human nature, and moral epistemology, see ch. 3 of my book *The Political and Legal Philosophy of James Wilson*.

54. *Works*, 133–67, 197–26, 628, 821, 147.

55. *Works*, 124.

56. *Works*, 125.

57. *Works*, 587.

58. *Works*, 617, 329.

59. *Works*, 150.

60. Brian Tierney, *The Idea of Natural Rights: Studies on Natural Rights, Natural Law, and Church Law, 1150–1625* (Grand Rapids, MI: Eerdmans, 1997). Of course, there is plenty of debate on the subject of when individual subjective rights arose. Even if one is convinced that Tierney is wrong, however, it is indisputable that some Christian thinkers have thought it possible to derive natural rights from a Christian conception of natural law. Twentieth-century proponents of this idea include Jacques Maritain, *The Rights of Man and Natural Law* (New York: Scribner, 1943), and John Finnis, *Natural Law and Natural Rights* (New York: Oxford, 1980).

61. Clinton Rossiter, *Seedtime of the Republic* (New York: Harcourt, Brace, and World, 1953), 369.

62. *Works*, 722, 589, 241, 753. On the connection between natural law and natural rights in America, see also Mortimer J. Adler and William Gorman, *The American Testament* (New York: Praeger Publisher, 1975), 33–41; and Ellis Sandoz, *A Government of Laws* (Baton Rouge: Louisiana State University Press, 1990), 162–217, esp. 189–97. Not surprisingly, the idea that natural rights are derived from natural law was accepted by all of Wilson's Neo-Thomistic interpreters. For a good example, of this see William F. Obering, "Our Constitutional Origins," *Thought* 11 (December 1937): 600. Wilson used the term *rights* to refer to "natural rights," "constitutional rights," and "legal rights." It is important, therefore, to examine closely the context in which he discussed rights. See, for example, *Works*, 93, 148, 153, 284, 325–26, 495, and 583–610.

63. Leo Strauss, *Natural Right and History* (Chicago: University of Chicago Press, 1950); Martin Diamond, "Democracy and *The Federalist*: A Reconsideration of the Framers' Intent," *American Political Science Review* 53 (March 1959): 52–68; and Walter Berns, "Judicial Review and the Right and Laws of Nature," *The Supreme Court*

Review, 1982, ed. Philip Kurland (Chicago: University of Chicago Press, 1983); Pangle, *The Spirit of Modern Republicanism*, esp. 122–23. See also Philip A. Hamburger, "Natural Rights, Natural Law, and American Constitutions," *Yale Law Journal* (January 1993): 907–60. Wilson is quite critical of Hobbes, but thinkers influenced by Strauss correctly point out that Hobbes had become so vilified even in his own lifetime that his followers would (or will) rarely identify with him (e.g. *Works*, 105, 464).

64. Velásquez, "Rethinking America's Modernity," 210, 193–96; *Works*, 609. Velasquez criticizes me for not discussing this claim in my book on Wilson (Velásquez, "Rethinking America's Modernity," 187). Although I do not discuss the passage, I do discuss Wilson's views regarding the right to preserve oneself (Hall, *Political and Legal Philosophy of James Wilson*, 57–58).

65. *Works*, 609. Velásquez neglects to note that Wilson appealed to Cicero's work as his authority for this claim.

66. Jean M. Yarbrough makes a similar argument with respect to Thomas Jefferson and then suggests that it applied to Wilson as well in *American Virtues: Thomas Jefferson on the Character of a Free People* (Lawrence: University Press of Kansas, 1998), 203,n86.

67. *Works*, 585.

68. *Works,* 592. Compare with John Locke, *Second Treatise,* ed. Peter Laslett (Cambridge: Cambridge University Press, 1960), 268–78, 283–86, 304.

69. *Works*, 72. Adler and Gorman translate the quote to read, "Law is the foundation of the liberty we enjoy. We are all servants of the laws in order that we can be free." Adler and Gorman, *The American Testament*, 118.

70. *Works*, 587.

71. *Works*, 592, 579, 587–88. Compare with Barry Shain, *The Myth of American Individualism: The Protestant Origins of American Political Thought* (Princeton, NJ: Princeton University Press, 1994). Yet, Wilson did not agree with all of the community restrictions discussed by Shain (esp. 153–92). For a good discussion of Wilson's views in this regard see Obering, *Philosophy of Law*, 99–100.

72. *Works*, 159.

73. *Works*.

74. *Works*, 587, 242, 71, 104, 579, and 649. Even Shain agrees that the founders had a fairly modern, expansive view of freedom of conscience (*Myth of American Individualism*, 30, 163–65, 176).

75. *Works*, 71, 104.

76. *Works*, 242, 579, 596, 649. With respect to religion, Wilson noted without comment that "[p]rofaneness and blasphemy are offenses, punishable by fine and imprisonment. Christianity is a part of the common law." Similarly, he remarked that certain "vicious and dishonorable" vices may be censored by the public (*Works*, 671, 242).

77. *Works*, 597.

78. *Works*, 596–97.

79. *Works*, 533–662, 653, 656, 657.

80. *Chisholm v. Georgia*, 2 U.S. (2 Dall.) 419, 455 (emphasis in original). Later in the opinion he wrote that "*Man himself*, free and honest, is, I speak as to this world, the noblest work of God." (emphasis in original, 463). Similarly, in his law lectures, he wrote that "the mind is of an order higher than that of the body, even more of the

wisdom and skill of the divine Architect is displayed in its structure. In all respects, fearfully and wonderfully are we made" (*Works* 202; Cf. Psalms 139: 13–14).

81. *Works*, 155.

82. *Works*, 818, 806, 661, 669.

83. *Works*, 721–46.

84. On this movement, see especially Michael Sandel, *Democracy's Discontent: America in Search of a Public Philosophy* (Cambridge, MA: Harvard University Press, 1996).

85. Sandel, *Democracy's Discontent*, 585. This is an important corrective to scholars who argue that the founders were primarily concerned with promoting their own self-interest, or that of their race, class, and gender.

86. Sandel, *Democracy's Discontent*, 133. I present this argument in detail in Mark Hall, "The Wilsonian Dilemma," *Southeastern Political Review* 25 (December 1997): 641–58.

87. *Works*, 329–30. For a detailed discussion, see Hall, *Political and Legal Philosophy of James Wilson*, chs. 4 and 5.

88. John McMaster and Frederick D. Stone, eds. *Pennsylvania and the Federal Constitution 1787–1788* (New York: Da Capo Press, 1970), 1:254.

8

George Mason's Pursuit of Religious Liberty in Revolutionary Virginia*

Daniel L. Dreisbach

Historians have exhaustively chronicled and rightly celebrated the contributions of Thomas Jefferson and James Madison to religious liberty in Virginia and the new nation. George Mason IV, by contrast, has received neither the credit nor the attention given to his more famous contemporaries for his contributions to the cause of religious freedom.[1] He was the principal draftsman of article XVI of the Virginia Declaration of Rights, a seminal, postcolonial statement on the rights of conscience. In legislative chambers and behind the scenes, Mason was a deft, untiring strategist in the bitter contests to guarantee religious freedom and to end the legal favors enjoyed by the established church in Virginia. Few among the founding generation have had such a significant and enduring influence on religious liberty, yet received as little public recognition as George Mason. He was a pivotal figure in the struggle to craft a distinctively American doctrine of religious liberty and church–state relations for both the commonwealth and the nation.[2]

A planter from Gunston Hall on the Potomac, George Mason was by all accounts a virtuous man. His biographers, unlike Jefferson's and Madison's, have written remarkably little about his religious faith and experience. The secondary literature is nearly devoid of

*An earlier version of this chapter was presented as a Liberty Lecture at Gunston Hall Plantation, Mason Neck, Virginia, on October 14, 1997, and published in *Virginia Magazine of History and Biography* 108, no. 1 (2000): 5–44. The author thanks the Virginia Historical Society for an Andrew W. Mellon Fellowship, which made possible additional research for this chapter.

any substantive discussion of his personal religious beliefs. Nonetheless, Mason's personal papers reveal glimpses of his piety. Moreover, as Josephine F. Pacheco has opined, "Mason more than any other revolutionary leader insisted on the necessity for morality in public life."[3] He confided to Patrick Henry, for example, that morality, "Justice & Virtue are the vital Principles of republican Government."[4] He was a lifelong member of the Church of England and, like many gentlemen of his social standing, served as a vestryman, an office with civic, as well as ecclesiastical, responsibilities. From 1749 to 1785, he was a vestryman of Truro Parish in Fairfax, Virginia. Shortly following his election to the vestry, he was designated a churchwarden.[5] He faithfully attended religious services and supervised the building of Pohick Church.[6]

From the earliest days of his adulthood, Mason exhibited an awareness of, and sensitivity to, the interests of religious citizens. For example, as officers of the Ohio Company of Virginia in 1753, Mason and his partners prepared an advertisement that included religious liberty among the inducements to attract Protestant immigrants to the company's vast western holdings. "That with regard to their religious Liberties," the recruitment document stated, "all foreign Protestants may depend on enjoying in this Government the Advantage of the Acts of Toleration in as full and ample manner as in any other of his Majesties plantations whatsoever, as great numbers of them have already experienced."[7] In short, he used religious freedom as an enticement to attract immigrants and increase profits for his land company. For another example, in "An Ordinance for Establishing a General Test Oath," framed in 1775 at the instruction of the Virginia Convention, Mason included a provision accommodating Quakers unable to swear an oath[8] for reasons of conscience by permitting them, in the alternative, to make solemn affirmation.[9] Such accommodation of the Quakers was not uncommon in the constitutions and laws of the late colonial and Revolutionary eras.

Unlike most gentlemen of his class and social standing, George Mason may have indirectly experienced the indignities of religious prejudice. His second wife, Sarah Brent, was the eldest daughter of George Brent of Woodstock in Stafford County. The Brents were a wealthy, devout Roman Catholic family with deep roots in Virginia, who, despite their prominence, were acquainted with the anti-Catholic laws and bigotry in Protestant Virginia.[10] George and Sarah, both in their early fifties, were married on April 11, 1780, in the Anglican Church.[11] Mason reported that he attended Roman Catholic services on more than one occasion, perhaps in the company of his wife, and once in Philadelphia, while a Virginia delegate to the Constitutional Convention of 1787.[12] His intimate exposure to a minority religious community undoubtedly made him more aware than most men of his social class of the tenuous place and restricted rights of religious dissenters in Virginia.

Although many historians have noted in passing Mason's legislative activities in behalf of religious liberty in Revolutionary Virginia, very little scholarship focuses specifically on Mason's contributions to the cause of religious freedom. This chapter seeks to rectify this omission. It first addresses the drafting of article XVI of the Virginia Declaration of Rights before turning to Mason's legislative role in defusing explosive church–state issues unleashed by that article, such as the legal rights of dissenters. Of particular interest are various legislative initiatives raised in late 1776 and 1779 to redefine church–state relations and religious liberty in Virginia. Next, the chapter chronicles Mason's behind-the-scenes involvement in the dramatic disestablishment struggle of the mid-1780s, which culminated in the passage of the Virginia "Bill for Establishing Religious Freedom." The conclusion acknowledges Mason's last great cause, his ardent advocacy for a federal bill of rights, and reflects on his legacy of liberty in Virginia and the nation.

ARCHITECT OF THE VIRGINIA DECLARATION OF RIGHTS

Today, George Mason is best known as the principal draftsman of the Virginia Declaration of Rights, adopted on June 12, 1776.[13] He was a Fairfax County delegate to the Virginia Convention, filling the seat vacated by George Washington when he became commander in chief of the Continental Army. The convention, which assembled in Williamsburg on May 6, 1776, was arguably the most noteworthy political body in the commonwealth's history.[14] Composed largely of veterans of the old House of Burgesses, the convention, on May 15, passed a resolution instructing the commonwealth's delegates at the Continental Congress to press for a declaration of independence from England.[15] The assembly also appointed a committee to prepare a state declaration of rights and plan of civil government.[16] Among those appointed to the committee were Mason and the young, untested delegate from Orange County, James Madison Jr.[17]

Mason, whose considerable talents were well known in the commonwealth, was the chief architect of the Declaration of Rights. Indeed, as Gaillard Hunt observed, "The master spirit of the Convention was George Mason."[18] In late May, Mason prepared a list of ten proposals to which others were added by Thomas Ludwell Lee and the committee.[19] The convention printed the Virginia Declaration in draft form and thoroughly debated and amended the document before it was passed unanimously on June 12. The singular achievement and genius of Mason's Declaration of Rights lies, as Thomas Jefferson said of his own Declaration of Independence, not in its "originality of principle or sentiment . . . [but rather in its] expression of the American mind" with its brilliant "harmonizing sentiments of the day."[20] William C. Rives characterized the Declaration as

> a condensed, logical, and luminous summary of the great principles of freedom inherited by us from our British ancestors; the extracted essence of Magna Charta, the Petition of Right, the acts of the Long Parliament, and the doctrines of the Revolution of 1688 as expounded by Locke,—distilled and concentrated through the alembic of [Mason's] own powerful and discriminating mind. There is nothing more remarkable in the political annals of America than this paper. It has stood the rude test of every vicissitude.[21]

The committee drafts of the Declaration were printed and circulated widely up and down the Atlantic seaboard in late May and June, and they had an immediate and "profound impact on other Americans [in nascent states] whose task it was to create new governments."[22] Robert A. Rutland observed,

> By the time the last cannonade of the Revolution sounded, every state either had fashioned a separate bill of rights or had passed statutes with similar provisions. In a good many cases the work was done with scissors, pastepot, and a copy of the Virginia Declaration—a fact that did not escape Mason's notice.[23]

It is, perhaps, not too much to acclaim the Declaration of Rights, which Mason boasted was the "first in America,"[24] as "an intellectual guidepost of the American Revolution."[25] This seminal document secured for Mason an honored seat among the literati of the Revolution.[26]

Drawing on principles expressed in John Locke's *Letter Concerning Toleration*,[27] Mason included an article on religion in the "first draught" of the Virginia Declaration. His original proposal declared,

> That as Religion, or the Duty which we owe to our divine and omnipotent Creator, and the Manner of discharging it, can be governed only by Reason and

Conviction, not by Force or Violence; and therefore that all Men shou'd enjoy the fullest Toleration in the Exercise of Religion, according to the Dictates of Conscience, unpunished and unrestrained by the Magistrate, unless, under Colour of Religion, any Man disturb the Peace, the Happiness, or Safety of Society, or of Individuals. And that it is the mutual Duty of all, to practice Christian Forbearance, Love and Charity towards Each other.[28]

The committee slightly amended Mason's initial version before laying it before the convention on May 27.[29] This iteration, although not the final text, was the draft printed and distributed widely in Virginia and in other colonies:

That religion, or the duty which we owe to our CREATOR, and the manner of discharging it, can be directed only by reason and conviction, not by force or violence; and therefore, that all men should enjoy the fullest toleration in the exercise of religion, according to the dictates of conscience, unpunished and unrestrained by the magistrate, unless, under colour of religion, any man disturb the peace, the happiness, or safety of society. And that it is the mutual duty of all to practice Christian forbearance, love and charity, towards each other.[30]

Although James Madison was certainly interested in all portions of the Virginia Declaration, only the final article "providing for religious toleration, stirred him to action." In "his first important public act,"[31] Madison objected to Mason's use of the word "toleration" because it dangerously implied that religious exercise was a mere privilege that the civil state could grant or revoke at its pleasure, rather than an equal, indefeasible right wholly exempt from the cognizance of the civil state and subject only to the dictates of a free conscience. Mason's proposal went further than any previous declaration in force in Virginia; it did not go far enough, however, to satisfy Madison. Madison wanted to replace "toleration" with the concept of absolute equality in religious belief and exercise. As early as 1774, Madison had come to think of religious toleration, the ultimate objective of most reformers of his day, as an inadequate halfway point on the road to religious liberty.[32] Madison eventually concluded that religious toleration, whether granted by the civil state or by a religious establishment, was inconsistent with freedom of conscience. Historically speaking, religious *toleration* stands in contrast to religious *liberty*. The former often assumes an established church and is always a revocable grant of the civil state rather than a natural, unalienable right.[33] In Madison's mind, the right of religious exercise was too important to be cast in the form of a mere privilege allowed by the ruling civil polity and enjoyed as a grant of governmental benevolence. Instead, he viewed religious liberty as a fundamental and irrevocable right, possessed equally by all citizens, that must be placed beyond the reach of civil magistrates.[34]

Madison's proposed revisions punctuated his aversion to the concept of mere toleration with a natural-rights argument that all men are equally entitled to the free exercise of religious belief. It is not certain when Madison offered his amendments, but they followed the committee revision of May 27. He first suggested as an alternative:

> That Religion or the duty we owe to our Creator, and the manner of discharging it, being under the direction of reason and conviction only, not of violence or compulsion, all men are equally entitled to the full and free exercise of it accord[in]g to the dictates of Conscience; and therefore that no man or class of men ought, on account of religion to be invested with peculiar emoluments or privileges; nor subjected to any penalties or disabilities unless under &c.[35]

Significantly, Madison retained the clause, "That Religion or the duty we owe to our Creator, and the manner of discharging it." The retention of this line suggests that both Mason and Madison construed "religion" as belief in a Creator and all of the duties arising from that belief. This notion is consistent with definitions of religion used historically in Virginia, and it included deists, but excluded atheists. Crucially, Madison replaced Mason's tentative statement "all Men should enjoy the fullest Toleration in the Exercise of Religion," with the phrase "all men are equally entitled to the full and free exercise of [religion]." He recognized that religious duties are prior to civil obligations. Madison thus jettisoned the language of toleration and embraced the concept of absolute religious liberty. The logic of Mason's phrasing was that because religion "can be governed only by reason and conviction, not by force or violence," for practical reasons all men "should enjoy . . . the fullest toleration." By contrast, the practical difficulty of governing religious opinion, whether by coercion or persuasion, concerned Madison less; rather, he sought to remove religion and matters of conscience from the cognizance of the civil state.[36] Key to Madison's restatement was the word "equally," which the convention retained in subsequent drafts. This language meant that the unlearned Separate Baptists of the central Piedmont had religious rights equal to those of the well-heeled Anglican aristocrats of the Tidewater.[37] Madison also dropped the word "enjoy" preceding the phrase "free exercise of religion." The word was reinserted in Madison's subsequent amendment, but it was stricken from the final version.

The clause stating "that no man or class of men ought, on account of religion to be invested with peculiar emoluments or privileges" was another radical feature of Madison's revision. It would have effectively terminated legal and financial support for the ecclesiastical establishment in Virginia. ("[M]an or class of men" is a reference to a clergyman or religious sect.) Religious assessments arguably would have been proscribed. Furthermore, by striking out "force" and replacing it with "compulsion," Madison was expanding the protection afforded religious citizens to include a prohibition on all pressure or interference by the civil state in matters of conscience. Madison's revision arguably would have deprived the commonwealth of legal and financial power to support any church or clergy or to control the religious beliefs of citizens in any way.[38]

This revision was unacceptable to most delegates and, perhaps, to most Virginians. Unable to muster sufficient support for passage of this amendment, Madison drafted a second alternative providing for the free exercise of religion, but carefully avoiding disestablishing the Anglican Church[39]:

> That religion, or the duty which we owe to our CREATOR, and the manner of discharging it, can be directed only by reason and conviction, not by force or violence; and therefore, that all men are equally entitled to enjoy the free exercise of religion, according to the dictates of conscience, unpunished and unrestrained by the magistrate, Unless the preservation of equal liberty and the existence of the State are manifestly endangered; And that it is the mutual duty of all to practice Christian forbearance, love, and charity towards each other.[40]

Although retaining a regime of equality and liberty in religious exercise, Madison's second revision abandoned the quixotic attempt to disestablish the church. He also dropped the word "compulsion," "thus giving up the specific prohibition of religious control through civil processes." Madison was successful, however, in cutting Mason's "clause on disturbance of the peace down to the Lockean principle of no interference with religion except to preserve civil society."[41] Mason had given the civil magistrate latitude to restrain religious exercise that disturbed "the Peace, the Happiness, or Safety" not only of society, but also of individuals. Madison, by contrast, would allow civil magistrates to infringe religious exercise only when it manifestly endangered the "existence of the State." By narrowing the state's interest in limiting religious exercise, Madison favored the claims of religious citizens.[42] The final version totally eliminated the clause qualifying religious exercise that is deemed a danger to the civil state.

Once again, delegates to the Virginia Convention declined to endorse Madison's amendment as a whole. They were uncomfortable with any suggestion that Madison's proposals might "sever the special relationship which bound Virginians to the church of their fathers."[43] The version finally adopted, however, included his clause declaring that "all men are equally entitled to the free exercise of religion." Madison apparently offered his amendments without sharp objection from Mason. In a letter to Mason's grandson in December 1827, Madison casually recounted that the term *toleration* "had been admitted into the original draught of the Declaration of Rights; but on a suggestion from myself was readily exchanged for the phraseology excluding it."[44] This episode, importantly, brought Madison to the attention of his fellow delegates and distinguished him, along with Mason and Jefferson, as an able spokesman for the cause of religious liberty.[45] In its final form, article XVI of the Virginia Declaration of Rights provided,

> That Religion, or the duty which we owe to our CREATOR, and the manner of discharging it, can be directed only by reason and conviction, not by force or violence; and, therefore, all men are equally entitled to the free exercise of religion, according to the dictates of conscience; and that it is the mutual duty of all to practise Christian forbearance, love, and charity, towards each other.[46]

The final version, observed L. John Van Til, linked "Creator," "religion," and "conscience."

> Religion is the way that a man relates to his Creator, but this relationship can be cared for only through conscience. Conscience employs reason and conviction, not force and violence; hence, conscience as the only way to discharge the duties of man toward his Creator must be at liberty. Significantly, the [article] adds that it is necessary therefore, to practice "Christian forbearance, love, and charity towards each other."[47]

This language rests on two important assumptions: first, that the rights of conscience envisioned by the Virginia Convention were to be exercised in a theistic context, and, second, that religious exercise involves not only the relationship between one man and his God, but also the relationship of each man to his neighbor.

The Virginia Convention thus embedded religious liberty in the organic law of the commonwealth. The effects of article XVI on law and policy were immediate, according to historian Hamilton James Eck-enrode. Notwithstanding the limited intentions of the legislature as manifested by its rejection of several of Madison's sweeping amend-ments, "[p]rosecution for religious causes ceased. Disabilities on ac-count of religion were removed. . . . Anglicans, Roman Catholics, Evangelicals, Jews, and unbelievers were placed on the same civil footing." Virginia, Eckenrode boasts, "was ahead of the world, . . . making the first legal statement of the principle of religious liberty."[48] Mason is rightly revered as the principal author of the Virginia Decla-ration of Rights, and it is his version of the article on religion, not Madison's, that was widely circulated and influential in the former colonies. Madison, it is recalled, did not offer his amendments until after the committee draft of the Virginia Declaration had been pub-lished and broadcast throughout the colonies and beyond. Mason wrote the initial script that, in the short term, was greatly imitated.[49] Yet, in the final analysis, it was the young James Madison who deliv-ered the memorable, felicitous lines that changed the way later gen-erations of Americans regarded religious liberty.

RELIGIOUS ESTABLISHMENT AND THE RIGHTS OF DISSENTERS IN REVOLUTIONARY VIRGINIA, 1776–1779

Although delegates to the Virginia convention may not have meant ar-ticle XVI to imply an end to the established church, religious dis-senters interpreted it that way. Accordingly, passage of article XVI un-leashed a torrent of petitions from clamoring religious dissenters demanding full equality in the exercise of religious belief and discon-tinuation of tax support and other special privileges granted to the commonwealth's established church. The dissenters' grievances were legion. In addition to advocating disestablishment and free exercise of religion, they protested specific practices and policies such as li-censure of the clergy, regulation of assemblies and meetinghouses, disposition of church buildings and glebe lands, incorporation of re-ligious societies, constitution and powers of vestries, and perfor-mance of legal marriages by dissenting ministers.[50]

The first republican legislature in Virginia, which convened in Williamsburg in early October 1776, was deluged by the dissenters' petitions. A poignant plea from the Presbyterian stronghold of Prince Edward County captured the spirit of these petitions:

> The last Article of the [Virginia] Bill of Rights we also esteem as the rising Sun of religious Liberty, to *relieve* us from a long night of ecclesiastical Bondage: and we do most earnestly request and expect that you would go on to complete what is so nobly begun; raise religious as well as civil Liberty to the zenith of Glory, and make Virginia an Asylum for free enquiry, knowledge, and the virtuous of every Denomination.

The petitioners asked the legislature, without delay, to "pull down all Church Establishments; abolish every Tax upon Conscience and private judgment."[51] In the words of another appeal, the petitioners, "haveing [*sic*] long groaned under the Burden of an Ecclesiastical establishment beg leave to move your Honourable House that this as well as every other yoke may be Broken and that the oppressed may go free."[52] Other memorialists petitioned "to put every religious Denomination on an equal Footing, to be supported by themselves independent one of another."[53] A letter from Augusta County, published in Purdie's *Virginia Gazette*, quoted the free-exercise language of article XVI and urged that the Virginia government give it immediate effect by placing all religious sects on the same basis, "without preference or preeminence" granted to any one church.[54] This outpouring was an immediate and practical consequence of article XVI. Indeed, many, if not most, of these petitions made direct appeal to the free-exercise language of the Virginia Declaration.

The ensuing battle over tax support for the established church was to prove long and rancorous. It prompted Jefferson to recollect in his retirement that the legislative infighting occasioned by these "petitions to abolish this spiritual tyranny . . . brought on the severest contests in which I have ever been engaged."[55] Mason, too, was drawn into the skirmish. The long-established order was reluctant to relinquish its legal privileges without a bruising fight. The fact that, as Jefferson noted, "although the majority of our citizens were dissenters . . . a majority of the legislature were churchmen" only deepened the acrimony.[56]

The Committee for Religion, to which the legislature had assigned these petitions, deadlocked while deliberating how to deal with the dissenters' demands. Thus, on November 9, 1776, the Virginia legislature relieved the committee of the task of considering these petitions and referred the matter to the house, sitting as a committee of the whole.[57] The house warmly debated the religion question and eventually adopted a set of sweeping resolutions on November 19.[58] These resolves called for the repeal of all acts of the British Parliament that criminalized religious opinion, refusal to attend religious services, or differing modes of worship. Other resolves exempted dissenters from all taxes or forced contributions to support the established church. They even removed any requirement that citizens contribute to the support of their own ministers except on a strictly voluntary basis. The resolves called for repealing several legislative acts that provided for clerical salaries, although all arrears of salary were to be paid present incumbents. The established church received in perpetuity the use of glebes, churches, chapels, and other possessions obtained from either public or private sources. "The net effect of these resolutions was to place all religious groups on a purely voluntary basis with respect to financial support, while giving the established church all the property and goods it possessed at the time," noted Thomas E. Buckley.[59]

The house appointed a committee of seventeen members, including Robert Carter Nicholas, a leading conservative churchman, and Jefferson, Madison, and Mason, to craft a bill in conformity with these resolutions.[60] In the ensuing deliberations, temporarily outmaneuvered by conservatives on the committee, Mason and his allies lost ground on the disestablishment issue, and the liberal tide of November 19 seemed to ebb.[61] The committee was instructed "to limit itself to those measures which pertained to tax exemption for dissenters and the reservation of the church property to the use of the establishment and to add provisions for the parish poor, the collection of the lists of tithables, and clerical salaries."[62] In short, the assembly withdrew from the committee the authority to address the more sweeping disestablishment aspects of the resolutions of November 19. The bill reported on November 30 confirmed that the "delegates had moved back into a position which unmistakably affirmed the existence of an established church in Virginia."[63] Jefferson, who in late November had been granted a special leave for the remainder of the legislative session, hurried back on December 4, possibly to salvage what he believed to be the most salient features of the November 19 resolutions.[64] In concert with Jefferson, Mason was instrumental in crafting compromise language that the house passed on December 5.[65] Mason's revision to the "Bill Exempting Dissenters from Contributing to the Established Church" deftly preserved some of the phraseology and much of the substance of the November 19 resolutions,[66] yet it stopped short of the complete, unequivocal disestablishment that Jefferson had desired:

WHEREAS several oppressive Acts of Parliament respecting Religion have been formerly enacted, and Doubts have arisen and may hereafter arise whether the same are in Force within this Common-Wealth or not, for Prevention whereof Be it enacted by the General Assembly of the Common-Wealth of Virginia, and it is hereby enacted by the Authority of the same, That all and every Act [or Statute either] of [the] Parliament [of England, or of Great Britain], by whatsoever Title known or distinguished, which renders criminal the maintaining of any Opinions in Matters of Religion, forbearing to repair to Church, or the exercising any Mode of worship whatsoever, or which prescribes punishments for the same, shall henceforth be of no Validity or Force within this Common-Wealth.[67]

The bill, which quickly passed in the House and Senate with minor amendments,[68] "repealed all laws requiring church attendance and exempted dissenters from direct tax support for the Anglican Church, but left untouched the Act of 1705 which maintained the symbolic established church."[69] The statute, Buckley reported, left

the established church in an ambiguous situation. No longer were the dissenters taxed to support a state church; nor were they forced to contribute to their own religious groups. The laity of the established church were also freed, at least on a temporary basis, from any taxation to support their own ministry. Religion in Virginia had become voluntary, and a man could believe what he wished and contribute as much or as little as he thought fit to whichever church or minister pleased him. He could also worship when and as he chose, within certain limits; for the Assembly maintained a measure of control over the external operations of the churches. The legislators had not officially yielded their authorization to license meetinghouses and dissenting preachers. Local magistrates, if they wished, might still claim a legal basis for restricting freedom of worship. However, the Revolutionary situation and popular sentiment for the rights of conscience precluded any consistent or widespread enforcement of these laws, and they effectually lapsed.[70]

Passage of the statute repealing the "oppressive acts of Parliament," observed Julian P. Boyd, editor of Jefferson's papers, "was due in large measure to the author of the [Virginia] Declaration of Rights. Even Mason, however, did not restore Jefferson's Resolution calling for the repeal of the Virginia Act of 1705, and their combined power was not equal to the task of disestablishing the Church of England."[71] Nonetheless, this legislation was a significant milestone on the road to eventual termination of an ecclesiastical establishment in Virginia. Jefferson's draft resolutions and legislation of late 1776 exempting dissenters from contributing to the support of the established church, refined by Mason's pen, were necessary precursors to, and direct forerunners of, the subsequent Virginia statute for establishing religious freedom.[72]

Among the issues deliberately left unresolved by the 1776 exemption act was the propriety of a general assessment for the support of all churches. The law concluded by stating that "nothing in this act contained shall be construed to affect or influence the said question of a general assessment, or voluntary contribution, in any respect whatever."[73] A typical general assessment proposal would tax all citizens for the support of religion, but permit each taxpayer to choose the church to which his assessment would be allocated. This arrangement, proponents argued, would encourage citizens to fulfill the "duty which we owe to our Creator" and promote the beneficent role of religion in public life, without forcing citizens to subsidize a specific church or form of worship that they disbelieved. Hence, they said, it was compatible with the free exercise of religion. Opponents, on the other hand, viewed the assessment as simply another odious form of religious establishment. This issue became the subject of bitter legislative battles in 1779 and again in the mid-1780s. And, once again, Mason played a decisive role in these contests.

The legislation of December 1776 permanently exempted dissenters from being taxed to support the established church but only temporarily suspended until the end of the next legislative session the collection of taxes from Anglicans to support their clergy. The legislature continued the suspension from one session to the next over the next several years. (The exemption created a loophole whereby Anglicans could escape paying their own minister's salary merely by declaring themselves "dissenters." The suspension of collecting taxes from Anglicans thus temporarily afforded all citizens, dissenters and Anglicans alike, tax relief.) By 1779, disestablishmentarians in the legislature agitated to make the suspension permanent and, thus, reach a more definite settlement of the church–state question. Numerous church–state issues had been percolating since long before independence, and with every passing year deferring resolution of these issues became increasingly difficult. Article XVI of the Declaration of Rights had been in force for nearly three years, raising questions concerning the precise nature of church–state arrangements in the commonwealth and the expectations of dissenters. Great uncertainty and turmoil arising from the suspension of salaries agitated the clerical ranks. Vestries were in a growing state of disarray and, indeed, faced calls for their complete dissolution. Thus, the 1779 spring session of the Virginia legislature was critical for church–state relations. As in earlier deliberations on church and state, Mason was as engaged in the 1779 legislative skirmishes as any other representative.

The legislature took up a variety of items important to organized religion. On May 17 the house instructed the Committee for Religion to examine and report on various requests to dissolve and reconstitute the vestries.[74] On June 4 the house appointed a committee, composed of John Harvie, George Mason, and Jerman Baker, to bring in a bill "for religious freedom."[75] The legislature also directed the trio to prepare a bill "for saving the property of the church heretofore by law established."[76] In response, on June 12 the committee submitted to the house two bills from Virginia's revised code: Jefferson's celebrated bill for establishing religious freedom and a bill for saving the property of the church heretofore by law established.[77] The house briefly considered the bills, but voted to defer further action on the measures.[78] The postponement afforded lawmakers ample time to canvass public sentiment on these matters. In early June, disestablishment forces in the legislature had lost their most effective advocate, Thomas Jefferson, who was elected to succeed Patrick Henry as governor.[79] The removal of his forceful voice from legislative deliberations frustrated the liberal campaign for church–state separation. In mid-June, the house ordered the Committee for Religion to prepare a bill "for farther [*sic*] suspending the payment of salaries heretofore given to the clergy of the Church of England."[80] The house received and promptly passed the bill on June 17.[81] Further discussion on a bill dissolving the vestries was shelved until the October session.[82] Thus, according to Eckenrode, "The [spring] session came to an end with the religious question in exactly the same position as before."[83]

The same church–state issues were, once again, prominent on the October legislative agenda. Petitions favoring and opposing Jefferson's religious freedom bill joined the steady stream of petitions on religion that had confronted the legislature since independence. By the time the legislature reconvened, "[t]he reaction in the press and the religious petitions clearly showed that the weight of public opinion favored some form of governmental intervention in religious matters, and this sentiment found support in the House of Delegates."[84] The house did not even consider Jefferson's controversial bill.

Not content merely to leave Jefferson's bill in legislative limbo, on October 25 the conservative defenders of state assistance for religion introduced a general assessment bill for the "encouragement of Religion and virtue" and for the "Support of Religious Teachers and places of Worship." The bill affirmed "that all persons and Religious Societies who acknowledge that there is one *God*, and a future State of rewards and punishments, and that *God* ought to be publickly worshiped, shall be freely tolerated." The bill specifically provided civil and religious privileges, such as the fruits of a general assessment and the right to incorporate, for those Christian societies and denominations that subscribed to five articles of faith (modeled on article XXXVIII of the South Carolina Constitution of 1778), including that "there is one Eternal God and a future State of Rewards and Punishments, . . . the Christian Religion is the true Religion, [and] . . . the Holy Scriptures of the old and new Testament are of divine inspiration, and are the only rule of Faith."[85]

Petitioners seeking robust legislative action to encourage Christianity and restore public virtue, presumed to be in decline since the commonwealth had begun dissolving its legal and financial bonds with the church, welcomed this initiative. Although eschewing the old, exclusive establishment model, the bill declared that "the Christian Religion shall in all times coming be deemed, and held to be the established Religion of this Commonwealth; and all Denominations of Christians demeaning themselves peaceably and faithfully, shall enjoy equal privileges, civil and Religious."[86] The legislature and the public warmly debated the bill, which was difficult to reconcile with article XVI of the Declaration of Rights. Clearly, the legislature and society were sharply divided on the merits of the general assessment proposal. In the end, neither Jefferson's bill nor the general assessment measure could muster sufficient momentum to gain passage that session. The general assembly set both aside for reconsideration by future legislatures.[87]

On November 18 Mason presented a bill "to repeal so much of the act for the support of the clergy, and for the regular collecting and paying the parish levies."[88] The bill repealed the provisions providing salaries for clergy and authorizing the collection and payment of parish levies that had been temporarily suspended since their enactment in December 1776. A brief preamble set forth the sweeping objectives of the proposal:

> To remove from the good People of this Commonwealth the Fear of being compelled to contribute to the Support or Maintenance of the former established Church, And that the Members of the said Church may no longer relye upon the Expectation of any Re-establishment thereof, & be thereby prevented from adopting proper Measures, among themselves, for the Support and Maintenance of their own Religion and Ministers.[89]

Mason and his liberal allies reclaimed the operative portion of the bill from the tabled general assessment bill. They affixed the unequivocal preamble to the repeal bill, perhaps to signal their repugnance for the assessment bill from which it was extracted and to dampen any prospects of reviving a general assessment scheme.[90] The measure, stripped of the preamble in the course of deliberations, passed on December 13.[91] This bill, in effect, permanently ended direct tax support for the formerly established church in Virginia. The Anglican Church had languished during the temporary suspension of clerical salaries. Supporters hoped that the church, stripped of tax subsidies and reorganized on a voluntary basis, would be energized by competition in the marketplace of ideas.

Mason, on November 26, introduced a somewhat revised bill "for saving the property of the church heretofore by law established to the members of the said church for ever."[92] This particular version of the bill, Eckenrode observed, "was presented by Mason and is in his handwriting, so it may be taken as his composition and as his method of solving the religious question."[93] Because the Anglican Church had acquired its property with taxes collected from the entire community, when not all citizens were members of that church, great controversy arose concerning the equitable dissolution of the temporal assets of the formerly established church. Many dissenters regarded church holdings as community, not solely Anglican, property.[94] The measure, in essence, respected the property interests of the formerly established church and gave parishioners significant control over important church matters, such as the removal of clergy. The proposal sought to balance some of the competing financial and governance interests manifested in the transition from establishment to disestablishment. Although the bill received a second reading, a postponement of further consideration until the next session effectively killed it.[95]

In late 1776, the legislature appointed a committee of prominent Virginians, chaired by Jefferson, to "revise, alter, amend, repeal, or introduce all or any of the said laws" of the commonwealth.[96] Their task, Jefferson reported, was to create for the newly independent commonwealth a legal "system by which every fibre would be eradicated of ancient or future aristocracy; and a foundation laid for a government truly republican."[97] In addition to Jefferson, the committee appointed on November 5, 1776, included Edmund Pendleton, George Wythe, George Mason, and Thomas Ludwell Lee.[98]

Despite this formidable brain trust, it was soon apparent that the thirty-three-year-old Jefferson would assume the lion's share of the work in framing the revised code.[99] Jefferson recounted in his *Autobiography* that when the committee

> proceeded to the distribution of the work, Mr. Mason excused himself, as, being no lawyer, he felt himself unqualified for the work, and he resigned soon after. Mr. Lee excused himself on the same ground, and died, indeed, in a short time. The other two gentlemen, therefore, and myself divided the work among us.[100]

Mason, indeed, resigned from the committee, but not before taking part in mapping out the revised code.[101] As Jefferson and Wythe reported to the Virginia legislature in June 1779,

> In the course of this work we were unfortunately deprived of the assistance and abilities of two of our associates appointed by the General Assembly, of the one by death [Lee], of the other by resignation [Mason]. *As the plan of the work had been settled, and agreeable to that plan it was in a considerable degree carried into execution before that loss*, we did not exercise the powers given us by the act, of filling up the places by new appointment, being desirous that the plan agreed on by members who were specially appointed by the Assembly, might not be liable to alteration from others who might not equally possess their confidence, it has therefore been executed by the three remaining members.[102]

It is not clear when Mason left the committee. He probably stepped down in early 1777, but possibly did so as late as 1778. It is clear, however, that Mason "did not let his interest in the committee's work flag despite his resignation."[103] By remaining in the Virginia legislature through the end of the decade, he exerted considerable influence on the revision of the laws of the commonwealth and brought before the legislature selected bills from the revised code. Because the plan of revision was "in a considerable degree carried into execution" before Mason's resignation and because he retained an interest in the revision after he departed the committee, "we may conclude that the code bears in some places the marks of his workmanship."[104]

The revised code contained several bills addressing religious concerns, but none was more celebrated than the "Bill for Establishing Religious Freedom," which was drawn in 1777, debated in the legislature in June 1779 and December 1785, and signed into law in January 1786.[105] Mason, who resigned from the Committee of Revisors, cannot be credited for this measure. He did not depart the committee, however, before the outline of a revised code had been agreed upon and "in a considerable degree carried into execution."[106] It is possible that Jefferson drafted this bill before Mason's resignation. Mason, it should be noted, was a member of the committee that on June 12, 1779, first presented Jefferson's bill to the Virginia legislature.[107]

Mason played a decisive role in the legislative debates of the late 1770s to redefine the commonwealth's postcolonial church–state policies. Article XVI commenced and, in many respects, framed the debate. He served on key legislative committees charged with addressing church–state concerns. In this capacity, he was instrumental in preparing, even drafting, important legislation. Most importantly, although allied with the liberal disestablishment camp, Mason stepped forward at critical junctures with creative compromises to bridge the gulf between various factions in the legislative debates concerning Virginia's evolving church–state arrangement. Between 1776 and 1780, no one in Virginia, not even Jefferson or Madison, was more engaged or more instrumental than Mason in the project to redefine church–state relations and promote religious liberty. Jefferson bitterly described these rancorous legislative battles as the "severest contests" of his public career[108]; surely the battles were no less arduous for Mason, who was engaged throughout in the same dramatic struggle. Mason represented Fairfax County until the end of the decade, when he retired from the legislature. A reluctant statesman who loathed the petty bickering and vexing delays of the legislative process, he was all too happy to relinquish the mantle of public office. During his brief tenure in the legislature, however, Mason left an indelible mark on church and state in Virginia.

THE STRUGGLE FOR RELIGIOUS LIBERTY IN VIRGINIA, 1784–1786

Passage of the "Bill for Establishing Religious Freedom"—Bill No. 82 of the revised code—was the culmination of a tumultuous and divisive legislative struggle that gripped the Virginia legislature for a decade. The battle began with the adoption of article XVI of the Declaration of Rights and smoldered until passage in 1786 of the "Bill for Establishing Religious Freedom." Jefferson's committee presented the revised code to the legislature in June 1779, the same month Jefferson was elevated to the governorship. Despite the bill's eloquence and the growing stature of its author, the house declined to enact the religious-freedom measure. It proved too radical for the times.[109]

While Jefferson, Madison, and Mason agitated to disestablish the state church, another influential group in the legislature championed an alternative approach to church–state relations, namely a general assessment for the support of all churches. Both groups professed the same objective, which was to increase the influence of religion in society as an instrument of social order and stability. On the one hand, disestablishmentarians believed true religion would flourish if freed from the control and monopoly of the civil state. Proponents of a general assessment, on the other hand, argued that, because religion is indispensable to social order and stability, the civil state has a duty to facilitate sustaining aid for religion lest religion's influence in the community atrophy for want of resources.

The general assessment scheme proposed to tax citizens, not for the support of a single, official church "by law established," but for the support and maintenance of ministers in the commonwealth's diverse Christian denominations. By 1779, the Virginia legislature had been inundated by petitions specifically requesting an assessment plan designed to rescue the financially strapped ecclesiastical institutions, as well as to enhance public morality. Public virtue, memorialists argued, had been in decline since the 1776 act exempting dissenters from contributing to the established church had suspended tax support for the Anglican Church and its clergy. Despite substantial proassessment sentiment in the commonwealth, the legislature enacted neither a general assessment measure nor Jefferson's bill in 1779. An epic legislative battle between supporters of the two statutory schemes raged for the next six years. The acrimonious contest climaxed in the mid-1780s and culminated in the enactment of the "Bill for Establishing Religious Freedom."

In the autumn session of 1784, the Virginia legislature again received numerous petitions requesting an assessment for the support of teachers of the Christian religion. These petitions told of nations that had fallen because of the demise of religion and portrayed the alarming decline of morals in the commonwealth. Some requests for an assessment argued that because religion was a general benefit to society, every citizen should be required to contribute to it. Petitioners observed that financial support was necessary to encourage good candidates to enter the ministry. Support for the declining ecclesiastical institutions, proponents asserted, was essential to maintaining republican virtues and preserving social order and stability.[110]

On November 11, 1784, the house went into a committee of the whole and held an in-depth debate on the assessment issue.[111] The debate, in many respects, replayed the battle in 1779 when the legislative chambers considered both Jefferson's religious freedom bill and a different, more sectarian assessment proposal. The delegates in favor of an assessment rallied behind the dominant personality in the house, Patrick Henry. With Jefferson in Europe serving as American minister to France, leadership of the opposition fell to James Madison. Many leading Virginians, including George Washington, John Marshall, and Richard Henry Lee, were allied with the proassessment movement.[112] Noting these influential statesmen's support for a general assessment, the eminent church–state scholar Anson Phelps Stokes wrote, "It is clear that most Protestants in Virginia at the time favored the encouragement of religion by the state through financial aid to the Christian churches."[113]

Patrick Henry won the first test of strength on the assessment issue by persuading his colleagues to adopt by a vote of 47 to 32 a resolution stating that "the people of this Commonwealth, according to their respectful [respective?] abilities, ought to pay a moderate tax or contribution, annually, for the support of the Christian religion, or of some Christian church, denomination or communion of Christians, or of some form of Christian worship."[114] Henry was promptly appointed the chair of a committee commissioned to draft a bill providing a plan for a general assessment. If the committee had prepared a proposal quickly, all indications are that it would have won swift passage in both chambers of the general assembly. Apart from Madison's opposition in the House, little organized resistance to an assessment was evident, and Henry effectively marshaled behind his cause delegates representing the most populous and wealthy constituencies in the commonwealth.

Alarmed at the growing support for Henry's assessment campaign and the perceived threat to religious liberty, Jefferson uncharitably suggested to Madison: "What we have to do I think is *devo[u]tly* to *pray* for *his* [Henry's] *death.*"[115] Madison, however, had a less final solution: remove Henry from the legislature by having him elected governor. Thus, with Madison's calculated support, on November 17, 1784, Henry won an uncontested election for the governor's seat.[116] With Henry removed from the legislative arena, advocates of a religious assessment lost the man whom one Virginia clergyman described as "the great Pillar of our Cause."[117] The forces for an assessment never regained the momentum lost with Henry's departure from the House. Henry's able rival, Madison, grasped the opportunity to defeat the elder statesman's project. By late November and into December, petitions opposing an assessment began to surface. Sensing a shift in sentiment, Madison jubilantly expressed doubt that the assessment bill would pass.[118]

Nonetheless, on December 2 Francis Corbin, the English-educated planter, lawyer, and delegate from Middlesex County, laid before the house a bill "establishing a provision for teachers of the Christian religion."[119] This bill, drafted under Henry's direction, provided for a moderate tax, with an unfixed rate, on all taxable property for the support of ministers, or teachers, of the Christian religion.[120] The bill permitted each taxpayer to designate the religious denomination that would receive this subsidy. Another provision directed undesignated revenues to "seminaries of learning" or other pious uses. This measure was very different from the 1779 general assessment bill. It did not explicitly proclaim Christianity to be the commonwealth's religion and, more importantly, it omitted the five creedal articles to which the earlier bill had required participating religious societies to subscribe. "While the 1779 bill had been directly oriented toward the public worship of God, the 1784 proposal was concerned with the religious instruction of man," wrote Thomas Buckley.[121]

The bill received a second reading the next day.[122] The House, sitting as a committee of the whole, debated the assessment bill again on December 22 and 23, 1784. According to Madison's account, "it was determined by a Majority of 7 or 8 that the word 'Christian' should be exchanged for the word 'Religious.' On the report to the House the *pathetic zeal of the late governor [Benjamin] Harrison* gained a like majority for reinstating discrimination."[123] Thus, a short-lived attempt to de-Christianize the bill by extending its benefits to all "who profess the public worship of the Deity," be they Muslims or Jews, failed.[124]

On December 23, at the conclusion of the two-day debate, Henry's bill was ordered by a close vote of 44 to 42 to be engrossed and read a third time. When the engrossed bill came up for its third reading the following day, opponents of an assessment moved to postpone the final reading until the next legislative session in November 1785. The motion passed by a vote of 45 to 38.[125] It was further moved that the measure "be published in hand-bills" and distributed throughout the commonwealth and "that the people thereof be requested to signify their opinion respecting the adoption of such a bill."[126] Madison's side had won a temporary victory that afforded them time to consolidate and mobilize the opposition to the assessment bill.

In the interval between legislative sessions, Madison was inclined to wait quietly for the growing popular opposition to an assessment to manifest itself.[127] But allies in the house, notably brothers Wilson Cary Nicholas and George Nicholas, did not share his optimism. Silence, warned George Nicholas, "would be construed into an assent."[128] Thus, Madison was persuaded to draft the "Memorial and Remonstrance against Religious Assessments" in the summer of 1785 and to circulate it anonymously.[129]

The Nicholas brothers and George Mason, who knew of Madison's authorship, distributed the "Remonstrance" across the commonwealth and orchestrated the successful drive to have it signed by their fellow citizens. Mason arranged and paid to have the "Remonstrance" printed and circulated throughout the Northern Neck. He also sent it to influential citizens for their endorsement. For example, in a letter to his neighbor, George Washington, Mason wrote,

> I take the Liberty of inclosing you a Memorial and Remonstrance to the General Assembly, confided to me by a particular Freind, whose Name I am not at Liberty to mention; and as the Principles it avows entirely accord with my Sentiments on the subject (which is a very important one) I have been at the Charge of Printing several Copys, to disperse in the different Parts of the Country. You will easily perceive that all Manner of Declamation, & Address to the Passions, have been avoided, as unfair in themselves, & improper for such a Subject, and altho' the Remonstrance is long, that Brevity has been aimed at; but the Field is extensive.
>
> If upon Consideration, you approve the Arguments, & the Principles upon which they are founded, your Signature will both give the Remonstrance weight, and do it Honour.[130]

Washington, declining to endorse the "Remonstrance," responded,

> Altho' no mans Sentiments are more opposed to *any kind* of restraint upon religeous principles than mine are; yet I must confess, that I am not amongst the number of those who are so much alarmed at the thoughts of making People pay towards the support of that which they profess, if of the denominations of Christians; or declare themselves Jews, Mahomitans or otherwise, & thereby obtain proper relief.[131]

Washington's ambivalence notwithstanding, the "Remonstrance" proved effective in galvanizing antiassessment sentiment. Specifically crediting Mason and George Nicholas, Madison reported that the "Remonstrance" was "so extensively signed by the people of every Religious denomination, that at the ensuing session, the projected [assessment] measure was entirely frustrated."[132] Madison was so successful in shielding his authorship of the "Remonstrance" and Mason so zealous in his support of it that some contemporaneous speculation attributed the document to Mason's pen.[133] In at least four sections, Madison quoted article XVI of the Declaration of Rights, which Mason had written for Virginia (these references may explain why some attributed the "Remonstrance" to Mason). Madison's "Remonstrance" was not alone among the petitions in this respect. As Rhys Isaac observed, "Almost every petition against establishment appealed to the Virginia Declaration—usually styled the 'Bill'—of Rights. This tablet of fundamental law served as the legitimation for demands directed from the spiritual domain of the evangelical churches into the secular realm of the legislature."[134]

Madison's argument was presented in the form of a "memorial" and "remonstrance," that is, a formal petition or complaint addressed to the legislature with an attached declaration of reasons. Thus, each of the document's fifteen numbered paragraphs begins with the word "because."[135] Madison argued that religion, or the duty owed the Creator, is a matter of individual conscience and not within the cognizance of civil government. All citizens are entitled to the full, equal, and natural right to exercise religion according to the dictates of conscience. "[T]he same authority which can establish Christianity, in exclusion of all other Religions," Madison warned, "may establish with the same ease any particular sect of Christians, in exclusion of all other Sects." The establishment of a particular church "violates that equality which ought to be the basis of every law." Furthermore, it is "an arrogant pretension" to believe "that the Civil Magistrate is a competent Judge of Religious Truth; or that he may employ Religion as an engine of Civil policy." Experience confirms that "ecclesiastical establishments, instead of maintaining the purity and efficacy of Religion, have had a contrary operation." The fruits of ecclesiastical establishment, Madison reported, have been "pride and indolence in the Clergy, ignorance and servility in the laity, in both, superstition, bigotry and persecution." Religious establishment in Virginia would be an unfortunate "departure from that generous policy, which, offering an Asylum to the persecuted and oppressed of every Nation and Religion, promised a lustre to our country, and an accession to the number of its citizens." Madison also rejected the notions that religion could not survive without the sustaining aid of civil government and that civil government could not preserve social order and stability without the support of an established church. He believed, to the contrary, that true religion prospered in the public marketplace of ideas unrestrained by the monopolistic control of the civil authority. He thought it a contradiction to argue that discontinuing state support for Christianity would precipitate its demise because "this Religion both existed and flourished, not only without the support of human laws, but in spite of every opposition from them. . . . [A] Religion not invented by human policy, must have pre-existed and been supported, before it was established by human policy." If Christianity depends on the support of civil government, then the "pious confidence" of the faithful in its "innate excellence and the patronage of its Author" would be undermined. The best and purest religion, Madison concluded, relied on the voluntary support of those who profess it, without entanglements of any sort with civil government, including those fostered by financial support, regulation, or compulsion.[136]

The "Remonstrance" was only one in the torrent of signed petitions opposing the assessment plan that deluged the legislature. The people had indeed, as their legislature requested, expressed their opinion on the matter. After only brief consideration in the fall of 1785, Henry's bill died quietly in committee. Hamilton James Eckenrode wrote that the "weight of [antiassessment] petitions settled the fate of the 'Bill for Establishing a Support for Teachers of the Christian Religion.'"[137] Madison's "Remonstrance," while only one, albeit the most eloquent and forceful,[138] of the many petitions addressing this issue drafted and circulated in the summer of 1785, may well have been decisive in this legislative battle.[139]

Emboldened by the demise of the general assessment plan, Madison brushed the dust off Jefferson's "Bill for Establishing Religious Freedom" and pushed it to passage by a comfortable margin.[140] Jefferson's bill, much to the author's dismay, had languished without legislative action since June 1779. The statute provided in its brief enabling clauses,

> that no man shall be compelled to frequent or support any religious worship, place, or ministry whatsoever, nor shall be enforced, restrained, molested, or burthened in his body or goods, nor shall otherwise suffer on account of his re-

ligious opinions or belief; but that all men shall be free to profess, and by argument to maintain, their opinions in matters of religion, and that the same shall in no wise diminish, enlarge, or affect their civil capacities.[141]

The "Bill for Establishing Religious Freedom" is one of the most profound and influential documents in American political history. Jefferson counted it supreme among his contributions to the commonwealth and the nation and selected his authorship of the statute as one of three achievements he wanted memorialized on his gravestone.[142] The passionate and artfully crafted document has proven for more than two centuries to be a manifesto for freedom of mind and conscience, not only in Virginia but also across the nation and around the world.[143]

Madison grandly proclaimed that the bill's passage "extinguished for ever the ambitious hope of making laws for the human mind."[144] The arguments advanced in the bill have been woven into the fabric of American political thought, and in the course of time the conventional interpretation of the bill as a manifesto for church–state separation has been adopted as the orthodox principle of American church–state relations.[145] As Harvard legal historian Mark DeWolfe Howe emphasized, however, Jefferson's bill did not "in its enacting clauses explicitly prohibit establishment."[146] Rather, the bill terminated compelled religious observance and removed civil disabilities against dissenters who publicly expressed their religious opinions. This measure, one historian observed, "is frequently referred to as the establishment of religious liberty in Virginia. But it contained no principle which had not already been more solemnly enacted in the [sixteenth article of the Virginia] Bill of Rights more than nine years before its passage."[147]

Madison's leadership and eloquence, reinforced by Mason's quiet, but effective, campaign behind the scenes, not only brought about the demise of Henry's general assessment measure but also revived Jefferson's long-endangered religious freedom bill.[148] Both the religious freedom bill and the "Remonstrance" grew from the fertile soil of article XVI of the Virginia Declaration of Rights. Indeed, Mason's article XVI and the acrid debate of 1776 that gave life to the bill exempting dissenters from contributing to the established church informed Jefferson's celebrated statute, written in 1777 and enacted in 1786. Virginia's struggle to redefine church–state relations in the mid-1780s set the stage for the church–state debate at the national level that culminated in the adoption of the First Amendment to the U.S. Constitution.

GEORGE MASON'S LEGACY OF LIBERTY

"[T]he year 1776," Elwyn A. Smith opined, "was perhaps the most significant in the history of the United States for the evolution of religious liberty."[149] In that year, Mason drafted, Madison amended, and the Virginia convention adopted article XVI of the Virginia Declaration. This seminal statement formulated the principles that framed much subsequent debate on the rights of conscience and free exercise of religion in both Virginia and the emerging nation. Mason and his contemporaries were keenly aware that article XVI "was but a beginning, not a conclusion."[150] In the months and years that followed, Mason played an often quiet, but decisive, role in the legislative battles to guarantee religious freedom and to terminate legal favors enjoyed by the established church in Virginia.

Although Mason initially framed article XVI in the language of religious toleration, he early came to embrace Madison's radical revision in favor of religious liberty. This vision of religious liberty sustained Mason in the bitter church–state battles of the late 1770s and 1780s and culminated in his enthusiastic endorsement of Madison's "Memorial and Remonstrance" and Jefferson's "Bill for Establishing Religious Freedom."

The denouement of Mason's lifelong commitment to religious liberty was his storied advocacy for a national bill of rights. If article XVI was the first grand, postcolonial declaration of religious liberty, then the First Amendment to the U.S. Constitution was the culmination of a concerted effort to recognize religious liberty in the organic law of the American people. Both measures bear Mason's imprint, although the nature of his involvement in these two statements differs greatly. The First Amendment, resting on the sturdy pillars of article XVI and the "Bill for Establishing Religious Freedom," was the capstone of a distinctively American doctrine of church–state relations and religious liberty. Through his leadership in the Virginia convention that produced article XVI and his zealous advocacy in the Constitutional Convention and subsequent ratification debate, Mason nurtured the fundamental principles that found expression in the First Amendment.

The story of Mason's opposition to the proposed national constitution of 1787 is well known and will not be rehearsed in detail here.

Mason, representing Virginia in the Philadelphia convention, spearheaded an effort to draw up a national bill of rights. The state delegations unanimously rejected this initiative.[151] The absence of support for Mason's proposal did not indicate hostility to the concept of rights. Rather, there was a consensus that the national government under the proposed constitution had no jurisdiction in matters pertaining to civil and religious liberties, and where no power had been granted, no need existed to check the abuse of power.[152] In the most famous utterance of his public career, Mason exclaimed "that he would sooner chop off his right hand than put it to the Constitution as it now stands," lacking a bill of rights.[153] "Col. Mason left Philad[elphi]a in an exceeding ill humour indeed," James Madison reported. "He considers the want of a Bill of Rights as a fatal objection."[154]

A truculent Mason returned to Virginia, where, in concert with Patrick Henry and William Grayson, he led the opposition to the proposed constitution in the Virginia ratifying convention. "No Bill of Rights" became the rallying slogan of Mason and the anti-Federalists.[155] The coalition to derail ratification lost by a narrow margin to the forces allied behind Madison, George Wythe, John Marshall, Edmund Pendleton, and Edmund Randolph (who declined to sign the Constitution in Philadelphia but emerged a key proponent of ratification in the Virginia debate).

The "anti-rats," as opponents of ratification were sometimes called,[156] succeeded in the Virginia ratifying convention in framing and recommending a bill of rights and amendments to the national constitution. The bill of rights proposed by the Virginia Convention, which followed closely Mason's Declaration of Rights,[157] included a revised version of article XVI of the Virginia Declaration.[158] Madison carried these proposals to the first federal Congress that convened under the authority of the Constitution. Fulfilling a campaign pledge that was key to his election to the first Congress, Madison doggedly led the fight to amend the national constitution. Although he perused all amendments proposed by the states, in the end the recommendations put forward by Virginia most influenced the draft amendments he submitted to the U.S. House of Representatives on June 8, 1789.[159]

Congress met in New York City in the sultry summer of 1789 and drafted a bill of rights that it sent to the states for ratification. Virginia's proposed amendment on religion was in essence the article Madison presented to Congress and that Congress, after much debate and revision, ultimately crafted into the First Amendment. While the first federal Congress was still debating amendments, Mason wrote, "I have received much Satisfaction from the Amendments to the national Constitution, which have lately passed the House of Representatives; I hope they will also pass the Senate. With two or three further Amendments . . . I cou'd chearfully put my Hand & Heart to the new Government."[160] Mason thus obtained a measure of satisfaction with the eventual ratification of the national Bill of Rights in December 1791.

Popular and scholarly accounts of the pursuit of religious liberty in Virginia and the new nation duly credit the prodigious contributions of Thomas Jefferson and James Madison. Curiously overlooked in many accounts are the consequential contributions of the gentleman planter from Dogue's Neck, George Mason. This is an egregious omission, indeed, for few, if any, Virginians were more engaged than Mason in the decade-long struggle between 1776 and 1786 to establish the equal and free exercise of religion. Starting with his authorship of article XVI of the Virginia Declaration, which eloquently and succinctly informed the themes and principles of all subsequent church–state debate in Virginia, continuing with his leadership in the 1776 and 1779 legislative debates on church–state policies, and culminating in the enactment of Jefferson's religious freedom bill facilitated by Madison's "Remonstrance," Mason was a pivotal figure in the epic struggle to ensure religious liberty in Revolutionary Virginia.

These labors in Virginia bore fruit in the new nation. Article XVI was widely studied and frequently imitated in other states, and, most importantly, it was a tentative "first draft" of a proposal eventually shaped into the First Amendment. It is a tortured logic that credits any one individual, party, or movement for the establishment of religious liberty in America. Liberals (such as Jefferson and Madison), evangelical Protestant dissenters, and anti-Federalists were among the diverse groups that agitated for religious liberty. Although motivated by different interests, all these advocates of freedom looked to and celebrated Mason's Declaration of Rights as a lodestar in their pursuit of religious liberty.

APPENDIX: VIRGINIA DECLARATION OF RIGHTS (SELECTED EXCERPTS)[161]

George Mason's First Draft, *circa* 20–26 May 1776

A Declaration of Rights, made by the Representatives of the good People of Virginia, assembled in full Convention; and recommended to Posterity as the Basis and Foundation of Government.

That all Men are born equally free and independant, and have certain inherent natural Rights, of which they cannot by any Compact, deprive or divest their Posterity; among which are the Enjoyment of Life and Liberty, with the Means of acquiring and possessing Property, and pursueing and obtaining Happiness and Safety.

That Power is, by God and Nature, vested in, and consequently derived from the People; that Magistrates are their Trustees and Servants, and at all times amenable to them.

That Government is, or ought to be, instituted for the common Benefit and Security of the People, Nation, or Community. Of all the various Modes and Forms of Government, that is best, which is capable of producing the greatest Degree of Happiness and Safety, and is most effectually secured against the Danger of mal-administration. And that whenever any Government shall be found inadequate, or contrary to these Purposes, a Majority of the Community had an indubitable, inalienable and indefeasible Right to reform, alter or abolish it, in such Manner as shall be judged most conducive to the Public Weal. . . .

That no free Government, or the Blessings of Liberty, can be preserved to any People, but by a firm adherence to Justice, Moderation, Temperance, Frugality, and Virtue and by frequent Recurrence to fundamental Principles.

That as Religion, or the Duty which we owe to our divine and omnipotent Creator, and the Manner of discharging it, can be governed only by Reason and Conviction, not by Force or Violence; and therefore that all Men shou'd enjoy the fullest Toleration in the Exercise of Religion, according to the Dictates of Conscience, unpunished and unrestrained by the Magistrate, unless, under Colour of Religion, any Man disturb the Peace, the Happiness, or Safety of Society, or of Individuals. And that it is the mutual Duty of all, to practice Christian Forbearance, Love and Charity towards Each other.

Final Version, June 12, 1776

A DECLARATION OF RIGHTS made by the Representatives of the good people of VIRGINIA, assembled in full and free Convention; which rights do pertain to them and their posterity, as the basis and foundation of Government.

1. That all men are by nature equally free and independent, and have certain inherent rights, of which, when they enter into a state of society, they cannot, by any compact, deprive or divest their posterity; namely, the enjoyment of life and liberty, with the means of acquiring and possessing property, and pursuing and obtaining happiness and safety.

2. That all power is vested in, and consequently derived from, the People; that magistrates are their trustees and servants, and at all times amenable to them.

3. That Government is, or ought to be, instituted for the common benefit, protection, and security of the people, nation, or community;—of all the various modes and forms of Government that is best which is capable of producing the greatest degree of happiness and safety, and is most effectually secured against the danger of mal-administration;—and that, whenever any Government shall be found inadequate or contrary to these purposes, a majority of the community hath an indubitable, unalienable, and indefeasible right, to reform, alter, or abolish it, in such manner as shall be judged most conducive to the publick weal. . . .

[. . .]

15. That no free Government, or the blessing of liberty, can be preserved to any people but by a firm adherence to justice, moderation, temperance, frugality, and virtue, and by frequent recurrence to fundamental principles.

16. That Religion, or the duty which we owe to our CREATOR, and the manner of discharging it, can be directed only by reason and conviction, not by force or violence; and, therefore, all men are equally entitled to the free exercise of religion, according to the dictates of conscience; and that it is the mutual duty of all to practise Christian forbearance, love, and charity, towards each other.

NOTES

1. For a brief historiographical essay on Mason, see Peter Wallenstein, "George Mason," in *Research Guide to American Historical Biography*, ed. Robert Muccigrosso et al., 5 vols. (Washington, DC: Beacham Publishing, 1988–1991), 5:2615–21. See also Peter Wallenstein, "Flawed Keepers of the Flame: The Interpreters of George Mason," *Virginia Magazine of History and Biography* 102 (April 1994): 229–32.

2. Although George Mason is an almost forgotten figure of the founding era, his contemporaries recognized him as, in the words of Thomas Jefferson, "one of our really great men, and one of the first order of greatness." Thomas Jefferson to Judge Augustus B. Woodward, April 3, 1825, in *The Writings of Thomas Jefferson*, ed. Andrew A. Lipscomb and Albert Ellery Bergh, 20 vols. (Washington, DC: Thomas Jefferson Memorial Association, 1905), 16:116 [hereinafter *Writings of Jefferson*]; see also Thomas Jefferson, *Autobiography*, in *The Life and Selected Writings of Thomas Jefferson*, ed. Adrienne Koch and William Peden, The Modern Library (New York: Random House, 1944), 43 [hereinafter *Life and Selected Writings of Jefferson*] (According to Jefferson, Mason was a formidable debater, "one [of the] most steadfast, able and zealous. . . . This was George Mason, a man of the first order of wisdom among those who acted on the theatre of the revolution, of expansive mind, profound judgment, cogent in argument, learned in the lore of our former constitution, and earnest for the republican change on democratic principles."); James Madison to George Mason, December 29, 1827, Virginia Historical Society, Richmond, Virginia (throughout the Constitutional Convention, "he [Mason] sustained . . . the high

character of a powerful Reasoner, a profound Statesman and a devoted Republican."); Philip Mazzei, *Memoirs of the Life and Voyages of Doctor Philip Mazzei,* trans. E. C. Branchi, *William and Mary College Quarterly Historical Magazine,* 2d ser., 9 (July 1929): 169 (Mason "is not well enough known. He is one of those brave, rare-talented men who cause Nature a great effort to produce,—a Dante, a Macchiavelli, a Galileo, a Newton, a Franklin, a Turgot, an Elvezio, and so on."). See also Robert Allen Rutland, *The Birth of the Bill of Rights, 1776–1791,* Bicentennial Edition (Boston: Northeastern University Press, 1991), 34 ("The comparatively low rank given him by later historians is in sharp contrast to his prominence among his contemporaries, who held his abilities in high esteem."); Gaillard Hunt, *The Life of James Madison* (New York: Russell & Russell, 1902), 3 ("His personal influence with men of consequence was probably as great as that of any man in Virginia"); Forrest McDonald, *E Pluribus Unum: The Formation of the American Republic, 1776–1790,* 2d ed. (Indianapolis, IN: Liberty Press, 1979), 265 (Mason "had prestige not drastically beneath Washington's and talent that far outweighed Madison's."); R. Walton Moore, "George Mason, the Statesman," *William and Mary Quarterly,* 2d ser., 13 (1933): 10 ("[Patrick] Henry considered him one of the two greatest statesmen he ever knew. Madison . . . thought, to use his own words, that Mason 'possessed the greatest talents for debate of any man he had ever seen or heard speak.'"). Even Mason's contemporaries lamented that he had not been accorded the recognition and honor due to him. Madison wrote, "It is to be regretted that highly distinguished as he was, the memorials of them on record or perhaps otherwise attainable are more scanty than of many of his contemporaries far inferior to him in intellectual powers and in public services." James Madison to George Mason, December 29, 1827, Virginia Historical Society.

3. Josephine F. Pacheco, "Introduction," in *The Legacy of George Mason,* ed. Josephine F. Pacheco (Fairfax, VA: George Mason University Press, 1983), 8.

4. George Mason to Patrick Henry, May 6, 1783, in *The Papers of George Mason, 1725–1792,* ed. Robert A. Rutland, 3 vols. (Chapel Hill, NC: University of North Carolina Press, 1970), 2:770 [hereinafter *Papers of Mason*].

5. Helen Hill Miller, *George Mason: Gentleman Revolutionary* (Chapel Hill, NC: University of North Carolina Press, 1975), 33.

6. See Helen Hill Miller, *George Mason, Constitutionalist* (Cambridge, MA: Harvard University Press, 1938), 57–72.

7. "Proposal to Settle Foreign Protestants on Ohio Company Lands," February 6, 1753, *Papers of Mason,* 1:28.

8. See Matthew 5:33–37; James 5:12.

9. "An Ordinance for Establishing a General Test Oath," August 19, 1775, *Papers of Mason,* 1:247. But see Robert L. Scribner and Brent Tarter, eds., *Revolutionary Virginia, The Road to Independence* (Charlottesville: Virginia Independence Bicentennial Commission; University Press of Virginia, 1977), 3:468n6 (questioning whether this was the ordinance Mason took the lead in drafting).

10. Pamela C. Copeland and Richard K. MacMaster, *The Five George Masons: Patriots and Planters of Virginia and Maryland* (Charlottesville: University Press of Virginia, 1975), 7–9, 208–9; Miller, *Mason: Gentleman Revolutionary,* 9, 208. See also "The Brent Family," *Virginia Magazine of History and Biography* 19 (1911): 94–95.

11. Copeland and MacMaster, *The Five George Masons,* 208–9.

12. Copeland and MacMaster, *The Five George Masons*, 228; George Mason to George Mason, Junior, May 20, 1787, in *Papers of Mason*, 3:881.

13. William Waller Hening, comp., *The Statutes at Large; Being a Collection of all the Laws of Virginia, from the First Session of the Legislature, in the Year 1619* (Richmond, VA: J. & G. Cochran, 1821), 9:109–12 [hereinafter *Statutes at Large*].

14. Hamilton James Eckenrode, *Separation of Church and State in Virginia: A Study in the Development of the Revolution* (Richmond, VA: Davis Bottom, 1910), 42; Hunt, *Life of Madison*, 2 (this was an "assemblage, not of young or untried men, but of the ablest, most experienced, and most trusted men in the colony.").

15. Julian P. Boyd et al., eds., *The Papers of Thomas Jefferson*, 30 vols. to date (Princeton, NJ: Princeton University Press, 1950–), 1:290–91 [hereinafter *Papers of Jefferson*].

16. The architects of the new, independent government of Virginia viewed "A Declaration of Rights . . . as the basis and foundation of government." Therefore, they drafted and adopted the Virginia Declaration *before* framing a "Constitution, or Form of Government." Hening, *Statutes at Large*, 9:109, 112. "It is significant," observed Virginia constitutional historian A. E. Dick Howard, "that provision for a bill of rights preceded mention of a plan of government. The members of the 1776 Convention, steeped in Lockean notions of the social contract, might well have considered themselves in a state of nature upon the dissolution of the bond with Great Britain." They thought a declaration of man's natural rights was a logical step toward framing a new social compact. A. E. Dick Howard, *Commentaries on the Constitution of Virginia*, 2 vols. (Charlottesville: University Press of Virginia, 1974), 1:34–35, and see 1:56–57 for a commentary on the preamble to the Virginia Declaration of Rights; Brent Tarter, "The Virginia Declaration of Rights," in *To Secure the Blessings of Liberty: Rights in American History*, ed. Josephine F. Pacheco (Fairfax, VA: George Mason University Press, 1993), 38–39 (arguing that the sequence of actions of the Virginia Convention followed the English precedent at the time of the Glorious Revolution of 1688–1689).

17. For more on the committee assignments, see Irving Brant, *James Madison: The Virginia Revolutionist* (Indianapolis, IN: The Bobbs-Merrill Co., 1941), 203–5; Rutland, *The Birth of the Bill of Rights*, 31–32.

18. Hunt, *Life of Madison*, 3. See also ibid. ("the chief work of the Convention fell to his hands."); Edmund Pendleton to Thomas Jefferson, May 24, 1776, in *Papers of Jefferson*, 1:296 ("Colo. Mason seems to have the Ascendancy in the great work" of forming a new government in Virginia).

19. Editorial Note, *Papers of Mason*, 1:275. Edmund Randolph recalled that, although "many projects of a bill of rights and constitution" were presented to the drafting committee, "[t]hat proposed by George Mason swallowed up all the rest. . . ." Edmund Randolph, *History of Virginia*, ed. Arthur H. Shaffer (Charlottesville: Virginia Historical Society; University Press of Virginia, 1970), 252.

20. Thomas Jefferson to Henry Lee, May 8, 1825, in *Life and Selected Writings of Jefferson*, 719; Editorial Note, *Papers of Mason*, 1:279.

21. William C. Rives, *History of the Life and Times of James Madison*, 2 vols. (Boston: Little, Brown and Co., 1859), 1:137. See also Brant, *Madison: The Virginia Revolutionist*, 241 ("The Virginia Bill of Rights . . . is an amalgam of human rights fused in the crucible of revolution. It comes from Magna Carta, from the British Bill of Rights, from the long struggle to establish parliamentary supremacy, from Locke

and Montesquieu, from Wycliffe and St. Augustine."); Howard, *Commentaries on the Constitution of Virginia*, 1:35.

22. Editorial Note, *Papers of Mason*, 1:276. See Brent Tarter, "Virginians and the Bill of Rights," in *The Bill of Rights: A Lively Heritage*, ed. Jon Kukla (Richmond: Virginia State Library and Archives, 1987), 6–7 (noting that it was the committee draft of the Virginia Declaration that was widely circulated); Miller, *Mason: Gentleman Revolutionary*, 142, 149–50 ("This draft, rather than the form finally adopted, was treated as the official version for many years.").

23. Robert A. Rutland, *George Mason: Reluctant Statesman* (Baton Rouge: Louisiana State University Press, 1961), 67 (footnote omitted). Another student of the Virginia Declaration observed:

> The most influential constitutional document in American history is . . . the committee draft of the Virginia Declaration of Rights, written by George Mason, and reported and printed "for the perusal" of the members of the Virginia Assembly on May 27, 1776. It was published in the *Virginia Gazette* of June 1, 1776, and thereafter republished in newspapers and magazines all over America, in England, and in Europe. It, and not the amended draft officially adopted on June 12, 1776, was the document from which Jefferson, Franklin, and Adams copied to make a preamble for the Declaration of Independence. Franklin copied it into the Pennsylvania and Adams copied it into the Massachusetts declarations of rights of 1776 and 1780, respectively. France copied it into her celebrated Declaration of Rights of 1789. All of the original American states that adopted declarations of rights copied from the committee draft. None copied from the official draft for around a half century. The official draft of the Virginia Declaration was never published in a bound volume with the bills of rights of the America states until after more than a score of editions had been published, and until Jonathan Foster of Winchester, Virginia published *The Constitutions of the United States* . . . to which the official Virginia Declaration was "prefixed" in 1811.
>
> The committee draft was published in French editions with other American constitutions and declarations while the official draft was not published beyond the boundaries of Virginia for a full half century. . . .
>
> Words, phrases and sentences copied from the committee draft of May 27, 1776, may be found in every Declaration of Rights adopted in America since May 1776, and in most of the other such declarations adopted elsewhere in the world. . . .
>
> Mason's original draft—not the official—was used as the basis not only for the proposals of the Pennsylvania minority, but by the Maryland minority and the Virginia, New York, North Carolina, and Rhode Island majorities, in their ratifying conventions of 1787–1790, which proposals later became the federal Bill of Rights.
>
> The committee draft of the Virginia Declaration of Rights of May 27, 1776, stands with Magna Charta and the English Bill of Rights of 1689, as one of the three most influential constitutional documents in all the history of liberty. . . . It is the most copied of the three.

R. Carter Pittman, Book Review, *Virginia Magazine of History and Biography* 68 (1960): 110–11. See also Robert Rutland, "George Mason and the Origins of the First Amendment," in *The First Amendment: The Legacy of George Mason*, ed. T. Daniel Shumate (Fairfax, VA: George Mason University Press, 1987), 90 ("Mason's draft of the Virginia Declaration of Rights is the grandfather of *all* the bills of rights. Not only is it one of the great state papers of the American Revolution, it is a milestone in the development of the worldwide Enlightenment."). See generally Miller, *Mason: Gentleman Revolutionary*, 153–55 (noting the influence of the Virginia Declaration of

Rights); Brent Tarter, "The Virginia Declaration of Rights," 47–52 (offering a cautious examination of the influence of the Virginia Declaration of Rights beyond the commonwealth).

24. Letter from George Mason, October 2, 1778, in *Papers of Mason*, 1:437, and see 1:434 ("this was the first thing of the kind upon the Continent, and has been closely imitated by all the other States."); Bernard Schwartz, *The Bill of Rights: A Documentary History* (New York: Chelsea House, 1971), 1:231 ("The Virginia Declaration of Rights of 1776 is the first true Bill of Rights in the modern American sense, since it is the first protection for the rights of the individual to be contained in a Constitution adopted by the people acting through an elected convention.").

25. Editorial Note, *Papers of Mason*, 1:291.

26. Referring to Mason's contributions to the Virginia convention of 1776, Kate Mason Rowland said "George Mason, then, may be called, with truth, the pen of the revolution in Virginia." Kate Mason Rowland, *The Life of George Mason, 1725–1792*, 2 vols. (New York, 1892), 1:234.

27. It has also been suggested that article XVI's language on the rights of conscience is reminiscent of the Independents in the Westminster Assembly. See Thomas Cary Johnson, *Virginia Presbyterianism and Religious Liberty in Colonial and Revolutionary Times* (Richmond, VA: Presbyterian Committee of Publication, 1907), 77; William Wirt Henry, *Patrick Henry: Life, Correspondence and Speeches*, 3 vols. (New York: Charles Scribner's Sons, 1891), 1:431; William Wirt Henry, "The Part Taken by Virginia, under the Leadership of Patrick Henry, in Establishing Religious Liberty as a Foundation of American Government," in *Papers of the American Historical Association; Report of the Proceedings, Third Annual Meeting* (New York: G. P. Putnam's Sons, 1887), II, no. 1:25; Douglas F. Kelly, *The Emergence of Liberty in the Modern World* (Phillipsburg, NJ: Presbyterian and Reformed Publishing Co., 1992), 134.

28. *Papers of Mason*, 1:278; *The Papers of James Madison*, ed. William T. Hutchinson et al., 17 vols. to date (Chicago: University of Chicago Press, 1962–), 1:172–73 [hereinafter *Papers of Madison*].

29. The committee deleted "as" preceding "Religion," "divine and omnipotent," and "or of Individuals." It also changed "governed" to "directed."

30. *Papers of Mason*, 1:284; *Papers of Madison*, 1:173.

31. Editorial Note, *Papers of Madison*, 1:171. See also Gaillard Hunt, "James Madison and Religious Liberty," in *Annual Report of the American Historical Association for the Year 1901*, 2 vols. (Washington, DC: GPO, 1902), 1:165; William Lee Miller, *The First Liberty: Religion and the American Republic* (New York: Alfred A. Knopf, 1986), 5 ("James Madison was first moved to revolutionary ardor by the issue of religious liberty."); Miller, *Mason: Gentleman Revolutionary*, 149 (Madison's action on this article described as "James Madison's first contribution to political theory.").

32. Irving Brant, "Madison: On the Separation of Church and State," *William and Mary Quarterly*, 3d ser., 8 (1951): 5.

33. See Charles Fenton James, *Documentary History of the Struggle for Religious Liberty in Virginia* (Lynchburg, VA: J. P. Bell Co., 1900), 201 ("By religious liberty is meant the right of every one to worship God, or not, according to the dictates of his own conscience, and to be held accountable to none but God for his belief and practice. It differs from religious toleration . . . in that toleration implies the right to withhold, or to refuse license, whereas religious liberty means that the civil power has

nothing to do with a man's religion except to protect him in the enjoyment of his rights."). For an extreme, secular expression of this view, see Thomas Paine's 1791 declamation in *Rights of Man*: "Toleration is not the *opposite* of Intolerance, but is the *counterfeit* of it. Both are despotisms. The one assumes to itself the right of withholding Liberty of Conscience, and the other of granting it. The one is the Pope armed with fire and faggot, and the other is the Pope selling or granting indulgences." Thomas Paine, *Rights of Man* (1791), in *The Writings of Thomas Paine*, ed. Moncure Daniel Conway, 4 vols. (New York: G. P. Putnam's Sons, 1894), 2:325.

34. In his so-called autobiography, Madison wrote, "Being young & in the midst of distinguished and experienced members of the Convention he [Madison, referring to himself in the third person] did not enter into its debates; tho' he occasionally suggested amendments; the most material of which was a change of the terms in which the freedom of Conscience was expressed in the proposed Declaration of Rights. This important and meritorious instrument was drawn by Geo. Mason, who had inadvertently adopted the word *toleration* in the article on that subject. The change suggested and accepted, substituted a phraseology which—declared the freedom of conscience to be a *natural and absolute* right." Douglass Adair, ed., "James Madison's Autobiography," *William and Mary Quarterly*, 3d ser., 2 (1945): 199 (emphasis in the original).

35. *Papers of Madison*, 1:174. Madison evidently meant that after "under" should follow the words of the committee's version—"colour of religion, any man disturb the peace, the happiness, or safety of society. And that it is the mutual duty of all to practice Christian forbearance, love and charity, towards each other."

36. Elwyn A. Smith, *Religious Liberty in the United States: The Development of Church–State Thought Since the Revolutionary Era* (Philadelphia: Fortress Press, 1972), 36–37.

37. Miller, *The First Liberty*, 5.

38. See Smith, *Religious Liberty in the United States*, 37 ("The legislature apparently recognized in Madison's substitution of 'violence or compulsion' for 'force or violence' a move against establishment itself, since to eliminate non-coercive methods amounted to the negation of enforcement altogether.").

39. *Papers of Madison*, 1:171.

40. *Papers of Madison*, 1:174–75.

41. Brant, *Madison: The Virginia Revolutionist*, 246.

42. See Michael W. McConnell, "The Origins and Historical Understanding of Free Exercise of Religion," *Harvard Law Review* 103 (1990): 1463.

43. Thomas E. Buckley, S.J., *Church and State in Revolutionary Virginia, 1776–1787* (Charlottesville: University Press of Virginia, 1977), 19. See also Hunt, *Life of Madison*, 9 ("as it was adopted . . . [article XVI] took no ground inconsistent with the existence of a state church.").

44. James Madison to George Mason, December 29, 1827, Virginia Historical Society, Richmond, Virginia. See also John T. Noonan Jr., *The Lustre of Our Country: The American Experience of Religious Freedom* (Berkeley: University of California Press, 1998), 70 ("Unexpectedly, Mr. Madison persuaded Mr. Mason that the new text said what Mr. Mason wanted to say."). Interestingly, "Madison, both in 1776 and in retrospect, attached more importance to his victory on the subject of toleration than to his defeat on immediate church disestablishment." Brant, *Madison: The Virginia Revolutionist*, 248.

45. For a thorough and illuminating examination of Madison's proposal in the 1776 Virginia convention, see "Editorial Note: Declaration of Rights and Form of Government of Virginia," *Papers of Madison*, 1:170–79; Brant, *Madison: The Virginia Revolutionist*, 242–50.

46. Hening, *Statutes at Large*, 9:111–12; *Papers of Mason*, 1:289; *Papers of Madison*, 1:175.

47. L. John Van Til, *Liberty of Conscience: The History of a Puritan Idea* (Phillipsburg, NJ: Presbyterian and Reformed Publishing Co., 1972), 163.

48. Eckenrode, *Separation of Church and State in Virginia*, 45. See also Brant, *Madison: The Virginia Revolutionist*, 249 ("The clause on religion [article XVI] asserted, for the first time in any body of fundamental law, a natural right which had not previously been recognized as such by political bodies in the Christian world."); Lance Banning, "James Madison, the Statute for Religious Freedom, and the Crisis of Republican Convictions," in *The Virginia Statute for Religious Freedom: Its Evolution and Consequences in American History*, ed. Merrill D. Peterson and Robert C. Vaughan (New York: Cambridge University Press, 1988), 112 ("In its final phrasing, Article XVI erected an ideal that no society had ever written into law."); Tarter, "Virginians and the Bill of Rights," 6 ("Boldly taking the first such step in modern Western civilization, Virginia removed all legal pretense for persecution or discrimination based upon religious differences.").

49. There is a tradition that attributes authorship of article XVI to Patrick Henry. This minority, if not discredited, view is based largely on Edmund Randolph's imperfect recollection of the convention recorded long after it had adjourned. See Randolph, *History of Virginia*, 254; Moncure Daniel Conway, *Omitted Chapters of History Disclosed in the Life and Papers of Edmund Randolph* (New York: G. P. Putnam's Sons, 1888), 30; Henry, *Henry: Life, Correspondence and Speeches*, 1:430–35; Rowland, *Life of Mason*, 1:235–39, 241; Brant, *Madison: The Virginia Revolutionist*, 236, 241–43; Eckenrode, *Separation of Church and State in Virginia*, 44; James, *Documentary History of the Struggle for Religious Liberty in Virginia*, 64–65. Randolph's faulty memory may have been based on the fact that Madison, who by his own admission was uncertain and inexperienced in legislative affairs and diffident about public speaking, apparently prevailed on Henry to present his amendment to the convention.

50. For a brief survey of key church–state controversies in late colonial and postindependence Virginia, see Charles Ramsdell Lingley, *The Transition in Virginia from Colony to Commonwealth* (New York: Columbia University Press, 1910), 190–211.

51. "Petition of Sundry Inhabitants of Prince Edward County," October 11, 1776, reprinted in *Virginia Magazine of History and Biography* 18 (1910): 41; *Journal of the House of Delegates of Virginia. Anno Domini, 1776*, October 11, 1776 (Richmond, VA: Samuel Shepherd, 1828), 7 [hereinafter *JHD*].

52. "The Petition of the Dissenters from the Ecclesiastical Establishment in the Commonwealth of Virginia," reprinted in *Virginia Magazine of History and Biography* 18 (1910): 265–66; *JHD*, October 16, 1776, 15.

53. "Dissenters Petition, Albemarle, Amherst and Buckingham," November 9, 1776, reprinted in *Virginia Magazine of History and Biography* 18 (1910): 257; *JHD*, November 9, 1776, 48; *Papers of Jefferson*, 1:587; *Papers of Mason*, 1:318n.

54. *Virginia Gazette* (Purdie), October 11, 1776, as quoted in Buckley, *Church and State in Revolutionary Virginia*, 22.

55. Jefferson, *Autobiography*, in *Life and Selected Writings of Jefferson*, 41.

56. Jefferson, *Autobiography*, in *Life and Selected Writings of Jefferson*, 41. See also Jefferson, *Notes on Virginia*, in *Life and Selected Writings of Jefferson*, 273 ("two-thirds of the people had become dissenters at the commencement of the present revolution"). But see Brant, *Madison: The Virginia Revolutionist*, 295 (challenging Jefferson's statement).

57. *JHD*, November 9, 1776, 48.

58. *JHD*, November 19, 1776, 62–63.

59. Buckley, *Church and State in Revolutionary Virginia*, 33.

60. *JHD*, November 19, 1776, 63.

61. *Papers of Mason*, 1:319n.

62. Buckley, *Church and State in Revolutionary Virginia*, 34; see also *JHD*, November 30, 1776, 76; Editorial Note, *Papers of Jefferson*, 1:527.

63. Buckley, *Church and State in Revolutionary Virginia*, 34.

64. Editorial Note, *Papers of Jefferson*, 1:528; *Papers of Mason*, 1:319n.

65. *JHD*, December 5, 1776, 83. See Editorial Note, *Papers of Jefferson*, 1:528, 533–34; *Papers of Mason*, 1:319n.

66. *Papers of Jefferson*, 1:534nn.

67. "Amendment to the Bill Exempting Dissenters from Contributing to the Established Church," December 5, 1776, *Papers of Mason*, 1:318. The bracketed material does not appear in Hening, *Statutes at Large*, 9:164.

68. *JHD*, December 9, 1776, 89–90; Hening, *Statutes at Large*, 9:164–67.

69. *Papers of Mason*, 1:319n.

70. Buckley, *Church and State in Revolutionary Virginia*, 36.

71. Editorial Note, *Papers of Jefferson*, 1:528.

72. Editorial Note, *Papers of Jefferson*, 1:525.

73. Hening, *Statutes at Large*, 9:165.

74. *JHD*, May 17, 1779, 11. A bill "for the dissolution of vestries" was introduced in late May. *JHD*, May 28, 1779, 26.

75. *JHD*, June 4, 1779, 34.

76. *JHD*, June 4, 1779, 34.

77. *JHD*, June 12, 1779, 44. See "Bill for Establishing Religious Freedom" (Bill No. 82) and "Bill for Saving the Property of the Church Heretofore by Law Established" (Bill No. 83), in *Report of the Committee of Revisors Appointed by the General Assembly of Virginia in MDCCLXXVI* (Richmond, VA: Dixon & Holt, 1784), 58–59.

78. *JHD*, June 14, 1779, 46.

79. *JHD*, June 1, 1779, 29.

80. *JHD*, June 15, 1779, 48.

81. *JHD*, June 17, 1779, 53; Hening, *Statutes at Large*, 10:111.

82. *JHD*, June 19, 1779, 59.

83. Eckenrode, *Separation of Church and State in Virginia*, 56.

84. Buckley, *Church and State in Revolutionary Virginia*, 56.

85. *JHD*, October 25, 1779, 24. The bill is reprinted in Buckley, *Church and State in Revolutionary Virginia*, appendix I, 185–88. Mason was one of nearly two dozen members of a committee ordered on October 15 to prepare this bill "concerning religion." *JHD*, October 15, 1779, 10.

86. Buckley, *Church and State in Revolutionary Virginia*, 185–88, and see generally 56–60; Miller, *The First Liberty*, 17–22.

87. Following its second reading, the House discussed the general assessment bill on numerous occasions. Finally, on November 15, the House voted to put off further discussion of the measure until the following March. *JHD*, November 15, 1779, 56.

88. *JHD*, November 18, 1779, 61. On November 15, the House directed Mason, along with French Strother and Beverley Randolph, to bring in this bill. *JHD*, November 15, 1779, 56–57.

89. "A Bill Repealing the Act to Support Ministers of the Established Church," November 18, 1779, *Papers of Mason*, 2:553.

90. Buckley, *Church and State in Revolutionary Virginia*, 61.

91. *JHD*, December 13, 1779, 87; Hening, *Statutes at Large*, 10:197–98.

92. *JHD*, November 26, 1779, 72; *Papers of Mason*, 2:590–92. Mason, along with James Henry and General Thomas Nelson, was directed on November 15 to bring in this bill. *JHD*, November 15, 1779, 57.

93. Eckenrode, *Separation of Church and State in Virginia*, 64. See also D. Rhodes, "The Struggle for Religious Liberty in Virginia" (Ph.D. dissertation, Duke University, 1951), 129 (attributing authorship to Mason).

94. See, for example, the claim of Baptist minister John Leland as reported in Buckley, *Church and State in Revolutionary Virginia*, 66.

95. *JHD*, December 11, 1779, 85–86.

96. Hening, *Statutes at Large*, 9:175–77; *Papers of Jefferson*, 1:562–63.

97. Jefferson, *Autobiography*, in *Life and Selected Writings of Jefferson*, 51.

98. *JHD*, November 5, 1776, 41. See *Papers of Jefferson*, 1:562–64.

99. See Editorial Note, *Papers of Jefferson*, 2:313 ("There can be no doubt that Jefferson was nominally and actually the leading figure in the revisal.").

100. Jefferson, *Autobiography*, in *Life and Selected Writings of Jefferson*, 45.

101. Rowland, *Life of Mason*, 1:242, 274–78.

102. Hening, *Statutes at Large*, June 18, 1779, 9:175–76n* (emphasis added). See also *JHD*, June 18, 1779, 56–57.

103. *Papers of Mason*, 1:332n.

104. Rowland, *Life of Mason*, 1:277, 242.

105. See Rowland, *Life of Mason*, 1:242 ("Among these laws [of the revised code], planned in part by George Mason, was the 'Act Establishing Religious Freedom.'").

106. Hening, *Statutes at Large*, June 18, 1779, 9:175n*.

107. *JHD*, June 12, 1779, 44.

108. Jefferson, *Autobiography*, in *Life and Selected Writings of Jefferson*, 41.

109. Miller, *The First Liberty*, 18.

110. For a description of the petitions and arguments circulated in support of a general assessment, see Eckenrode, *Separation of Church and State in Virginia*, 75–76, 83–84, 88–90, 111–13; Buckley, *Church and State in Revolutionary Virginia*, 74, 80–81, 90, 94–95, 98–99, 141–47.

111. *JHD*, November 11, 1784, 19.

112. See Hunt, "James Madison and Religious Liberty," 168; Miller, *The First Liberty*, 27; Rives, *History of the Life and Times of Madison*, 1:602; Marvin K. Singleton, "Colonial Virginia as First Amendment Matrix: Henry, Madison, and Assessment Establishment," *Journal of Church and State* 8 (1966): 351–52.

113. Anson Phelps Stokes, *Church and State in the United States*, 3 vols. (New York: Harper and Brothers, 1950), 1:390.

114. *JHD*, November 11, 1784, 19. See Eckenrode, *Separation of Church and State in Virginia*, 86; Buckley, *Church and State in Revolutionary Virginia*, 91–92.

115. Thomas Jefferson to James Madison, December 8, 1784, in *Papers of Madison*, 8:178.

116. *JHD*, November 17, 1784, 26–27. See Buckley, *Church and State in Revolutionary Virginia*, 100–102; Irving Brant, *James Madison: The Nationalist, 1780–1787* (Indianapolis, IN: The Bobbs-Merrill Co., 1948), 345–46; Singleton, "Colonial Virginia as First Amendment Matrix," 355.

117. The Reverend Samuel Sheild to the Reverend David Griffith, December 20, 1784, David Griffith Papers, Virginia Historical Society, Richmond, Virginia.

118. See James Madison to James Madison, Sr., November 27, 1784, in *Papers of Madison*, 8:155; James Madison to James Monroe, December 4, 1784, in *Papers of Madison*, 8:175 ("The bill for the Religious Asst. was reported yesterday and will be taken up in a Come. of the Whole next week. Its friends are much disheartened at the loss of Mr. Henry. Its fate is I think very uncertain.").

119. *JHD*, December 2, 1784, 51.

120. The term *teacher* in this context referred to the minister of a church. See Chester James Antieau, Arthur T. Downey, and Edward C. Roberts, *Freedom from Federal Establishment: Formation and Early History of the First Amendment Religion Clauses* (Milwaukee, WI: Bruce, 1964), 33.

121. Buckley, *Church and State in Revolutionary Virginia*, 108.

122. *JHD*, December 3, 1784, 52.

123. James Madison to Thomas Jefferson, January 9, 1785, in *Papers of Madison*, 8:229.

124. *JHD*, December 22–23, 1784, 80–81. See generally Eckenrode, *Separation of Church and State in Virginia*, 102; Buckley, *Church and State in Revolutionary Virginia*, 108; Daniel L. Dreisbach, "Thomas Jefferson and Bills Number 82–86 of the Revision of the Laws of Virginia, 1776–1786: New Light on the Jeffersonian Model of Church–State Relations," *North Carolina Law Review* 69 (1990): 167n45.

125. *JHD*, December 24, 1784, 82.

126. *JHD*, December 24, 1784, 82.

127. Brant, *Madison: The Nationalist*, 348; Eva T. H. Brann, "Madison's 'Memorial and Remonstrance': A Model of American Eloquence," in *Rhetoric and American Statesmanship*, eds. Glen E. Thurow and Jeffrey D. Wallin (Durham, NC: Carolina Academic Press, 1984), 12.

128. George Nicholas to James Madison, April 22, 1785, in *Papers of Madison*, 8:264.

129. In his "Detached Memoranda," written late in life, Madison recalled that it was "[a]t the instance of Col: George Nicholas, Col: George Mason & others, the memorial & remonstrance agst it [the assessment bill] was drawn up, . . . and printed Copies of it circulated thro' the State, to be signed by the people at large." Elizabeth Fleet, ed., "Madison's 'Detached Memoranda,'" *William and Mary Quarterly*, 3d ser., 3 (1946): 555.

Although a copy of the "Remonstrance" was printed as early as 1786 under Madison's own name, "[s]o successful was he [Madison] in maintaining anonymity that a few libraries still have a printed version with speculative attributions of the work to other public men." Editorial Note, *Papers of Madison*, 8:295. Madison did not publicly acknowledge his authorship of the document until 1826.

130. George Mason to George Washington, October 2, 1785, in *Papers of Mason*, 2:830–31. See also George Mason to Robert Carter, October 5, 1785, in *Papers of Mason*, 2:832–33.

131. George Washington to George Mason, October 3, 1785, in *Papers of Mason*, 2:832.

132. James Madison to George Mason, July 14, 1826, Virginia Historical Society, Richmond, Virginia. See also James Madison to Thomas Jefferson, January 22, 1786, in *Papers of Madison*, 8:473–74; James Madison to General Lafayette, November 24, 1826, in Robert S. Alley, ed., *James Madison on Religious Liberty* (Buffalo, NY: Prometheus Books, 1985), 86; Fleet, "Madison's 'Detached Memoranda,'" 556 (the number of signatures added to the "Remonstrance" "displayed such an overwhelming opposition of the people that the proposed plan of a genl assessmt was crushed under it."); Rives, *History of the Life and Times of Madison*, 1:632 ("When the Assembly met in October, the table of the House of Delegates almost sunk under the weight of the accumulated copies of the memorial sent forward from the different counties, each with its long and dense column of subscribers. The fate of the assessment was sealed. The manifestation of the public judgment was too unequivocal and overwhelming to leave the faintest hope to the friends of the measure. It was abandoned without a struggle."); Hunt, "James Madison and Religious Liberty," 169 ("There are few instances recorded where the tide of public opinion has been so completely turned by a single document as it was in this instance by Madison's remonstrance."); Brant, *Madison: The Nationalist*, 350 ("The political effect of this remonstrance was staggering. By the time the legislature convened the flow of petitions had become a tidal wave.").

133. Rowland, *Life of Mason*, 2:87; *Papers of Mason*, 2:835n; Editorial Note, *Papers of Madison*, 8:296.

134. Rhys Isaac, *The Transformation of Virginia, 1740–1790* (Chapel Hill: Institute of Early American History and Culture; University of North Carolina Press, 1982), 292.

135. "This petition is presented in the form of a *remonstrance*, that is, a protest, suggestively, of the 'faithful,' but it is not a mere protest, as are most present-day petitions. It is also a *memorial*, a declaration of reasons—every paragraph begins with a 'because'—in the tradition of the Declaration of Independence." Brann, "Madison's 'Memorial and Remonstrance': A Model of American Eloquence," 16.

136. Madison, "Memorial and Remonstrance," *Papers of Madison*, 8:298–304.

137. Eckenrode, *Separation of Church and State in Virginia*, 113.

138. Madison's biographer, Irving Brant, wrote: "This remonstrance against religious assessments continues to stand, not merely through the years but through the centuries, as the most powerful defense of religious liberty ever written in America." Brant, *Madison: The Nationalist*, 352. Significantly, U.S. Supreme Court justices Hugo L. Black and Wiley B. Rutledge relied on the "Remonstrance" in the landmark case of *Everson v. Board of Education*. The latter described it as "the most concise and the most accurate statement of the views of the First Amendment's author concerning what is 'an establishment of religion.'" *Everson v. Board of Education*, 330 U.S. 1, 37 (1947) (Rutledge, J., dissenting).

139. For a canvassing of the petitions filed in this legislative contest, see Rhys Isaac, "'The Rage of Malice of the Old Serpent Devil': The Dissenters and the Making and Remaking of the Virginia Statute for Religious Freedom," in *Virginia Statute for Religious Freedom*, 146–56.

140. On October 31, 1785, Madison reintroduced in the Virginia House of Delegates Bill No. 82 from the revised code—"A Bill for Establishing Religious Freedom." *JHD*, October 31, 1785, 12–15. The measure was specifically brought to the attention of the House on December 14 and passed on December 17 by a convincing majority of 74 to 20. *JHD*, December 17, 1785, 92–93, 96. The bill was read in the Senate for the first time on Saturday, December 17, 1785. *Journal of the Senate of the Commonwealth of Virginia* (Richmond: Thomas W. White, 1827), December 17, 1785, 54. On Friday, December 23, the Senate voted narrowly to replace the preamble with article XVI of the Virginia Declaration of Rights. *Journal of the Senate*, December 23, 1785, 61. The bill was read for the third time, passed, and returned to the House of Delegates. Unable to reconcile differences between the House and Senate versions of the bill, a conference committee was formed early in the new year. *Journal of the Senate*, January 9, 1786, 81. On January 16, 1786, the House considered and, perhaps reluctantly, accepted relatively minor Senate amendments. *JHD*, January 16, 1786, 143–44; *Journal of the Senate*, January 16, 1786, 92. The speaker signed the act on January 19, 1786. *JHD*, January 19, 1786, 148.

141. Hening, *Statutes at Large*, 12:86; *Virginia Code, Annotated* (repl. vol. 1986), § 57–1. Jefferson's bill is reprinted in *Papers of Jefferson*, 2:545–47.

142. See Paul Leicester Ford, ed., *The Works of Thomas Jefferson*, Federal Edition, 12 vols. (New York: G. P. Putnam's Sons, 1905), 12:483. Jefferson also wished to be remembered as the author of the Declaration of American Independence and the father of the University of Virginia.

143. See *Bond v. Bond*, 144 W.Va. 478, 492, 109 S.E.2d 16, 23 (1959) ("[T]he Virginia Statute of Religious Freedom . . . is said to have formed a model for statutes and constitutional provisions throughout the land."). In a letter to Madison, written shortly after the bill was enacted, Jefferson proudly reported that "The Virginia act for religious freedom has been received with infinite approbation in Europe, and propagated with enthusiasm." Thomas Jefferson to James Madison, December 16, 1786, in *Life and Selected Writings of Jefferson*, 408–9.

144. James Madison to Thomas Jefferson, January 22, 1786, in *Papers of Madison*, 8:474.

145. C. Randolph Benson noted that Jefferson's church–state views "in the course of time became the official American position." C. Randolph Benson, *Thomas Jefferson as Social Scientist* (Rutherford, NJ: Fairleigh Dickinson University Press, 1971), 190–91. See generally Daniel L. Dreisbach, "A New Perspective on Jefferson's Views on Church–State Relations: The Virginia Statute for Establishing Religious Freedom in Its Legislative Context," *American Journal of Legal History* 35 (1991): 172–204; Daniel L. Dreisbach, "Thomas Jefferson and Bills Number 82–86 of the Revision of the Laws of Virginia, 1776–1786," 159–211.

146. Mark DeWolfe Howe, *The Garden and the Wilderness: Religion and Government in American Constitutional History* (Chicago: University of Chicago Press, 1965), 44.

147. Henry, "The Part Taken by Virginia, under the Leadership of Patrick Henry, in Establishing Religious Liberty as a Foundation of American Government," II, no. 1:27. See also Hunt, *Life of Madison*, 9–10 (arguing that had Madison's amendments to article XVI been adopted there would have been no "occasion for the famous bill for religious freedom which Jefferson wrote.")

148. Most historians of the era have characterized Jefferson's "Bill for Establishing Religious Freedom" as incompatible with, if not directly opposed to, the various general assessment bills considered by the Virginia legislature. See, for example, Leonard W. Levy, *Constitutional Opinions: Aspects of the Bill of Rights* (New York: Oxford University Press, 1986), 160 ("Confronted by two diametrically opposed bills [Jefferson's bill for complete separation between religion and government and a 1779 general assessment bill], the Virginia legislature was deadlocked, and neither bill could muster a majority.") This characterization, however, may inaccurately depict the way many Virginians viewed these proposals at the time. Some Virginians, including religious dissenters, saw no contradiction between supporting Jefferson's bill and requesting the Virginia legislature to enact a general assessment. See *Papers of Jefferson*, 2:548n (presenting evidence that some dissenters supported both a general assessment and Jefferson's bill); Buckley, *Church and State in Revolutionary Virginia*, 74 (noting a petition calling for both religious toleration and a general assessment); Singleton, "Colonial Virginia as First Amendment Matrix," 361 ("[I]t should be noted that some dissenters had, during the late 1770s, petitioned simultaneously for Jefferson's bill and for a common assessment."). The 1779 general assessment plan was more extreme than the 1784 version in the sense that the 1779 scheme outlined specific requirements of Christian doctrine and worship.

149. Smith, *Religious Liberty in the United States*, 35–36.

150. Smith, *Religious Liberty in the United States*, 40.

151. Max Farrand, ed., *The Records of the Federal Convention of 1787* (New Haven, CT: Yale University Press, 1911), 2:587–88.

152. See James Wilson, "State House Yard Speech," October 6, 1787, in Paul Leicester Ford, ed., *Pamphlets on the Constitution of the United States* (Brooklyn, NY, 1888), 156 (arguing that since the federal government did not have enumerated powers to infringe certain rights, it was unnecessary to have a bill of rights stipulating that the federal government could not violate such rights). In *The Federalist Papers*, No. 45, James Madison observed that "[t]he powers delegated by the proposed Constitution to the federal government are few and defined. Those which are to remain in the State governments are numerous and indefinite. . . . The powers reserved to the several States will extend to all the objects which, in the ordinary course of affairs, concern the lives, liberties, and properties of the people, and the internal order, improvement, and prosperity of the State." Clinton Rossiter, ed., *The Federalist Papers* (New York: Mentor Books, 1961), 292–93.

153. *Papers of Mason*, August 31, 1787, 3:973. This intemperate outburst contrasts with his earlier assertion that "he would bury his bones" in Philadelphia rather than see the convention fail. *Papers of Mason*, July 5, 1787, 3:920.

154. James Madison to Thomas Jefferson, October 24, 1787, in *Papers of Madison*, 10:215; *Papers of Jefferson*, 12:280.

155. The absence of a bill of rights was the first deficiency Mason identified in his "Objections." Mason, "Objections to this Constitution of Government," *ca.* September

16, 1787, *Papers of Mason*, 3:991. See generally Rutland, *Birth of the Bill of Rights*, 120–25. Other scholars have questioned the emphasis placed on Mason's advocacy of a bill of rights, because the absence of a bill was not his sole or even primary reason for opposing ratification of the Constitution. See Brent Tarter, "George Mason and the Conservation of Liberty," *Virginia Magazine of History and Biography* 99 (1991): 292–95; Wallenstein, "Flawed Keepers of the Flame," 238–42, 256–58.

156. See Joseph Gales, ed., *The Debates and Proceedings in the Congress of the United States*, 42 vols. (Washington, DC: Gales and Seaton, 1834–1856), 1st Cong., 1st sess. (August 15, 1789), 1:731.

157. In drafting his own proposals for a federal bill of rights, Madison "leaned heavily on the Virginia Declaration of Rights. . . ." Rutland, *Birth of the Bill of Rights*, 202.

158. *Papers of Mason*, 3:1071, 1119. Jon Kukla, "Yes! No! And If . . . Federalists, Antifederalists, and Virginia's 'Federalists Who are for Amendments'," in *Antifederalism: The Legacy of George Mason*, ed. Josephine F. Pacheco (Fairfax, VA: George Mason University Press, 1992), 59 ("Mason coordinated the compilation of the forty amendments, a bill of rights and twenty structural changes, adopted by the convention on the day it adjourned."). Successive drafts of these amendments are printed in *Papers of Mason*, 3:1054–57, 1068–72, 1115–20.

159. See Schwartz, *Bill of Rights*, 2:765 ("the importance of the Virginia Ratifying Convention's proposed Bill of Rights is shown by the fact that . . . every specific guarantee in the Virginia-proposed Bill of Rights [save one] later found a place in the federal Bill of Rights. . . .").

160. George Mason to Samuel Griffin, September 8, 1789, in *Papers of Mason*, 3:1172. But see George Mason to John Mason, July 31, 1789, in *Papers of Mason*, 3:1164 (Mason dismissed Madison's proposed amendments as mere "Milk & Water Propositions . . . by Way of th[r]owing out a Tub to the Whale."); Linda Grant De Pauw, "The Roots of American Federalism," in *Federalism: The Legacy of George Mason*, ed. Martin B. Cohen (Fairfax, VA: George Mason University Press, 1988), 57–58 (Mason was among those who "were not satisfied with the Bill of Rights voted by Congress even though the first eight of the ten amendments can be traced directly to the Virginia Bill of Rights, which Mason had drafted in 1776."); Tarter, "George Mason and the Conservation of Liberty," 301 (arguing that the "two or three further amendments" Mason had in mind were so sweeping that this statement cannot be construed as complimentary of the Constitution or federal Bill of Rights); Wallenstein, "Flawed Keepers of the Flame," 256–58.

161. Robert A. Rutland, ed., *The Papers of George Mason, 1725–1792*, 3 vols. (Chapel Hill: University of North Carolina Press, 1971), 3:274–91; Hening, *Statutes at Large*, 9:109–12.

9

Catholic Politics and Religious Liberty in America

The Carrolls of Maryland

James R. Stoner

Since the modern jurisprudence of the no establishment clause of the First Amendment was inaugurated in the 1947 case of *Everson v. Board of Education*,[1] the touchstone of constitutional and scholarly debate about religious liberty in the United States has been the account of separation of church and state developed by Thomas Jefferson and James Madison in the disestablishment controversy in Virginia in 1785–1786. In *Everson*, the Court split five to four on the question of whether New Jersey's law permitting the township of Ewing to reimburse the parents of private (largely Catholic) school children the cost of transportation to school was a violation of the Constitution—Justice Black for the majority thought that because transportation, not instruction, was at issue, the law could stand, but the justices all agreed that Jefferson and Madison were the authorities to be consulted. Indeed, Justice Rutledge reprinted Madison's "Memorial and Remonstrance" as an appendix to his dissent. Turning to Jefferson and Madison to elucidate the meaning of the amendment must have seemed self-evident to the justices. Madison, a few years after the Virginia Statute for Religious Freedom, introduced what became the First Amendment in Congress, and Jefferson thought so highly of the statute that he famously listed it, together with his authorship of the Declaration and his founding of the University of Virginia, in his epitaph. As presidents Jefferson and Madison sought in their own ways to apply a strict separationism in their official acts, and they were, of course, founders of the political party—or at any rate the immediate ancestor of the political party—by whose nomination every member of the Court in 1947 had received his post.

The *Everson* Court helped ratify what various strains of midcentury scholarship sought to establish: that the critical influence behind religious liberty in America was the secular Enlightenment. To make Jefferson and Madison the authorities on the meaning of the First Amendment was to make John Locke its philosopher, or rather, to make its arbiter the liberal philosophy that Locke helped initiate, but that developed over the course of the nineteenth and twentieth centuries in ways that Locke, limited by the continued establishment of Protestant Christianity in his time, was unwilling or unable to go. Since *Everson*, a voluminous scholarship has emerged calling into question the adequacy of Jefferson and Madison as authoritative spokesmen for the religion clauses, most especially by bringing to light the extensive involvement of religion in the political life of the federal and particularly the state governments from the time of the founding through the nineteenth and early twentieth centuries.[2] However persuasive these studies have proven in historical terms, and however useful in the rare case when the Court finds the inertia of tradition a barrier to its own logic,[3] the proponents of Enlightenment secularism have found such evidence easy to dismiss. No one doubts that Protestant Christianity played an important role in the settlement of the country and that its influence remained strong through the nineteenth century; what the secularists claim is that there is no constitutional warrant for reviving this role once historical change led to the apparent collapse of the old Protestant "establishment." Indeed, to the modern liberal, religious liberty is significant not because it serves the specifically religious needs and aims of human beings, but because it was the paradigm out of which developed the idea of personal autonomy that defines the modern self and the idea of constitutional limits that chastens political ambition to prescribe the human good.[4]

Into the gap between these incompatible readings of the First Amendment, I want to insert an observation that at once complicates the story of its original intention and suggests a way to approach our predicament today: I want to draw attention to the role of Catholics in the founding of the United States and in the design of religious liberty as it was then understood. More particularly, I want to focus on the contribution of the most prominent Catholic family among those who made the Revolution and established the Constitution, the Carrolls of Maryland. In many, if not most, modern accounts of the founding, their role has been neglected, not only by secular scholars, but by Catholics themselves.[5] In part, I suspect, this is due to developments in the nineteenth century, when church–state controversies often took the form of Catholic resistance to Protestant nativism, and the native Catholic heritage was overlooked on both sides; in part, I suspect, the Declaration of Religious Liberty promulgated by the Second Vatican Council, in which the church seemed to reverse its preference for the confessional state at the urging of American Catholics, has made Catholic arguments in favor of religious liberty as a constitutional right seem a new development. Whatever the case, the Carrolls recognized that the political situation of the eighteenth century made their participation in the new American constitutionalism of religious liberty the course of political prudence and the proper expression of their Catholic faith. Why that was so and what it has to teach us today will be the burden of my brief and all too preliminary remarks.

THE CARROLLS

Three members of the Carroll family played an important role in the American founding, and they emerged on the political stage youngest first.[6] The eldest, however, was Daniel Carroll, whose father had immigrated from Ireland around 1725 and established himself as a planter and merchant in Prince George's County, Maryland. Educated at St. Omer's School, run by English Jesuits in Flanders, then under France—the school of choice for wealthy Maryland Catholics, although colonial law apparently forbad their attendance—Daniel returned to Maryland in 1748, only to find himself three years later managing the family fortune upon his father's death. Barred as a Catholic from holding office and even from voting in Maryland until 1776, Daniel later sat in the Maryland Senate, served in the Continental Congress, attended the federal convention in Philadelphia in 1787 (after his cousin Charles declined to go), served as one of Maryland's original elected representatives under the Constitution, and was then appointed by President Washington to the commission overseeing the establishment of the District of Columbia, where he had owned what was to become Capitol Hill.

John Carroll was Daniel's younger brother. His formal education began at an illegal, but tolerated, Catholic school for boys on Maryland's eastern shore, and when his elder brother returned from St.

Omer's, he was sent across the ocean to study there himself. He did not see America again for twenty-five years, succeeding in his studies, moving on to the English Jesuit seminary at Liege, becoming ordained a Jesuit priest, and apparently teaching at both schools he had attended until they were closed when the Jesuits came under persecution by the king of France. Accompanying the son of an English Catholic on a tour of Europe, he arrived in Rome in 1773 as the Jesuits were disbanded by the pope under pressure from various Catholic monarchs. After declining an offer to serve as family chaplain to an English lord and with full awareness of political developments in his homeland, he returned to America in 1773 and served as priest to his family and neighbors in Maryland. In 1776, at the request of Congress, he accompanied Benjamin Franklin, Samuel Chase, and his cousin Charles on a diplomatic mission to Quebec, which failed to gain Quebec's concurrence in the Revolution, but gave him occasion to earn Franklin's respect. After independence was won and thanks in part to Franklin's communications with Vatican diplomats in Paris, John became the Catholic superior of the mission in the new United States, with responsibility for overseeing Catholic priests; in May 1789, with Vatican permission and subsequent assent, he was elected bishop by his fellow priests and the next year went to England to be ordained among the friends of his youth. He served as bishop, then when other sees were established in America, as archbishop, of Baltimore for twenty-five years until his death in 1815. His success in this role is testimony to no small skill in human governance, as America attracted many priests fleeing the troubles in Revolutionary Europe, who were not unknown to cause troubles of their own. Among the many institutions John Carroll helped to found were Georgetown University and St. Mary's Seminary, and he served as well as a trustee of numerous other Maryland institutions that were not specifically Catholic, including St. John's College and the University of Maryland.

Charles Carroll of Carrollton was born in 1737, related to Daniel and John by blood through an Irish ancestor and later as well by marriage. His grandfather had trained as a lawyer in the Inns of Court in London and came to Maryland in 1688 as attorney for the proprietor, Lord Baltimore. Although the effects of the Glorious Revolution in the colony progressively narrowed the political rights of Catholics like Charles Carroll the Settler, their property rights were on the whole respected, and as a loyal servant to the Calvert family and son-in-law to the proprietor's chief agent, Carroll acquired extensive colonial lands;

indeed, the nearly 50,000 acres he owned at his death in 1720 made him the largest landowner in Maryland. His son and heir, Charles Carroll of Annapolis, built up this fortune, not only developing landed and creditor interests, but helping to found the profitable Baltimore Iron Works. Charles of Carrollton was heir in turn to this fortune, and his father prepared him for this charge with an extensive European education, sending him along with his cousin John to St. Omer's in 1748, then to college in Rheims and Paris, to study civil law in Bourges and Paris, and finally to London to study common law at the Inns of Court. His father visited him once in Paris, in 1757, between young Charles's taking his degree from the College of Louis le Grand and beginning his study of law, and the senior Charles sent the junior on a tour of Europe after the end of the Seven Year's War in 1763, allowing him finally to return to Maryland the following year after his unsuccessful courtship of a young English lady. In 1773 Charles of Carrollton won popular acclaim for getting the better of Daniel Dulany in a war of letters in the Maryland *Gazette* over fees levied by the royal governor without assembly assent. The following year he was elected to the Maryland convention, where he quickly earned the respect of his colleagues. Although not chosen to be a delegate to the first Continental Congress, he went to Philadelphia for a couple weeks anyway and apparently joined in the informal evening sessions at the local tavern. Over the course of the next several years, he was elected and reelected to the Maryland conventions, which as extralegal bodies were not considered bound by the Catholic disability acts. After the mission to Quebec, he played a leading role in persuading the convention to send instructions to their delegates at the second Continental Congress authorizing a vote for independence, and he was himself elected delegate in time to sign the parchment Declaration in August, thus wagering what was reputed the largest fortune among the signers upon the success of the new United States. Moving back and forth during the Revolution between eastern Pennsylvania and central Maryland, Carroll served on the congressional Board of War, where he staunchly supported (and gently prodded) General Washington, while playing a critical role in Maryland, where he helped design its aristocratic Senate while serving on the convention's constitutional committee and fought, unsuccessfully, the legislature's paper money scheme. He was elected to the Maryland Senate for the next twenty-four years and served as its chair. He declined election to the federal convention in Philadelphia in 1787, although he sent his thoughts on government along with his cousin Daniel, and without giving up his Maryland office, Charles became one of the state's original U.S. senators, drawing the two-year lot and retiring to state office in 1791. Defeated even from that in the Jeffersonian rout of 1800—the family were staunch Federalists—he left public service to concentrate on the management of his estates. He survived Jefferson and Adams to become the last living signer of the Declaration, finally succumbing in 1832 at the age of ninety-five, although not before meeting Alexis de Tocqueville during his journey to America the year before.

As befits men of the world, the Carrolls carried on an extensive correspondence, much of which has found its way into print in recent years. My concern here, however, will be with their few public essays, which inevitably touch on Catholic themes, specifically the "Antilon"–"First Citizen" exchange between Charles Carroll and Daniel Dulany in 1773 and several published writings and a public address by John Carroll.

CHARLES CARROLL AS "FIRST CITIZEN"

Charles Carroll established his political reputation as a leader in the patriot cause through a series of four letters published in the Maryland *Gazette* in the first half of 1773, each in response to a letter published under the pseudonym "Antilon," but widely known to be by Daniel Dulany, identified by the modern editor of the exchange as "the towering intellect of colonial Maryland and one of the finest lawyers in the colonies . . . in his fiftieth year and, as provincial secretary and unofficial 'minister of Maryland,' at the peak of his power."[7] Son of the onetime leader of the antiproprietary party in the colonial assembly who had later served in a number of appointed offices, the younger Dulany had earned his reputation as author of one of the most successful pamphlets making the colonial case against the Stamp Act in 1765 as an exercise of taxation without representation. Like his father, he was soon after on Governor Eden's council and apparently its leading member. The specific issue that precipitated the published quarrel with Carroll was a dispute between the lower house and the governor concerning the fees of tobacco inspectors, a matter that touched the colony's chief export. The lower house, thinking the schedule of fees established some years before too high, allowed the act authorizing the fees to expire in 1770 and refused to pass another at the rate the governor and his council desired. After the governor prorogued the assembly that year, he issued a proclamation establishing a new schedule of fees, claiming set fees were needed to forestall extortion by his agents. Members of the lower house denounced the proclamation as a violation of the constitution of the colony and an instance of taxation without representation, and in subsequent assemblies addresses on this score moved among the branches of Maryland government, without any resolution of the issue to the satisfaction of all parties and, thus, without the passage of legislation.

Apparently to discredit the opposition party's charges of "Court-influence and Corruption," Dulany published in early 1773 a dialogue between a "first citizen" and a "second citizen," in which the former speaks in generalities about "the Cause of Freedom" and government corruption, while the latter defends the wise policy of the government, explains the dangers of excited appeals to the people, and expresses his regret that politicians in the course of "electioneering" "have divided a house against itself, and kindled the inextinguishable flames of hatred and animosity, even in the hearts of brothers."[8] No scholar I know has suggested that the narrator's pretense to have overheard the conversation reported in Dulany's letter was anything other than a literary device, but Carroll assumes Dulany's character and brings his "first citizen" to life in a dialogue of his own published a month later in the same journal. Here the governor's proclamation is compared to Charles I's notorious policy of raising ship money without parliamentary approval, Antilon (Dulany's pseudonym) is accused of corruption for having persuaded the governor to issue the unconstitutional proclamation, which was financially to his own benefit as an officeholder who would receive fees, and the honor of lawyers and assemblymen is defended, not least against Antilon's earlier charge that assemblymen who speak of liberty and denounce the government readily seek places for themselves in the governor's charge.

While minute accounting of the constitutional argument between Antilon and First Citizen is beyond the scope of this chapter, the outlines of the dispute elucidate Carroll's clear and confident statement of his constitutional principles, at once careful and precise in a lawyerly sense, uncompromising in its adherence to the popular cause, and attuned to a sophisticated understanding of the British constitution. After the first exchange, both authors drop the dialogic form, with each presenting his side of the issue and answering quite specifically the other's charges. Carroll cites the authority of Sir Edward Coke to show that fees are taxes and so must be approved by Parliament—or its colonial analog, the assembly—unless the fees are ancient and traditional. On the strength of this finding, he holds the governor's proclamation establishing fees to be analogous to Charles I's demands for ship money: Both executives sought sources of income that would be legal if approved by the legislature, but in demanding them on executive authority alone, they exceeded their right. Dulany finds the suggestion preposterous, insisting that numerous courts and authorities in England set their own fees, claiming that there was ample precedent in Maryland for gubernatorial fee setting and expounding on the benefit of the proclamation in insuring smooth administration of tobacco inspection laws. Carroll responds that the English instances of fee setting principally involve the houses of Parliament themselves, who come under their own law rather than general common law, and that Parliament recently investigated such fee setting by other courts as an abuse; he gives evidence that there was only a single precedent before 1770 for fee setting by proclamation; and he thinks that adequate fees in the absence of legislation could either be agreed upon by the parties or determined by a jury in the course of ordinary litigation in the case of a dispute. The problem with the proclamation is that it awards the fees to the people who set the fees, and moreover, because in colonial Maryland the governor was also chancellor, the courts that might be called upon to judge the legality of the fees would involve the same people who proclaimed and collected them. Citing Montesquieu on the need to separate judicial, executive, and legislative power, and quoting Coke's opinion in *Doctor Bonham's Case* on the ability of common law to control even an act of Parliament that makes a man judge in his own cause,[9] Carroll defends his objection, and not only abstractly: "Antilon," known to be Dulany, is charged with corruption precisely for his role in setting fees he will soon collect, or more precisely, for seeking to pervert the constitution of the colony to insure his personal fees.

Carroll's argument thus takes the colonial argument that had been pressed against the Stamp Act and the Townsend Duties a step further, applying American constitutional principles not against the British ministry or Parliament acting from afar, but against the royal officials operating in the colonies themselves. Dulany laughs on the page when Carroll invokes the maxim that "the king can do no wrong" to protect the governor and accuse his chief advisor, saying that the governor is also the king's minister and that appeal to any colonial decision lies open to the council in London. But Carroll insists on a strict analogy of the British constitution and the colonial constitution of Maryland: The governor is the king's representative, not his mere minister, and the Maryland assembly is as much as Parliament entitled to insist upon its rights in relation to him. At issue in the question of fees and taxes, after all, is the right of property, and if taxes can be collected without legislative consent, then property is taken as it were without due process. Property is such only if it is protected by law, and law governs only if the principles of the constitution are sound and respected. There is nothing, besides perhaps the pen name, in Carroll's "First Citizen" letters that presages independence from England as yet, but there is a presumption that runs throughout of the equality of English and American institutions, that is, of an equality of the rights of Englishmen in the New World with those in the Old.

Carroll is well aware that this equality is not simply a matter of immemorial custom; indeed, he is aware that the principles of the British constitution for which he contends are themselves not altogether immemorial. In the fourth and final letter, he treats at some length the constitutional development of England, and although he briefly praises the ancient Saxon order and denounces its suppression by the Norman Conquest, he does not, like Jefferson, rest everything upon remote antiquity. Instead, drawing on Hume, he offers an encapsulated history of the constitution, commenting equally on abuse by the kings and neglect by the parliaments; over the years, the constitution has improved, but ironically, the complacency this induced has enabled Parliament to relax its vigilance and grow corrupt in the hands of the king's ministers. Repeating Hume, he says, "The necessities of the English kings, which constrained them to have frequent recourse to parliamentary aid, first gave rise to, then gradually secured, the liberty of the subject."[10] Applying this principle or observation to the situation in Maryland explains why the matter of tobacco inspection fees, which might seem trivial or particular, in fact ought to precipitate a constitutional crisis: With the upper house of the assembly "composed of officers dependent on the proprietary and removable at pleasure," the delegates have nothing but their right to control provision of government officials that ensures them in practice a say in their own government. Carroll's argument, then, is defensive, but it is based on a constitutional understanding that contains the seeds of constitutional development and growth.

There is nothing, or next to nothing, in the constitutional controversy Carroll engages that directly implicates the question of religious liberty. Indeed, that may have been part of what prompted him to enter the debate, for he could not be accused of the self-interested use of public debate that he could charge his opponent with. But Dulany, misjudging Carroll's equanimity or his audience's prejudices, or both, cannot resist insinuation and even invective against Carroll as a Catholic. In his second letter, and so first response, he belittles Carroll's St. Omer's in contrast to his own Cambridge; in rebuking Carroll's alliance with the lower house of the assembly, he reminds him that that House had not so long before reiterated the anti-Catholic spirit that had imposed disabilities at the turn of the century and adds that he (Dulany) had then been one of the few to object. Carroll is magnanimous in his response, expressing his willingness to let the past be forgiven, although suspicious of Dulany's motives in bringing such matters up, as they appear not to touch upon the constitutional issue in question. By his final letter, however, Dulany sets aside all restraint, denouncing as suspect Carroll's express endorsement of the Glorious Revolution. To Carroll's statement that "his speculative opinions, in matters of religion, have no relation to, or influence over, his political tenets," Dulany retorts,

> But we are taught otherwise and put on our guard by our laws, and constitution, which have laid him under disabilities, because he is a papist, and his religious principles are suspected to have so great influence, as to make it unsafe to permit his interference, in any degree, when the interests of the established religion, or the civil government, are concerned. . . . It is as little my wish, as the Citizen's, to rekindle extinguished animosities; tho' I think his conduct, very inconsistent with the situation of a man, who owes even the toleration, he enjoys, to the favour of government.[11]

Carroll's response is carefully measured, and in drawing attention to Carroll's endorsement of the Glorious Revolution, Dulany helps make clear how his involvement in the present controversy touches upon the question of religious liberty. In his own final letter, Carroll expands on his earlier defense of the Glorious Revolution, writing now "that the national religion was in danger under James the 2d, from his bigotry and despotic temper." He proceeds,

> The nation had a *right* to *resist*, and to secure its civil and religious liberties. I am as averse to having a religion crammed down peoples throats, as a proclamation. These are my political principles, in which I glory; principles not hastily taken up to serve a turn, but what I have always avowed since I became capable of reflection. I bear not the least dislike to the church of England, though I am not within her pale, nor indeed to any other church; knaves, and bigots of all sects and denominations I hate, and I despise.[12]

The carefully calibrated insistence on balance and impartiality that informs Carroll's account of the constitution, in other words, likewise defines his approach to religious liberty. His cautious optimism about the possibility of constitutional improvement and the dignity of his replies to Dulany's appeals to establishment prejudice made him a leader among the Maryland patriots and made religious liberty, in the sense of removal of religious disability, a patriot cause.

JOHN CARROLL, PATRIOT PRIEST

A similar temper of self-restraint and skill of precise expression characterize the writings of John Carroll. Having seen the distinguished order in which he had been ordained a priest suppressed, as it were, before his eyes in Rome, Fr. John can hardly be supposed to have felt indebted to the old regime in Europe, which gave privileges to the Catholic clergy only to make them subject to the despotic will of purportedly Catholic monarchs. The trials of the Church under Napoleon must only have confirmed this opinion, as indeed his letters express. Returning to an America which he understood to be on the road to independence in 1773 was a declaration of republicanism on his part, and with his acceptance (albeit after protest of his unsuitability) of the diplomatic mission to Quebec, he cast his lot with the Revolution. Although he knew well from his many English friends of the persecution of Catholics in England, there was no rancor in his patriotism. When he was chosen to be the United States' first bishop in 1789, he chose to go to England rather than Quebec or France to be ordained, and he was pained in the last years of his life to find his country at war with those he saw as the valiant enemies of Bonaparte, the true menace to liberty in the world. Still, if his patriotism seems natural enough given his family connections and his European experience, the pre-dominant religious orientation of American revolutionaries was not Catholic; indeed, if Nathan Hatch is correct, the New England clergy first formulated their notion of "the sacred cause of liberty" in the colonial war of the 1750s and 1760s against the Catholic French.[13]

Like his cousin, John Carroll rarely wrote for the public press, but an early pamphlet gives a glimpse of his religious convictions and the meaning for republican liberty that he thought they entailed. Written in 1784, just as he was assuming leadership of the nascent American church, Carroll's "Address to the Roman Catholics of the United States of America by a Catholic Clergyman"[14] was occasioned by the distribution in the United States of Charles Wharton's "Letter to the Roman Catholics of Worcester." Like Carroll, Wharton was a native Marylander who was ordained a Jesuit priest; instead of re-turning to Maryland when the Jesuits were disbanded, he went to England and served as a chaplain in Worcester. There he went over to the Church of England, married, and ended up in Delaware as an Episcopalian minister, publishing his reasons for leaving Catholicism as a critique of a number of its doctrines. Apparently fearing the cor-rosive effect the argument of an ex-Catholic might have on Catholics, Carroll wrote a careful, but forceful, rejoinder that proves him a loyal son of Rome. Citing Bellarmine and others, although apologizing for the paucity of sources at his disposal in the United States, Carroll de-fends the antiquity of the doctrine of transubstantiation and of the practice of auricular confession; explains the importance of tradition as authoritative, not least in the establishment of the biblical canon; insists on the infallibility of the Church as conveyor, not only of the fundamentals, but also of the integral whole of the Catholic faith; and clearly distinguishes infallibility on points of doctrine from impecca-bility on the part of Catholic clergy, even at the highest levels, which of course he does not claim. He offers a sophisticated account of the development of doctrine over the course of the Church's history in response to changing situations and new heresies, and he precisely delineates what Catholics were obliged to believe as authoritative doctrine in different eras. (Whether his cousin's account of constitu-tional change, discussed above, is colored by a similar understand-ing of doctrinal development is a matter worth investigating.) He is lucid on the difference between the private interpretations of the-ologians, even those canonized as saints, and the public dogma of the universal Church.

Carroll puts at the very beginning of his long essay the discussion that will be of most immediate interest to American ears skeptical of theological controversy: the relation of Catholic doctrine to liberty of conscience. He starts by insisting that it is Catholic teaching that obedience in matters of faith must be reasonable, citing the Protestant John Leland when explaining that reasonableness need not involve the suspension of faith itself, much less of its practice, only "a mind open to conviction, and a disposition to embrace truth, on which side soever it shall appear, and to receive the evidence that shall arise in the course of the trial." The various papal bulls that forbad the reading of Protestant authors he dismisses as "no prejudice to free inquiry" in practice. To the claim that Catholics teach that non-Catholics cannot be saved and thus justify persecution as being for the sake of salvation, he replies with Bellarmine's distinction between being in communion with the Catholic Church and being a member of that Church; the first is restricted to those who are united in the sacraments, but the second consists of "all those, who with a sincere heart seek true religion, and are in an unfeigned disposition to embrace the truth, whenever they find it," and while Catholic doctrine restricts salvation to the latter, it never has to the former.[15] As for persecution, he says the following:

> If, then, we do not hold the doctrine of exclusive salvation, can the horrible tenet of persecution, which, he says, is the consequence of it, be imputed to us? I do not indeed see their necessary connexion; but I know that Protestants and Catholics equally deviate from the spirit of their religion, when fanaticism and fiery zeal would usurp that control over men's minds, to which conviction and fair argument have an exclusive right.[16]

The sentiment here expressed seems as full of equanimity as anything in Locke, although the calculation of the wager is different: While Locke insists that the stakes of salvation are so high as to lead no man to trust another's judgment over his own, Carroll suggests that with so much riding on the choice and reason being limited in its metaphysical capacity, the rational course is for a man to trust that faith that can best prove its continuity with Christ.

John Carroll's other venture into the public press came in the form of an article in John Fenno's *Gazette of the United States* on June 10, 1789, under the pseudonym "Pacificus," which is notable as a politically orthodox defense of religious liberty.[17] Carroll here writes in answer to "E. C.," whose essay "The Importance of the Protestant

Religion Politically Considered" is characterized by Carroll's modern editor as "a very early statement of the popular nineteenth century theme of Protestant Nationalism."[18] Carroll denounces the essay as an attempt "to revive the odious system of religious intolerance," despite its professions of toleration, for he reads its assertion that "[t]he Protestant religion is the important bulwark of our Constitution" to imply the need for religious disabilities in political life.[19] Carroll opens his case with the Constitution's forbidding religious tests and its support for the "firm persuasion that [Americans] were to retain when associated [in 'one great national union'], every natural right not expressly surrendered."[20] Not only Protestants fought and died in the Revolution, he reminds his readers; nor were Protestant dissenters the only ones who came to America in colonial times seeking religious liberty; nor was the country from whom independence was won not itself Protestant; nor have the arts and sciences flourished only under Protestantism; and so forth. The "rights of conscience and liberty of religion" depend not on the clergy of any particular religion but on "luminous principles"; but

> the constitutions of some of the States continue still to intrench on the sacred rights of conscience; and men who have bled, and opened their purses as freely in the cause of liberty and independence, as any other citizen, are most unjustly excluded from the advantages which they contributed to establish.[21]

America must "rest the preservation of her liberalities and her government on the attachment of mankind to their political happiness, to the security of their persons and their property, which is independent of religious doctrines, and not restrained by any."[22] A clearer endorsement from a Catholic pen of a rather strict separation of church and state is hard to imagine.

Carroll was bishop when Washington died—like his cousin he had been Washington's friend and in fact had dined with the former president at Mount Vernon barely six months before his passing—and urged his brother priests to accede to the government's request for a day of mourning on February 22, 1800. The oration he gave that day was lavish in its praise of the deceased and insightful in its catalog of his virtues.[23] The themes were providence and wisdom: Carroll stressed Washington's belief in the former and his dedication to the latter, quoting as if it were Washington's creed a passage from the book of Wisdom, which is not canonical in Protestant scripture and so might be a text that Washington had never read. He paraphrased as well the Farewell Address's admonition "that nations and individuals are under the moral government of an infinitely wise and just providence; that the foundations of their happiness are morality and religion; and their union among themselves their rock of safety; that to venerate their constitution and its laws is to ensure their liberty."[24] The height of political virtue that Carroll describes in Washington was not specifically Catholic, and Carroll does not begrudge him that. It is interesting to note, as the editor of *The John Carroll Papers* makes easy to see, that in writing to his clergy about the duty to honor Washington that day, he carefully reminds them that their talk should not be a sermon on a biblical text, but should take the form of an oration, and that if they choose to speak in church, "where the H[oly] Sacr[amen]t is usually kept, it will be proper to remove it previously, with due honor, to some decent place."[25]

CONCLUSION

What conclusions might one draw from this brief investigation of the thoughts and deeds of the Carrolls on religious liberty in young America? First, it is important to note that both men were convinced of the perfect compatibility of a staunch Catholic faith and the American settlement on religious liberty. These were highly educated men, aware of and versed in Enlightenment literature, but they confidently took from that literature its conclusions regarding religious liberty without its premises challenging the Christian faith. Second, and perhaps as a consequence, their support for separation of church and state, while consistent with a nondenominationalist reading of the First Amendment, nevertheless reflected as well their distrust of generalized Protestant accounts of religious liberty and of the liberal tendency to conflate the freedom of the individual conscience from political coercion with the autonomy of the individual from church authority in matters of belief. They thought, in other words, that an impartial constitutionalism was possible even in the face of metaphysical difference. The sentiment here is precisely what one finds in Washington's famous letters "to the Roman Catholics in the United States" (in response to a letter the Carrolls had helped draft) and "to the Hebrew Congregation in Newport"—indeed, so precisely that one wonders whether it did not grow from the close personal association between Washington and the Carrolls over the years.[26] And it is hard not to imagine that de Tocqueville's understanding of American religious liberty, in particular of how separation of church and state can strengthen religion, was forged, or at least confirmed, at his fellow Catholic's hearth.[27]

Finally, the Carrolls' willingness to join their fellow citizens in venturing into new political arrangements regarding church and state, while preserving their spiritual bonds with the Catholic Church, reflected a training in a form of political prudence that was not dependent on modern ideology, but reached back to the whole of the Western tradition. How this meeting of ancient prudence and modern theory fared as American democracy developed, as the American people (including the Catholic laity and clergy) became more democratic, and as liberal principles militated against institutions, such as slavery, that ancient prudence had allowed, is a question for another generation of Carrolls and for us another time.

APPENDIX: LETTER OF JOHN CARROLL, WRITING AS PACIFICUS, "TO JOHN FENNO OF THE *GAZETTE OF THE UNITED STATES*," JUNE 10, 1789[28]

EVERY friend to the rights of conscience, equal liberty and diffusive happiness, must have felt pain on seeing the attempt made by one of your correspondents, in the Gazette of the United States No. 8, May the 9th, to revive an odious system of religious intolerance.—The author may not have been fully sensible of the tendency of his publication, because he speaks of preserving universal tolerance. Perhaps he is one of those who think it consistent with justice to exclude certain citizens from the honors and emoluments of society, merely on account of their religious opinions, provided they be not restrained by racks and forfeitures from the exercise of that worship which their consciences approve.—If such be his views, in vain then have Americans associated into one great national union, under the express condition of not being shackled by religious tests; and under a firm persuasion that they were to retain when associated, every natural right not expressly surrendered.

It is pretended that they, who are the objects of an intended exclusion from certain offices of honor and advantage, have forfeited by an act, or treason against the United States, the common rights of nature, or the stipulated rights of the political society, of which they form a part? This the author has not presumed to assert. Their blood flowed as freely (in proportion to their numbers) to cement the fabric of independence as that of any of their fellow-citizens: They concurred with perhaps greater unanimity than any other body of men, in recommending and promoting that government, from whose influence America anticipates all the blessings of justice, peace, plenty, good order and civil and religious liberty. What character shall we then give to a system of policy, for the express purpose of divesting of rights legally acquired those citizens, who are not only unoffending, but whose conduct has been highly meritorious?

These observations refer to the general tendency of the publication, which I now proceed to consider more particularly. Is it true as the author states, that our forefathers abandoned their native home; renounced its honors and comforts, and buried themselves in the immense forests of this new world, for the sake of that religion which he recommends preferable to any other? Was not the religion which the emigrants to the four Southern States brought with them to America, the pre-eminent and favored religion of the country which they left? Did the Roman Catholics who first came to Maryland, leave their native soil for the sake of preserving the Protestant church? Was this the motive of the peaceable Quakers in the settlement of Pennsylvania? Did the first inhabitants of the Jerseys and New York, quit Europe for fear of being compelled to renounce their Protestant tenets? Can it be even truly affirmed that this motive operated on all, or a majority of those who began to settle and improve the four eastern States? Or even if they really where [*sic*—were] influenced by a desire of preserving their religion, what will ensue from the fact, but that one denomination of Protestants fought a retreat from the persecution of another? Will history justify the assertion that they left their native homes for the sake of the Protestant religion, understanding it in a comprehensive sense as distinguished from every other?

This leading fact being so much misstated, no wonder that the author should go on bewildering himself more and more. He asserts that the *religion* which he recommends, *laid the foundation of this new and great empire*; and therefore contends it is entitled to pre-eminence and distinguished favor. Might I not say with equal truth, that the religion which he recommends exerted her powers to crush this empire in its birth, and still is laboring to prevent its growth? For, can we so soon forget, or now help seeing, that the bitterest enemies of our national prosperity possess the same religion as prevails generally in the United States? What inference will a philosophic mind derive from this view, but that religion is out of the question? That it is ridiculous to say, THE PROTESTANT RELIGION IS THE IMPORTANT BULWARK OF OUR CONSTITUTION? That the establishment of the American empire was not the work of this or that religion, but arose from a generous exertion of all her citizens to redress their wrongs, to assert their rights, and lay its foundations on the soundest principles of justice and equal liberty.

When he ascribed so many valuable effects to his cherished religion, as that she was the nurse of *arts and sciences*, could he not reflect, that *Homer* and *Virgil, Demosthenes* and *Cicero, Thucydides* and *Livy, Phidias* and *Apelles* flourished long before this nurse *of arts and sciences* had an existence? Was he so inconsiderate as not to attend to the consequences, favorable to Polytheism, which flow from his reasoning? Or did he forget that the Emperor Julian, the subtle and inveterate enemy of Christianity, applied this very same argument to the defense of Heathenish superstition? The recollection of that circumstance may induce him to suspect the weight of his observation, and perhaps to doubt of the fact, which he assumed for its basis.

But he tells us that Britain owes to *her religion her present distinguished greatness*: a gentle invitation to America to pursue the same political maxims, in heaping exclusive favors on one, and depressing all other religions!

But does Britain owe indeed the perfection and extent of her manufactures, and the enormous wealth of many individuals to the cause assigned by this author? Can he so soon put it out of his mind, that the patient industry so natural to English artificers, and the long monopoly of our trade, and that of their dependencies, by increasing the demand and a competition among her artizans, contributed principally to the perfection of the manufactures of Britain? And that the plunder of Indian provinces poured into her lap the immense fortunes which murder and rapacity accumulated in those fertile climes? God forbid that religion should be instrumental in raising such greatness!

When the author proceeds to say, that the clergy of that religion, which operated such wonders in Britain, *boldly and zealously stepped forth and bravely stood our distinguished sentinels to bring about the late glorious revolution*, I am almost determined to follow him no further: He is leading me on too tender ground, on which I chuse not to venture. The clergy of that religion behaved, I believe, as any other clergy would have done in similar circumstances: But the voice of America will not contradict me, when I assert that they discovered no greater zeal for the revolution, than the ministry of any other denomination whatever.

When men comprehend not, or refuse to admit the luminous principles on which the rights of conscience and liberty of religion depend, they are industrious to find out pretences for intolerance. If they cannot discover them in the actions, they strain to cull them out of the tenets of the religion which they wish to exclude from a free participation of equal rights. Thus, this author attributes to his religion the merit of being *the most favorable to freedom*, and affirms that not only *morality* but *liberty* likewise must expire, if his clergy should ever be *contemned* or *neglected*: all which conveys a refined insinuation, that liberty cannot consist with, or be cherished by any other religious institution; and which therefore he would give us to understand, it is not safe to countenance in a free government.

I am anxious to guard against the impression intended by such insinuations; not merely for the sake of any one profession, but from an earnest regard to preserve inviolate for ever, in our new empire, the great principle of religious freedom. The constitutions of some of the States continue still to intrench on the sacred rights of conscience; and men who have bled, and opened their purses as freely in the cause of liberty and independence, as any other citizens, are most unjustly excluded from the advantages which they contributed to establish. But if bigotry and narrow prejudices have prevented hitherto the cure of these evils, be it the duty of every lover of peace and justice to extend to them no further. Let the author who has opened this field for discussion, be aware of slyly imputing to any set of men, principles or consequences, which they disavow. He perhaps may meet with retaliation. He may be told and referred to Lord Lyttleton, as zealous a Protestant as any man of his days, for information, that the principles of nonresistance *seemed the principles* of that religion which we are not [*sic*—now] told is *most favorable to freedom*; and that its opponents *had gone too far in the other* extreme!

He may be told farther, that a Reverend Prelate of Ireland, the Bishop of Bloyne, has lately attempted to prove, that the Protestant Episcopal Church is best fitted to unite with the civil constitution of a mixed monarchy, while Presbyterianism is only congenial with republicanism. Must America then yielding to these fanciful systems, confine her *distinguishing* favors to the followers of Calvin, and keep a jealous eye on all others? Ought she not rather to treat with contempt these idle, and generally speaking interested speculations, refuted by reason, history, and daily experience, and rest the preservation of her liberalities and her government on the attachment of mankind to their political happiness, to the security of their persons and their property, which is independent of religious doctrines, and not restrained by any?

NOTES

1. 330 U.S. 1.

2. For the most recent examples, see Philip Hamburger, *Separation of Church and State* (Cambridge, MA: Harvard University Press, 2002), and Daniel L. Dreisbach, *Thomas Jefferson and the Wall of Separation between Church and State* (New York: New York University Press, 2002). See also Barry Alan Shain, *The Myth of American Individualism: The Protestant Origins of American Political Thought* (Princeton, NJ: Princeton University Press, 1994).

3. E.g., *Marsh v. Chambers*, 463 U.S. 783 (1983), upholding the constitutionality of prayer at the opening of legislative sessions. Cf. then Justice William Rehnquist's dissenting opinion in *Wallace v. Jaffree*, 472 U.S. 38 (1985), at 91 ff., and Justice Thomas's concurrence in *Zelman v. Simmons-Harris*, 536 U.S. 639 (2002), n4.

4. See, e.g., John Rawls, *A Theory of Justice* (Cambridge, MA: Harvard University Press, 1971), sect. 33.

5. An exception, albeit in magazine format, is Matthew Spalding, "Faith of Our Fathers," *Crisis* (May 1996): 30–34. In his recent book, *On Two Wings: Humble Faith and Common Sense at the American Founding* (San Francisco: Encounter Books, 2002), Michael Novak includes the Carrolls among "the forgotten founders" in his appendix and discusses the compatibility of Catholic thought and the American settlement at some length, but he does not explore the possibility that the Carrolls played a conscious role in forming American religious liberty to be compatible with Catholic faith.

6. For information on Daniel and John Carroll, I have relied on Annabelle M. Melville's fine biography, *John Carroll of Baltimore: Founder of the American Catholic Hierarchy* (New York: Charles Scribner's Sons, 1955). The most extensive biography of Charles is Thomas O'Brien Hanley, S.J., *Charles Carroll of Carrollton: The Making of a Revolutionary Gentleman* (1970; Chicago: Loyola University Press, 1982), and *Revolutionary Statesman: Charles Carroll and the War* (Chicago: Loyola University Press, 1983), but a new biography has just appeared: Scott McDermott, *Charles Carroll of Carrollton: Faithful Revolutionary* (New York: Scepter Publishers, 2002). Much useful information can be found in the introductions, notes, and appendixes of the first published volumes of the Charles Carroll papers: Ronald Hoffman, ed., *Dear Papa, Dear Charley: The Papers of Charles Carroll of Carrollton, 1748–1782*, 3 vols. (Chapel Hill: University of North Carolina Press, 2001). See also Hoffman's *Princes of Ireland, Planters of Maryland: A Carroll Saga, 1500–1782* (Chapel Hill: University of North Carolina Press, 2000).

7. Peter S. Onuf, ed., *Maryland and the Empire, 1773: The Antilon—First Citizen Letters* (Baltimore: Johns Hopkins University Press, 1974), 15.

8. Onuf, *Maryland and the Empire*, 45, 43, 50.

9. Onuf, *Maryland and the Empire*, 141.

10. Onuf, *Maryland and the Empire*, 213–14, with an editor's note to Hume's *History of England*, 6:142.

11. Onuf, *Maryland and the Empire*, 188.

12. Onuf, *Maryland and the Empire*, 225–26.

13. Nathan O. Hatch, *The Sacred Cause of Liberty: Republican Thought and the Millennium in Revolutionary New England* (New Haven, CT: Yale University Press, 1977).

14. In Thomas O'Brien Hanley, S.J., ed., *The John Carroll Papers* (Notre Dame, IN: University of Notre Dame Press, 1976), 1:82–144.

15. Hanley, *The John Carroll Papers*, 1:85, 86, 87.

16. Hanley, *The John Carroll Papers*, 1:92.

17. Hanley, *The John Carroll Papers*, 1:365–69.

18. Hanley, *The John Carroll Papers*, 1:369.

19. Hanley, *The John Carroll Papers*, 1: 365, 367.

20. Hanley, *The John Carroll Papers*, 1:366.

21. Hanley, *The John Carroll Papers,* 1:368.

22. Hanley, *The John Carroll Papers,* 1:368.

23. Hanley, *The John Carroll Papers,* 2:297–308.

24. Hanley, *The John Carroll Papers,* 2:306.

25. Hanley, *The John Carroll Papers,* 2:296.

26. In William B. Allen, ed., *George Washington: A Collection* (Indianapolis, IN: Liberty Classics, 1988), 546, 547. Thanks to Matthew Spalding and Paul Carrese for drawing this to my attention.

27. See Alexis de Tocqueville, *Democracy in America,* trans. Harvey C. Mansfield and Delba Winthrop (Chicago: University of Chicago Press, 2000), esp. 1:282–88.

28. From Hanley, *The John Carroll Papers,* 1:365–68.

Afterword

Revolutionary-Era Americans: Were They Enlightened or Protestant? Does It Matter?

Barry Alan Shain

A central question of continuing interest to students of the American founding concerns the nature of the ideas and values that guided Americans into and out of their war of independence. Many political scientists contend that what was and "remains America's deepest and so far most abiding commitment" is primarily an enlightened "natural-rights philosophy" that shaped eighteenth-century Americans' understanding of things political.[1] Other scholars, in the main historians, argue that a particular slice of pagan thought inherited from Greece and Rome and transformed by Renaissance thinkers, known as civic humanism or classical republicanism, shaped Americans' political and social views of the period. And still others, a minority by all accounts, hold that the central organizing principles of American social and political life were derived, either immediately or indirectly, from varying and changing forms of Protestant Christianity.[2]

Although classical republicanism enjoyed great influence among American historians for much of the last two or three decades, recently it has waned in importance.[3] Accordingly, the debate regarding the nature of moral and political thought during the American founding has become a binary one, with the traditionalist defenders of an Enlightened America on one side and those who give pride of place to Protestantism on the other. Of course, there is much to be found in the historical record that can offer encouragement to both sides, but what is most surprising, given its limited public visibility, is how powerful the evidence is supporting the Protestant reading of American foundational political culture. Yet, in spite of the comparative strength of the evidence marshaled by its defenders and its timely utility in explaining important differences between the cultural norms of much of Western Europe and America, this perspective has heretofore been largely relegated to the margins of the nation's self-understanding.[4] If the evidence for a Protestant America even approaches the power of that offered by those who argue for an Enlightened America, how can one explain the disparity in the national recognition that each perspective enjoys?

However one views such concerns, one might ask, "why be concerned with such antiquarian interests?" In response, I would answer that these are, in truth, questions worth asking and answering. Thus, I would like to examine in brief the strengths of these competing ways of viewing America's foundational political culture and to consider in particular evidence of America having been effectively founded as a Protestant nation; to consider whether the most important personal right, that of religious conscience, was Enlightened or Protestant in spirit; to examine the enduring importance in America of the Christian dogma of original sin; and then to pause to look at patterns of elite thought. Finally, I will consider why the Protestant-inclined historiography has not enjoyed comparable standing to that of secular accounts, and conclude by very briefly highlighting the continuing importance of getting this history right.

PROTESTANTISM VERSUS ENLIGHTENMENT INFLUENCES

In comparing the influence of the Enlightenment and Protestantism on late eighteenth-century Americans, one must begin by recognizing that, even among the most highly respected historians, there is little debate as to which of these, in a general sense, was dominant.[5] Thus, we find the preeminent historian of the Enlightenment in America, Henry May, observing that "many, probably most, people who lived in America in the eighteenth and nineteenth centuries" did so outside the contours of Enlightened thought.[6] Almost all Americans, rather, were localist, parochial, and communal Christians whose world was shaped by the tenets of Reformed and Pietist Christianity; by their provincial and local political experiences of sometimes over 150 years; and by the demands and constraints of agricultural production. If this were the case, what, then, demands further consideration? It is, of course, the nature of the thought that guided those political actors who shaped state-level and national-level politics, most particularly, those men who shaped institutions of enduring importance. It is the thought of this political class, not the thought of the Protestant family farmer who made up 95 percent of the European-descended population, about which knowledgeable students of the period are likely to disagree.

Yet, with the remarkable exception of Publius, the author of *The Federalist*, and a few like-minded elites, those we ordinarily view as cosmopolitan "founders" held to political and social commitments that, even if not religiously orthodox in any simple sense, stood at a sizable distance from those of the leaders of the British and French Enlightenments.[7] In support of this contention, consider a brief comparison of salient Enlightenment and American political and social commitments to gauge whether the positions endorsed by various Enlightenment authors correspond with those held by those founders most visible on the national and international stage. Although there are many areas we might examine in outline, let me suggest three broad categories that almost all will recognize as important areas of social and political thought: constitutional design, the centrality of religion, and progressive perspectives on commercial life. Of course, such a comparison must, at best, be cursory; still, if the findings fit poorly with popular notions of an Enlightened eighteenth-century America, this exercise may prove instructive.

Concerning essential constitutional design, by the 1770s, most leading Enlightenment thinkers embraced unicameralism. In America, however, there were only two short-lived state experiments in unicameralism. Even among the intercolonial elite, Americans adhered to the necessity of the bicameralism with which they had grown to maturity under the British crown. Conversely, American federalism and continued localism were ridiculed by the leading lights of the Enlightenment, virtually all of whom defended centralization and nationalization. Turgot, most famously, objected that "instead of collecting all authority into one center, that of the nation, they have established different bodies" and, thus, it is now necessary for them to strive "to unite them [the states] by bringing them to one uniform set of principles."[8] Similarly, reflecting their differing logic, Enlightened authors as different as Adam Smith and Turgot defended a professional military, while almost all Americans staunchly defended militias.[9] In short, Americans born and raised in a Reformed Protestant culture of congregational autonomy were incapable of embracing the centralizing theories of men born in a world dominated by Anglican and Catholic theories of hierarchy and episcopacy.

On still more strictly religious issues, the differences between the leading lights of America and Europe are even starker. With the exception of Montesquieu and some English Unitarians, almost every eighteenth-century Enlightened author, from Voltaire to Beccaria, viewed Christianity as a central source of human evil and proposed its gradual or rapid eradication. Yet, almost no eighteenth-century American joined publicly in this secular crusade. The one exception was a nominal American, Thomas Paine, and he paid severely in widespread condemnation for his boldness.[10] As well, the centrality of the concept of original sin as a theological and political organizing principle insured that Americans would continue to adhere to Augustinian Christianity until at least the end of the eighteenth century.[11] Their European colleagues, like Condorcet, were well on their way to envisioning a benign human nature and even a perfectible one free of original sin.[12] In short, Enlightened authors had embraced an anthropocentrism and anticlericalism in opposition to Americans' continuing theocentrism and broad public respect for pious religiosity; indeed, late-eighteenth-century Americans were living between two religious revivals moving America in an increasingly pietistic and heartfelt direction.[13] And, accordingly, one should not be surprised by the continuing cultural, political, and religious differences readily found today in the contrasting norms of Western Europe and America.

Next, consider that in France and Britain many Enlightened authors, although surely not all, enthusiastically defended the role of luxury and avaricious merchants as valuable in the positive transformation of society.[14] Indeed, the defense of commercialism was of great interest to most Enlightened authors and, in most instances, was met with wholesale approbation. Americans, however, refused to defend in print or recorded speech the production and consumption of luxury goods. As well, they were generally unwilling to defend in public the avarice of merchants and the selfishness, if you will, of the radically modern thought of Bernard Mandeville in which human passions are defended as necessary for the good life, rather than viewed as hindrances that must be overcome.[15] One is far more likely to find simplicity and selflessness lauded by American editorialists and pamphleteers—that is, an economics congruent with the agrarian and self-overcoming tenets of Christianity and classical republicanism.

And again, with the exception of Publius and select elites, one finds few if any American authors arguing that virtue and self-denying control over one's passions is unnecessary in the maintenance of republican government.[16] Rather, what one finds in Revolutionary-era America, even among those we would today view as leading political figures, are political, religious, and economic views that one would expect to find among a Protestant people who wished to be guided not by the stark reason of the late Enlightenment, but by revelation or inner illumination. Nor is this surprising, for they were not Christians in name only: "the majority of inhabitants continued to go to church . . . [and] the preaching colonists heard most of the time—remained consistently otherworldly."[17] Such differences, then, should be expected because Americans were not searching for a perfected society created by the hand of man, as counseled by late Enlightenment authors, but rather they continued to look for the intercession of Christ and the Holy Spirit in their private and public lives, for only through God's intercession could man be freed from sin, above all his disfiguring selfishness, lusts, and passions.[18]

AMERICA: A PROTESTANT NATION

Importantly, such distinctly different aspirations, contrary to the claims of those who would relegate Christianity to the sidelines of American life, are readily discoverable not only in the sermons of the pastors and the private confessions of common folk, but as well in the legal codes and social practices publicly articulated by the cosmopolitan elite. For example, to the dismay of European Enlightened authors, only one of the thirteen states, Virginia, failed to require a religious test for those wishing to hold public office. All other states required that state officeholders, including federal senatorial electors, be Protestant (in Connecticut, Rhode Island, Georgia, Massachusetts, New Hampshire, New Jersey, North and South Carolina, and Vermont), be Trinitarian Christian (in Delaware), accept the truthfulness of scripture (in Pennsylvania and Vermont), be Christian (in Maryland), or be non-Catholic (in New York). Indeed, Delaware's constitution demanded that officeholders "profess faith in God the Father, and in Jesus Christ His only Son, and in the Holy Ghost." Nonetheless, the state code most reprinted and most often read by high school and

college students is the anomalous constitution of Virginia. Most Americans might have surmised as much without reading the arresting research of Paul Vitz, who has explored the antireligious nature of contemporary high school and college curricula.[19]
Looking back only a few years from the creation of a new American federal government to the time of the Revolution, we find a situation even less in accord with the Enlightenment standards regularly attributed to late-colonial Americans. During the era of the War of Independence, we discover that

> only three colonies allowed Catholics to vote. They were banned from holding public office in all New England colonies save Rhode Island. New Hampshire law called for the imprisonment of all persons who refused to repudiate the pope, the mass, and transubstantiation. New York held the death penalty over priests who entered the colony; Virginia boasted that it would only arrest them. Georgia did not permit Catholics to reside within its boundaries; [and] the Carolinas merely barred them from office.[20]

And yet, such a world, we are led to believe by leading modern American authors and public spokesmen, was one guided by Enlightenment sensibilities.
More in keeping with the historical record, careful students of the period like James Hutson find that during the War of Independence many of the new elites, such as Secretary of the Congress Charles Thompson, "retired from public life to translate the Scriptures from Greek to English" and that the famous pamphleteer John Dickinson "also retired from public life to devote himself to religious scholarship." Much the same was true of three of the Congress's presidents: Elias Boudinot, Henry Laurens, and John Jay.[21] And under their leadership, one should not be surprised to learn that thirteen times Congress unapologetically, via proclamations for days of fasting and humiliation, sought on behalf of the young nation the intervention of Jesus Christ and the Holy Ghost.
Indeed, the Continental Congress on March 14, 1781, even appointed young James Madison, a favorite of the secularists, to serve on a committee of three "to prepare a recommendation to the states for setting apart a day of humiliation, fasting and prayer" that was delivered on March 20, 1781, for May 2. As Daniel Dreisbach has demonstrated,[22] like Jefferson in Virginia in the 1770s and 1780s, Madison was involved in the close working together of church and state in Revolutionary America. Not surprisingly, then, this same Congress acted in support of Protestantism in its daily prayers, its appointment of military

chaplaincies, its collective attendance at Protestant worship services, its ordering that an American bible either be imported or published, and its persistent efforts to bring American Indians to Christ.[23]

Yet, in still other ways the early national and state governments, led by a putatively enlightened American political elite, displayed an ample willingness to patronize Protestantism in ways that can only be described as unimaginable to the authentic men of the Enlightenment. Thus,

officials donated land and personalty for the building of churches, religious schools, and charities. They collected taxes and tithes to support ministers and missionaries. They exempted church property from taxation. They incorporated religious bodies. They outlawed blasphemy and sacrilege, [and] unnecessary labor on the Sabbath and on religious holidays.[24]

Well into the nineteenth century, states and localities were comfortable in "endorsing religious symbols and ceremonies," crosses were common on statehouse grounds, holy days were official holidays, chaplains continued to be "appointed to state legislatures, military groups, and state prisons," thanksgiving prayers were offered by governors, subsidies were given to Christian missionaries, the costs of bibles were underwritten, tax exemptions were provided to Christian schools,

public schools and state universities had mandatory courses in the Bible and religion and compulsory attendance in daily chapel and Sunday worship services . . . [and] polygamy, prostitution, pornography, and other sexual offenses . . . were prohibited. Blasphemy and sacrilege were still prosecuted. . . . and other activities that depended on fate or magic were forbidden.[25]

Justice Story, thus, concluded that in America "it is impossible for those who believe in the truth of Christianity as a divine revelation to doubt that it is the special duty of government to foster and encourage it among all the citizens and subjects."[26] In opposition to the most cherished hopes of Enlightened authors, throughout the nineteenth century, Protestantism was simply an accepted and protected part of American life and law.

THE RIGHT OF RELIGIOUS CONSCIENCE: ENLIGHTENMENT OR PROTESTANT?

There was, however, one freedom in America that was natural and uniquely individual, and the defenders of the Enlightenment might well claim it as evidence of the Enlightenment's pervasive influence—the freedom of religious conscience. But it is useful to remember that at the beginning of the Revolutionary years, the protection awarded religious conscience was a manifestation of Americans' deep religiosity rather than a reflection of some form of Enlightenment theorizing. Not surprisingly, then, this hallowed right did little to limit the local community's exercise of corporate religious oversight. And by such, wholly unenlightened communities required attendance at the preaching of God's word, that respect be paid to the Sabbath (even forbidding inappropriate travel and leisure activities) and God's revealed dictates and commandments, that the rights of political participation be limited, and that one be taxed, church member or not, to retain a teacher of the community's (frequently established) Protestant faith. Indeed, in many areas of life, communities encroached on matters of personal choice well beyond narrowly understood matters of conscience. Thus, for example, there were religiously motivated (or at least supported) laws forbidding theater attendance, balls, masques, dice playing, cock fighting, and horse racing.[27] It should not be surprising, then, to remember how shocked the provincial Adams and Jefferson, among America's most "enlightened" citizens, were by the sophisticated and degenerate lives of the Enlightened members of the ancien régime they observed while serving their young country as ambassadors in decadent France. Only the cosmopolitan Franklin and Gouverneur Morris seemed unfazed.[28]

It is, nonetheless, true that during the years surrounding America's War of Independence, freedom of religious conscience had become a well-accepted aspect of liberty.[29] But it remained the only truly unalienable individual right (there were also corporate rights that were beginning to be viewed as unalienable).[30] In comparison, there were many political rights that governments or communities could "ask" citizens to surrender on appropriate occasions.[31] Not surprisingly, then, excepting the right to religious conscience,[32] more than two-thirds of the states made no mention of natural rights, often described as Enlightenment individual rights in their constitutions; once again, Virginia's was the exception.[33] Delaware's declaration of rights, for example, begins by holding that "all government of right originates from the people, is founded by compact only, and [is] instituted solely for the good of the whole." Only the right of conscience is then described as a possession of "all men." The Maryland declaration follows that of Delaware and begins with the same communal, rather than individualistic, rights language, and in its description of the right of conscience is more restrictive still. In Maryland, only those "professing the Christian religion, are equally entitled to protection in their religious liberty." Not only are atheists excluded from enjoying this most basic Enlightenment right, but all non-Christian believers are as well.

North Carolina's constitution also begins with a declaration of popular sovereignty and then claims "that the people of this State ought to have the sole and exclusive right of regulating the internal government and police thereof." And, as one might expect, the only individual right that is described as natural and unalienable in this constitution is that of conscience (section 19). All other rights, taken as they are from the English common law, are couched as recommendations, described in the language of "ought," and, thus, wholly subject to the vagaries of popular democratic will. Finally, New Hampshire's late constitution of 1784, borrowing its language from those that preceded it in other states, reminds its citizens that when "men enter into a state of society, they surrender up some of their natural rights to that society, in order to insure the protection of others." However, "among the natural rights, some are in their very nature unalienable, because no equivalent can be given or received for them. Of this kind are the RIGHTS OF CONSCIENCE."[34]

Clearly, then, the right of religious conscience enjoyed an unparalleled status in the minds' of eighteenth-century Americans as the only individual right that could not be surrendered or transferred as one moved from a state of "nature" to one of civil society.[35] One should not assume, therefore, that documents defending this right, such as Madison's famous "Remonstrance," were couched in the language of the Enlightenment. It is far more likely, as is the case with Madison's petition, that they were written in a language that appealed to America's Protestant electorate. And all other natural rights not easily confused with that of conscience, but readily associated with the Enlightenment, were of lesser importance and, thus, were fungible and subject to corporate oversight and restrictions.[36]

ORIGINAL SIN: AN ENDURING PROTESTANT INFLUENCE

The enduring influence of the hallowed status attached to the individual right of conscience is not the only Protestant presence that shaped American culture and politics of the late eighteenth century. For in any attempt to understand the American political and social thought and practices of the period, one must take note not only of the freedom of religious conscience and those individual rights that followed in its religious train, but also of the American understanding of the controlling power over society and men of the Christian understanding of original sin. As president of Princeton, a long-serving member of Congress, and a man of the moderate Scottish Enlightenment, John Witherspoon held that "nothing can be more absolutely necessary to true religion than a clear and full conviction of the sinfulness of our nature and state."[37] Politically, this demanded that governments help the individual to master his otherwise uncontrollable passions, lusts, and, most particularly, selfishness. In opposition, thus, to varying streams of Christian humanism and the closely associated ideas of their Enlightenment brethren, most Americans adhered to an understanding of human flourishing that rested on corporate oversight and, still more importantly, on rebirth in Christ.

This teaching, an Augustinian Christian perspective, and particularly a Reformed Protestant or Calvinist one, holds that man's sinful condition makes it impossible without grace for him to live a life of ordered freedom, one that he would have been able to enjoy eternally if not for his fall. Exactly this strong sense of limits derived initially from the Christian concept of original sin largely determined, even if not quite as openly as it had in the seventeenth century,[38] the understanding of things both religious and political in eighteenth-century America. And according to Edmund Morgan, even as late as the years surrounding the Revolution,

> the intellectual center of the colonies was New England, and the intellectual leaders of New England were the clergy, who preached and wrote indefatigably of human depravity and divine perfection . . . and the purpose of government was to restrain the sinfulness of man, to prevent and punish offenses against God.[39]

Not unexpectedly, then, the case for the centrality of original sin is nearly as strong in early national American political culture as in its religious history.[40]

Again, Witherspoon gave voice to this in his rejection of the late Enlightenment optimism regarding human goodness. He held that "the Enlightenment image of a virtuous society seemed extremely cloudy. 'Others may, if they please, treat the corruption of our nature as a chimera: for my part, . . . I see it everywhere, and I feel it every day.'"[41] Such relatively modest assertions concerning human depravity are best appreciated when compared both to bolder claims made concerning man's absolute depravity by America's still dominant orthodox Calvinist denominations (Congregational, Presbyterian, and some Baptist) and to the rare American radical Enlightenment figures like Elihu Palmer, Thomas Paine, and Ethan Allen,[42] as well as their plentiful European brethren, who argued by the end of the century in defense of human perfectibility.[43]

The American humanistic elite, both republican and Christian, to say nothing of the more pious Protestant and more conservative average American, rejected the optimistic sentiments of the late Enlightenment and instead adhered to some version of the Protestant axiom of original sin.[44] Even according to the celebrated liberal apologist Louis Hartz, "Americans refused to join in the great Enlightenment enterprise of shattering the Christian concept of sin, [and] replacing it with an unlimited humanism."[45] At the end of the century, when indeed the advocates of the French Revolution widely championed bold ideas of human perfectibility, the moderate pillars of American provincial society continued to distance themselves from any rejection of the concept of original sin. Thus, as late as 1798, Israel Woodward compared the worldviews of the French and the American elite, so different in their relationship to Christianity, and wrote,

> The *liberties* of the American and French nations, are grounded upon totally different and opposite principles. In their matters of civil government, they adopt this general maxim, that mankind are virtuous enough to need no restraint; which idea is most justly reprobated by the more enlightened inhabitants of the United States, who denominate such liberty, licentiousness.[46]

This rejection of secular optimism in human perfectibility in favor of Reformed Protestant pessimism was, and would long continue to be, part of American orthodoxy and, still today, does much to distinguish American nonelite culture from that of Western Europe.

Similarly, American antipathy toward the political and ecclesiastic hierarchy, often taken to be native to certain strains of British "country" ideology, was in truth derived from Reformed Protestant thought. This, importantly, helps explain the centrality of localism in American political thought. It is too often forgotten that equally at the center of the Reformation, along with the theology of grace, was the ecclesiastic concern with localism and laity-based, rather than episcopacy-based, church governance. Indeed, in England, as Hooker emphasized with such clarity, preeminently ecclesiastical rather than theological concerns divided the English church deeply.[47] And Americans, reaching back to their Brownist roots in the Plymouth colony, had developed remarkably localist and congregational patterns of secular and church governance that continued in the eighteenth century to shape political as well as religious sensibilities. For Reformed Protestants, no sinful man, no matter how socially elevated, could be trusted with corrupting power and, thus, long chains of hierarchy, be they in church or state, had to be resisted.

As a result of their continued adherence to the Protestant dogma of original sin and their localist ecclesiology, eighteenth-century Americans, elite and common alike, believed that man was destined to live always under the restraints of government. For as the rather progressive James Madison had written, "if men were angels, no government would be necessary."[48] The even more progressive Jefferson believed that "the human character . . . requires in general constant and immediate control, to prevent its being biased from right by the seduction of self-love."[49] Or, in the words of Andrew Eliot, "the necessity of government arises wholly from the disadvantages, which, in the present imperfect state of human nature [fallen], would be the natural consequence of unlimited freedom."[50]

The most important political implication of their Calvinist-inspired belief in the sinful nature of all men, however, might have been the imperial crisis itself. By passing the Declaratory Act on March 18, 1766, and demanding from Americans "unlimited submission" in "all cases whatsoever," the British Parliament had created a situation that Americans as Congregationalists were obligated to resist.[51] For, as Calvin's teacher Butzer had written in his *Lectures on the Book of Judges*, "wherever absolute power is given to a prince, there the glory and the dominion of God is injured. The absolute power, which is God's alone, would be given to a man liable to sin."[52] By demanding unlimited submission, Parliament, an external body of sinful men, had effectively "set itself alongside God's Word as a competing sovereign."[53] Americans, as a Reformed Protestant people, were committed to submitting only to local self-control and through this medium to God and his word—"and only God's word—in all aspects of life and faith"; thus, their response should have been predictable.[54] The members of Parliament had framed the debate in such a way that most Americans immediately understood it in quasimillennial terms as a struggle between eternal life and perpetual damnation.[55] Accordingly, American pastors could effectively use the themes of freedom of religious conscience, human sinfulness, and fear of an episcopacy for wartime mobilization.[56]

THE ELITE: HOW EXCEPTIONAL?

One must still confront the exceptional thought of Publius in *The Federalist*. Here one confronts a full-throated defense of May's moderate Enlightenment, although at the time it was authored by Publius, even this text lagged far behind the leading edge of French, English, and Scottish Enlightened thought. That is, *The Federalist* embodied the liberal moral, political, and economic theory developed by Hume and Montesquieu fifty years earlier. And in this earlier phase of Enlightenment thought, these authors, in many ways seminal conservatives, had emphasized a balance of power and the rule of law; a low but solid expectation for political life with little concern with corporate encouragement of virtue in either citizen or ruler; an acceptance of and reliance on the avaricious and ambitious nature of man; and a willingness to make commercial development one of the featured goals of political life.

Indeed, Publius not only embraced and followed the teachings of Hume and Montesquieu, but in addition made important contributions in his own right to what would become modern liberal political theory. That is, in his understanding of how to balance power between governmental branches, without the benefit of king or governmentally recognized class distinctions, Publius developed a new understanding of this matter in which the private passions of the individual would be tied to the public activities of governmental institutions.[57] However, in creating this brilliant new theory with which to replace the traditional conceptualization based on formal estates or on publicly inculcated virtue, and his concern with advancing individual rights, Publius was wholly anomalous in America. It is impossible to find in earlier or even contemporaneous accounts a comparable commitment to the moderate Enlightenment's rejection of the necessity of selfless virtue and minority rights.[58]

But, in considering Publius as an exception to the argument advanced above, two further considerations must be borne in mind. First, most of the soon-to-be liberal elite were still, during the years surrounding America's War of Independence, as publicly committed to religion and the dogma of original sin as any of the pastors or publicists cited above.[59] Although many of these men, particularly some of those described as founders, understood Christian religiosity in a wholly instrumental fashion, this does not vitiate the power of their commitment to it for wholly secular reasons. "Men like Jefferson and Madison," according to Thomas Pangle, who frequently criticizes defenders of America's foundational Protestant character, "did honor religion," although "not for its theological richness or theoretical insight, but for its moral value."[60] Other students of the period—like Miller, Levy, and Curry—have demonstrated that the founders understood religion to be "an essential precondition of social order and a crucial prop for the novel sort of government they were creating." The elite forces supporting establishment in many of the new states, thus, commonly argued for the continuation of establishments in terms of bourgeois morality, rather than godly ends.[61] But recognizing this does not imply that the vast majority of Americans, who most certainly were not privy to the private thoughts of the elite, would have understood that the religion that the founders so vociferously supported was, in fact, strikingly different from that preached by their pastors and regularly asserted by themselves.[62]

Second, most of the elite who were personally not religious were careful about keeping their personal views private and were not hesitant to advise others to do the same. For example, the English philosopher and Unitarian, Richard Price, in responding to a request from Dr. Benjamin Rush to keep his religious views private, refused and added,

> [Y]ou observe that in writing to the citizens of America it would be necessary that I should be silent about the disputed doctrines of Christianity, and particularly the Trinity. I am afraid that were I to write again, I should find this a hard restraint . . . I hope your countrymen will learn not only to bear but to encourage such discussions.[63]

Clearly, in the view of the well-placed Rush, most Americans did not welcome heterodox views on the Trinity. To most Americans, then, the elite's embrace of religion, whatever they personally believed, must have seemed to be of the same: a Protestant recognition of original sin and damnation that could only be overcome by faith in Christ, self-examination, and God's freely given and wholly undeserved grace.

It seems safe to conclude, therefore, that Christianity in America, which until the end of the eighteenth century meant Protestant Christianity, is a political and cultural resource that is central to a correct understanding of American historical political thought and institutions.[64] Moreover, it is wrong to confuse Christianity, even in its most humanistic or pietistic modes, with Enlightenment humanism and anticlericalism. Such differences, in fact, are still of importance in helping to explain the continuing differences that separate contemporary American and Western European culture.

THE SOCIAL PRODUCTION OF AMERICAN HISTORY

If this is so, why then, in America's high schools and colleges, is the Protestant foundation of America's political institutions and culture so rarely taught?[65] I would suggest two overlapping reasons that help explain this troubling situation: one is a reflection of the tension-ridden standing that Christianity enjoys in contemporary American elite culture and the second reflects the difficulty of studying eighteenth-century American political and social thought.

First, it must be recognized that in spite of the anomalous religious character of American society among all contemporary advanced-industrial countries, our cultural and intellectual leaders (although not political) differ little from their counterparts in Europe in their lack of, and even contempt for, religious belief. Accordingly, if one is to be accepted by the various standard bearers of elite culture, one must appropriately limit the sweep and scope of one's embrace of Christianity to an appropriately liberal range of social concerns in which the Second Table (that directing us to love our neighbors) of values overwhelms a forgotten First Table (that demands, above all, that we first love God with all our heart). Seemingly, however, it is not only concerning contemporary matters that the appropriate level of secularism must be observed, but, because of the potent symbolism and juridical standing attached to American founding principles, the elite, even the Christian elite, are encouraged to describe the American founding in ways that underemphasize the centrality of Christianity if they are to continue to enjoy respectability and funding. Thus, we find that elite Christian authors, when writing for national elite audiences, often ignore the lived religious and legal practices and values of late-eighteenth and early-nineteenth-century Americans, or they at least ask their readers to privilege the thought of progressive secular authors like Madison, whose perspective is more in accord with the liberal sensibilities of these authors and their elite audiences.[66] In short, elite Christian authors in particular often seem embarrassed by much of America's authentic religious past as they write to provide an appropriately secular portrait of American history that speaks to the vitiated religious sensibilities of their elite audience.[67]

And, not surprisingly, much the same is true of most non-Christian intellectuals who are also committed to underreporting the Protestant character of eighteenth-century American political thought and culture. Accurate accounts could, if widely accepted, potentially legitimate streams of political thought that American intellectual and cultural elites find repugnant. Given our system of constitutional jurisprudence, it is clearly "dangerous" to bring undue attention to potentially "destabilizing," if historically accurate, religiously dominated patterns of thought and behavior from our past because of their uncontrollable potential. It is far better to pretend that Reverend Falwell's remarks after September 11 blaming our nation's suffering on what he claimed was our religious and moral degeneracy were anomalous, rather than confront and wrestle with the utter normalcy of them in the broad sweep of American history.

Of course, with a far weaker evidentiary foundation, no comparable qualms were experienced during the past few decades by scholars shaped by 1960s radicalism in their highlighting the influence of classical republicanism in eighteenth-century American thought. And, even when historians work hard to get the history right, as for example concerning the authentically communal, rather than individualistic, nature of the Bill of Rights,[68] they seem to exercise a limited power in disseminating their understanding to the broader public whose knowledge of such matters is informed primarily through mass-media outlets. In short, the Protestant foundation of American political thought and culture is a story because of its potential political and juridical power, which most who control the dissemination of ideas in both secular and elite Christian outlets would prefer to see relegated to the sidelines of American intellectual life.

Still, there is a second reason that helps explain the limited influence enjoyed by a history that emphasizes the Protestant nature of American political institutions and culture. This one is the least obvious and results from the nature of the evidence available and the training of intellectual historians and political theorists. That is, late-eighteenth-century Americans produced no secular texts dedicated to an exploration of their understanding of the political good, and no full-time moral or political theorists of note. Even their most renowned political work, *The Federalist*, only addresses questions of the good elliptically and surreptitiously in a series of newspaper editorials. Accordingly, those texts in which light is likely to be shed on such matters often go unread, and those that are read were written for more limited political ends.

Many political theorists have been trained to approach their subject by principally reading texts that are considered canonical. It would not be surprising, then, that when they find little that passes as normative political theory and nothing at all of stature, they would declare Americans bereft of a political theory of the good and, thus, by necessity secular and by default "liberal." This overlooks the fact that in order to extract the normative teaching embedded in most eighteenth-century texts, even in *The Federalist*, one must be prepared to hunt, uncover, and reconstruct their theory of the good. This effectively is a different activity than the exegesis of focused works of political philosophy. The studying of American normative political theory, particularly when it is most likely to be buried in political sermons, is akin to archaeology, and because of the way the professions are structured, is not an activity encouraged among those working in political theory or American history.[69]

It is true, however, not only that eighteenth-century Americans were more likely to discuss matters in print that are best described as political science or jurisprudence (rather than moral or political philosophy), but also that scholarly treatment has followed suit and has examined in detail the pamphlets concerned with such matters. Indeed, the normative political theory of Revolutionary-era America, surprisingly, is still an underresearched area. And this situation has led to the conflating of highly visible secular theories about regimes and political institutions with much harder-to-uncover Protestant-inspired American views of the good.[70] Americans' abundantly researched concerns about governmental abuse of power and how best to provide needed limits against it have been taken to demonstrate their embracing of a secular liberal theory of the good. This seems natural enough, particularly given that the former materials are so readily available and the latter so inaccessible.

Nevertheless, such an association is likely mistaken in two ways. First, we would be assuming wrongly that their institutional visions are only correctly associated with liberal constitutionalism, when, in fact, these same concerns are readily associated as well with ancient and medieval theorists.[71] Indeed, the true essence of liberalism, according to many of its adherents, is not its strictures regarding institutional arrangements. Rather, it is its belief that reasonable people tend to differ and disagree about the nature of the good life and that, therefore, the public must play a limited role in determining the ends to be pursued by individuals. This may be more readily associated with certain institutional designs, but it is not primarily institutionalist in its focus. And these institutions that have become commonplace under liberal regimes are, nonetheless, equally compatible with other political visions.

Second, assuming for the moment that the particular institutional arrangements embraced by Americans were uniquely liberal, we would be wrong to conclude that their theory of the good must likewise be secular and liberal. Americans could very well have adhered to what we now describe as secular and liberal theories of how to limit central governmental power vis-à-vis the people, while continuing to believe that the government, especially at the state and local levels, had been appropriately empowered by the people to protect and foster their communal and Protestant vision of human flourishing. Indeed, isn't that what federalism allows for? Thus, it is conceivable that those who describe America's constitutional arrangements as liberal and those of us who find that their localist theory of the good was Protestant and communal are both correct.[72] But if this proves true, theories of the good and those of regimes, Plato notwithstanding, may be less tightly linked than is often assumed by his contemporary admirers.

Moreover, this confusion between political theories of regimes and those of the good, I suspect, is not peculiar to America, but rather broadly descriptive of contemporary theorizing about the seventeenth and eighteenth centuries. Although we have immediate access to typologies of different regimes (for example, monarchies versus republics), we have no vocabulary for describing early-modern social and political theories of the good that is comparable to classical republicanism, Catholic organicism, or modern liberalism. Is it, as suggested by Pocock, that Protestant thinkers produced no social and political theories to fill the void that existed between the efflorescence of Renaissance republicanism in the sixteenth century and the self-conscious emergence of individualism in the nineteenth century?[73] I doubt it because it is clear that at least one Protestant nation in the seventeenth and eighteenth centuries did defend a communal and reformed Protestant theory of the good—America. But this confusion points to yet one more reason why the Protestant foundations of American political thought are likely to go unrecognized.

WHY GETTING FOUNDATIONAL AMERICAN HISTORY RIGHT MATTERS

Finally, such unreliable historical accounting is troubling not only because it has falsely reified Enlightenment secularism into America's chosen political ideology, but because a long, rich, and authentic tradition of American political thought has been rendered falsely illegitimate and "un-American." As noted above, for good or bad, the history of the period with its norms and practices continues to exercise a remarkable hold on the American political and legal consciousness. That an openly Evangelical Christian like George W. Bush can be elected president is evidence of this. Indeed, in America, foundational history matters, and those who are its keepers control a potent set of symbols and icons. America's intellectuals have attempted, although clearly only with limited success, to make illegitimate a normative theory of the good political life that is enduring, democratic, Christian, and communal—that is, Reformed Protestant. American history has been constantly revised so that it now appears that this earlier political vision, with its self-overcoming intentions, never existed, or in a more moderate version of this historical fable, that we are a people that are gladly and willingly relinquishing our Protestant inheritance for more acceptably secular and enlightened alternatives.

America's democratic and localist Reformed Protestant inheritance, however, is its most enduring political tradition. To understand American politics and history well, one must explore its role in shaping and limiting the range of political options that were available to political actors throughout the nineteenth and twentieth centuries and its continuing ability to produce political outcomes that astound and dismay Western Europeans. Without such an understanding, so much in American history, from lynchings to referenda to the moralism of our domestic and international policies, is incomprehensible. Admittedly, this tradition is not the humanistically self-satisfying secular past pursued by many republican revisionists, and it is not without moral features that many might find troubling.

Neither, however, is it illusory. This authentic and powerful inheritance still resonates with the religious and social beliefs of many Protestant Americans. Accordingly, this living, communal tradition may contain within it modes of analysis and approaches to political and moral problems that might help solve some of America's most nagging social problems and tools that might help Europeans better understand the ways of many average Christian Americans. And with an expansion of what is recognized as authentically American, our range of options with which to confront our public challenges must necessarily increase. For all but the most intolerant secularists, this might be viewed as a welcome change.

NOTES

1. Michael P. Zuckert, *The Natural Rights Republic: Studies in the Foundation of the American Political Tradition* (Notre Dame, IN: University of Notre Dame Press, 1996), 95, 175.

2. For their survey of these varying literatures, see Joseph P. Viteritti and Gerald J. Russello, "Community and American Federalism: Images Romantic and Real," *Virginia Journal of Social Policy & the Law* 4 (Spring 1997): 683–742.

3. See Daniel T. Rodgers, "Republicanism: The Career of a Concept," *Journal of American History* 79 (June 1992): 12–38; and Robert E. Shalhope, "Republicanism and Early American Historiography," *William and Mary Quarterly* 39 (1982): 334–56.

4. See Barry Shain, "One Nation, Under God," review essay of *Religion and The Continental Congress, 1774–1789* by Derek H. Davis and of *Religion and the American Constitutional Experiment* by John Witte Jr., in *Books & Culture* (July/August 2001): 29–32; and Stanley Fish, "Why We Can't All Just Get Along," *First Things* (February 1996): 18–40.

5. Ironically, given the broad agreement concerning the Protestant character of Americans, this fact is often set aside and otherwise overlooked by students of the period. See Stanley N. Katz, "Legal and Religious Context of Natural Rights Theory: A Comment," in *Party and Political Opposition to the Revolution*, ed. Patricia U. Bonomi (Tarrytown, NY: Sleepy Hollow Press, 1980), 36–7, who observes that "curiously, however, neither the 1920's nor the 1960's interpretations took *religious* ideas seriously as a component of American opposition ideology . . . in what was, after all, still an intensely religious society"; Michael Novak, *On Two Wings: Humble Faith and Common Sense at the American Founding* (San Francisco: Encounter Books, 2002); James H. Hutson, *Religion and the Founding of the American Republic* (Washington, DC: Library of Congress, 1998); and Norman Hampson, *The Enlightenment: An Evaluation of its Assumptions, Attitudes and Values* (1968, repr. New York: Penguin Books, 1986), 131, who writes of the eighteenth century that "it is something of an historical impertinence to consider the century as the age of Enlightenment since religion exercised a far greater hold over most sections of every society than it does today."

6. Henry F. May, *The Enlightenment in America* (New York: Oxford University Press, 1976), xiv, and see 45–46, where he continues that "for most inhabitants of the American colonies in the eighteenth century, Calvinism was . . . in the position of laissez-faire in mid-nineteenth-century England or democracy in twentieth-century America."

7. Barry Alan Shain, *The Myth of American Individualism: The Protestant Origins of American Political Thought* (Princeton, NJ: Princeton University Press, 1996), 145. M. E. Bradford argues in *Founding Fathers: Brief Lives of the Framers of the United States Constitution,* 2d rev. ed. (Lawrence: University Press of Kansas, 1994), that the majority of the framers were, in fact, religiously orthodox.

8. Turgot, "Letter to Richard Price [March 22, 1778]," in *Correspondence of Richard Price,* ed. D. O. Thomas, 3 vols. (Durham, NC: Duke University Press, 1991), 2:13.

9. Turgot, "Letter to Richard Price," in *Correspondence of Richard Price,* 2:13; Adam Smith, *An Inquiry into the Nature and Causes of the Wealth of Nations,* ed. R. H. Campbell and A. S. Skinner, 2 vols. (Indianapolis, IN: Liberty Classics, 1981), 2:699–700.

10. See Jack Fruchtman Jr., *Thomas Paine: Apostle of Freedom* (New York: Four Walls Eight Windows, 1994), 393–435.

11. See H. Richard Niebuhr, "The Idea of Original Sin in American Culture," in *H. Richard Niebuhr—Theology, History, and Culture: Major Unpublished Writings,* ed. William Stacy Johnson (New Haven, CT: Yale University Press, 1996); Barry Shain, "Religious Conscience and Original Sin: America's Protestant Foundations" (unpublished manuscript); and H. Shelton Smith, *Changing Conceptions of Original Sin: A Study in American Theology Since 1750* (New York: Charles Scribner's Sons, 1955).

12. See Antoine-Nicolas de Condorcet, *Progress of the Human Mind,* trans. June Barraclough (Westport, CT: Hyperion Press, 1979), 184.

13. See generally, Hutson, *Religion and the Founding of the American Republic.*

14. For example, see David Hume, "Of the Rise and Progress of the Arts and Science," in *Political Essays,* ed. Knud Haakonssen (Cambridge: Cambridge University Press, 1994); and Voltaire, *Letters on England,* trans. and ed. Leonard Tancock (London: Penguin Books, 1980).

15. See Bernard Mandeville, "Inquiry into the Origin of Moral Virtue," in *Fable of the Bees,* ed. Phillip Harth (London: Penguin Books, 1970).

16. See Barry Shain, "Understanding the Role of Virtue in *The Federalist*: Old and New Interpretations," unpublished manuscript, currently under review.

17. Harry Stout, *New England Mind, New England Soul: Preaching and Religious Culture in Colonial New England* (New York: Oxford University Press, 1986), 6; see also James H. Hutsor, *Forgotten Features of the Founding: Themes in the Early American Republic* (Lanham, MD: Lexington Books, 2003), 111–32.

18. See Perry Miller, *The New England Mind: From Colony to Province* (Cambridge, MA: Belknap Press, 1983), 69, who follows Augustine's *Confessions* where it is argued that "whenever God converts a sinner, and translates him into the state of grace, he freeth him from his natural bondage under sin, and by his grace alone enables him freely to will and to do that which is spiritually good"; and Augustine, "On Grace and Free Will" and "On the Predestination of Saints," in *Basic Writings,* ed. Whitney J. Oates (Grand Rapids, MI: Baker Book House, 1993), 771, 779–85.

19. See Paul C. Vitz, "Religion and Traditional Values in Public School Textbooks," *The Public Interest* 84 (Summer 1986): 79–90.

20. Derek Davis, *Religion and the Continental Congress, 1774–1789: Contributions to Original Intent* (Oxford: Oxford University Press, 2000), 153.

21. Hutson, *Religion and the Founding of the American Republic*, 49.

22. See Daniel L. Dreisbach, "Another Look at Jefferson's Wall of Separation, A Jurisdictional Interpretation of the 'Wall' Metaphor," *Witherspoon Fellowship Lectures* (August 2000): 5; Daniel L. Dreisbach, "A New View on Jefferson's Views on Church–State Relations: The Virginia Statute for Establishing Religious Freedom in its Legislative Context," *American Journal of Legal History* 35 (April 1991): 172–204; and generally, Daniel L. Dreisbach, *Thomas Jefferson and the Wall of Separation between Church and State* (New York: New York University Press, 2002).

23. See, for example, *Journals of the Continental Congress*, November 11, 1775, 3:351; and generally, Hutson, *Religion and the Founding of the American Republic*.

24. John Witte Jr., *Religion and the American Constitutional Experiment: Essential Rights and Liberties* (Boulder, CO: Westview Press, 2000), 53.

25. Witte, *Religion and the American Constitutional Experiment*, 97–98.

26. Joseph Story, *Commentaries on the Constitution of the United States,* 2:603; see also 2:602–9 where Story writes that "the right of a society or government to interfere in matters of religion will hardly be contested," for "the great doctrines of religion . . . never can be a matter of indifference in any well-ordered community." Indeed, "the real object of the First Amendment was not to countenance, much less to advance, Mahometanism, Judaism, or infidelity, by prostrating Christianity; but to exclude rivalry among Christian sects." See also James McClellan, *Joseph Story and the American Constitution: A Study in Political and Legal Thought* (1971; repr. Norman: University of Oklahoma Press, 1990), 118–59; and A. G. Roeber, "Long Road to *Vidal*: Charity Law and State Formation in Early America," in *The Many Legalities of Early America*, eds. C. L. Tomlins and Bruce H. Mann (Chapel Hill: University of North Carolina Press, 2001), 417.

27. See Ann Fairfax Withington, *Toward a More Perfect Union: Virtue and the Formation of American Republics* (New York: Oxford University Press, 1991), 184, who describes the Continental Congress's embrace of such prohibitions, and Roeber, "Long Road," 435, who writes that even in 1794 Pennsylvania passed a bill that "assaulted gaming, violation of Sunday rest, profanity and blasphemy, and other affronts to the moral quality of society. The conviction that the common law of Pennsylvania should reflect broadly Christian patterns of behavior seemed quite clear."

28. See Gouverneur Morris, *Diary of the French Revolution*, ed. Beatrix Cary Davenport and George G. Harrap, 2 vols. (Boston: Houghton Mifflin, 1939), 1:5–61.

29. See Shain, *Myth of American Individualism*, 193–240.

30. See Shain, *Myth of American Individualism*, 243–58, concerning the corporate right of self-government declared so boldly in America's Declaration of Independence.

31. See the Federal Farmer, "Letter VI," in *The Anti-Federalist*, ed. Herbert J. Storing (Chicago: University of Chicago Press, 1985), 70, who writes that "of rights, some are natural and unalienable, of which even the people cannot deprive individuals: Some are constitutional or fundamental; these cannot be altered or abolished by the

ordinary laws; but the people, by express acts, may alter or abolish them—These, such as the trial by jury, the benefits of the writ of habeas corpus, etc. . . . and some are common or mere legal rights, that is, such as individuals claim under laws which the ordinary legislature may alter or abolish at pleasure."

32. Five of the original thirteen state constitutions had no declaration of rights: Connecticut (1776), Georgia (1777), New York (1777), Rhode Island (1663), and South Carolina (1778). Four others, Delaware (1776), New Hampshire (1784), North Carolina (1776), and Maryland (1776), had declarations of rights, but failed to make any mention of individual natural rights.

33. This is not true of the declarations of rights of Virginia (1776), Pennsylvania (1776), Vermont (1777), or Massachusetts (1780). That of Virginia famously begins that "all men are by nature equally free and independent, and have certain inherent rights, of which, when they enter into a state of society, they cannot by any compact, deprive or divest their posterity." Often overlooked, though, is that this formulation is a traditional usage of natural-rights language, which stipulates the just relationship between generations (one of three conditions under which natural law or rights rather than civil law was controlling) and not between an individual and the society at large. Only in regard to the right of religious conscience (section 16) is the relationship constrained between the individual and his or her society. Similarly, it is often ignored that the Pennsylvania declaration privileges in all instances the community's needs over those of the individual, except in regard to conscience (and even then atheists are excluded).

34. In Benjamin Perley Poore, ed., *The Federal and State Constitutions, Colonial Charters, and Other Organic Laws of the United States*, 2d ed., 2 vols. (Washington, DC: Government Printing Office, 1878; repr. Union, NJ: Lawbook Exchange, 2001), 2:1280–1. New Hampshire then continues without any sense of tension in Article VI to sustain its taxation "for the support and maintenance of public Protestant teachers of piety, religion and morality."

35. See Shain, *Myth of American Individualism*, 181–93.

36. In truth, though, it is not even clear that most Enlightenment authors forcefully defended natural rights. This, too, seems to be a retrospective invention of later historians.

37. John Witherspoon, *The Dominion of Providence over the Passions of Men* (Philadelphia: R. Aitken, 1776), 7–8.

38. See Perry Miller, "Religion and Society in the Early Literature of Virginia," in *Errand into the Wilderness* (Cambridge, MA: Harvard University Press, 1956), 129 and 132, who writes that in both Virginia and Massachusetts, "political doctrine was founded on the premise of original sin" and that the authoritarian character of their governments was "the logical consequence of a theology of depravity and enslavement of the will."

39. Edmund S. Morgan, "The American Revolution Considered as an Intellectual Movement," in *Essays on the American Revolution*, ed. David L. Jacobson (New York: Holt, Rinehart and Winston, 1970), 29.

40. See Nathan O. Hatch, *The Sacred Cause of Liberty: Republican Thought and the Millennium in Revolutionary New England* (New Haven, CT: Yale University Press, 1977), 125, who writes that "the primary purpose of government" for the

Standing Order of New England, "was to restrain the corruptions of human nature"; and Michael Zuckerman, *Peaceable Kingdoms: New England Towns in the Eighteenth Century* (New York: Alfred A. Knopf, 1970), 116–17.

41. Gordon S. Wood, *Creation of the American Republic* (Chapel Hill: University of North Carolina Press, 1969), 114–15.

42. To gauge better the moderate character of these stances, consider Phillip Greven, *The Protestant Temperament: Patterns of Child-Rearing, Religious Experience, and the Self in Early America* (New York: New American Library, 1977), 65–6, for a description of the centrality of "the doctrine of original sin and of innate depravity" to the thought of eighteenth-century American evangelical Christians; for them "human nature was corrupt, not in part but totally. Sinful men, said Jonathan Edwards, 'are totally corrupt, in every part, in all their faculties . . . There is nothing but sin, no good at all.'"

43. See May, *Enlightenment in America*, 231, who discusses the few radical deists in America, like the blind preacher Elihu Palmer, who adhered to the belief that man was perfectible and that "this great truth, the new deists tirelessly explained, had been hidden from mankind by the sinister alliance of priests and kings, whose chief reliance had always been the absurd doctrine of original sin."

44. See Shain, *Myth of American Individualism*, 225–28, 231–33.

45. Louis Hartz, "American Political Thought and the American Revolution," *American Political Science Review* 46 (June 1952): 324.

46. Israel B. Woodward, *American Liberty and Independence: A Discourse* (Litchfield: T. Collier, 1798), 8.

47. Richard Hooker, "Preface," in *Of the Laws of Ecclesiastical Polity*, ed. Arthur Stephen McGrade (Cambridge: Cambridge University Press, 1989), 24.

48. Alexander Hamilton et al., *The Federalist: A Commentary on the Constitution of the United States*, ed. Edward Mead Earle (Indianapolis, IN: Modern Library, 1937), 337.

49. Thomas Jefferson to P. S. Dupont de Nemours, April 24, 1816, in *Writings*, ed. Merrill D. Peterson (New York: Library of America, 1984), 1386.

50. Andrew Eliot, *Massachusetts Election Day Sermon* (Boston: Green & Russell, 1765), 8–9.

51. See Max Weber, *The Protestant Ethic and the Spirit of Capitalism*, trans. Talcott Parsons (New York: Charles Schribner's Sons, 1958), 255–6, who has written of the "sinfulness of the belief in authority, which is only permissible in the form of an impersonal authority, the Scriptures, as well as of an excessive devotion to even the most holy and virtuous of men, since that might interfere with obedience to God. . . . It is also part of the historical background of that lack of respect of the American which is, as the case may be, so irritating or so refreshing"; and Zuckerman, *Peaceable Kingdoms*, 248–49.

52. Cited by Hans Baron, "Calvinist Republicanism and Its Historical Roots," *Church History* 8 (1939): 37.

53. Here, I am largely following Stout, *New England Mind, New England Soul*, 7.

54. Stout, *New England Mind, New England Soul*, 259.

55. See Keith Thomas, "Politics Recaptured," *New York Review of Books*, May 17, 1979, 28, who writes "Lutherans and Calvinists alike continued to represent resistance to unsatisfactory rulers as a religious duty rather than a political right."

56. See Alice M. Baldwin, *New England Clergy and the American Revolution* (Durham, NC: Duke University Press, 1928).

57. See Edmund S. Morgan, "Safety in Numbers: Madison, Hume, and the Tenth *Federalist*," *Huntington Library Quarterly* 49 (Spring 1986): 110; and Barry Shain, "Reading *The Federalist*: Brilliant and Precocious, Madison's Political Theory Uncovered," (unpublished manuscript).

58. See Larry D. Kramer, "Madison's Audience," *Harvard Law Review* 112 (January 1999): 611–79.

59. The early modern rationalists shared in common with their more religious brethren a belief in objective moral truth and rational ethical standards. They no more countenanced arbitrary, in effect, sinful behavior than the more religious members of the elite. See Gordon S. Wood, *The Rising Glory of America, 1760–1820* (New York: George Braziller, 1971), 17, who writes that "although nature had been important to Revolutionary Americans, it was not the wilderness or landscape they had sought to celebrate, but the natural order of a Newtonian universe."

60. Thomas Pangle, *Spirit of Modern Republicanism: The Moral Vision of the American Founders and the Philosophy of Locke* (Chicago: University of Chicago Press, 1988), 81.

61. See May, *Enlightenment in America*, 257, who writes that "all the New England High Federalists [in the main Unitarians] believed morality essential . . . and religion essential to morality."

62. See May, *Enlightenment in America*, 274, who writes that "it is almost impossible to find any Republican, from Jefferson down who defended or admitted the deist views of the Republican candidate"; and John M. Mason, *Voice of Warning to Christians on the Ensuing Election of a President* (New York: G. F. Hopkins, 1800), 8–9, who, in great frustration, attempts to offset the propaganda efforts of the republicans so that the electorate would believe, what we now know to be true, that Jefferson would not have been considered a Christian. He draws attention to how well kept this secret was at the time. See also Benjamin Hale, *Liberty and Law: A Lecture* (Geneva, NY: Ira Merrell, 1838), 23, who writing in 1837 could boldly emphasize without embarrassment how different the irreligiosity of men believed to be infidels like Paine was from the "true founders of our national independence [who] were religious men."

63. Richard Price, "Letter to Rush [September 30, 1786]," in *Richard Price and the Ethical Foundation of the American Revolution: Selections from His Pamphlets, with Appendices*, ed. Bernard Peach (Durham, NC: Duke University Press, 1979), 337.

64. See John G. West, *The Politics of Revelation and Reason: Religion and Civic Life in the New Nation* (Lawrence: University Press of Kansas, 1996).

65. See Paul C. Vitz, *Censorship: Evidence of Bias in our Children's Textbooks* (Ann Arbor, MI: Servant Books, 1986).

66. See James Madison, "Madison's 'Detatched [sic] Memoranda,'" ed. Elizabeth Fleet, *William and Mary Quarterly*, 3d ser., 3 (October 1946): 551–62, for his anticlerical thought. Still, this essay was not published by Madison and was written sometime following Madison's retirement from the presidency in 1817.

67. See generally, Fish, "Why We Can't All Just Get Along," and Shain, "One Nation, Under God."

68. See Akhil Reed Amar, *The Bill of Rights: Creation and Reconstruction* (New Haven, CT: Yale University Press, 1998).

69. See Shain, "On Reading 18th-Century American Political Theory," in *The Myth of American Individualism*, 14–18; and Donald Lutz, *A Preface to American Political Theory* (Lawrence: University Press of Kansas, 1992).

70. This is a theme also explored by Joshua Mitchell, *Not by Reason Alone: Religion, History, and Identity in Early Modern Political Thought* (Chicago: University of Chicago Press, 1993).

71. See M. Stanton Evans, *The Theme Is Freedom: Religion, Politics, and the American Tradition* (Washington, DC: Regnery, 1994).

72. See George W. Carey, *The Federalist: Design for a Constitutional Republic* (Urbana: University of Illinois Press, 1989), 159–60, 165, who advances a version of this argument.

73. See J. G. A. Pocock, *The Machiavellian Moment: Florentine Political Thought and the Atlantic Republican Tradition* (Princeton, NJ: Princeton University Press, 1975), 507.

Bibliography

Abzug, Robert H. *Cosmos Crumbling: American Reform and the Religious Imagination.* New York: Oxford University Press, 1994.

Adams, Arlin M., and Charles J. Emmerich. *A Nation Dedicated to Religious Liberty: The Constitutional Heritage of the Religion Clauses.* Philadelphia: University of Pennsylvania Press, 1990.

Aldridge, Alfred Owen. *Benjamin Franklin and Nature's God.* Durham, NC: Duke University Press, 1967.

Alley, Robert S., ed. *James Madison on Religious Liberty.* Buffalo, NY: Prometheus Books, 1985.

Baldwin, Alice M. *The New England Clergy and the American Revolution.* Durham, NC: Duke University Press, 1928.

Boller, Paul F., Jr. *George Washington and Religion.* Dallas, TX: Southern Methodist University Press, 1963.

———. "George Washington and Religious Liberty." *William and Mary Quarterly,* 3d ser., 17 (1960): 486–506.

Bradford, M. E. *Founding Fathers: Brief Lives of the Framers of the United States Constitution.* 2d rev. ed. Lawrence: University Press of Kansas, 1994.

———. "Religion and the Framers: The Biographical Evidence." *Benchmark* 4, no. 4 (1990): 349–58.

Bradley, Gerard V. *Church–State Relationships in America.* Westport, CT: Greenwood Press, 1987.

Brown, Richard D. "The Founding Fathers of 1776 and 1787: A Collective View." *William and Mary Quarterly,* 3d ser., 33 (1976): 465–80.

Buckley, Thomas E., S.J. *Church and State in Revolutionary Virginia, 1776–1787.* Charlottesville: University Press of Virginia, 1977.

———. "The Political Theology of Thomas Jefferson." In *The Virginia Statute for Religious Freedom: Its Evolution and Consequences in American History,* edited by Merrill D. Peterson and Robert C. Vaughan. New York: Cambridge University Press, 1988.

Cherry, Conrad, ed. *God's New Israel: Religious Interpretations of American Destiny*. Englewood Cliffs, NJ: Prentice Hall, 1971.

Clebsch, William A. *From Sacred to Profane America: The Role of Religion in American History*. New York: Harper and Row, 1968.

Conkin, Paul K. "The Religious Pilgrimage of Thomas Jefferson." In *Jeffersonian Legacies*, edited by Peter S. Onuf. Charlottesville: University Press of Virginia, 1993.

Cord, Robert L. *Separation of Church and State: Historical Fact and Current Fiction*. New York: Lambeth Press, 1982.

Cornelison, Isaac A. *The Relation of Religion to Civil Government in the United States of America: A State without a Church, but not without a Religion*. New York: G. P. Putnam's Sons, 1895.

Cousins, Norman, ed. *"In God We Trust": The Religious Beliefs and Ideas of the American Founding Fathers*. New York: Harper and Brothers, 1958.

Curry, Thomas J. *The First Freedoms: Church and State in America to the Passage of the First Amendment*. New York: Oxford University Press, 1986.

Davis, Derek H. *Religion and the Continental Congress, 1774–1789: Contributions to Original Intent*. New York: Oxford University Press, 2000.

Dreisbach, Daniel L. *Thomas Jefferson and the Wall of Separation between Church and State*. New York: New York University Press, 2002.

Eidsmoe, John. *Christianity and the Constitution: The Faith of Our Founding Fathers*. Grand Rapids, MI: Baker Book House, 1987.

Evans, M. Stanton. *The Theme Is Freedom: Religion, Politics, and the American Tradition*. Washington, DC: Regnery, 1994.

Fiering, Norman S. "Benjamin Franklin and the Way to Virtue." *American Quarterly* 30 (Summer 1978): 199–223.

Foote, Henry Wilder. *The Religion of Thomas Jefferson*. Boston: Beacon Press, 1947.

Gaustad, Edwin S. *Faith of Our Fathers: Religion and the New Nation*. San Francisco: Harper and Row, 1987.

———. *Sworn on the Altar of God: A Religious Biography of Thomas Jefferson*. Grand Rapids, MI: William B. Eerdmans, 1996.

Gould, William D. "The Religious Opinions of Thomas Jefferson." *Mississippi Valley Historical Review* 20 (1933): 191–208.

Hall, David W. *The Genevan Reformation and the American Founding*. Lanham, MD: Lexington Books, 2003.

Hall, J. Lesslie. "The Religious Opinions of Thomas Jefferson." *Sewanee Review* 21 (1913): 164–76.

Hall, Mark David. *The Political and Legal Philosophy of James Wilson*. Columbia: University of Missouri Press, 1997.

Hamburger, Philip. *Separation of Church and State*. Cambridge, MA: Harvard University Press, 2002.

Hart, Benjamin. *Faith and Freedom: The Christian Roots of American Liberty*. Dallas, TX: Lewis and Stanley Publishers, 1988.

Hartnett, Robert C. "The Religion of the Founding Fathers." In *Wellsprings of the American Spirit*, edited by F. Ernest Johnson. New York: Cooper Square, 1964.

Hatch, Nathan O. *The Sacred Cause of Liberty: Republican Thought and the Millennium in Revolutionary New England*. New Haven, CT: Yale University Press, 1977.

Healey, Robert M. *Jefferson on Religion in Public Education.* New Haven, CT: Yale University Press, 1962.

Holmes, David L. *The Religion of the Founding Fathers.* Charlottesville, VA: Ash-Lawn-Highland; Ann Arbor, MI: The Clements Library, 2003.

Hood, Fred J. *Reformed America: The Middle and Southern States, 1783–1837.* Tuscaloosa: University of Alabama Press, 1980.

Humphrey, Edward Frank. *Nationalism and Religion in America, 1774–1789.* Boston: Chipman Law Publishing Co., 1924.

Huntley, William B. "Jefferson's Public and Private Religion." *South Atlantic Quarterly* 79 (1980): 286–301.

Hutson, James H. *Forgotten Features of the Founding: The Recovery of Religious Themes in the Early American Republic.* Lanham, MD: Lexington Books, 2003.

———. *Religion and the Founding of the American Republic.* Washington, DC: Library of Congress, 1998.

———, ed. *Religion and the New Republic: Faith in the Founding of America.* Lanham, MD: Rowman & Littlefield, 2000.

Hyneman, Charles S., and Donald S. Lutz, eds. *American Political Writing during the Founding Era: 1760–1805.* 2 vols. Indianapolis, IN: Liberty Press, 1983.

Ives, J. Moss. *The Ark and the Dove: The Beginning of Civil and Religious Liberties in America.* New York: Longmans, Green, and Co., 1936.

Ketcham, Ralph. "James Madison and Religion—A New Hypothesis." *Journal of the Presbyterian Historical Society* 38 (June 1960): 65–90.

Knoles, George Harmon. "The Religious Ideas of Thomas Jefferson." *Mississippi Valley Historical Review* 30 (1943): 187–204.

LaHaye, Tim. *Faith of Our Founding Fathers.* Brentwood, TN: Wolgemuth & Hyatt, 1987.

Lambert, Frank. *The Founding Fathers and the Place of Religion in America.* Princeton, NJ: Princeton University Press, 2003.

Levy, Leonard W. *The Establishment Clause: Religion and the First Amendment.* 2d ed. Chapel Hill, NC: University of North Carolina Press, 1994.

Lindsay, Thomas. "James Madison on Religion and Politics: Rhetoric and Reality." *American Political Science Review* 85 (1991): 1321–37.

Littell, Franklin Hamlin. *From State Church to Pluralism: A Protestant Interpretation of Religion in American History.* Garden City, NY: Doubleday, 1962.

Mapp, Alf, Jr. *The Faiths of Our Fathers: What America's Founder's Really Believed.* Lanham, MD: Rowman & Littlefield, 2003.

Meyer, Donald H. "Franklin's Religion." In *Critical Essays on Benjamin Franklin,* edited by Melvin H. Buxbaum, 147–67. Boston: G. K. Hall & Co., 1987.

Miller, Perry. *Errand into the Wilderness.* Cambridge, MA: Harvard University Press, 1956.

Miller, William Lee. *The First Liberty: Religion and the American Republic.* New York: Alfred A. Knopf, 1986.

Moore, Frank, ed. *The Patriot Preachers of the American Revolution, 1766–1783.* New York, 1860.

Morris, B. F. *Christian Life and Character of the Civil Institutions of the United States, Developed in the Official and Historical Annals of the Republic.* Philadelphia: George W. Childs, 1864.

Morrison, Jeffry Hays. "John Witherspoon and 'The Public Interest of Religion.'" *Journal of Church and State* 41 (Summer 1999): 551–73.

Muñoz, Vincent Phillip. "George Washington on Religious Liberty." *The Review of Politics* 65 (Winter 2003): 11–33.

———. "James Madison's Principle of Religious Liberty." *American Political Science Review* 97 (February 2003): 17–32.

Nichols, James Hastings. "John Witherspoon on Church and State." *Journal of Presbyterian History* 42 (1964): 166–74.

Noonan, John T., Jr. *The Lustre of Our Country: The American Experience of Religious Freedom.* Berkeley: University of California Press, 1998.

Novak, Michael. *On Two Wings: Humble Faith and Common Sense at the American Founding.* San Francisco: Encounter Books, 2002.

Oberg, Barbara B., and Harry S. Stout. *Benjamin Franklin, Jonathan Edwards, and the Representation of American Culture.* New York: Oxford University Press, 1993.

Perry, William Stevens. *The Faith of the Signers of the Declaration of Independence.* Tarrytown, NY: William Abbatt, 1926.

Peterson, Merrill D., and Robert C. Vaughan, eds. *The Virginia Statute for Religious Freedom: Its Evolution and Consequences in American History.* New York: Cambridge University Press, 1988.

Plumstead, A. W., ed. *The Wall and the Garden: Selected Massachusetts Election Sermons, 1670–1775.* Minneapolis: University of Minnesota Press, 1968.

Sandoz, Ellis. *A Government of Laws: Political Theory, Religion and the American Founding.* Baton Rouge: Louisiana State University Press, 1990.

———, ed. *Political Sermons of the American Founding Era: 1730–1805.* Indianapolis, IN: Liberty Press, 1991.

Sanford, Charles B. *The Religious Life of Thomas Jefferson.* Charlottesville: University Press of Virginia, 1984.

Schaff, Philip. *Church and State in the United States; or, The American Idea of Religious Liberty and Its Practical Effects.* New York: G. P. Putnam's Sons; American Historical Society, 1888.

Shain, Barry Alan. *The Myth of American Individualism: The Protestant Origins of American Political Thought.* Princeton, NJ: Princeton University Press, 1994.

Sheldon, Garrett Ward, and Daniel L. Dreisbach, eds. *Religion and Political Culture in Jefferson's Virginia.* Lanham, MD: Rowman & Littlefield, 2000.

Sheridan, Eugene R. "Liberty and Virtue: Religion and Republicanism in Jeffersonian Thought." In *Thomas Jefferson and the Education of a Citizen*, edited by James Gilreath. Washington, DC: Library of Congress, 1999.

Singer, C. Gregg. *A Theological Interpretation of American History.* Rev. ed. Phillipsburg, NJ: Presbyterian and Reformed Publishing Co., 1981.

Smylie, James H. "Madison and Witherspoon: Theological Roots of American Political Thought." *Princeton University Library Chronicle* 22 (Spring 1961): 118–32.

Stokes, Anson Phelps. *Church and State in the United States.* 3 vols. New York: Harper and Brothers, 1950.

Stout, Harry S. *The New England Soul: Preaching and Religious Culture in Colonial New England.* New York: Oxford University Press, 1986.

Swanson, Mary-Elaine, *The Education of James Madison: A Model for Today.* Montgomery, AL: The Hoffman Center, 1992.

Tait, L. Gordon. *The Piety of John Witherspoon: Pew, Pulpit, and Public Forum.* Louisville, KY: Geneva Press, 2001.

Thornton, John Wingate, ed. *The Pulpit of the American Revolution; or, the Political Sermons of the Period of 1776.* Boston: Gould and Lincoln, 1860.

Velasquez, Eduardo. "Rethinking America's Modernity: Natural Law, Natural Rights and the Character of James Wilson's Liberal Republicanism." *Polity* 29 (Winter 1996): 193–220.

West, John G., Jr. *The Politics of Revelation and Reason: Religion and Civic Life in the New Nation.* Lawrence: University Press of Kansas, 1996.

———. "George Washington and the Religious Impulse." In *Patriot Sage: George Washington and the American Political Tradition,* edited by Gary L. Gregg II and Matthew Spalding. Wilmington, DE: ISI Books, 1999.

Witte, John, Jr. *Religion and the American Constitutional Experiment: Essential Rights and Liberties.* Boulder, CO: Westview Press, 2000.

Index

About the Contributors

Thomas E. Buckley, S.J., is professor of American religious history at the Jesuit School of Theology Berkeley/Graduate Theological Union and author of *Church and State in Revolutionary Virginia, 1776–1787*.

Daniel L. Dreisbach is professor of justice, law, and society at American University and author of *Thomas Jefferson and the Wall of Separation between Church and State*.

Mark D. Hall is associate professor of political science at George Fox University and author of *The Political and Legal Philosophy of James Wilson, 1742–1798*.

Howard L. Lubert is assistant professor of political science at James Madison University and author of an essay on Thomas Hutchinson and James Otis in *History of American Political Thought*.

Jeffry H. Morrison is currently James Madison Visiting Fellow in the Department of Politics at Princeton University and associate professor of government at Regent University. He is author of the forthcoming *John Witherspoon and the Founding of the American Republic*.

Vincent Phillip Muñoz is assistant professor of political science at North Carolina State University and Civitas Fellow in Religion and

Public Life at The American Enterprise Institute. His articles have appeared in the *American Political Science Review* and the *Review of Politics*.

Michael Novak is the George Frederick Jewett Chair in Religion and Public Policy at the American Enterprise Institute and author of *On Two Wings: Humble Faith and Common Sense at the American Founding*.

Barry Alan Shain is associate professor of political science at Colgate University and author of *The Myth of American Individualism: The Protestant Origins of American Political Thought*.

Garrett Ward Sheldon is the John Morton Beaty Chair of Political Science at the University of Virginia's College at Wise and author of *The Political Philosophy of James Madison*.

James R. Stoner is professor of political science at Louisiana State University and author of *Common Law and Liberal Theory: Coke, Hobbes, and the Origins of American Constitutionalism*.

John Witte Jr. is Jonas Robitscher Professor of Law and Ethics at Emory University and author of *Religion and the American Constitutional Experiment: Essential Rights and Liberties*.